Death by Design

Craig Haney

Death by Design

Capital Punishment as a
Social Psychological System

OXFORD
UNIVERSITY PRESS

2005

OXFORD
UNIVERSITY PRESS

Oxford University Press, Inc., publishes works that further
Oxford University's objective of excellence
in research, scholarship, and education.

Oxford   New York
Auckland   Cape Town   Dar es Salaam   Hong Kong   Karachi
Kuala Lumpur   Madrid   Melbourne   Mexico City   Nairobi
New Delhi   Shanghai   Taipei   Toronto

With offices in
Argentina   Austria   Brazil   Chile   Czech Republic   France   Greece
Guatemala   Hungary   Italy   Japan   Poland   Portugal   Singapore
South Korea   Switzerland   Thailand   Turkey   Ukraine   Vietnam

Copyright © 2005 by Oxford University Press, Inc.

Published by Oxford University Press, Inc.
198 Madison Avenue, New York, New York 10016

www.oup.com

Oxford is a registered trademark of Oxford University Press

Library of Congress Cataloging-in-Publication Data
Haney, Craig.
Death by design : capital punishment as social psychological system / Craig Haney.
    p.   cm.—(American psychology-law society series)
Includes bibliographical references and index.
ISBN-13: 978-0-19-518240-8
ISBN 0-19-518240-5
1. Capital punishment—United States.   2. Capital punishment—Moral and ethical aspects—
United States.   3. Discrimination in capital punishment—United States.   I. Title.   II. Series.
HV8699.U5H365 2005
364.66'0973—dc22   2004023583

9 8 7 6 5 4 3 2 1

Printed in the United States of America
on acid-free paper

To my parents, Bill, Irene, and Nan

Series Foreword

Ronald Roesch, Series Editor

This book series is sponsored by the American Psychology-Law Society (APLS). APLS is an interdisciplinary organization devoted to scholarship, practice, and public service in psychology and law. Its goals include advancing the contributions of psychology to the understanding of law and legal institutions through basic and applied research; promoting the education of psychologists in matters of law and the education of legal personnel in matters of psychology; and informing the psychological and legal communities and the general public of current research, educational, and service activities in the field of psychology and law. APLS membership includes psychologists from the academic research and clinical practice communities as well as members of the legal community. Research and practice are represented in both the civil and criminal legal arenas. APLS has chosen Oxford University Press as a strategic partner because of its commitment to scholarship, quality, and the international dissemination of ideas. These strengths will help APLS reach its goal of educating the psychology and legal professions and the general public about important developments in the field of psychology and law. The focus of the book series reflects the diversity of the field of psychology and law as we will publish books on a broad range of topics. Books currently in production provide analyses and reviews of a number of areas, including trial consulting and civil litigation.

Preface

In his eloquent critique of capital punishment, Albert Camus described the death penalty as something modern society keeps "smothered under padded words" to discourage the public from honestly debating its legitimacy. He argued that these padded words have prevented us from "examin[ing] the penalty in reality" and thwarted any attempt to say what capital punishment "really is and then say whether, being what it is, it is to be considered necessary."* This book is a modest attempt to deflate at least some of the padded words that substitute for honest debate over the death penalty. It does so by bringing to bear an array of social science data that is intended to examine capital punishment "in reality." The reality I have in mind is a psychological one, and I approach the topic of the death penalty's legitimacy from the perspective of average citizens, voters, and jurors who frequently think about and react to the threat of violent crime and criminals, who often form beliefs and express preferences about the use of capital punishment in the hope of making society safer, and who sometimes deliberate and render decisions about whether and when the death penalty should be imposed.

I have been conducting research and writing about various death-penalty-related topics for about 25 years. Although the specific topics have varied, my previous research always has focused on some discrete aspect or narrow feature of the death-sentencing process. Like many other social scientists, I have tried to use empirical data as a way of measuring the fairness

*A. Camus, Reflections on the Guillotine. In *Resistance, Rebellion, and Death* (pp. 131–189). New York: Modern Library (1960), p. 134.

or effectiveness of one or another particular death-penalty-related procedure or doctrine by isolating individual components in the overall system of capital punishment. In this book I have drawn heavily on that research and writing, updating and in some instances expanding the scope of some of those earlier analyses. But I have focused more intently here on something that my prior work did not and could not do: make a series of interconnections between various individual pieces of research and relate them to the larger system of death sentencing of which they are all a part. Thus, this book represents an attempt to step back and view the system of capital punishment as a whole, formed by the various parts and pieces of the death-sentencing process that I and numerous other social scientists have spent many years scrutinizing through discrete studies and focused research.

Although posing critical questions at many junctures, at virtually every turn, I have tried to couch my inquiry in terms of the social facts of capital punishment, relying heavily on my own empirical research and that of others to raise concerns about the inherent fairness of the current system of death sentencing. My own views on these issues have evolved over the years as a result of extensive, direct experience with the criminal justice institutions and legal procedures by which capital punishment is implemented and through the social science research I have conducted on the manner in which the death penalty is deliberated and sometimes imposed. Those experiences and that research form the basis for the conclusions I reach in the pages that follow.

It is important to state at the outset that I make one basic assumption that is central to the entire discussion that follows. It is that our system of capital punishment asks normal people to participate in what, under normal circumstances, would be regarded as extraordinary, prohibited acts. Most people are not routinely capable of thoughtfully considering or enthusiastically advocating domestic social and political policies that are, in the final analysis, intended to take the lives of other persons. Nor are they capable of rationally contemplating and calmly deciding to themselves actually pursue a course of action that, ultimately, is designed to result in someone's death. Yet the death penalty asks them—whether as citizens, voters, or capital jurors—to do precisely these things. Of course, the request to take these extraordinary courses of action comes with varying degrees of clarity and urgency and often is made in ways that blur the connection between act and consequence. But death is the bottom line of it. It is only the padded words with which we have surrounded capital punishment that could make it appear otherwise.

Although concentrating on the lethality of the system of death sentencing, it is important to note that I do not intend to equate the actions taken by ardent death penalty supporters, pro-death judges, legislators, or prosecutors, or death-sentencing jurors with the violence of capital defendants themselves who are the intended targets of these policies or who are placed on trial in capital cases. Mine is a more basic and less controversial point. It is, simply, as I have said, that the actions that are taken by our society to support, enact, implement, and impose the death penalty are designed to bring about the deaths of other human beings, and that this is something that, under normal circumstances, normal people cannot easily do. As basic, uncontroversial, and simple as this point is, it has been covered by padded words so effectively and for so long that we often forget or ignore it.

With this assumption in mind, I analyze the various mechanisms by which our system of death sentencing goes about creating the extraordinary conditions and special states of mind that enable widespread public partici- pation in forms of behavior that modern society otherwise would regard as odious and even condemnable. Note that the process of preparing citizens for the various roles they play in this peculiar kind of "death work" begins long before any one of them is asked to decide how to vote in an election in which capital punishment may be at issue or is called to serve as a juror in a capital case where someone's life is at stake. No matter their role in the process, few people approach the task of death sentencing as *tabula rasa*. Even though citizens typically lack real firsthand experience with the criminal justice system, most—I will argue—have been deeply immersed in a popular culture that is replete with reasonably consistent messages and very powerful images that help to distort the perceived necessity and true nature of capital punishment. It could be said, then, that the media systematically miseducates average citizens about many of the issues I address in this book, and that miseducation facilitates their participation in the death-sentencing process.

Citizens rely on the media for much of their knowledge about the crim- inal justice system. However, media portrayals of violent crime are not neu- tral. A vast audience is repeatedly exposed to what are often politically or economically motivated campaigns about crime and punishment. Its mem- bers are bombarded with messages that are as graphic and dramatic and emotionally engaging as they are consistent and, too often, consistently wrong. Many misleading story lines and dramatic images reach most people unchallenged, lacking critical perspectives or alternative points of view against which to measure their validity or representativeness. As a result, the audience comes to believe that these media accounts of crime and punish- ment are simply commonsense, the way things are, a part of the natural order of things. People regularly form beliefs based on this consistent but inaccurate information and, if the beliefs go unchallenged, they can motivate and shape what people do and decide as voters, and certainly as jurors, on matters of crime and punishment.

Especially over the last several decades, these images and myths have become more powerful and frightening and unrelenting. They have been used to engender an unprecedented high level of punitiveness in citizens, voters, and jurors in the United States. Yet even these powerful images and myths are not enough to allow a democratically administered system of death sentencing to function smoothly. To be sure, this inherently democratic na- ture—the fact that in the United States the death penalty not only needs the periodic assent of the electorate but, at crucial junctures, always requires average citizens to actively participate in imposing it—is what makes a more elaborate and overarching set of social psychological forces so essential.

Our legal system plays an important role in setting these additional social psychological forces in motion, often building on and amplifying many erroneous views. Too often, the system does nothing to correct the media-based and politically inspired popular myths or to ensure that participants in the death-sentencing process approach their tasks with a balanced mindset. At its worst, the system employs practices that select for and further exaggerate already biased stereotypes about the causes of crime, the nature of violent perpetrators, and the need to respond with state-sanctioned violence of its own.

To begin telling this story, chapter 1 suggests that the death penalty creates tensions and strains in our legal culture that are managed largely through a process of collective denial. That is, that the image of fairness and procedural propriety with which we cloak the death penalty is too often contradicted by a reality of unfairness, unpredictability, and morally disengaged decision making. In some quarters, this reality is so troublesome and painful to systematically analyze and fully recognize or acknowledge that legal decision makers do not try. I discuss one important aspect of this process— the way in which the courts now distort or ignore social science data that contain much of the bad news about how the system actually functions. The U.S. Supreme Court, in particular, has created several de facto doctrines that carefully circumscribe and minimize the legal and constitutional significance of these social science data (in the limited number of cases where they refer to them at all).

Chapter 2 addresses a topic—the role of the media in creating myths and stereotypes about the nature of capital violence and capital punishment—whose importance is implicit in much of what I have already said. I suggest that, especially over the last quarter century, the media's increasing obsession with crime and punishment has saddled the American public with a number of widely held myths and misconceptions. Indeed, an especially troublesome combination has been created: a mass audience that believes it knows a great deal about the criminal justice system but that has learned most of what it knows through highly misleading and inaccurate media story lines. Because these story lines are pursued so consistently for their entertainment and economic value rather than for the genuine information they impart, there is little or no accountability to the facts and few opportunities for a corrective or counter-narrative to be introduced.

In chapter 3, I draw on some of my own research to illustrate several of these points. Rather than talking about the media in general, these studies examine several aspects and consequences of news coverage in capital cases in particular. I report first on a study that analyzed a sample of newspaper stories about actual capital cases published in the California press in the mid-1990s. The second study discussed in this chapter is one that analyzed a large database created in conjunction with change-of-venue motions in death penalty cases where community surveys were used to estimate the impact of pretrial publicity on the mind-set of the potential capital jury pools. Taken together, this and other research I discuss suggest that there is a distinct bias or slant in the way in which death penalty cases are reported by the press *and* that potential voters and jurors are much affected by the publicity to which they are exposed.

Chapter 4 looks more carefully at some of the public opinion consequences of the media's treatment of crime and punishment-related issues and the highly politicized messages that have been disseminated about death penalty policy over the last several decades. Historically, there have been many times when the mood and preferences of the citizenry played an unusually significant role in shaping political and legal debates about capital punishment. However, the virtual absence of meaningful debate over the death penalty in the United States over the last several decades—the lack of alternative perspectives or critical points of view to consider—has left the public to embrace a set of widely held myths about it. I illustrate some of these myths with data from national surveys on the topic and with a detailed discussion of an elaborate public opinion poll that my colleagues and I conducted in California some years ago. Among other things, it demonstrated the unsettling fact that people who know most about the death penalty generally support it least.

As people who are close to the day-to-day administration of capital punishment are well aware, the legal system further facilitates death sentencing by the way it selects the people who are eligible to sit as actual jurors in death penalty cases. There are special challenges posed by jury selection or "voir dire" in capital cases that come about because of the high levels of publicity that often surround death penalty trials. In addition, capital jurors are subjected to a unique process, known as "death qualification," that significantly narrows the group of persons eligible to participate in these kinds of cases. Chapter 5 reviews existing legal and empirical analyses of both aspects of the jury selection process, concentrating on the way they skew the composition of the group of remaining jurors deemed eligible to serve on a capital case.

In chapter 6, I examine separate but related research on the "process effects" of death qualification—the way in which simply being exposed to questioning about one's willingness and ability to impose the death penalty can change attitudes and shape expectations about the trial that will follow. Both the composition and process effects occur in tandem in the jury selection that precedes an actual capital case, of course, and the research shows that together they serve not only to increase the likelihood that a capital defendant will be sentenced to death following conviction but also to elevate his chances of being convicted in the first place.

Once a capital jury finally has been selected, its members move closer to the morally and psychologically complex question of whether they should vote to take the defendant's life. An excruciatingly delicate balance must be struck: On the one hand, jurors must be brought nearer to this ultimate question in order to answer it. On the other hand, they must be kept at a psychologically safe distance from its human implications and from too closely confronting the harshest details of the process by which state-sanctioned killing is accomplished.

Thus, chapter 7 looks much more carefully at practices and procedures that occur in the normal course of capital trials to "morally disengage" jurors from the reality of what they are being asked to do. Concentrating on what I term "structural aggravation"—those things that are structured into the very nature of a typical death penalty trial that facilitate the death-sentencing behavior of the jury—this chapter examines four basic features of the process: the dehumanization of defendants, exaggerating differences between them and the jurors who will decide their fates, highlighting the defendants' dangerousness, and minimizing the extent to which jurors can consider the social and human costs of a death verdict. All serve to accomplish these moral distancing effects.

In chapter 8 I turn attention to a much-studied issue in the recent law and psychology of capital punishment—the incomprehension of death penalty sentencing instructions. Since the mid-1970s, when the U.S. Supreme Court reinstated the death penalty as a constitutionally acceptable punishment, the courts have placed tremendous faith in capital jury sentencing instructions to properly guide the jury's decision-making process. Yet, despite the use of reformed and revised capital statutes, scholars and researchers have shown that troublesome patterns of arbitrariness and racial discrimination in death sentencing persist.

In part to better understand this phenomenon, in the mid-1980s my students and I began to study the difficulties many people encounter in simply understanding the new sentencing instructions. Many other researchers now have examined this issue as well. The aggregate data from my own and these other studies paint a clear and consistent picture: there is a widespread lack of comprehension of capital sentencing instructions that compromises the jury's ability to engage in a process of fair and reliable decision making. Because no one can be guided by what he or she does not understand, the lack of comprehension is significant and raises broad questions about whether the modern system of death sentencing is capable of consistently achieving the kind of guided but discretionary decision making on which it is supposed to be founded.

Chapter 9 addresses in more detail some of the ways that the various separate parts of the system of death sentencing that have been described in previous chapters accumulate and fit together in particular kinds of cases. Although these effects are structural and generic—applying to capital cases in general—in this chapter I look at the especially problematic consequences that are created in capital cases in which the defendants are African American. To examine this issue, I review the concept of mitigation and note that, given the continuing correlation between race and a number of adverse, potentially harmful, and even criminogenic experiences in our society, African American defendants have a store of "structural mitigation" that is inscribed into their life histories. Yet, in part because of the effects of the various practices and procedures I have discussed, and in part because of the way an "empathic divide" separates jurors from capital defendants, and especially so from African American defendants, this mitigation does not play the role that it should. As a result, I believe, these defendants continue to be sentenced to death at higher rates than their life histories would otherwise explain.

Chapter 10 concludes my analysis of the social psychological "design" of our system of death sentencing by proposing a series of comprehensive, interlocking reforms that are closely derived from the empirical analyses presented in the previous chapters. I argue that these reforms are needed to bring our system of capital punishment closer to the values and ideals of the legal system in which it functions. Because the overarching, cumulative nature of the process of death sentencing produces its most powerful effects, piecemeal changes are not likely to ensure the required level of fairness. Systemic problems like the ones outlined in the preceding chapters will require comprehensive, system-oriented solutions.

This observation about the overarching, systemic effects of the various social psychological components that facilitate death sentencing leads to an important clarification. In the pages that follow I repeatedly use terms such as "systemic" and "structural" and "by design" to refer to the overall operation of the death penalty in the United States. As I have noted, I do so by way of suggesting that the whole of the system is much more powerful and problematic than the sum of its constituent parts. But I do not mean to imply or suggest anything definitive about the level of intentionality with which this system operates. Whether, when, and how much of the "design" of the death-sentencing process is specifically intended by anyone to accomplish the effects I describe in this book are seemingly unanswerable questions. In any event, they are beyond the scope of my analysis.

Determining what, exactly, is "intended" as opposed to merely inadvertent, or perhaps the known but regrettable or unavoidable consequence of a practice pursued for other reasons, is less important than the real task at hand—frankly evaluating the problematic effects of this overall system, created for whatever reason and in whatever name. A system like this does not have to be the product of a grand conspiracy or even a conscious strategy for its components to operate cumulatively and interactively, and to have real psychological force and effect over those who participate in it.

Indeed, it may be that without this elaborate, effective, and legally supported social psychological network of practices and procedures, capital punishment would no longer be viable in our society. It is possible that too few normal, healthy citizens now would be capable of regularly and sometimes enthusiastically calling for the death of their fellows, let alone, as jurors, taking steps designed to bring those deaths about. This, I suppose, is an empirical question whose answer may become clearer in the coming years, if and when we move closer to having a system of death sentencing that genuinely embodies the legal and constitutional values even many of its most ardent supporters agree it should.

Of course, notwithstanding this speculation about the future viability of the system of capital punishment, I am also well aware that it has a long and storied history in the United States. Virtually all the legal jurisdictions in the American colonies quickly embraced and implemented death penalty laws even before the nation formally began. Moreover, there have been thousands of people executed, often with widespread public support and even outright rejoicing in some circles. Yet there has always been a sense of collective ambivalence. Even in the nation's early embrace of the death penalty there were substantial numbers of people who did not support it—so many that, as I discuss in a later chapter, they had to be removed from juries well before a capital trial began. And I am aware that our laws have advanced slowly but inexorably to drastically limit the circumstances under which the death penalty is even a possibility, and that we continue to reform the manner in which executions are finally accomplished (in ways that seem, at least, designed to lessen their obvious painfulness and apparent cruelty). Times have changed and, along with them, the nature of modern sensibilities. To me, these evolving standards of decency mean that the system of death sentencing depends even more heavily now than in the past on the social psychological forces I address in the following pages.

Finally, I believe that it is possible to analyze the social psychological design of our system of death sentencing without arguing one way or another about whether the death penalty is necessarily morally "wrong" or ethically unacceptable. My expertise is in social science and not moral philosophy. I have my own opinion about the morality of the death penalty, of course, but that opinion is neither the focus of nor the driving force behind this book. I know that other thoughtful persons have reached opposite conclusions and I respect their right to do so. However, I do think it is important for death penalty supporters and opponents alike to take Camus's suggestion seriously—to make sure we know what the death penalty really is before we reach conclusions about whether it is really necessary or really not. And, whatever else it is, the death penalty is about taking lives. This book is one perspective on the fairness and authenticity of the process by which we go about doing it.

Acknowledgments

I have had the good fortune of working with and around some of the most skilled and capable lawyers and legal thinkers in the country as well as many insightful, fair-minded judges. There are far too many of them to mention by name; they know who they are. I hope some of what I have written here has done justice to the many things they taught me.

Over many years of teaching at Santa Cruz, an institution I dearly love, I also have been blessed with many extremely talented graduate students who worked with me on death-penalty-related issues, including Lawrence White, Cathy Johnson, Laura Sweeney, Sally Costanzo, and Carmel Benson. I have worked especially closely with two of my former students—Lorelei Sontag, who now provides expert consultation and testimony in actual death penalty cases, and Mona Lynch, who has developed a impressive, independent scholarly career of her own but still manages to collaborate with me on death penalty research from time to time. Two recently graduated students, Susan Greene and Amy Smith, also have worked with me on a number of capital-punishment-related projects and now begun their promising careers in psychology and law. I am grateful to all of them for the many contributions they made to the research that I describe in this book.

Ron Roesch, APLS book series editor, was extremely gracious, patient, and wise throughout this entire project. It certainly would not have been completed without his help.

Finally, to my large and loving family—Lynne, Erin, Matt, Arcelia, Bonnie, and Chanel—and, especially, to my wife Aida, who has made so many of the good things in my life possible, I owe an immeasurable debt.

Contents

Death by Design

1

Blinded by the Death Penalty
The Supreme Court and the Social Realities of Capital Punishment

There have not been here only writers hungering for reality and brilliant narrators whose "dazzling" verve carries off a man's head; whatever the degree of guilt of the accused, there was also the spectacle of a terror which threatens us all, that of being judged by a power which wants to hear only the language it lends us . . .
—Roland Barthes, "Dominici, or the Triumph of Literature" (1972)

Historian Douglas Hay has written that the death penalty was once "the climactic emotional point of the criminal law—the moment of terror around which the system revolved."[1] Although times have changed dramatically since 18th-century England, when some 200 crimes were punishable by death, this climactic emotional point still plays a central role in the administration of justice in our society. Moreover, our ambivalence about honestly and fully contemplating the "moment of terror" and everything that leads up to it often skews the way many of us talk and think about capital punishment, the way we study it, and the way our courts reason about it.

Perhaps because of a deep-seated moral and psychological ambivalence about capital punishment in our culture, many people—even some who are strongly in favor of the death penalty—find themselves saying one thing and doing another on this issue. Legal decision makers, especially, find that their support of the death penalty increasingly requires them to ignore a growing gap between many of their stated values and ideals and the patterns and practices by which they are routinely implemented in this area of law. The present chapter addresses some of these issues.

The death penalty presents American society with a mass of contradictions. In the contested terrain of capital punishment, citizens, voters, and jurors are pulled in different directions by a series of unresolved and often unnamed tensions. There is, of course, the core tension that characterizes any system of death sentencing—that, in order to demonstrate the degree to which we value human life, we take life. But there are others. Many citizens in the United States regard themselves as members of the world's most ad-

nane democracy. Our government often presses human rights
'r nations and condemns presumably less advanced countries
quent lapses in this regard. Yet we are one of the very few
:ies that still regularly executes its own citizens—even per-
...riously mentally ill, and, until very recently, children and the
...ally retarded.[2]

Some of these tensions and contradictions are played out vividly in our capital jurisprudence as well. We like to boast, often with good reason, about our remarkably elaborate and expensive system of justice, one that may extend more due process rights and provide better access to courts to more people than any other in history. Nowhere are the claims about these elaborate procedures to ensure fairness made grander or voiced more strongly than with respect to the death penalty. Those who defend our system of capital punishment insist that it affords every feasible procedural safeguard and spares no reasonable expense to uphold the rights of persons whose very lives are at stake in the criminal process.

Indeed, as often as not, these claims about the quest to provide "perfect justice" in death penalty cases are voiced by critics who argue that the procedural protections are excessive, that they have become far too elaborate, time-consuming, and unduly solicitous of the rights and interests of the truly undeserving. Justice Scalia, for example, has complained forcefully and often about what he calls a "death is different jurisprudence," one that is purchased only "at great expense to the swiftness and predictability of justice." It is a jurisprudence that Scalia and others think has been won through a "guerilla war" that is being waged by death penalty opponents hoping to make capital punishment "a practical impossibility."[3]

Yet, if truth be told, we do little to ensure that the full panoply of impressive rights that exist on paper is provided in reality to *all* capital defendants. There is much evidence documenting our shortcomings in this regard. For example, by the mid-1980s, two researchers had begun to uncover an unsettling portrait of what they called "the dark figure of innocence"—the number of cases in the United States in which an innocent person was convicted of a potentially capital crime.[4] In recent years, with the help of DNA and other forensic technologies, the size of that dark figure has reached unexpected proportions. As I write this, for example, there are an estimated 119 documented cases of innocent persons being freed from an American death row since the reinstating of capital punishment in the mid-1970s.[5]

Moreover, factually innocent death-sentenced prisoners appear to be just the most dramatic, visible tip of a much larger problem that is submerged throughout the criminal justice system—ineffectively represented and badly defended capital defendants who do not actually deserve the death penalty but who receive it nonetheless. Thus, although the issue is less publicly acknowledged, our system of death sentencing also is severely compromised whenever the process of assigning *penalty* is flawed, when persons are sentenced to die who, if they had been properly represented in the sentencing phases of their capital trials, would have received life sentences instead.

"Mitigating evidence"—typically in the form of information about the background and character of the defendant that helps to explain his past behavior and puts his criminal acts in a larger social context—gives jurors legally supported reasons to spare a defendant's life. Under modern death penalty statutes, once a defendant has been convicted of a potentially capital crime, mitigating evidence is the only thing that stands between him and a death sentence. Yet in too many cases this information is never properly gathered or effectively presented to the jurors who must decide the defendant's fate.[6]

These flaws—condemning persons for crimes they did not commit and sentencing others to death in cases in which fully informed jurors would have spared them—are the legacy of a system in which lawyers often are badly trained, their work poorly funded, and their performance inadequately monitored. For these reasons, instead of a shiny edifice of "super due process for death,"[7] many jurisdictions appear to have built what James Liebman and his colleagues have termed a "broken system," one that they have convincingly shown produces wrong outcomes more often than it is right.[8] Yet many courts have chosen to ignore these troublesome realities in their capital jurisprudence, preferring to depict, rely on, and legitimize an idealized version of the death-sentencing process that, in certain respects, is more reassuring than it is accurate.

In a related way, the warp of the death penalty has created barriers for scholars and researchers who would seek to apply social science to law. We now have at our disposal the most sophisticated research methods and statistical tools ever available for gathering and analyzing data. Many researchers have training in both social science and law, and have sharpened their skills at structuring precise, legally relevant empirical questions. A whole range of jurisprudential issues are open to factual analysis. The effects of various legal procedures and the quality of the law's decision-making processes can now be assessed in ways that were not possible in the past. Perhaps nowhere in law and social science have these methods and skills been applied more often and with more illuminating effect than in the study of the death penalty.

Despite this expertise, our courts and lawmakers now regularly ignore or minimize what such research reveals about the nature and consequences of our society's system of death sentencing. After a brief period of openness in which capital punishment was empirically scrutinized and debated in factual terms, many judges and legislators have become hostile toward or wary of death-penalty-related data. They appear to prefer insulating the capital punishment status quo from reforms whose need has been increasingly well documented by social scientists and others.

This last set of tensions—between social science data and death-penalty-related decisions—has produced a number of dissonant legal chords that

rate throughout the rest of this book. In this chapter I try to address
f them, and in a way that frames several of the issues that are devel-
,~~ ... the chapters that follow.

Empirical Truths and Death Penalty Law

Roland Barthes once wrote that the first step in all "legal murders" is to "rob
a man of his language."[9] In a sense, the first step in preserving our system of
death sentencing has been to gain control over the language by which it is
described, challenged, and defended. The courts, especially, have narrowed
and neutralized the legal significance and public impact of meaningful critical
analyses of the real nature and overall consequences of capital punishment.
Many critics would argue that the modern system of death sentencing has
been maintained through the widespread unwillingness of death penalty supporters and pro-death-penalty legal decision makers to acknowledge fully
and openly all of what is now known about the worst aspects of the system
itself. This has allowed many citizens to support the death penalty without
really understanding how it operates overall, and many courts to give their
imprimatur to a system that is repeatedly but often incorrectly represented
as fair, reliable, and necessary.

Especially over the last several decades, there has been a "conspiracy of
silence" of sorts in which those who are in a position to know most about
the system, and who are perceived to be in some sense above the partisanship
that often dominates the resolution of individual capital cases, have isolated
themselves from its realities. In fact, in the course of preserving our system
of death sentencing, the U.S. Supreme Court has established a number of
legal precedents that exclude many of the most critical facts from its own
view and, in turn, from the view of persons who might look to the Court for
some understanding of how the death penalty actually functions. Because of
the narrowing effect of the Court's doctrines on the nature and scope of
relevant evidence, broad-based social scientific analyses of how the system
really works—including many of its systemic flaws, procedural imperfec-
tions, and sometimes irreparable consequences—have been excluded from
consideration.

The Court, in particular, has refused to consider, acknowledge, or be
influenced by social research that describes a system that is too often plagued
by error and tilted toward death. Many of the Justices have refused to talk
candidly in their opinions about the problems that undermine the fair administration of the death penalty. As a result, the language by which they
describe the system of capital punishment has been robbed of much of its
truth-telling power. The Court's insistence on depicting an idealized rather
than accurate version of the system of death sentencing has contributed to a
number of widespread misunderstandings and misperceptions that I discuss
in a number of subsequent chapters. Because the Court has elected to pre-

serve the death penalty, in part by denying the problems that stil
administration, few authoritative correctives have been or can b
the public's misguided sense of how this system actually functic

To make this nexus a bit clearer, I need to say a few words abou ...
role of the Supreme Court as a communicator of legal values and a legiti-
mator of legal practices. Elsewhere I have written about the Supreme Court's
moralizing influence, and its capacity to set the terms of almost any discussion that is important to the nation's legal self-image. More than any other
institution in our society, the Court manages a "symbolic legality" that embodies our legal and cultural values and represents what most people believe
are the core principles upon which our agencies of justice are based and are
supposed to operate. Not surprisingly, the Constitution stands at the center
of that symbolic legality.[10] If constitutional scholar Sanford Levinson is right
to compare reverence for the Constitution to a "civil religion" in the United
States,[11] and I think he is, then certain of the Court's opinions—especially
those that address matters of importance to all citizens, such as civil rights,
abortion, and the death penalty—are directives from the religion's highest
priests on how to understand and think about certain pressing social and
moral issues. Although I am well aware that this is not the Court's explicit
or official institutional role, it is a function that it performs nonetheless.[12]

When the Justices talk publicly and write in their opinions about a system of capital punishment that is slow to act because it affords *too many*
rights to defendants, they create the misleading impression that the process
of death sentencing is free of certain kinds of errors. When they conclude
that death penalty laws are administered in a racially fair manner, despite a
disproportionate number of African Americans on death rows throughout
the country (and on the lists of those who have been executed), they imply
that bias and prejudice no longer taint the nation's criminal justice institutions. And when the Court summarily approves death sentences or refuses
to stay executions, often without comment, it implies that the legal process
that produced them was so obviously proper and reliable that no justification
of their life-ending consequence is necessary.

The cumulative effect of these decisions is to create the impression that
the overall system of death sentencing has been carefully and comprehensively scrutinized and that it has been pronounced, as a normative matter,
procedurally correct and just in its outcomes. As I have noted, however,
systematic studies of this decision-making process consistently show these
impressions to be false. In this sense, much death penalty doctrine has come
to deny the social reality of death penalty imposition. Although it serves to
maintain a system of death sentencing that otherwise might receive intolerable levels of criticism, this denial nonetheless comes at a steep price. Of
course, it is uniquely costly for the intended targets of capital punishment.
But it also exacts something important from those members of the general
public who seek guidance about how the death penalty really functions in
our society and who want to know whether and when it is really necessary.

Realism About Constitutional Law:
The Promise of *Brown* and *Furman*

Among other things, denying the realities of death penalty imposition and ignoring a great deal of social science evidence about how capital punishment functions in our society have placed the Justices at odds with a long-lasting and important trend in American law. In contemporary times, courts and legislatures have come to rely heavily on specialized expertise to inform themselves about a wide range of issues that once were trusted to "common sense." Given the gravity of the issues they deliberate, it is entirely appropriate that they do. Moreover, when a judicial decision or legal rule depends on one or another conception of the *social* facts that are relevant to the outcome—the real-world impact of a rule or procedure, the actual consequences of a particular practice, and so on—those social facts typically are established by drawing on expertise from disciplines outside the law. For many such legal questions and issues, social scientists possess the most specialized knowledge and relevant expertise needed to inform and enrich the decisions at hand.[13] Of necessity, then, modern-day courts have become accustomed to relying on social science expertise to establish and evaluate essential social facts.

This was not always the case. In the late 19th and early 20th centuries, as the social sciences were emerging as distinct disciplines with recognized areas of expertise, there was substantial resistance from many lawyers and judges who were reluctant to acknowledge any influence from outside the law itself. However, the nation's most important jurisprudential movement—legal realism—ameliorated many early concerns about the propriety of relying on social science in legal decision making. Realism came to dominate American legal education and jurisprudential thinking from the 1930s on, and it paved the way for courts to premise many of their decisions on established social facts—facts that often could be developed only with the empirical methods of social science.[14]

As one commentator more recently put it, the primary goal of much realist thinking was "to displace the speculation and intuition of the traditional common law method with a conscious reliance on empirical methods."[15] Although there were many pockets of continuing resistance, the goal of creating both heightened awareness of and increased reliance on empirical facts was more or less realized in most legal contexts in the United States. Indeed, it was realized in so complete a way that, in an oft-quoted comment, legal historian William Twining could observe: "Realism is dead; we are all realists now."[16]

Moreover, as social science achieved more widespread legitimacy and acceptance, and attained increasingly greater sophistication, this trend intensified. Thus, as the expertise of social scientists from various disciplines came to pertain more directly to legal questions and issues, and as society in general became more accustomed to using social science to inform its understanding of the social world, the increased reliance by legal decision makers—including reluctant members of the judiciary—was inevitable. As two commentators put it, "[o]nce heretical, the belief that empirical studies can influence the content of legal doctrine is now one of the few points of general agreement among jurists."[17]

As most scholars in psychology and law well know, the use of social science in constitutional decision making achieved real prominence in the historic *Brown v. Board of Education* case.[18] In the litigation that preceded *Brown*, the NAACP Legal Defense Fund pressed the social realities of segregation on the federal courts by using, among other things, testimony and data that had been assembled by a number of social science experts. The Supreme Court made passing reference to social science data in a footnote in the *Brown* decision, and empirical research was cited as one basis for the Court's conclusion that segregation was psychologically harmful to the children who were subjected to it.[19] Whether or not the footnoted citations were critical to the outcome of the case, social science knowledge *was* pivotal to the way the Court answered the key legal question that was posed: Why condemn the practice of segregation now when the Supreme Court in the past had found it unproblematic? Chief Justice Warren's answer was simple but decisive—"[w]hatever may have been the extent of psychological knowledge at the time" that the earlier decision was made, times had changed. The Court's revised view of the matter was now "amply supported by the weight of modern authority"[20]—authority that was largely social scientific in nature.

Among other things, in the Court's opinion, this reference to "the weight of modern authority," and the intense focus that was brought to these issues in the wake of the *Brown* decision taught the public much about the system of segregated education in the United States and its harsh consequences for the many African American children who had lived under it. Although many people no doubt knew or suspected that this kind of racial discrimination was widespread and understood intuitively that it was hurtful, the decision in *Brown* brought a measure of undeniability to this social reality. Thus, the mandate to change this pernicious system was made more compelling by the Court's attention to the social facts by which it could be characterized.

In the 1960s, the same organization that had successfully litigated the desegregation cases—the NAACP Legal Defense Fund—began to address another topic of critical importance to African Americans: the administration of the death penalty. Social science would play at least as important a role in this litigation as it had in the desegregation cases. This was in part because the attorneys chose not to challenge the morality of capital punishment per se—as some death penalty opponents might have preferred—but rather to question the way in which the death penalty actually was being administered. That is, they focused on what they contended was the irrationality, unreliability, and unfairness of the *system* of death sentencing.

Legal Defense Fund attorneys and others pressed these arguments by making empirical claims of the sort that social scientists were uniquely suited to address: Did the death penalty deter? If not, were there any other legitimate penological purposes it served? Was it being meted out haphazardly and unreliably? Were death sentences often the product of bias and, particularly, racial prejudice? Did unique aspects of death penalty law result in persons who were facing capital punishment being treated less rather than more fairly than other criminal defendants?[21] These were *all* inherently empirical questions that seemed impossible for the courts to answer without relying heavily on social science research. They were questions that the Supreme Court finally addressed in the 1972 landmark case *Furman v. Georgia.*[22]

As important as *Brown* was in establishing a potential role for social scientists in helping to document many of the social facts on which key constitutional questions were based, *Furman* produced even greater optimism among modern legal realists and others about the important function that research might serve in constitutional decision making. *Furman* seemed to signal that the U.S. Supreme Court was prepared to make extensive use of social science data in grappling in serious, scholarly ways with the social factual context of even its most contentious decisions. The case was notable in many respects. Of course, it is best known for the stunning result it reached—a declaration that death penalty statutes across the country were unconstitutional as they then were being applied. There were nine separate opinions written in the narrow 5–4 decision, and it was the longest single opinion in the history of the Court. But *Furman* also contained the most extensive discussion of social fact data and the greatest number of explicit references to social science research in any decision before or since.

Unlike the single footnote in *Brown*, the various opinions written by the individual Justices in *Furman* included over 60 footnotes citing published social science research, statistical data, and expert social science opinions and commentaries. Although the Justices quoted social science when it was helpful, and ignored it when it was not, and repeatedly disagreed with one another about the social fact data and their implications, their use and application of empirical science and their debates over what it meant were prolonged, serious, and thoughtful. The discussion seemed to acknowledge the obvious— that no conscientious evaluation of the constitutionality of a vast sociolegal system such as capital punishment could be done without careful consideration of the social facts that described how it operated and with what effect. Accordingly, the debate in *Furman* proceeded in a way that seemed unmistakably to legitimize the enterprise of law and social science itself.

Among other things, the style of reasoning that characterized *Furman* suggested that the real facts and actual operation of the system of capital punishment would be at the forefront of any future litigation and judicial decisions that pertained to its constitutionality. To paraphrase Camus, the Justices appeared committed to examining what the death penalty really was and, only then, deciding whether it was really necessary. Of course, this meant that the Court would provide the American public—as an important audience for its opinions on matters such as these—with accurate information about the nature and effect of the death penalty. Even as the Justices openly and strongly disagreed with one another, the empirical terms of the debate—including a number of social factual questions that remained to be answered—were established.

In the final analysis, the Court's decision finding death penalty statutes unconstitutional turned on the view of a plurality of the Justices that these laws were being applied haphazardly, through the "unbridled discretion" of juries whose members operated without legal standards or formal guidance with which to decide which defendants lived and which died. The pattern of irrationality that plagued the sentencing process, the fact that the particular considerations that might tip the balance in one direction or another seemed to be left to chance—that "there [was] no meaningful basis for distinguishing the few cases in which it [was] imposed from the many cases in which it [was] not"[23]—meant that the penalty itself was excessive and in violation of the Eighth Amendment.

Learning From *Furman*: The Legal Mechanics of Denial

When the Court, in essence, "reinstated" the death penalty four years later—in *Gregg v. Georgia* and several companion cases[24]—its implicit message about whether and how it would rely on social science changed dramatically. In addition to their more obvious and dramatic doctrinal consequences, *Gregg* and the related 1976 death penalty decisions signaled a profound shift in the nature of the Court's reasoning about capital punishment. Starting with these cases, it seemed as though the social facts of capital punishment had become too troublesome and inconvenient for the majority Justices (who had decided to uphold the death penalty) to acknowledge. Perhaps because of the deep ambivalence about capital punishment to which I earlier alluded, and because of the profound nature of what is at stake in any death penalty case, the Court began to deal with these troublesome and inconvenient social facts simply by declaring them irrelevant. From this point on, a majority of the Justices seemed to turn Camus's advice on its head: Because they had decided the death penalty was "really necessary," they would refuse to examine what it really was or, in the wake of the new laws they continued to approve, what it was becoming.

Legal scholars and death penalty lawyers know that the *Gregg* Court not only ruled that "the punishment of death does not invariably violate the Constitution,"[25] but also shifted the entire framework that would be used to examine the constitutionality of capital punishment. Justice Stewart focused attention on what he termed "objective indicia that reflect the public attitude toward a given sanction,"[26] and he relied on these indicia to conclude that "it is now evident that a large proportion of American society continues to regard [the death penalty] as an appropriate and necessary criminal sanction."[27] In addition to the importance of public support, however, Stewart acknowledged that the death penalty also had to achieve some legitimate penological purpose. He dealt summarily with what that might be.

Stewart first asserted that the death penalty served "two principal social purposes: retribution and deterrence." To establish the legitimacy of retribution, he began by quoting his own opinion in *Furman* to the effect that "[t]he instinct for retribution is part of the nature of man," and that the death penalty "promot[ed] the stability of a society governed by law." Indeed, he asserted that the absence of the death penalty somehow would sow "the seeds of anarchy," even promote acts of vigilantism, and—of all things—lynching.[28] These fundamentally empirical claims were offered without the benefit of any social scientific citations or references to social fact data to support them. Moreover, they begged the real question of whether and why the retributive effect of the punishment of *death* was uniquely capable of satisfying this "instinct" and forestalling anarchy and lynchings. As retributive theorists often do, Stewart mistakenly substituted a justification for inflicting *some* punishment in place of a justification for imposing a *particular* punishment (in this case, death).

From a social science perspective, his handling of the next issue—deterrence—was even less satisfactory. The issue of whether the death penalty was an effective deterrent had been hotly debated in *Furman*. In fact, Justice White had termed the deterrence issue "most important," and it was the one on which his pivotal vote in *Furman* had seemed to turn. In Stewart's *Gregg* opinion, however, deterrence was dispensed with in less than two pages. He referred only in passing to the substantial body of empirical research that pointed almost without exception to the *lack* of any measurable deterrent effect. Without any detailed or meaningful discussion of the data themselves, Stewart declared the numerous studies "inconclusive." Quoting a law professor—not a social scientist—he embraced the notion that a " 'scientific'—that is to say, a soundly based—conclusion is simply impossible, and no methodological path out of this tangle suggests itself."[29]

This view, of course, is simply wrong, and it was at the time Justice Stewart expressed it. There were a variety of methodological paths by which sound conclusions about the deterrent effect of the death penalty not only could be reached but already had been. Justice Stewart's assertion that "there is no convincing empirical evidence either supporting or refuting" the unique deterrent effect of the death penalty certainly was not corroborated by the standard acknowledged in *Brown*—"the weight of modern authority."[30]

In fact, *Gregg* was the beginning of a long line of capital cases in which a majority of Justices made it increasingly clear that they simply were not interested in the social realities of capital punishment. Thus, with respect to deterrence, Justice Stewart opined in *Gregg* that it was a "complex factual issue the resolution of which properly rests with the legislatures which can evaluate the results of statistical studies in terms of their own local conditions and with a flexibility of approach that is not available to the courts."[31] Other important death-penalty-related social fact issues got similar cursory treatment or less.

Notwithstanding the Court's mishandling of the social fact issues, the legal centerpiece of *Gregg* and the related 1976 cases was the Justices' approval of an approach to death sentencing that was designed to better structure the death-sentencing process itself. Recall that it was the nature and amount of discretion afforded to capital jurors that had troubled many of the Justices in *Furman*. In approving statutes that ostensibly were designed to address this problem, the *Gregg* Court talked repeatedly about an "individualized" sentencing process in which capital jurors would be instructed to consider aggravating and mitigating factors—legally acceptable reasons for imposing either a death or life sentence—in reaching their penalty verdicts.

This sentencing scheme was untested and unevaluated at the time the Court approved it. Consistent with what appeared to be a newfound lack of interest in or respect for death-penalty-related social science data, *Gregg* made no mention of the empirical vacuum on which the Court's approval rested. The majority did not attempt to answer the social fact question that was at the core of the case—whether the new penalty-phase procedures actually warranted the faith the Court was placing in them. In fact, Justice White chastised the petitioners in *Gregg* for even raising it. He suggested that their challenge to the revised death-sentencing procedures reflected little more than "an assertion of lack of faith in the ability of the system of justice to operate in a fundamentally fair manner."[32] But White's own opinion and that of the Justices who joined him in approving of Georgia's new statute were based on the opposite wholly faith-based view. That is, that the centuries-old system of death sentencing—the one that, just a few years earlier, the Court had declared was so lacking in fundamental fairness that it was cruel and unusual—now had been made so obviously reliable and fair that the Justices did not need the benefit of any further empirical scrutiny before giving it their blessing.

McCleskey: Denying the Social Realities of Discrimination

There was one more systemic challenge to Georgia's death penalty laws that seemed to epitomize the Court's new approach to the social realities of capital punishment. In the history of the death penalty in the United States, African Americans have been sentenced to die in numbers that greatly exceeded their percentages in the population at large. Historian Stuart Banner has noted that even before the American Revolution the southern colonies managed their captive slave workforces by relying on "ever-increasing lists of capital statutes" that were applied to blacks and not whites.[33] The legacy of this early system has persisted well into modern times. At the time of *Furman*, for example, 405 blacks had been executed for the crime of rape over the preceding 40 years, compared to 45 whites.[34]

Nonetheless, the Court in *Furman* had split over the issue of whether capital punishment was being discriminatorily imposed on African American defendants. Several Justices were reluctant to conclude anything about apparent racism in the administration of capital punishment, in part because they believed that the discriminatory practices that gave rise to these racial disproportions in the past had been remedied—perhaps in the course of the ongoing civil rights movement and struggle for racial fairness in which the Court itself had played a prominent role. Yet even most of the skeptical and reluctant Justices seemed to concede that more recent and appropriate evidence on this question might well be persuasive. For example, although Chief Justice Burger dismissed the data on racial disparities that had been presented in *Furman* because it was based on practices "in the distant past," he noted that "[d]ata of more recent origin are essential," that "a strong showing would have to be made," and that a convincing study would have to take "all relevant factors into account."[35]

Similarly, Justice Powell noted that an equal protection argument "might well be made" if it could be shown that blacks were being "singled out" for the death penalty at a higher rate than others.[36] He quoted an appellate court opinion that had been written by Justice Blackmun several years earlier (when Blackmun was a member of the Court of Appeals for the Eighth Circuit), to the effect that the courts were "not yet ready" to uphold such a claim "on the basis of broad theories of social and statistical injustice."[37]

Blackmun's earlier decision and Powell's *Furman* opinion were predicated on the notion that an "improper state practice of the past does not automatically invalidate a procedure of the present."[38] Powell was explicit in asserting (on the basis of what appeared to be little more than his own private view of the matter) that "[t]he segregation of our society in decades past, which contributed substantially to the severity of punishment for interracial crimes, is now no longer prevalent in this country. . . . Because standards of criminal justice have 'evolved' in a manner favorable to the accused, discriminatory imposition of capital punishment is far less likely today than in the past."[39] Presumably, though, if data were presented showing a *recent* pattern of precisely the kind of widespread discrimination that Powell believed was "no longer prevalent," he could be persuaded. Otherwise why all this emphasis on past versus present discrimination?

The opportunity came 15 years after *Furman,* and some nine years after the Court reinstated the death penalty in *Gregg.* The case was *McCleskey v. Kemp,*[40] and it gave the Court a chance to examine the system of death sentencing that had been put into operation since those two earlier, landmark opinions. The facts and claims raised in *McCleskey* provided a realistic look at the joint effects of economic and racial injustice—being poor and being black—which, in American society, so often co-occur. Petitioner Warren McCleskey and his NAACP Legal Defense Fund attorneys presented the Su-

preme Court with strong evidence documenting the discriminatory imposition of the death penalty.

To be sure, there was a historical context for race-based death-sentencing
practices in Georgia in particular. For example, between 1930 and 1977,
Georgia had executed 62 men for the crime of rape, 58 of whom were black.[41]
But more recent data collected in Georgia and elsewhere indicated that racial
factors continued to influence the administration of the death penalty. Thus,
a substantial amount of post-*Furman* data showed that blacks in different
jurisdictions across the country still were more likely to receive the death
penalty once they had been convicted of a potentially capital crime.[42] In
addition, another strong pattern emerged in this research—defendants of
either race were less likely to receive the death penalty when their victims
were black rather than white. As Samuel Gross and Robert Mauro put it,
"racial factors, in particular the race of the victim, have large aggregate effects
on capital sentencing."[43] Thus, blacks appeared to be overpunished as capital
defendants and undervalued as victims of capital crime. A number of these
studies suggested that the influence of racial factors was persistent and that
it infected many of the decision points in the process by which the death
penalty eventually was imposed.[44]

Warren McCleskey was a black man who had been convicted and sentenced to die in Georgia. His appeal was based largely on an elaborate social
science study by Professor David Baldus and his colleagues examining death-
sentencing practices in the state. The pattern of racial discrimination that
Baldus identified was highly significant.[45] As table 1.1 shows, for example,
prosecutors were more than twice as likely to seek a death sentence against
a black accused of killing a white victim—fully 70% of the cases—as when
the defendant was white. When black defendants in Georgia were convicted
of killing white victims, they were sentenced to death at nearly 22 times the
rate of blacks convicted of killing blacks and more than seven times the rate
of whites who killed blacks (22% death verdicts vs. 3%).

Baldus's study was sophisticated and detailed. It employed a meticulous
design and utilized advanced statistical techniques. To address the concern

Table 1.1
Death Penalty and Discrimination in Georgia

		Percent of Cases That Prosecutors Seek Death				Percent of Cases That Juries Return Death	
		Race of Victim				Race of Victim	
		White	Black			White	Black
Race of defendant	White	32%	19%	Race of defendant	White	8%	3%
	Black	70%	15%		Black	22%	1%

From Baldus, Woodworth, & Pulaski, 1990.

that some factors other than race might be accounting for what appeared to be clear racial differentials, Baldus took as many as 230 variables into account in various multiple regression analyses.[46] No matter how the data were analyzed or what additional factors were added into the regression equations, patterns of racial discrimination were identified. They appeared to be at the heart of the death-sentencing process in Georgia.

Although the data and analysis Baldus provided in *McCleskey* struck "at the heart" of Georgia's criminal justice system, as the Court itself acknowledged,[47] they struck even more at the heart of the Court's own earlier, hopeful reasoning in *Gregg*. That is, the troubling implications of the Baldus data for the system of death sentencing that the Court previously had approved now seemed clear—the use of narrowing statutes and sentencing instructions to guide capital juries and ensure that they exercised their discretion in fair and unbiased ways appeared to have failed, at least in Georgia. Other similar studies done in other jurisdictions suggested that this approach to eliminating racial discrimination in death sentencing was unsuccessful elsewhere as well.[48] However, instead of acknowledging this seemingly inescapable and troublesome fact, the Court chose to reject the clear implication of the overall pattern of discriminatory death sentencing that the *McCleskey* case brought to its attention.

To do so, however, the Justices had to dismiss the very evidentiary foundation on which McCleskey's claim was based—social scientific data about the overall operation of the system of death sentencing. Justice Powell, who had seemed open in *Furman* to a study of present rather than past discrimination, now focused on an entirely different set of concerns. He began by "assuming" that the Baldus study was "statistically valid."[49] Even so, Powell said, the pattern of overall discrimination that Baldus had documented did not mean that "the study shows that racial considerations actually enter into any sentencing decisions in Georgia." That was because "even a sophisticated multiple regression analysis" like the one Baldus had done could "*only* demonstrate a risk that the factor of race entered into capital sentencing decisions and a lesser risk that race entered into any particular sentencing decision."[50] Of course, social science studies that examine overall patterns of aggregate data reach conclusions that are based entirely on risks and probabilities—the *tendency* of a system or process to produce one kind of outcome versus another. That is their greatest strength. Yet Powell argued that it was their fatal flaw.

This and other passages in the *McCleskey* opinion underscored the Court's unwillingness to examine problematic systemic patterns and structural deficiencies in the way that death penalty cases were being decided by jurors who were choosing between life and death in Georgia (and, by implication, in other states as well). Quite clearly, the collective outcomes of a *system* of capital sentencing were being depicted in Baldus's data, and McCleskey's case provided the appropriate vehicle with which to precipitate a broad-based response to this systemic problem. It was a response that the

Court was uniquely positioned to provide. Yet because McCleskey was unable to offer "evidence *specific to his own case* that would support an inference that racial considerations played a part in his sentence,"[51] Powell said, he could not prevail.

The Court added another requirement that, practically speaking, would prove fatal to future constitutional challenges based on social scientific analyses of patterns of unequal treatment. Justice Powell wrote that capital defendants would have to show intentional or purposeful discrimination in order to succeed on claims that they had been treated in ways that were racially unfair. That is, "to prevail under the Equal Protection Clause," a defendant "must prove that the decision makers in *his* case acted with discriminatory purpose."[52] The Court left no doubt about how exacting a standard it would apply to such claims: "Because discretion is essential to the criminal justice process, we would demand *exceptionally clear* proof before we would infer that the discretion has been abused."[53]

The practical implications of this requirement were obvious. Because persons who are most prejudiced often are least aware of their biases and, when they are aware, are least willing to disclose them, requiring clear proof of intentional discrimination meant that it would be difficult if not impossible for a future petitioner ever to succeed.[54] Moreover, *conscious* prejudice— certainly a consciousness of bias manifested in ways that led to "exceptionally clear" proof—is merely one aspect of racially unfair treatment. A system of death sentencing could operate with little conscious awareness on any one person's part that he or she was bringing racial prejudice to bear on the discretionary criminal justice decisions being made. Yet structural, implicit, and nonconscious biases still could produce outcomes that were no less discriminatory or invidious. The *McCleskey* decision left death penalty petitioners with no remedy for these kinds of prejudices.

Moreover, the warp of the death penalty to which I earlier alluded appeared to play a significant role in shaping the rhetoric with which the Court surrounded its holding in *McCleskey*. Justice Powell simply could have left his analysis of the fairness of this aspect of the death-sentencing process where it stood—data about systemic discrimination were not enough in death penalty challenges and evidence of discriminatory intent was the threshold for an equal protection claim of this sort (no matter how elusive it might be to obtain). Yet he continued in an unusual and unusually revealing way. That is, he set about to describe at length all of the due process "protections" that capital defendants were afforded. Presumably, these were things with which McCleskey (and other African American capital defendants like him) should have been satisfied, no matter how racially discriminatory the final outcomes in their collective cases.

After all, Powell noted, "numerous features of the . . . Georgia statute met the concerns articulated in *Furman*."[55] The opinion neglected to mention that the *Furman* Court had "concerns" about the *outcomes* of death penalty cases and the "features" of the new statutes were no more than the hopeful means to fairer, less arbitrary and discriminatory ends. Nonetheless, Powell explained to McCleskey that even though some discretion had to be left to the jury, "the discretion to be exercised is controlled by clear and objective standards so as to produce non-discriminatory application."[56] No further word about the highly discriminatory pattern of death sentencing established in McCleskey's appeal. Instead, the Court had only more due process to offer. It reminded McCleskey that the Georgia Supreme Court was required "to review each sentence to determine whether it was imposed under the influence of passion or prejudice," and that these reviews were aided by the trial judge's answers to a questionnaire about, among other things, "whether race played a role in the trial."[57]

Justice Powell continued, praising a system that afforded defendants "the inestimable privilege of trial by jury," by giving them "fundamental 'protection of life and liberty against race or color prejudice.' " Indeed, Powell noted that the Court required the profoundly important judgments made in capital cases to reflect a "diffused impartiality," one that brought to bear "the conscience of the community on the ultimate expression of life or death."[58] This touting of due process advantages was repeated a short time later when he noted again that the "jury sentence reflects the conscience of the community as applied to the circumstances of a particular offender and offense" and reminded readers that "[d]iscretion in the criminal justice system offers substantial benefits to the criminal defendant."[59] There was still more reassurance, a few pages later, to the effect that the Court consistently had required that the process of determining guilt and assigning punishment in capital cases be "*surrounded* with safeguards to make it *as fair as possible*" by relying on various procedures that were "designed to *minimize* racial bias in the process."[60] And, as if McCleskey still might not be convinced (and given the Baldus data it is hard to see how he could be), Powell asserted with apparent pride, "[b]ecause of the risk that the factor of race may enter the criminal justice process, we have engaged in 'unceasing efforts' to eradicate racial prejudice from our criminal justice system."[61]

The juxtaposition of these numerous procedural reassurances against the backdrop of the Baldus data on racial disparities seemed anomalous. It was as though Justice Powell wished to use the litany of due process-type safeguards to prove somehow that discriminatory death sentencing was simply impossible, no matter what the evidence showed. He seemed to invoke all of the impressive due process rights and then to repeat them as a kind of fairness incantation to ward off the reality of unequal treatment that the troublesome social science data had revealed. Focusing so much attention on the due process issues allowed him to ignore many aspects of the equal protection claims at the core of the case. Because Powell already had declared the patterns of discriminatory death sentencing irrelevant, he did not have to struggle with an explanation for *why* they persisted under the newer and presumably fairer system of death sentencing. Nor did he have to grapple with the most problematic aspects of a criminal justice system that was still capable of generating the kinds of disparities that Baldus's research uncovered.

Indeed, Justice Powell's opinion in *McCleskey* spared the Court the task of examining the inequalities in life circumstances that continued to divide the races in the United States, or acknowledge the ways in which the nexus between race, poverty and unemployment, and crime virtually ensured racial disparities in the imposition of the death penalty. In a related way, the opinion sidestepped the issue of whether the elaborate procedural protections with which the Court presumably had surrounded the death penalty would be of any real use to Warren McCleskey and others like him if they did not have the means with which to implement them. McCleskey had a lawyer, to be sure, but like virtually all capital clients, he could not afford to pay him for his time. Instead, he was defended at trial by a court-appointed attorney who, in Georgia and many other states—especially in the southern "death belt"—was overworked, underpaid, and very likely unqualified to handle the increasingly complex challenges posed by a death penalty defense.

There was much evidence at the time—none of which the Court acknowledged—that many death penalty lawyers lacked the training and resources to properly defend their clients. In Virginia, for example, capital defense lawyers at the time *McCleskey* was decided were being paid an average of $687 per case—cases that, if done properly, should take many hundreds (often thousands) of hours to prepare and present. Similarly, Alabama set the statutory limits for indigent defense trial expenses at $500 in capital cases, and the state supreme court upheld this limit.[62]

Not surprisingly, then, only the least experienced and least sought after attorneys handled capital cases in many states. Ironically, rather than calling attention to this problem and requiring states to address it, the Court itself had contributed to it. That is, by creating a number of doctrines that punished capital defendants for the sloppy or untimely legal maneuvers of their lawyers, the Court made the consequences of poor performance by *attorneys* literally fatal for their *clients*. Thus, if lawyers failed to take full advantage of all of the due process protections that the Court's "unceasing efforts" made available to them (by, among other things, objecting to procedural irregularities at trial), then those claims were regarded as having been "defaulted" or waived by the capital clients themselves (even if the claims otherwise would have been meritorious).[63] This meant that as the rules of due process became more elaborate and complex, not only were attorneys who were underfunded, undertrained, and inexperienced less able to make use of them, but many of the lawyers' failures could not be corrected at a later time. The Court neglected to discuss any of this.

The Failure to Present Mitigation:
Skewing the Death-Sentencing Equation

As I have suggested, in many ways *McCleskey* was as revealing for what it did not say about the system of death sentencing as for what it did. In fact, however, this was true of several of the Court's other landmark death penalty cases as well. In each instance, critical aspects of the inadequacies in the way capital defendants were being represented were literally ignored by the Court. These omissions had a major impact on the way capital cases continued to be handled in trial courts across the country. They also likely undermined the public's understanding of the nature of capital punishment and the factors that should govern its imposition.

Perhaps the most glaring oversight concerned one of the most important components in the capital sentencing process. Recall that *Gregg* had approved new death penalty laws that provided for a separate penalty trial and the introduction of aggravating and mitigating testimony. "Aggravation"—evidence that would incline jurors toward death sentences—usually comes in the form of heinous facts about the crime itself and evidence of criminal behavior in which the defendant engaged in the past. Typically, this kind of evidence is straightforward for prosecutors to find and present, and it often represents powerful evidence in favor of a death verdict. Indeed, graphic details about the crime for which the defendant is being tried usually are introduced in the guilt phase of the case. Similarly, if the defendant has a criminal history, it usually is well documented and readily accessible through law enforcement records. Further, aggravation requires little explanation. That is, jurors intuitively understand the negative implication of this kind of evidence and why it suggests that a death sentence may be appropriate.

On the other hand, mitigation—evidence that would incline jurors toward life sentences—is often difficult to obtain and requires special effort on the part of defense attorneys to locate, analyze, and present. Unlike a criminal history, mitigation is less often well documented and rarely is found in an easily accessed, centralized location. Instead, it requires painstaking and time-consuming investigation to acquire. Defense team members must locate and interview an often large number of potential witnesses and comb through diverse sources of information. This kind of mitigation is critical to the outcome of a capital case and to any semblance of fair and reliable death sentencing. In most cases it represents the *only* real hope defendants have of avoiding the death penalty. As one well-known death penalty scholar summarized it: "According to defense attorneys who specialize in capital cases, the best way to be successful at the penalty stage is to present a dramatic psychohistory of the defendant to the jury."[64] But the Supreme Court's handling of this aspect of the death-sentencing process has done little to facilitate the public's understanding of mitigation or to ensure that lawyers grasp and discharge their duty to find and present it.

To be sure, the Georgia statute that was approved in *Gregg* and under which Warren McCleskey was sentenced to die did not explicitly prevent capital defendants from finding and presenting virtually all of the mitigating evidence they could. Unfortunately, however, in Georgia as in many other states—especially in the South—defense attorneys were provided with virtually no resources with which to acquire and analyze such evidence—evidence that typically takes many hundreds of hours to locate, develop, refine, and present in a way that has any hope of being persuasive. This accounts in part for the fact that many defense attorneys fail to make full and effective use of the due process right to present a wide range of mitigation. In fact, in a number of capital cases, *no* such evidence is introduced.

The importance of mitigation to the outcome of capital cases notwithstanding, the Supreme Court has failed to acknowledge the widespread lack of training, experience, and resources that accounts for attorneys failing to effectively find or present mitigating evidence during death penalty trials. Indeed, it took nearly 30 years since *Gregg* reinstated the death penalty in the United States for the Court to require capital defense attorneys to uncover and introduce this kind of potentially lifesaving evidence.[65]

The three landmark Georgia capital cases—*Furman, Gregg,* and *McCleskey*—are illustrative in this regard. The petitioner in *Furman*—William Henry Furman—was sentenced to die in 1968. He had only a sixth-grade education and suffered from a number of psychological problems. While awaiting trial in his death penalty case, Furman was sent to a state institution for a psychiatric evaluation. He was diagnosed as "mentally deficient" with convulsive disorder and psychotic episodes. His mental problems were serious enough for the hospital staff to notify the court that he was presently incompetent to stand trial. About six weeks later the hospital reported that, although his competency had been restored, he still suffered from the previously diagnosed mental deficiency and mental illness. For some reason, however, Furman's court-appointed counsel never put *any* information about his client's mental impairments before the jury that eventually sentenced him to death.

Under Georgia practice at the time, indigents like Furman were entitled to appointed counsel who received a total of $150 for defending him in this capital murder case. His attorney's requests for additional funds to hire an investigator and to be compensated for the additional time and expenses that would be needed "to prepare a case of this kind" were all denied by the judge. The trial itself was exceedingly brief. The entire proceeding—from the start of jury selection to the jury's rendering of a death sentence—was accomplished between 10 A.M. and about 5 P.M the same day. As Justice Brennan noted, "[a]bout Furman himself, the jury knew only that he was black and that, according to his statement at trial, he was 26 years old and worked at 'Superior Upholstery.' "[66]

Of course, Furman's case had come to trial under the "old," unconstitutional system, the one that presumably had been reformed by the time the next landmark case—*Gregg*—was decided. The petitioner in *Gregg v. Georgia*—Troy Gregg—was the beneficiary of the new and improved death penalty system. The Georgia statute that governed his case included the various special protections that the Court used as the basis for deciding that capital punishment once again was constitutional in the United States. Gregg was convicted of a less sympathetic crime than Furman—killing two men who had given a ride to him and friend as they were hitchhiking. Although Gregg claimed later that he had acted in self-defense, the prosecutor successfully contended that he intended to rob the two victims. Despite the fact that his trial was a bit more elaborate than Furman's had been, the entire proceeding—including the special, new sentencing hearing—still lasted only four days. Here, too, except for the details of the serious crime of which they convicted him, the jurors learned *nothing* about Troy Gregg or the kind of life he had lived.

Indeed, at Gregg's separate sentencing hearing—the very procedural innovation on which the Supreme Court had placed so much emphasis when it decided that the constitutional defects in the death penalty had been remedied—Gregg's court-appointed attorney presented no evidence whatsoever. When it came time for their all-important consideration of "aggravating" and "mitigating" evidence in order to decide whether Gregg should live or die and their exercise of the "guided discretion" that would become the touchstone of modern capital jurisprudence, members of his jury likely had an easy time of it. No specific "mitigating circumstances" were listed or defined anywhere in the Georgia statute, and no mitigating testimony had been presented in Gregg's sentencing hearing. In fact, his court-appointed attorney presented *no* evidence in Gregg's entire trial (except to place his client on the witness stand to deny that he committed the murders in the course of a robbery).

And then there was Warren McCleskey's case. McCleskey was a young black man who was convicted of killing a police officer in the course of the robbery of a furniture store. His case was tried even later in a post-*Gregg* world where bifurcated capital trials and specific sentencing instructions were commonplace and supposedly guided the jury to consider a broad range of factors that would preclude arbitrary or discriminatory death sentencing. Indeed, as I noted earlier, the Supreme Court had trumpeted many of these new due process protections from which McCleskey presumably had benefited.

Recall that Justice Powell's *McCleskey* opinion had pointed early and often to the central role of mitigation in insuring the fairness of the existing state death-sentencing systems, noting that "a capital sentencing jury may consider *any* factor relevant to the defendant's background, [and] character."[67] Thus, Powell underscored the importance of Georgia's bifurcated capital trial process, one that was used "so that the jury can receive *all relevant information* for sentencing without the risk that evidence irrelevant to the defendant's guilt will influence the jury's consideration of that issue." This allowed "the defendant to introduce *any relevant mitigating evidence* that might influence the jury not to impose the death sentence."[68] Indeed, as I noted earlier, Justice Powell seemed to justify McCleskey's own death sentence by pointing to the care with which it presumably had been meted out—of course, in accord with sentencing procedures in Georgia that followed the mandate of *Gregg* to focus the jury's discretion "on the particularized characteristics of the individual defendant."[69]

Remarkably, despite the Court's repeated reassurances about the centrality of mitigation to the new system of death sentencing, Warren McCleskey's attorney, in fact, had offered *no* mitigating evidence on his client's behalf. Moreover, in the course of its lengthy peroration on the elaborate due process protections available to McCleskey, the Court did not see fit to mention the fact that the one protection he most needed—a competent attorney who did everything possible to amass and present mitigating evidence to his jury—was one he did not have. Notwithstanding all the talk about the importance of judging "the particularized characteristics of the individual defendant," the jury that sentenced Warren McCleskey to die knew nothing at all about his background or social history or life experiences or particularized characteristics of any kind.

In fact, the only thing the jury knew about the defendant's background was the aggravation that the prosecutor had introduced—that McCleskey previously served time in prison for prior armed robberies. The jurors likely concluded the same thing that a legal commentator later inferred from the trial record in the case—that "McCleskey seemed the stereotype of the violent black felon so feared by contemporary American society. A seemingly sociopathic armed robber."[70] It was a view McCleskey's attorneys never bothered even to attempt to rebut. No one in a position to decide his fate—certainly not the jury that sentenced him to die—would ever know whether it was true.[71]

Capital defendants Furman, Gregg, and McCleskey certainly were not unique in having their death sentences rendered by juries that knew nothing about them except for the crimes they had committed. Especially in southern states, court-appointed defense lawyers routinely handled capital cases for so little compensation that the least experienced and least skilled attorneys were likely to defend criminal defendants in precisely those cases where the stakes were highest. As one commentator put it: "Many of these lawyers had little or no experience trying capital cases; many had no experience in criminal matters at all; some lacked any conception of what they were supposed to do. Many made no effort to gather evidence that might help their clients avoid the death penalty."[72] There is little evidence to indicate that the situation has changed appreciably over time in many jurisdictions.[73] Yet, as I say, for nearly all of the almost 30 years since *Gregg*, Supreme Court decisions have remained silent about all of this.

Conclusion

What does this long discussion of Supreme Court doctrine and the role of social science in constitutional decision making have to do with how citizens, voters, and jurors approach our system of death sentencing? Note that the Supreme Court's modern death penalty jurisprudence has accomplished several things, each of which is crucial to the public's understanding of the nature of capital punishment and to the maintenance of our system of death sentencing. For one, the Court effectively has shielded the death-sentencing process from most of the broad-based social scientific analyses that have uncovered many of its potential constitutional flaws. Instead of a social fact-oriented and empirically based discussion of the realities of the system of death sentencing, the Court substituted an idealized but inaccurate account of how capital punishment actually operates in the Unites States.[74]

In a similar vein, the Court has legitimized capital punishment not only by relying on procedures that were supposed to afford defendants a surplus of due process rights but also by placing much emphasis on an elaborate framework of penalty-phase decision making that it claimed allowed capital juries to "receive all relevant information for sentencing," including a full range of "compassionate or mitigating factors stemming from the diverse frailties of humankind."[75] Nonetheless, after the Court reinstated capital punishment—and did so largely on the basis of these procedures and this framework—it did little or nothing to ensure that defendants actually received the benefits of these same reforms.[76] Precisely because the Court rejected broad-based challenges to the overall system of death sentencing—insisting first that capital punishment was really necessary and then never bothering to examine what it really had become—capital defendants in many jurisdictions and in many cases never enjoyed the fair process to which the Court had said they were entitled.

Of course, combined with the rhetoric about the "unceasing efforts" to which it had gone to make the death penalty fair and reliable, the Court's death penalty decisions left the public with a number of mistaken impressions. Citizens, voters, and potential jurors who lacked firsthand experience with the system of death sentencing could infer from the way the Court wrote about capital punishment that it was administered in an excessively fair fashion, that it tailored sentencing outcomes according to nuanced considerations and unique factors that applied to individual defendants and particular cases, and that it was responsive to any and all possible mitigating factors that could be brought to bear on a defendant's behalf. Yet in many cases—in some jurisdictions they were the normative cases by far—none of these things were true.

If citizens could not rely on the Court for an accurate understanding of the workings of the death penalty, and to help them reach conclusions about whether there was a genuine need for capital punishment to safeguard the communities in which they lived, then they would turn to other sources. In these ways, then, the Court's abdication of its role as a careful analyst of the realities of capital punishment meant that, increasingly, the public was especially vulnerable to the kind of myth and misinformation that I discuss in the next two chapters.

2

Frameworks of Misunderstanding
Capital Punishment and the American Media

Crime-related issues . . . are socially and politically constructed;
they acquire their meaning through interpretive, representational,
and political processes.
—Katherine Beckett, *Making Crime Pay: Law and Order in
Contemporary American Politics* (1997)

This chapter develops a theme that serves as an important backdrop for the
chapters that follow: namely, that the mass media in our society play a central
role in the creation of erroneous beliefs and preconceptions about crime and
punishment that have real consequences for death penalty policies and practices. Given the ubiquity and power of the mass media in American society,
it has become difficult to intelligently analyze *any* important public policy
issue without some reflection on the potential influence of the media.[1] As
members of the public formulate their views of the death penalty—in their
roles as citizens, voters, and jurors—they are especially likely to be affected
by media messages about violent crime and capital punishment. This chapter
explores some of the dimensions of that influence and sets the stage for the
more data-based chapters that follow. It is admittedly more impressionistic
than my subsequent discussion of the system of death sentencing, but it is
no less important.

All Crime, All the Time

No matter which form of media they prefer, American audiences are immersed in crime-related themes and stories. Crime dominates the newspapers
and airwaves, and its dominance is long-standing. Because "[t]he mass media
always are on the alert for dramatic, personalized stories that will command
public attention,"[2] crime has been a prominent feature in both print and
electronic news and drama. In fact, crime is the single most popular story

50-year history of television, with between one-quarter and
television shows estimated to be crime-related.[3] This popu-
ned in recent years. In 2003, for example, there were more
rime shows broadcast regularly on prime-time television.[4]
ns a central focus of news coverage as well as dramatic
........ming. Not surprisingly, perhaps, one study of well over 100,000
stories covered in network evening newscasts during the decade of the
1990s found crime to be the single most frequently addressed topic.[5] Crime
dominates other media outlets as well. As one commentator put it, if the
United States "could be said to have a national literature, it is crime mel-
odrama."[6]

Studies suggest that the media's focus on crime is not necessarily tied
to actual crime rates. That is, the amount of media crime coverage is not
a simple function of the amount of crime that plagues the community in
which it is disseminated.[7] In fact, Christopher Jencks noted a persistent
bias within the media to depict crime rates as ever increasing.[8] That is, as
part of a "very selective approach to crime statistics," media gatekeepers
tend to ignore or downplay a decrease in crime rates but interpret any increase "as a portent of things to come and give it a lot of play."[9] Jencks
suggested that this helps to create a public atmosphere in which crime
rates feel like they are on the rise even when they are not. This perception
tends to increase crime fears and give the impression that the nation is
perpetually losing the battle against crime. Over the last several decades
many politicians have been quick to blame the sometimes illusory but
(seemingly) ever-rising tide of criminality on lenient sentencing policies.
This has served as a powerful, built-in argument in favor of harsher punishments like the death penalty.

In fact, the media continued to promote heightened fears about crime
well into the 1990s, long after crime rates in the United States were on the
decline. For example, in just one month at the start of 1994, after the nation
had experienced several years in a row of *falling* crime rates, the covers of all
three of the national news magazines carried frightening crime-related messages. Specifically, *Newsweek*'s January 10, 1994, cover story reported on
"Growing Up Scared: How Our Kids Are Robbed of Their Childhood," and
argued that the fear of violent crime had become so pervasive in our society
it was radically transforming the very nature of childhood. The next week,
U.S. News & World Report's January 17, 1994, cover depicted a shattered glass
window that had been pierced by several bullets. This disturbing image was
overlaid with the words "The Truth About Violent Crime, What You Really
Have to Fear." And just a few weeks later, the February 7, 1994, cover of
Time displayed a dramatic rendering of a criminal locked into an old-
fashioned pillory painted in the colors of the American flag. Beneath the
image were the words "Lock 'Em Up and Throw Away the Key, Outrage
Over Crime Has America Talking Tough." (See figure 2.1.)

As crime rates continued to decline in the 1990s, however, there came

Figure 2.1 Fear Factor: The covers of the major national news magazines carried alarmist messages about crime during just a single month period at the start of 1994, despite the fact that the crime rate in the United States had already begun its decade-long steady decline. (Top) *Newsweek* © 1994 Newsweek Inc. All rights reserved. Reprinted with permission. (Middle) *Time Magazine* © 1994 Time Inc. Reprinted with permission. (Bottom) *U.S. News & World Report* © 1994 U.S. News & World Report, L.P. Reprinted with permission.

a point where the downward trend could not be ignored. Still, many of the news reports about the declining crime rates speculated about an impending "upturn" sometime in the "near" future. For example, in 1996, the *New York Times* reported: "Despite recent reports that crime is decreasing, violent crime in the United States is a 'ticking time bomb' that will explode in the next few years as the number of teenagers soars, an organization of prosecutors and law-enforcement experts said in a report yesterday." The author of the report, conservative criminologist John DiIulio, expressed the concern that recent drops in violent crime rates were nothing more than the "lull before the crime storm," and he advocated more "aggressive" crime-fighting tactics to ward off the crime wave yet to come.[10] Alarmist forecasts like these kept pressure on lawmakers to continue to support increasingly harsh punishment that included longer prison sentences and the expanded use of the death penalty. In fact, these kinds of laws were passed throughout the 1990s, despite what blossomed into a full decade of decreasing crime rates. The "ticking time bomb" fortunately never materialized, but neither did any in-depth media analysis of how and why the dire predictions had proven incorrect.

Media Agenda Setting and the Fear of Crime

The process by which the media highlight those issues around which there is heightened public awareness, debate, and concern has been termed its "agenda setting" function. The topic has spawned a substantial amount of academic writing and empirical research.[11] Since Walter Lippmann observed many years ago that the media played a significant role in creating many of "the pictures inside our heads,"[12] few scholars have doubted the influential effect of media messages and images on public opinion. Studies have documented the relationship between the amount of news coverage given to particular topics and the significance the public subsequently attaches to these same topics.[13]

Both the print and electronic media appear to play significant roles in this process. Although television news and drama reach more people, and are capable of more dramatic images, newspapers still affect public discourse and opinion. Not surprisingly, what is reported in the local press is significantly correlated with what people in the community report reading and talking about.[14] Indeed, one study indicated that the agenda-setting effect of television news actually was enhanced by the viewers' exposure to print media. That is, persons who read the newspapers also apparently tend to watch television and—perhaps because newspapers provide a consistent but richer context with which to interpret typically briefer television news broadcasts— they are more influenced by it than those who do not.[15]

The media are especially powerful in shaping attitudes and beliefs about those things with which members of the public have little direct experience—

like the causes of crime, the nature of violent criminality, and the most effective strategies for addressing crime-related problems.[16] Studies of media coverage of crime-related topics bear this out. According to at least one relatively recent survey, the media were the *most important* source of information about the crime problem for 90% of the respondents.[17] In addition, many researchers have observed that the media not only focus extensively on crime but also report it in ways that distort and exaggerate its prevalence and significance.[18] Among other apparent distortions, homicides are grossly overrepresented in media accounts of crime.[19]

Distorted or not, crime news coverage and crime-related drama appear to have real effects on the public. As researchers have noted, "[b]ecause most people do not have direct experience with the serious violent crimes that they most fear, the role of the media in generating such fear becomes particularly important."[20] For example, studies have demonstrated a direct relationship between the amount of newspaper space devoted to violent crime and the likelihood that neighborhood residents selected crime as their community's most serious problem.[21] One found that "media-supplied crime experience is a significant predictor of general fear of crime for both male and female subjects."[22] In addition, readers of newspapers with the largest amount of crime reporting also expressed higher levels of fear of crime than residents of other communities where there was less coverage.[23] In fact, some researchers have found that actual experience with crime may *reduce* one's fear of it.[24]

Subsidized Crime News, Biased Media Messages, and Criminal Justice Policy

Skewed crime rate reporting may be a symptom of a larger structural bias in modern news-gathering practices that stems from the symbiotic relationship that has been formed between the media and law enforcement organizations. Just as the public learns about crime primarily from the media, the media learn about crime primarily from the police and other criminal justice officials who become, in essence, the "gatekeepers" of crime news. Over the last two decades, it has become standard for criminal justice agencies to appoint "public information officers" whose job it is to "coordinate the flow of information to the news media while promoting a positive image of the organization."[25] Crime reporters correspondingly have become dependent on these regular sources for the information on which they base their stories. A tight circle of mutual self-interest is thus created. In this sense, then, statements made by law enforcement officials often serve as the fundamental building blocks of crime news.[26]

For example, one study reported that almost three-quarters of network news sources were political leaders or governmental officials.[27] Others have analyzed the role of governmental agencies in providing so-called "subsidized news" stories that are based directly on press releases from public information officers. These practices help to account for the frequency of crime stories as well as their lack of connection to specific crime problems in the local communities in which they are published.[28] One researcher found that the state department of justice was the most prolific source of press releases, as well as the source of the greatest number of subsidized news stories. Not surprisingly, stories about justice and public safety accounted for close to 50% of all subsidized stories in that state during the period under study.[29] In addition, local police agencies as well as high-level state agencies have become increasingly "media savvy." For example, one group of researchers who studied the way in which images of crime and punishment were constructed in the media noted that "[p]olice officers of all ranks emphasized that the force was becoming increasingly oriented to the media."[30] Others have commented on the reorganization of public affairs units within police departments themselves that include the hiring of "civilians experienced in journalism and public relations" to better assist in the task of managing their public, media image.[31] As one such police public affairs manager conceded: "Our primary public relations tool is the media. My job is to try and manage the public image of the police department. . . ."[32]

If we make the reasonable assumption that public information officers present news releases that reflect their state agency's point of view, then the media's crime coverage agenda will be influenced by the agenda of the state agency providing the subsidized news. In one important study, for example, sociologist Katherine Beckett found not only that crime-related news stories were likely to come from state-sponsored sources, but also that this common practice appeared to significantly influence the content of the stories themselves. State-sponsored stories predominated in the media coverage Beckett analyzed and predominately conveyed what she termed "respect for authority" themes.

Specifically, these themes consistently suggested that the only way to control the human propensity for "evil" was to maximize a potential wrongdoer's fear of punishment and to hold individuals completely responsible for their transgressions. The percentage of stories containing such messages (62%) was more than three times the number containing the message that poverty causes crime, and more than six times the number that suggested a balancing of short-term enhancement of effective law enforcement while simultaneously pursuing ways to eradicate the root causes of crime.[33]

Other structural factors are likely to compound this particular bias. For example, a number of analysts have argued that that the economic structure of the mass media constrains the messages it disseminates and subverts its editorial content. These commercial interests help to ensure that the media will reflect a largely homogenized view of reality that is most attractive to relatively affluent readers and viewers.[34] Thus, the ways in which current structural arrangements and economic policies may contribute to chronic poverty, the impact of deep poverty on the day-to-day lives of the poor, or the role of poverty in the genesis of socially problematic behavior (such as crime) tends to be deemphasized or ignored altogether.

Indeed, a number of studies have documented the way in which the influence of broad social and economic contexts on criminality typically are ignored in crime reporting.[35] From this perspective, the heavy concentration on individual responsibility to the exclusion of poverty or a lack of equal opportunity as explanations for criminal behavior is not surprising. But the framework for understanding crime that is conveyed to the audience that consumes these messages will be unnecessarily narrow and misleading. Citizens, voters, and potential jurors may be steered in the direction of favoring individualistic crime control policies (including the death penalty)—rather than, say, socioeconomic reform—as a result.

Thus, as figure 2.2 helps to illustrate, the media's handling of crime-related issues not only may influence citizens' fear of crime but also their beliefs about the causes of criminal behavior and the desirability of one or another approach to crime control. Admittedly, the interrelationships between the media, members of the public, politicians, and crime-related social policy are complex. Moreover, there are many very real crime and punishment issues that are of intrinsic interest to the public at large. To be sure, the fear of criminal victimization is not an irrational figment of the media's imagination. At the same time, however, the media have the capacity to create or reorder public priorities. This power—especially when it is influenced by politically motivated operatives who seek to promote one or another crime-related agenda—is substantial.

Of course, it is difficult to specify precisely how—in any given case—all

Figure 2.2 Certain crimes generate intense media coverage that can surround a case with a powerful prejudicial atmosphere. The defendants in this case were all convicted but years later were released from prison because of a lack of evidence. (First image) *New York Post*. Reprinted with permission from the *New York Post*, April 21, 1989, © NYP Holdings, Inc. (Remaining images) *New York Daily News*. © New York Daily News, L.P. Reprinted with permission.

this translates into the actual policies that are implemented by legal and political decision makers. As two communications researchers have characterized the mutual influence of these various forces: "Once shaped by the media agenda, the public agenda may in turn influence the policy agenda of elite decision makers, and, in some cases, policy implementation. Of course, in some instances the media agenda seems to have direct, sometimes strong, influence upon the policy agenda of elite decision makers, and, in some cases, policy implementation."[36]

Yet whether any particular public concern, framework of understanding, or policy agenda comes originally from citizens, politicians, or pundits, the media can and often do effectively amplify certain points of view. The media also select and give legitimacy to particular perspectives, help to set national priorities by increasing the visibility of some issues and not others, and create a sense of urgency about solving certain social problems over a range of other competing claims.

Beckett's previously mentioned study illustrated the way in which existing political agendas, biased media coverage, and a relatively malleable body of public opinion played mutually reinforcing roles in creating and maintaining harsh crime control policies.[37] She found that certain politicians were able to use the media to implement their own agenda over the last several decades by framing the crime problem largely "as the consequence of insufficient punishment and control."[38] The media communicated this particular—and highly debatable—view of the problem so effectively and so uncritically that it had a real impact on public opinion. That is, the media's biased or selective coverage of crime issues was joined with effective political rhetoric and accompanying policy initiatives to produce *subsequent* increases in public concern about crime.

Media crime coverage not only shapes public perceptions and heightens concerns over the nature and frequency of victimization and the magnitude of the crime problem but also appears to influence judgments people make about whether to use punitive strategies in order to solve it. For example, in one study, researchers compared sentencing views among persons who reviewed several case-related court documents with another group that reviewed several newspaper articles about the same case. Those who read the newspaper articles were more than three times as likely to regard the sentence meted out to the defendant as "too lenient."[39] Another study found that crime-related publicity increased participants' recommended levels of punishment even when the crime for which they rendered a sentence (e.g., theft) was very different from the one they read about (e.g., homicide).[40] As one literature review concluded: "[P]references for highly punitive sanctions in the criminal justice system are one consequence of the media's predilection for covering violent and sensational crimes."[41]

Television Crime Drama: Blurring Fact and Fiction

Of course, media effects are not restricted to news reporting. Consistently high and increasing levels of fear and concern over crime appear related to the nature and amount of *television crime drama* that has dominated network programming over the last several decades. Indeed, as early as 1951 television critic Charles Morton observed that "[c]riminality is still the backbone of broadcasting."[42] However, the manner in which television depicts criminality has changed since the 1950s in ways that appear to have influenced public attitudes about punishment. Thus, Steven Stark reviewed a number of studies concerning the effects of television viewing and concluded that "it is undeniable that in the 1970s, television helped solidify 'crime control' values in the culture at large."[43]

Another commentator similarly argued that between the years 1968 and 1976—a period in which overall public support for punitive crime control in general, and capital punishment in particular, increased significantly[44]—television crime drama underwent an important transformation: "[T]elevision turned back to more conservative police shows in this period. . . . Like radio in the Depression, societal unrest caused television to trigger a conservative backlash, and a number of series that legitimated 'the system.' In broadcast terms, the 1970s became a broader-scale rerun of the 1930s."[45] This trend continued through the decades that followed. In the 1980s, networks increased the diet of police shows served up to the viewing public. By the mid-1980s there 28 police and private detective shows on prime-time television alone.[46]

So-called "cop shows" became a staple of prime time programming, and conveyed a consistent point of view. As a number of commentators have reported, "[b]y the early 1970s the cop show had entirely supplanted the Western as the dominant genre of narrative fiction on U.S. television."[47] Some of the conservative backlash that occurred during this period was reflected in the way that criminality was depicted in the police shows themselves: "In the seventies, the easily understood and clearly identified mobsters and crime czars of the past had been replaced in the public's mind by more amorphous, but equally frightening forces. Criminals were often violent madmen and urban delinquents with no stake in society."[48] In particular, violent crime was depicted as the product of the permanent, intractable traits of perpetrators who, in turn, were seen as largely disconnected from the context in which they acted.

Indeed, when John Manzolati and I systematically analyzed television crime drama broadcast in the midst of these trends in the mid-1970s, we found much the same thing with respect to the way criminality was depicted. In fairly consistent ways, television criminals were portrayed largely without social context, life connections, relationships with others, or normal human needs, wants, or hardships. They were, in short, nonpeople.[49] Instead, television criminals were represented by the dastardly deeds they were shown committing (along with whatever other incidental but odious traits could be depicted in the first few minutes of the drama) and little else. In fact, in nearly 40% of the programs that Manzolati and I scored, crime was committed in the first three minutes of the show, before any time *could* be devoted to establishing the perpetrator's background, showing the context from which he came, or presenting the powerful situational forces to which he might have been reacting.

Because television criminals seemed to have no personal history, no human relationships, and no social context, there was no explanation for what they did—except, of course, for their own personal evil. This theme often was underscored in another way. In on-screen dramas villains typically were depicted as deviant in as many ways as possible and then juxtaposed with the law enforcement officials who pursued them. The police were portrayed in an elaborate network of normal-looking human interactions, mundane situations, and caring personal relationships. In fact, much of the dramatic tension in the shows we analyzed drew on this very juxtaposition: basic human good versus unmitigated, uncomplicated, and incomprehensible evil.

We also found that television crime drama gave a very consistent but largely inaccurate picture of *why* crimes were committed. Thus, the crime we analyzed was almost never remotely justified or justifiable in terms of the situations or circumstances in which it occurred. James Carlson found much the same thing. He noted: "[C]rime shows are morality plays that transmit the simple message that legal compliance is an important norm and that violations of the law are always punished. On crime shows there are never any mitigating circumstances that might justify illegal behavior. Not surprisingly, heavy viewers of crime shows are disposed to support the legal system. . . ."[50] To be sure, television crime is rarely committed for reasons or motives that would generate much sympathy or understanding among members of the audience.

Thus, Manzolati and I also found that crime on television was almost never the product of social contextual influences, situational pressures, or the force of circumstance. Instead, television criminals were depicted in ways entirely consistent with the earlier mentioned themes of individualism and personal blameworthiness. That is, the causes of crime in television police drama were almost exclusively *personal,* relating directly to the traits or dispositions of the individual lawbreaker and to little else. It was individual pathology and never pathological social conditions that caused the television crime and violence we analyzed. For example, in less than 5% of the shows Manzolati and I coded was *unemployment*—an important situational determinant of crime in real life—even remotely implicated as an explanation for the crimes that were committed.

Not only did television drama blame crime almost exclusively on the traits or characteristics of its perpetrators, but it also was highly selective in *which* traits or characteristics were employed as explanations. Specifically,

Manzolati and I found that *two* motives accounted for over 70% of the crimes depicted on the screen: Television criminals engaged in crime either because they were "crazy" or because they were pathologically greedy. The crazy or insane criminal was either explicitly labeled as such (e.g., the police sergeant tells the young rookie cop that the murderer they are looking for "had a mental breakdown"), or it was depicted in such a way as to make the inference of mental disturbance inescapable (the culprit is shown behaving bizarrely with strangers in a context unrelated to the crime). In some shows a psychiatrist appeared on a regular basis to do on-the-spot psychoanalyses of the often elusive and irrational criminals.[51] Pathological greed, on the other hand, was generally communicated indirectly. These criminals were shown living in relatively posh surroundings—expensive homes, clothes, and cars— yet they continued to pursue high-stakes economic crime (or violent crime with economic payoffs).

Because television almost never presents viewers with the harsh life circumstances from which many perpetrators come, it fails to promote any real empathetic awareness. Regular viewers will get no help in imagining how they might behave in the face of grim poverty or a lifetime of racially discriminatory treatment, or how their psychological adaptations to a legacy of brutal abuse at the hands of their parents might impair prosocial behavior. The audiences for these shows rarely if ever see these criminogenic patterns play out in television crime drama or witness the connections between traumatic social histories and adult criminality that exists in real life. Thus, television does little to promote genuine insight or understanding about the origins of much criminal behavior. This one-sided perspective not only diverts the public's attention away from the importance of criminogenic situations but also encourages the audience to favor individualistic approaches to crime control over preventive interventions that might, for example, address poor social conditions.

Manzolati and I used the term "television criminology" to underscore the way in which the public's sense of the imminence and importance of the crime problem and the viability of different strategies of crime control depend in large part upon what viewers "learned" from media outlets about the threat of criminal victimization, the causes of crime, and the characteristics of those persons who commit it. In this context, the agenda-setting function of the media likely plays a role in keeping the death penalty at the forefront of public concern over crime. Capital punishment is implicitly promoted as one of society's most rational responses to what television often depicts as an otherwise uncontrollable threat to public safety.

To get some idea of whether or not people actually internalized the television criminology to which they were exposed, Manzolati and I administered a questionnaire to several hundred persons, asking them about a variety of criminal justice issues, as well as how much television they watched. We found that people who watched a great deal of television ("heavy viewers" watching for four or more hours each day) had theories about crime that almost perfectly reflected the views presented in television crime drama.[52] For example, heavy viewers were significantly more likely to employ individualistic, personal, or "dispositional" explanations for crime than persons who watched less television ("light viewers" who looked at two or less hours per day). Heavy viewers in our study were also more likely than light viewers to discount the role of unemployment in crime causation, and they were more likely to associate crime with "abnormality" (although they were no more willing than light viewers to absolve criminals of responsibility because of "mental disturbance"). Not surprisingly, they believed crime was irrational and rarely if ever justified by the circumstances.

Again, it is not difficult to speculate about how such distortions might translate into attitudes about crime control policy, including support for the death penalty. For example, Robert Young has examined whether attitudes toward the death penalty are significantly related to people's beliefs about the motivations of criminals. He suggested that even though individuals "may be equally likely to acknowledge the causal agency of convicted criminals, they may differ in the extent to which they hold them completely responsible for their acts and consequently in their willingness to impose the ultimate punishment."[53] Specifically, Young found that among white Americans the belief that "crime pays" is positively related to support for the death penalty, while support for the proposition that "poverty causes crime" is negatively related. Both of these lessons—that crime pays and that poverty does not cause crime—are regularly taught by television crime drama (the latter, albeit, by dramatic omission). Thus, in these indirect ways, high levels of exposure to television criminology may contribute to higher levels of death penalty support.

Demonizing Violent Offenders

Death penalty cases present citizens, voters, and capital jurors with stark choices about human nature, ones in which the causes of the violence and the redemptive potential of the perpetrator are placed explicitly at issue. If increasing numbers of people become convinced that violent crime is the product of monstrously defective criminals, then the prospect of taking their lives is easier to tolerate. Indeed, it may even be perceived as a necessary form of societal-level protection against a criminal menace that cannot be controlled in any other way. Media trends toward depicting violent crime as the product of the permanent and intractable traits of perpetrators may be especially influential in helping to generate support for the death penalty.

Thus, there are additional dimensions to the influence that the media may have on levels of death penalty support. John Sloop analyzed the media's portrayals of criminal offenders over the period 1950–1993. He found evidence of a dramatic shift away from depicting offenders as redeemable or subject to personal growth and change. Instead, there was a growing tendency to show prisoners as irrational, predatory, dangerous, and beyond reform. Violent offenders, in particular, tended to be shown as having "animalistic and senseless" characteristics that stemmed from their "warped personalities."[54]

As one legal commentator has observed, demonizing offenders in these ways helps to simplify the difficult task of assigning moral blame and to "condemn beyond what is deserved." Persons perceived as fundamentally different from us are easier to hurt and, in an ultimate sense, to condemn to death. When apparent differences are exaggerated and "essentialized," they increase the temptation "to ignore the moral complexities [inherent in the process of judging another] and declare the person and his act entirely evil." Too often, the media encourage us to "assign the offender the mythic role of Monster, a move which justifies harsh treatment and insulates us from moral concerns about the suffering we inflict."[55]

Thus, terrorists and domestic criminals alike are depicted as "isolated from their historical and social context, denied legitimacy of conditions or cause, and portrayed as unpredictable and irrational, if not insane" so that they come to "symbolize a menace that rational and humane means cannot reach or control."[56] And, as one television historian observed, television drama "rarely invited the viewer to look for problems within himself. Problems came from the evil of other people, and were solved . . . by confining or killing them."[57]

In addition, internal tensions created within the story lines themselves often push audiences to demand a decisive triumph of good over the evil, one for which they have been prepared to react emotionally. Psychoanalyst Erik Fromm has even explained the fascination with crime drama in terms of a "deep yearning for the dramatization of the ultimate thing in human life, namely life and death, through crime and punishment."[58] A "just" and satisfying ending permits nothing less than the clear-cut elimination of the wicked: "And there is no ending more uncompromising than the death of one's antagonist. In the police story, justice is indefinitely suspended, the decisive combat postponed, until that final, cathartic scene in which the hero's previous inability to 'speak' the definitive reply to the criminal violence is suddenly cured. . . . In this moment of purifying violence, all the frustrations of the hero's plot are focused into a gun barrel, all the delays of justice exploded by a single righteous bullet into the body of the criminal."[59]

Conditioned by repeated exposure to these manipulative morality plays from the 1970s to the present, many members of the public have come to regard anything less than these "moments of purifying violence" as a denial of justice. The violence of the death penalty gives cathartic voice to a public frustrated by the real world's inability to deliver the "definitive reply" they have been led by the media to expect.

Film provides one of the few mediums through which any kind of in-depth study of criminal behavior is even attempted for public consumption. Yet, almost invariably, such films sensationalize the nature of criminality, pander to the worst conceivable popular stereotypes, and are similarly un-informed by any realistic analysis of the social contextual and personal historical causes of crime. Indeed, the American public has learned many of its "deepest" lessons about crime and criminality through watching mythically frightening cinematic figures such as Hannibal Lecter—"Hannibal the Cannibal," the sadistically mad killer, played with Oscar-winning skill by Anthony Hopkins in *The Silence of the Lambs*.[60] Absent any alternative, equally compelling narratives, the large audiences for films like that learn that murders are committed by persons who truly relish their deadly work; plot brilliantly, diabolically, and joyfully to perform it; and would just as easily polish off a meal of their victim's liver with a little Chianti as give you the time of day.[61]

Thus, along with prime-time television crime drama, Hollywood delivers sensationalized, graphic lessons in media criminology on a more or less regular basis. For example, in Oliver Stone's *Natural Born Killers*,[62] which appeared just a few years after the success of *Silence of the Lambs*, Mickey and Mallory—Stone's gratuitously, mindlessly, unbelievably violent couple—were not only apparently "born to kill" but also were depicted as engaging in violence for the sheer joy of it. Their violence was portrayed as an act of self-expression, and they were shown carving up bodies and dispensing flesh-tearing gunshots much as an artist might creatively decorate a canvas. Despite Stone's claim of satiric intent, many who watched his film could reasonably infer that *this* was what capital punishment was about: people whose evil was so profound that it defied any attempt at rational explanation and challenged even a creative filmmaker's cinematic skills to depict it.

Indeed, Mickey and Mallory's frenetic addiction to violence was so inhuman that filmmaker Stone was forced numerous times to resort to animated cartoon figures because no *real* human being could adequately capture the extraordinary and grotesque distortions of body and soul he wished to convey. Stone was forced at one point to stencil the word "DEMON" across his psychopathic protagonist's chest to make sure he got the point across. Yet Stone's film failed as the satire he had hoped to produce because, despite all its seemingly obvious distortions and exaggerations, it still came far too close to representing the public's dominant view of criminality to be seen in satiric terms.

That is, to appreciate satire, audiences must have an alternative, competing vision of the truth against which to measure the satirist's exaggerations. Too few of them did, perhaps in large part because of the extensive media miseducation they had received over the preceding several decades. In fact, in the increasingly politicized atmosphere of the 1990s, scholarship came to imitate this strange and misleading brand of "art," with supposed expert commentators referring to "natural born killers" as if they represented a scientific category rather than the product of a Hollywood filmmaker's imagination.[63]

The bizarre and simplistic caricatures of criminal behavior that are so common in television and film may be supplemented by written works of fiction where, in theory, the public can get access to more nuanced, in-depth, and accurate accounts. Yet such writing typically reaches a much smaller audience. Moreover, rather than conveying more subtle, textured themes, many authors seek to maximize their appeal by relying on the same distorted stereotypes and images employed in the popular broadcast media. For example, one novel published in the 1990s, ironically titled *Mitigating Circumstances*, opened with its main character—a veteran woman prosecutor—referring to criminal defendants as "vermin" and describing repeat offenders as "rotten pieces of meat viler than when first digested."[64] Not surprisingly, when she speculated about how to handle the crime problem, the death penalty came immediately to mind: "She thought of the guillotine, wondering if it had really been barbaric. They certainly didn't reoffend."[65]

The book ended on a similar note, as a seasoned police officer reassured the prosecutor that her personal act of vengeance—the shotgun murder of a man she believed had victimized her daughter (the essence of the "mitigating circumstances" from the book's title)—was entirely justified because: "The world doesn't need [them], the Bobby Hernandezes. You stepped on a cockroach. There are thousands more. They're in all the cabinets, under the sinks, crawling under every stinking toilet."[66] Avid fiction readers hoping to glean a deeper and more accurate understanding of the kind of "mitigating circumstances" that had been made a formal part of death penalty statutes across the country would have to look elsewhere.

Even otherwise respectable journals of news, information, and opinion have added to the mix of misinformation to which the public is regularly exposed. In recent years, for example, *Newsweek* magazine has carried numerous sensationalistic articles about supposed trends in violent crime fashioned from little more than random anecdotes and base stereotypes, and often devoid of representative statistics, accurate expert analyses, or contextual information about the backgrounds and social histories of the perpetrators. For example, one several-page spread, complete with dramatic, color mug shots, was titled "The Incorrigibles: They Rape and Molest. They Defy Treatment. How Can Society Protect Itself?"[67] A later cover story showed a teenager running with a rifle, headlined "Teen Violence: Wild in the Streets," with an article that began: "Murder and mayhem, guns and gangs: a teenage generation grows up dangerous. . . ."[68]

The *Newsweek* stories are typical of those that have appeared in other magazines, even those geared toward more specialized and seemingly progressive audiences. For example, one cover story from a magazine devoted to "new age lifestyle" read, "Children Without a Conscience: An Inside Look at a Hidden Epidemic and Its Controversial Cure."[69] Many of the themes and images that are firmly implanted in the public's consciousness go beyond sensational headlines, suggesting the overwhelming threat that violent crime represents in our society. They contain implicit causal messages about "incorrigible," "wild," and "dangerous" young criminals who are intent on mayhem, defy treatment, and lack a conscience. For the most part, these messages are conveyed without benefit of a single reliable scholarly citation to valid, replicated scientific research on the nature of criminal violence.

Such misleading messages are not restricted to the glossy magazines that thrive on mass circulation. There are enough consumers of images and accounts of violent crime that a number of commercial enterprises have arisen to meet their needs. These industries treat criminality as merchandise and cater to a clientele that seeks lurid details and sensationalized accounts of gruesome criminal acts. Here, too, the emphasis is on the diabolical and salacious rather than accurate, sober accounts that are grounded in research or based on in-depth scholarly analysis. For example, Time-Life Books used a national mailing to advertise its series on mass and serial murderers. The envelope that hundreds of thousands of potential buyers received depicted a pair of deep-set eyes above the red letters: "Have You Ever Looked Into the Eyes of a Killer?" Recipients were further enticed—before they had even opened the envelope—with the promise: "Inside: a unique chance to probe the twisted minds and deeds of America's most violent criminals!"

Not to be outdone, Columbia House Video Library's mass mailer promised recipients that they could "own this one-of-a-kind glimpse into the darkest side of the 20th century" by purchasing "one extraordinary video series [that] explores the shocking true stories of America's most notorious criminals." Among other things, the series promised to answer the question: "What goes on inside the twisted mind of a serial killer?" Of course, none of these "inside stories" grappled honestly or accurately or expertly with the developmental or social contextual causes of violent crime, concentrating instead on the graphic, sordid details of the criminal behavior itself and the apparent deep-seated pathology and twisted motives of the perpetrators.

Media outlets otherwise known for their thoughtful approach to complex social problems sometimes echo these same stereotypical, misleading views. For example, one issue of a respected journal of book reviews carried this offhanded observation, feeding the mystique that the roots of capital violence are simply impossible to fathom: "A problem with psychopathic killers, both for the law and for their biographers, is that they take their baggage with them. They profess innocence or create new excuses right up to the very end so that evidence of their deeds and even the basic facts of their lives are a confusing mass of contradictions. We know them only by the damage they leave behind, as though we were pursuing someone who had left the ransacked room just a moment before we arrived."[70]

Despite the authoritative tone, it is hard to conceive of a more normatively incorrect account of the lives of capital defendants. The truth is that many of them admit to their wrongdoing and, as a group, they leave remarkably detailed documentary histories as well as numerous percipient witnesses who typically can testify to early traumatic experiences and forms of extreme childhood and adolescent mistreatment, in addition to often ill-fated attempts to overcome these legacies and even, in many cases, what can only be interpreted as fairly desperate cries for help.[71]

It is easy to understand how the audiences exposed to even a small portion of the broad range of misinformation could come to believe that they really grasped important truths about the nature of criminal violence. Similarly, it would be easy for many of them—operating as voters or as jurors—to reach the conclusion that the death penalty was the *only* answer to the individualized, menacing evil so often depicted in mainstream mass media. For many members of the public, intense media exposure is likely to create a subjective sense of expertise, what many no doubt experience as a "common-sense" understanding of these issues. Yet this sense of expertise and common-sense understanding may be based on media messages that are constructed with an eye toward market share as much or more than empirical truth.

Conclusion

People's direct contact with crime and criminals understandably shapes their fears and perspectives. Yet there are other, seemingly more powerful influences at work. As Richard Sparks put it, "crime and justice carry cultural and political meanings which precede and extend beyond our direct encounters with them."[72] Of course, those cultural and political meanings are typically carried to citizens by the mass media. This process can have direct consequences for a range of crime control policies.

Media programmers apparently act on the belief that by individualizing and sensationalizing violent crime and demonizing violent criminals they will attract larger audiences than if they undertake the task of providing more complex, balanced, and informative narratives that include some of the structural and contextual factors that help to cause crime. To be sure, there is no reason to believe that the media have any particular interest in degrading the quality of due process or reducing the full measure of justice that is afforded criminal defendants. Yet these and other problematic outcomes may be the unintended criminal justice consequences of an overdependence on subsidized news combined with programming decisions that are made for largely economic reasons.

Indeed, in our culture, some of the explanations for the consistent slant and pervasive bias in coverage do appear to be economic in nature. For one, the economic mandate of television broadcasting seems to dictate a false clarity in depictions of crime and punishment. Only story lines in which pure good triumphs over pure evil leave audiences comfortably reassured: "[P]olice dramas offered a sense of security to their audiences. In theory that made them better consumers, which from a sponsor's view is the real purpose of all programming. . . . Consequently, the new crime shows and commercial television were a perfect match."[73]

However, in addition to the economic incentive, there are psychological factors at work. Demonizing the perpetrators of certain kinds of crimes absolves the larger society for widespread attitudes and practices that implicitly promote and condone violence. For example, as one theorist has argued, "in myriad ways, the culture regularly doublethinks a distance between itself and sexual violence, denying the fundamental normalcy of that violence in a male supremacist culture and trying to paint it as the domain of psychopaths and 'monsters' only."[74] And, because the media present us with the most distorted and extreme possible versions of violence—individual grotesques that bear so little relationship to the rest of us that no one in the audience can identify with them—we are saved the unpleasant task of confronting the potential for violence that we all share.[75]

In this context, it becomes justifiable "to kill those who are monsters or inhuman because of their abominable acts or traits, or those who are 'mere animals' (coons, pigs, rats, lice, etc.) . . ." because they have been excluded "from the universe of morally protected entities."[76] But locating the causes of capital crime exclusively within the offender—whose evil must be distorted, exaggerated, and mythologized—not only makes it easier to kill them but also to distance ourselves from any sense of responsibility for the roots of the problem itself.[77] If violent crime is the product of monstrous offenders, then our only responsibility is to find and eliminate them. On the other hand, genuine explanations for crime that include its psychological, social, and economic causes—because they sometimes connect individual violent behavior to the broader and more subtle forms of violence that inhere society itself—implicate us all in the crime problem.

Many of the effects I have described in this chapter are indirect and "atmospheric." None of the media messages—even ones as biased and one-sided as some of those I have cited here—necessarily determine public opinion, dictate the outcomes of elections in which death-penalty-related issues are in play, or compel verdicts in capital trials. Yet these misleading and sensationalized messages do help to establish the general atmosphere within which the rest of the system of death sentencing operates. Because there are so few other sources of information to which the public can turn in attempting to make informed death-penalty-related decisions, it is not far-fetched to suggest that collective immersion in these media-based images and story lines leads many persons to develop distorted but influential views of violent crime and criminal defendants. These views, in turn, are likely to affect how subsequently obtained information is processed—including information that is presented as supporting evidence for crime- and punishment-related political positions and even evidence that is introduced as the basis for capital jury verdicts.

To be sure, these sensationalized images and simplistic frameworks have become very much a part of the public's "knowledge" about crime and punishment, despite their fictional quality. Because they represent media-based views that at least some citizens bring into voting booths and courtrooms across the country, they undoubtedly do wield some influence over actual legal decisions, including, in some unspecified number of cases, matters of life and death.

3

Constructing Capital Crimes and Defendants
Death Penalty Case-Specific Biases
and Their Effects

There remains [an inherent] discrepancy between what criminal
events mean at the moment of their commission and what they
stand for once they have entered the widening circles of
punishment, rhetoric and rebuttal, election platforms and the
multitude of communicative exchanges which compose the public
sphere.
—Richard Sparks, *Television and the Drama of Crime: Moral Tales
and the Place of Crime in Public Life* (1992)

The media's intense focus on crime-related issues and the tendency to concentrate on unrepresentative, sensational crimes help to heighten the public's
fear of crime and to elevate the importance that citizens attach to crime
control as a pressing social and political issue. As suggested in the last chapter,
in addition to this agenda-setting function, the media's coverage of crime-
related issues shapes the broad climate of opinion in which beliefs about
crime control policy are formed. Beyond exaggerating the nature and amount
of violence in our society and increasing fears of victimization, the media
often portray violent crime as the exclusive product of evil, depraved, even
monstrous individual criminals. This framework of understanding, in turn,
helps to convince many citizens that only the harshest, most punitive sanctions—including the death penalty—are likely to be effective in the war
against crime.

The media's general "theory" about the nature of crime and the motivations of its perpetrators serves as a constant backdrop when members of
the public make judgments about individual crimes and criminals in their
communities. At the same time, because capital cases involve very serious
crimes, most of them generate substantial amount media attention of their
own. That is, the typical capital case is surrounded by some degree of case-
related publicity that focuses on its *specific* facts and circumstances. Thus, in
addition to the general effects of the media-created atmosphere surrounding
crime and punishment in our society, it also is important to consider whether
and how the public may be influenced by case-specific news coverage of
actual death penalty cases.

Sociologist Kai Erikson noted the changes that occurred in the manner in which legal punishment was imposed in both England and colonial America. Originally, criminal penalties were conducted in public and in ways that "afforded the crowd a chance to participate in a direct, active way." The spectacle of punishment invited a collective response. As Erikson observed, the shift to a more private and less participatory way of imposing criminal sanctions "coincided almost exactly with the development of newspapers as a medium of mass information." As the public came to have less direct personal contact with these events, newspapers and, later, radio and television, provided much "the same kind of entertainment as public hangings or a Sunday visit to the local gaol."[1]

Steven Box has made a similar point: "Newspapers make redundant the need for large gatherings of persons to witness punishments; instead individuals can stay home and still be morally instructed."[2] In the course of this early transformation active public participation gave way to a more passive and emotionally distant form of civic engagement. The realities of crime and punishment were filtered through the media in a way that allowed citizens to experience them at a step removed, and on their own terms (or, as I suggested in the last chapter, terms supplied entirely by the media). Other commentators suggested that the move away from public executions was part of a changing sensibility—that the middle classes were troubled by such direct contact with the harsh realities of criminal justice and welcomed the experiential barriers that were interposed.

Yet, in the several centuries that have passed since this change occurred, another kind of transformation appears to have taken place. Nowadays not only do citizens get their information about the criminal justice system directly from the media, but the media's crime-related messages also have become ever-present, extremely potent, and personally engaging. As I suggested in the last chapter, and as most people in the United States acknowledge, the news media are their primary source of general information about crime.[3] But multiple media outlets have become far more sophisticated in proactively pursuing audiences and saturating the culture with sensational images and powerful messages. Instead of having to actively seek lessons about crime and punishment, citizens find that it is increasingly difficult to avoid exposure to this information.

Thus, rather than providing a more passive and emotionally distanced way for citizens to participate in issues of crime and punishment, the modern media have learned to draw citizens in, to generate interest and emotional reactions, and to personally engage the pubic in unprecedented ways. This may be especially true when the crime-related subject matter concerns local cases that directly implicate personal safety and where community interests and standards may be brought to bear on the outcome of the case. Because death penalty cases involve the most serious violent crimes that can be committed within a community, they have special significance to the local media, law enforcement officials, and the residents where they occur. Commentators have cited the fact that death penalty cases often involve "high profile crimes that attract enormous media attention" as one of the important factors that contributes to "high error rates in convicting and sentencing innocent people to death row."[4] The publicity that surrounds a particular capital case puts enormous pressure on the police to find a culprit, and on prosecutors to gain a conviction and death sentence.

In addition, however, death penalty cases have some unique legal features that may alter the nature of media coverage and its potential impact on local citizens, voters, and jurors. Capital trials involve more than determining who is legally responsible for the crime that has been committed—the traditional issue of guilt or innocence around which all other kinds of criminal trials revolve. In death penalty cases, jurors are asked to represent the "conscience of the community" in deciding which punishment to impose. In making the choice between life and death, of course, the law requires jurors to take a whole range of additional factors into account, including the background and character of the defendant. Whether and how well the media fairly and comprehensively inform the public about these additional factors can influence the nature of the death-sentencing process that results.

In this chapter, I suggest that the nature and amount of publicity that surrounds many death penalty cases often miseducate citizens, voters, and potential jurors. The media coverage generates and intensifies community interest in the case and heightens concern over the outcome, but only in a very selective way. Often only certain aspects of the case are addressed and very narrow points of view represented to the exclusion of many others. To illustrate some of these points, I discuss two studies that my colleagues and I conducted, focusing on some of the ways that case-specific news and publicity help to shape people's understanding of capital crimes and influence the mind-set with which jurors approach their death-penalty-related decision making.

Creating Biased Frameworks: Newspaper Reporting on Capital Cases

In the first of these studies, Susan Greene and I examined media portrayals of capital trials and capital defendants in published newspaper stories about specific cases.[5] Reasoning that citizens would get their frameworks of understanding for capital crime from media stories about actual death penalty cases in local jurisdictions, we content-analyzed news stories published about a representative sample of such cases. We were concerned primarily with the nature of the information that would be available to careful readers of the news, and whether many of the biases that plagued media crime drama and crime reporting in general were corrected by the way in which the news media handled these specific actual cases.

In addition, we wondered whether the kind of information that a knowledgeable voter or capital juror might need in order to formulate thoughtful opinions and make reasoned judgements with respect to important death penalty issues could be found in local publicity about specific capital cases. Finally, we were interested in what kind of information the public at large and prospective capital jurors received about the nature of the decision-making process that governs capital trials. Specifically, we wondered whether the key concepts that are supposed to guide jury verdicts in these cases were communicated to the public in an accurate, informative, and even-handed way.

Precisely because citizens and jurors are supposed to bring to bear a broader understanding—to judge the defendant and his life, not just his crime—in deciding whether someone convicted of a potentially capital crime should live or die, information that the news media provide about these broader issues (for example, who commits capital crime and why, what kinds of life experiences capital defendants may have in common that help to explain their behavior, etc.) is especially relevant and important to death penalty cases.

With these issues in mind, Greene and I and several of our students coded various dimensions of the case-related publicity we had sampled. Specifically, we examined the coverage of 26 capital trials (13 that resulted in death, 13 in life without parole sentences), randomly selected from a list of all such cases that went to verdict in California between 1995 and 1997. We used a newspaper search service to find over 300 newspaper articles ($N = 321$) published about the 26 cases, which came from different geographical locations around the state. What we found was troublesome in a number of respects and raised serious concerns about the way in which capital cases were being depicted.

First, Greene and I tried to determine which stages of a capital case were most often covered in published news stories—pretrial, guilt phase, penalty phase, and sentencing. Reasoning that only certain information was available at certain stages of a case, we wondered whether there might be a built-in bias in the content of crime reporting that stemmed from the *timing* of the stories themselves. Other studies had found that the media tended to concentrate only on the beginning stages of criminal justice system processing (i.e., crime incidents, arrests, and charges being lodged against suspects), and that the overwhelming majority of details contained in news stories pertained to the commission of the crime itself.[6] On the other hand, because of the central role that a capital defendant's life story is supposed to play in the sentencing process that determines his fate, this lopsidedness should not necessarily occur in reporting about death penalty cases. Unfortunately, Greene and I found that it did. In fact, the bias was nearly as pronounced in this sample of newspaper stories about capital cases as any reported elsewhere in the literature.

As table 3.1 illustrates, more than half of all the newspaper articles published about the cases in our overall sample appeared during the pretrial

Table 3.1
Percent of Articles Focused on Phase of Case

Stage	Total Articles (%)	"Life Without Parole" Verdict Cases (%)	Death Verdict Cases (%)
Pretrial	53	54	53
Guilt phase	24	30	20
Penalty phase	7	4	9
Sentencing	15	9	18
Posttrial	3	4	2

stages of the case. Indeed, well over 90% of the articles focused on stages of the case *other* than the penalty phase—the stage where humanizing and explanatory information about the defendant and his social history ordinarily would be presented. In fact, the press was twice as likely to report on the sentencing stage of the case—typically a single, brief event in which either a sentencing verdict was returned by the capital jury or the judge formally pronounced the sentence of the court—than they were to report on the sometimes lengthy penalty trials that led up to the sentencing verdicts.

We found a few important differences between press coverage of cases that ultimately resulted in death verdicts versus those that ended with life sentences. For one, there were nearly twice as many stories written about cases that resulted in death verdicts than there were about cases in which life verdicts were rendered (207 vs. 114). There also were differences in the stages of the cases on which the press focused. As table 3.1 shows, the major differences between the life verdict and death verdict cases pertained to the likelihood of reporting about the penalty trial and the sentencing in the case: The press was more than twice as likely to report on the penalty phase of a case that resulted in death than life (9% vs. 4%) and also twice as likely to report on the pronouncement of sentence in a death than a life verdict case (18% vs. 9%).

These differences may result from the fact that, as a rule, the death verdict cases are more likely to contain aggravating facts that are more easily sensationalized than those in life cases, and also because death verdicts apparently are regarded by the press as more "newsworthy" than life verdicts. Whatever the reason, note that life verdict cases—ones in which, by definition, there should be more mitigating than aggravating evidence presented about the defendant—got comparatively little press coverage overall and even less penalty-phase coverage. Moreover, the press was much less likely to report the fact that a life verdict had been rendered. This may convey the misleading impression that such verdicts are rare (when, in fact, they occur more often than death verdicts).[7]

Greene and I also examined the sources that the press cited for the information that was contained in the case-specific news coverage. As I noted earlier, many people have described the heavy (sometimes exclusive) reliance by crime news reporters on the police and other law enforcement agencies— the so-called subsidized news feature of crime reporting.[8] Again, there are reasons why capital crimes should be an exception. Because of their higher news profile and greater perceived importance to the community, Greene and I speculated that a different and more independent approach to news gathering and reporting might be used for capital cases. If not, of course, the otherwise routine overreliance on law enforcement sources would be especially problematic. That is, because the only information the police typically have pertains to the crime itself and the defendant's criminal record, stories derived primarily from police sources would lack detailed knowledge about the defendant and likely omit any information about his social history or noncriminal background. In short, police and other law enforcement sources would be likely to describe crimes in ways that would reinforce a narrowly individualistic view of crime causation.

As table 3.2 illustrates, we found that the press relied overwhelmingly on the police and other law enforcement personnel as the sources cited for the information contained in the articles we coded. Thus, the police were the single most frequently cited source in the articles in our sample, and they were cited more than twice as often as defense attorneys. Not surprisingly, the police often were quoted providing seemingly objective details about the case and the defendant. But they also frequently made statements that included especially damaging characterizations, ones that—in the exact form in which they were quoted—would be inadmissible at trial. For example, one story noted that "cops say [the defendant] has the street cunning of a longtime criminal."[9] In another case, the press quoted a police officer's lengthy description of the defendant characterizing him as "an extremely

Table 3.2
Percent of Cited Sources in Published Articles

Overall	Total Articles (%)	"Life Without Parole" Verdict Cases Only (%)	Death Verdict Cases Only (%)
Police/law enforcement	36	28	40
Prosecutors	25	28	23
Judges	6	6	7
Defense attorneys	14	16	14
Defendants (confessions/ admissions)	5(4)	7(6)	4(3)
Lay witnesses			
Prosecution	11	13	9
Defense	3	2	3

dangerous man with an exceptionally violent background and no regard for positions of authority . . . a treacherous type of criminal who has the know-how to be extremely dangerous."[10]

Although prosecutors tended to be cited somewhat less often than the police overall, they were the next most frequent source of the information contained in the news stories we analyzed. Prosecutors, too, were quoted in the press providing especially negative and damaging characterizations of the defendants, such as: "To the prosecutor, [the defendant] is a 'predatory beast,' who deserves to be executed,"[11] or "[the prosecutor] described a cool and calculated robber who at times 'appeared to be having a good time' during the crimes."[12] In another case, a federal prosecutor was quoted as warning her state counterpart about a particular capital defendant's "violent nature" and recommending "extreme caution" in transferring him.[13] Another was quoted as saying that, after having deliberated for several days before returning a death verdict, jurors in the case told him they had "been searching for something good" about the defendant that might justify sparing his life, but "they could not find a hint of humanity in him."[14] Of course, much like the citations to statements by police officers, quoting prosecutors—seen by many as "officers of the court" who represent "the people"—lends the accounts and descriptions of defendants a degree of credibility that they otherwise would not have.

Judges tended to be cited sparingly in the newspaper articles we coded—they were about 6% of identified sources overall. The percentage did not vary significantly for life without parole versus death verdict cases. However, because judges tended to be cited at the time of sentencing, their quoted statements were not always neutral or dispassionate. For example, one judge, in the course of sentencing a defendant to death, was quoted by the newspaper as saying, "[the defendant] showed he wants to 'satisfy his lust and anger only on those weaker than himself.' "[15] Even in the cases of defendants sentenced to life without parole, judges were sometimes quoted characterizing defendants or their crimes in especially harsh, demonizing terms. Judges virtually never commented on the way in which a defendant's traumatic and troubled life might have led to his criminal behavior or acknowledged the role of compassion or mercy in the sentencing decision that was rendered in the case.

In addition, although newspaper accounts generally did not include many statements that were attributed directly to lay witnesses, there was a clear bias in the orientation of those witnesses who were cited. Thus, prosecution witnesses were referenced as sources more than three times more often than defense witnesses overall. On a number of occasions, lay witnesses were quoted characterizing defendants in terms that seemed designed to justify the charges against them. For example, in a story about one suspect who was wanted for murder, the newspaper reported that his "ex-wife . . . suggested he committed crimes for the thrill and sense of power" and that he possessed a "dark side" that had emerged soon after they were married.[16]

Only about 5% of the information in the stories we analyzed was attributed to the defendants themselves. Even here, however, the overwhelming majority (almost 80%) of such references were to the defendants' confessions or to other damaging admissions that they had made (most often quoted directly from police interrogations).

When we combined the citation of police sources with the number of times that prosecutors were cited, the slant of the articles became even more apparent. Thus, in the overall sample of cases, police and prosecutors were cited more than four times as often as defense attorneys. The magnitude of the prosecutorial bias was even more apparent when several other frequently cited sources were aggregated. Four of them—law enforcement (36%), prosecutors (25%), prosecution lay witnesses (11%), and self-incriminating statements made by the defendant (4%)—accounted for fully 76% of the sources cited in the articles in our overall sample.

In addition to the stage of the case on which the articles were focused and the sources cited for the information they contained, we coded the content of the articles themselves. Because these were potential death penalty cases in which jurors would be asked to pass judgment on the defendant's entire life as well as the heinousness of the crime for which he was convicted, we were interested in the relative emphasis on the crime facts versus the facts of the defendant's life.

Perhaps not surprisingly, literally *every* article we coded made reference to the crime for which the defendant was being tried and sentenced. In most instances, the articles made many repeated references to the crime, often with carefully crafted language that further dramatized already emotionally charged events. As table 3.3 indicates, information about the defendant's background or social history was dwarfed by the newspapers' focus on the crime facts. Crime facts were mentioned between six to seven times more frequently than any background or social history information.

We also found that this pattern did not vary much as a function of whether the case ultimately resulted in a life rather than a death sentence. If one makes the reasonable assumption that the case verdict reflects something about the actual heinousness of the crime compared to the sympathetic facts of the defendant's life, this constancy in press coverage would seem to reflect

Table 3.3
Focus on Crime Facts Versus Background/Social History

	Total Mentions Overall	
	No.	Per Article
Crime facts	2409	7.5
Social history facts	382	1.2

The total ratio of crime to social history facts per article is 6.3:1.

Table 3.4
Nature of Background/Social History Factors Cited

Social History Factors Mentioned	Overall % of Total Mentions	By Case Outcome	
		"Life Without Parole" Verdict Articles (%)	Death Verdict Articles (%)
Prior gang affiliations	32	38	29
Prior drug use	26	41	20
Mental illness	30	15	34
Cognitive deficits	5	0	7
Victim of abuse/neglect	3	3	4
Parental substance abuse	1	3	1
Exposure to violence	3	0	4

something about news reporting in general, something largely independent of the facts of a particular capital case, crime, or defendant.

As can be seen from table 3.4, however, even these numbers understate the magnitude of the crime focus as compared to *sympathetic* social history information about the defendant's background in the newspaper stories in this sample. That is because the overwhelming majority of social history or background facts about the defendant were *negative* and actually pertained to past criminality. The past criminality tended to be either prior drug use or prior involvement with gangs. Remotely sympathetic background information that might have conveyed an explanation of the defendant's criminal behavior in terms of past trauma, an especially deprived or abusive upbringing, or some other social contextual factors was almost entirely absent from newspaper coverage. Indeed, except in one especially high-profile death verdict case where the possibility of mental illness was raised extensively, drug use and gang involvement were the only "background" factors to be mentioned with any regularity. Overall, we calculated that only 10% of the articles included *any* mitigating social history information.

Of course, as I have noted, the law *requires* that jurors in capital cases be allowed to consider the background and character of the defendant in reaching a decision about whether he should live or die. But if and when they encounter this information in an actual capital trial, they will have had little advance preparation about what to do with it. That is, based on our analysis, it did not appear that citizens, voters, or potential jurors were given much meaningful prior information by the press about the important role of social historical influences and the "risk factors" that often play such a significant role in shaping the course and direction of a capital defendant's life.

In particular, despite the fact that these were capital cases in which the ultimate question of whether the defendant lived or died was supposed to be based on a consideration of the defendant's entire life as well as the heinousness of the crime for which he was convicted, the heavy emphasis on crime facts to the near-exclusion of background information provided the public with no framework with which to do so. Moreover, the omission of background and social history issues from the press coverage indirectly may have suggested that such information was irrelevant to understanding the nature of the crime, judging the character and blameworthiness of the person who committed it, and ultimately to deciding on the appropriate punishment to be meted out in this or any capital case. Yet each of these impressions would be legally as well as psychologically incorrect.

Finally, Greene and I looked directly at the relative emphasis on aggravating versus mitigating information in the newspaper articles. In their content analysis of pretrial publicity of capital cases, Marla Sandys and Steven Chermak found aggravating factors mentioned in 78% of their articles.[17] Our numbers were even higher; overall, 95% of the articles we analyzed included some aggravation (usually in the form of aggravating aspects of the crimes or prior instances of criminality on the part of the defendants). For example: "Redd [previously] was arrested for bank robbery and wounding a police officer,"[18] and "Kelly had been arrested at least five times of rape charges."[19]

We also found that aggravating factors were mentioned over four (4.55) times as often as mitigating factors in the news coverage we analyzed. The majority of such aggravation referred to prior crimes involving force or violence. When we grouped the articles by case verdict, we found that the ratios did not change much in the articles pertaining to defendants who were sentenced to death as opposed to those written about defendants sentenced to life.

It seems reasonable to assume that cases that result in death verdicts actually have more aggravation than those resulting in life sentences. Note also that, by definition, cases that result in life sentences presumably have more mitigating factors than aggravating ones (in California, as a "weighing" state, jurors are instructed to return life sentences when mitigation outweighs aggravation). Yet, even in the reports written about these life-verdict cases, the news coverage we analyzed contained a disproportion of aggravation—indeed, as I say, the ratio was still about four aggravators for every one mitigator that appeared in the press. Thus, the bias in the focus of news reporting was still substantial.

In sum, Greene and I found that the newspaper reporting about these capital cases reflected a disproportionate emphasis on the earliest stages of the case—when there were active police investigations under way, and when all that typically was known about the case was the nature of the crime that had occurred and, usually, the identity of the perpetrator). Although the cases we examined were from California jurisdictions in the 1990s, the results of other studies suggest that this is a stable feature of crime coverage in other parts of the country. For example, Sanford Sherizen's content analysis of newspaper crime reporting in Chicago during selected months in 1975 showed that over two-thirds of the articles related to only the beginning stages of criminal justice system processing (crime incidents, arrests, charges being lodged against suspects), that commission of the crime itself accounted for the major details contained in the articles, and that later stages of criminal justice processing were seldom mentioned.

Sherizen concluded that the "world view or public belief system developed by the media limits the perspectives of the audience to certain limited aspects of the crime phenomena and, in the process of limiting its coverage, certain features of considerable importance are excluded from comprehension."[20] Similarly, our analysis also revealed that many issues that were "of considerable importance" to a balanced, informed, and legally fair understanding of the case, trial, and verdict were left out of these stories. As noted, for example, there was surprisingly little attention given to the all-important penalty phase of the case in which information is presented that provides jurors with the basis for choosing between life and death. As indicated earlier, Greene and I found that the press devoted much more coverage to the sentencing stage of these cases—the point at which a sentencing verdict actually was returned or at which the judge formally imposed the sentence—than to the often long and involved penalty trials on which sentencing verdicts themselves are based.

Yet even the sentencing stage of the cases tended to get little real fanfare in the press, and rarely anything that could be interpreted as a careful explanation or analysis of the legal basis for the choice between life and death. In this aspect, contemporary news reporting appears to differ significantly from press coverage in past times. According to historian Stuart Banner, the moment of sentencing in capital cases once occupied a great deal of the public's attention. As he described it in the 19th century:

> [T]he phase of the trial that seems to have been the most popular was sentencing, the part most similar to the old public hanging. Sentencing involved no suspense. The jury had already returned a verdict requiring a death sentence. As in a hanging, everyone knew how it would come out in the end. The drama resided in the emotion of the moment, in the words chose by the judge and in the reaction of the condemned person. . . . Like a hanging, it was a moment of dramatic community condemnation, but it was an event the respectable could still feel good about attending.[21]

If the press attention given to the sentencing phases of the cases that we analyzed can serve as any measure, the press no longer encourages the public to participate as intensely or invest quite the same degree of symbolic meaning in this form of community condemnation. For whatever reason—perhaps because the judicial act of sentencing someone to death is a too-pointed reminder of what capital punishment is really about—the press seems to lose some of its previously intense interest.

As I noted, Greene and I also found that more than 75% of the sources cited were law enforcement and prosecutorial in nature. This disproportion was perhaps the direct result of the press focus on earlier stages of the case, and perhaps also due to the continued heavy dependence by reporters on subsidized news even in death penalty cases.[22] As indicated earlier, crime reporters come to depend upon the police as their primary source of information about crime. Indeed: "Crime reporters differ from other journalists by the time they spend with non-journalists as well as their socialization with and reliance upon the police. Crime reporters become more like the police than like other reporters while the police, to a large degree, remain constant to their police occupational identity."[23]

If subsidized news is at the bottom of much crime reporting in general, the articles we analyzed seemed to confirm its influence in capital cases in particular. Newspapers cited explicitly to law enforcement and prosecutorial officials for most of the information contained in their stories. This, too, may help to explain the heavy focus on earlier stages of the cases (as well as vice versa). That is, police and prosecutors typically have less new information that they can reveal to press contacts as a case gets closer to trial. Trial coverage, on the other hand, is difficult to accomplish via subsidized news. Newspapers typically must send reporters to trials rather than rely on press releases alone. Moreover, social history and mitigation evidence is not likely to be supplied in the form of subsidized news, which may help to account for its absence in newspaper stories.

In addition, Greene and I found that the various details of the crime and portrayals of defendants that came from law enforcement sources typically were asserted as "objective fact," as if newspaper reporters were acting simply as conduits of uncontested information. Yet such details are not necessarily unambiguous or factual in nature. Indeed, in most cases many of them will be vigorously disputed. As LaFree observed, "legal agents, no less than other human beings, must actively construct their own perceptual world 'as it really is' . . . the distance between perception and reality is likely to be especially great in the case of the criminal-selection process, because legal agents most often respond to events that they did not actually observe."[24] Still, the police, especially, are typically perceived as credible and their accounts of "what happened" are rarely questioned. As our content analysis showed, these accounts are duly (and repeatedly) reported in a high percentage of cases.

In fact, the articles Greene and I analyzed not only tended to repeat the details of the crime but also routinely focused the reader's attention on their most heinous aspects or features. Even in these newspaper accounts (where, at least compared to televised news, one would expect sensationalism to be at a relative minimum), graphic language was often employed in ways that seemed designed to evoke an emotional response. On the other hand, as I noted, very little information was reported from which readers could develop a structural or contextual interpretation of the crime, or glean any thoughtful insights into the social historical roots of the defendant's criminality, or feel even a minimum of compassion for defendants who often had experienced troubled and traumatic lives.

Thus, as noted, there was very little reporting of the penalty phase of the case—the stage of the trial during which the explanatory evidence is introduced so that jurors can make a meaningful and principled choice between life and death. The little social history information that was reported tended to be overwhelmingly negative. Indeed, there was far more aggravation than mitigation contained in the news stories—on average, more than four times as much. Moreover, much of the small amount of mitigation that was reported related to initial, largely pro forma claims of "not guilty," which, given the convictions that subsequently occurred, would have been only marginally relevant or persuasive in the penalty phases of most cases.

Of course, the lack of published information about the defendant's background would make it difficult for readers to gain any real understanding of the social historical and structural causes of capital crime in general or this capital crime in particular. Press coverage repeatedly depicted the crimes in question as having occurred without context; stories focused instead on the numerous specific details of the acts themselves. If it is true that many citizens get not only specific bits and pieces of information from the media but also develop frameworks of understanding for the broader issues and problems that form the context of capital crime, then the press did little in these cases to meaningfully educate them about these important matters.

The amount of attention given to the crime itself, the focus on the most dramatic or heinous features of the crime, and the redundancy with which they were described likely evoked feelings of anger and outrage that could be directed at only one obvious target—the (necessarily) unsympathetic defendant. Among other things, the lack of coverage of the personal histories or backgrounds of defendants seemed to deny the humanity of the persons who were charged with capital crimes. The one-sidedness of the coverage meant that the press repeatedly highlighted the heinousness of their crimes and consistently ignored the reality of their personhood.[25]

Thus, the articles we coded often repeated criminal descriptors that "essentialized" the defendant's identity as a criminal, in terms such as "thrill killer," "career criminal," "escapee," "fugitive," "inmate," "serial date rapist," or "an urban predator" who would not "hesitate to kill again."[26] For many capital defendants, the sensationalized details of the crime became their identities—a totalizing description of who they were—as though they had done or experienced nothing outside their criminal behavior. For example, one defendant was described as "an animal, not a person,"[27] and another was reported to commit crimes "for the thrill and sense of power."[28]

Case-Specific Prejudice: Estimating the Effects of Media Reporting in Capital Cases

In the content analysis of newspaper articles that Greene and I conducted we were able to examine only what was reported in the articles, not necessarily what readers gleaned from them. Our study did not address whether and how readers were affected by the content of the capital-case-related news to which they were exposed. This issue is difficult to examine directly and precisely, in part because media influences are so repetitious and widespread in our society. Most people are exposed to multiple news reports and fictional crime dramas each day, over periods of many years. Separating out the effects of any particular set of media messages from those that address crime or the death penalty in general is methodologically daunting. My colleague Hiroshi Fukurai and I attempted to overcome some of these methodological challenges by examining several related issues in a study designed to shed some light on whether and how media reports about *particular* capital crimes actually influence the beliefs of persons who are exposed to them.[29]

Specifically, Fukurai and I used the results of community surveys done in conjunction with change-of-venue motions in capital cases in California to assess whether and how media coverage affected certain aspects of the death-sentencing process. We reasoned that this was one way to approach the important question of whether citizens, voters, and potential jurors were not only exposed to case-related publicity in death penalty cases but were actually affected by it in ways that might compromise the fairness with which capital trials were being conducted.

Previous research on noncapital criminal cases has indicated that pretrial publicity *does* have biasing effects on potential jurors.[30] Among other things, this kind of publicity appears to give potential jurors a pro-prosecution orientation,[31] negatively bias their perceptions of the defendant, increase their belief in the strength of the prosecution's case[32] and lead them to be more punitive toward defendants.[33] Researchers have suggested that many persons regard the publicity to which they are exposed as accurate and legitimate at the time they receive it, and that they store it uncritically in their memories. Once information has been received and integrated into memory this way, the process is difficult for people to reverse.[34] The very high level of publicity that often surrounds capital cases, in particular, led Fukurai and I to examine whether similar problems arose in death penalty trials.

To do so we analyzed the results of 26 public opinion surveys that were conducted between 1980 and 2002 and pertained to 19 separate death penalty cases. The surveys reflected a geographically diverse population, having been drawn from 15 different California counties. The surveys themselves were conducted over the telephone,[35] and they were designed to examine the effects of exposure to pretrial publicity on the public's awareness of the particular case and the tendency to prejudge the defendant's guilt in advance of trial. Modern sampling techniques (random digit dialing, or "RDD") were employed to maximize the representativeness of the sample of jury-eligible adult respondents in each of the counties in which the surveys were conducted.[36] All the community surveys involved relatively highly publicized capital cases where the levels of pretrial publicity led to concerns over whether the defendant's ability to get a fair trial had been compromised. Each individual survey consisted of a representative sample of approximately 300–400 persons. Overall, our analysis is based on the survey responses of nearly 10,000 jury-eligible respondents.

The format of the surveys had been standardized so that respondents were first asked a series of general criminal justice attitude questions that oriented them to the general subject matter of the survey and also provided us with useful data about their law-related beliefs that could be used in additional analyses. These items were followed by several questions about the particular case that had been publicized in their community. Then, to determine whether the level of media exposure was related to the respondents' level of case-related knowledge and to their tendency to prejudge the case, each person was asked several questions about the frequency with which he or she read newspapers, watched television news, and listened to news on the radio.[37] Finally, respondents were asked a series of demographic questions, including several questions designed to screen for eligibility for jury service in the California counties in which the surveys were conducted.

Obviously, the measurement of respondents' "case awareness"—whether persons recognized the case at all—was crucial to our analysis. It was based on a two-part, case-specific question in which respondents were asked if they had "read or heard" anything about this case (typically described in a single sentence that contained a few case-related facts to cue possible recognition). If they had not, they were given another few facts about the case to potentially jog their memories. To further assess the degree to which potentially prejudicial publicity may have penetrated the community, those respondents who were aware of the case also were asked whether they had heard or read about several case-specific items of publicity that had been printed or broadcast about the case. Interviewers prefaced these questions by telling respondents: "As you may know, the media—newspapers, radio and television—have reported a number of things about this case. Some people may remember some facts, while others may remember other facts. We're interested in what you may have seen or heard about this case." The respondent then was asked whether or not he or she had read or heard about each item of publicity. The items of publicity were selected to provide a range of responses—some items had been repeated often in the publicity surrounding the case, others much less so.

Assessing "prejudgment" also was critical in each case. All the surveys used exactly the same question: "Based on what you have read or heard in the news or from other sources, do you think [the defendant] is *definitely not guilty, probably not guilty, probably guilty* or *definitely guilty?*" To eliminate potential order effects, interviewers alternately reversed the direction of the response options that were read, beginning either with "*definitely guilty*" or "*definitely not guilty.*"

Because the effects of pretrial publicity are expected to be greater among persons more regularly exposed to it, we anticipated that the respondents' level of media exposure would influence their case awareness, their recognition of specific prejudicial publicity, and their tendency to prejudge the

case. Thus, after the respondents had indicated any awareness or prejudgment, several questions were used to measure general exposure to the news
media.

Note that unlike the randomly selected, representative sample of cases
whose newspaper coverage Susan Greene and I examined in the first study
that I reported on earlier in this chapter, the cases that Fukurai and I analyzed
were all very highly publicized—at least enough to be candidates for change-
of-venue motions. Just as in the earlier study, however, they were all potentially capital cases—ones in which the prosecution had announced an intention to seek the death penalty.

Not surprisingly, in light of the amount of publicity that surrounded the
cases, the level of community awareness about each case was substantial. In
fact, the results of the surveys indicated that, long before the particular death
penalty trials were scheduled to take place, most community residents were
well informed about the local case in question. An average of about three of
four respondents recognized each of the cases in their community and, in
fact, in a third of the surveys, 90% or more of the community residents
acknowledged that they knew about the case well before the trial commenced.

Levels of prejudgment—a respondent's belief in the guilt of the defendant in advance of trial—also tended to be high. In a few of the least highly
publicized cases in our sample, only about a third of the persons who were
aware of the case had reached the conclusion that the defendant was probably
or definitely guilty. However, in virtually all the others, nearly half or more
had prejudged the defendant as guilty. In fact, in one of the cases fully 90%
of community residents who were aware of the case expressed the belief that
the defendant was guilty.

In addition to calculating these high overall levels of awareness and prejudgment, we were interested in determining whether there was a clear relationship between media exposure and the apparent effects of the publicity.
That is, did people who regularly read newspapers, watched television news,
or listened to news on the radio tend to be more affected by the publicity?
As we expected, the level of exposure to both newspapers *and* TV/radio news
had a statistically significant impact on case awareness, with standardized
regression coefficients indicating that the greater respondents' exposure to
the media, the more likely they were to be aware of the particular case about
which they were asked.

As might be expected, the respondents' level of exposure to newspapers
and to TV/radio news was significantly related to the number of specific items
of publicity about the case that they recognized. That is, those persons with
more media exposure tended to recognize more specific items of case-related
publicity. These patterns generally held through each of the individual case
analyses as well as for the sample overall. Thus, in virtually each case, the
more a respondent had been exposed to media in general (especially to newspapers), the more likely he or she was to be aware of the particular case and
to recognize more specific items of case-related publicity.

Table 3.5
Case Awareness, Recognition of Negative Publicity Items, Media Exposure, and Prejudgment[a]

Dependent Variable	Negative Publicity Recognized	Mass Media Exposure			
		Newspapers	TV/Radio	Intercept	R^2
Case awareness		−.041 (−.156)**	−.027 (−.063)**	0.977	.031
Negative publicity recognized		−.265 (−.207)**	−.141 (−.067)**	1.050	.261
Prejudgment	.163 (.329)**	.016 (.026)*	−.050 (−.049)*	3.040	.207

[a]Ordinary least square regression analyses. Figures in parentheses show standardized regression coefficients.
*$p < .01$, **$p < .001$.

Fukurai and I also analyzed the effects of these publicity-related variables on the most serious kind of pretrial prejudice—the respondents' tendency to prejudge the individual cases. In the overall analysis, we found that the number of items of publicity that respondents recognized had a statistically significant impact on prejudgment, so that persons who recognized more items of case-related publicity were more likely to believe that the defendant was guilty. The direct effects of exposure to newspapers and TV/radio on prejudgment also were statistically significant, suggesting that those who were exposed to more media were more likely to prejudge the case. (These overall statistical relationships are summarized in table 3.5.)[38]

Finally, we found that a number of the general criminal justice attitudes that we measured were significantly related to media exposure, case awareness, recognition of negative publicity, and prejudgment. People with certain beliefs about the criminal justice system appeared to be more likely to have been exposed to the media, and more likely to be affected by this exposure than others. For example, we found that respondents who favored the death penalty were more likely to be aware of the case and also to recognize more items of publicity. It is possible that death penalty supporters take a keener interest in the publicity that surrounds capital cases, or that persons who more often immerse themselves in such publicity come to favor the death penalty.

Among other things, Fukurai and I concluded that case-specific media coverage can have a powerful effect on how people think about particular capital cases that are being tried in their communities. Thus, we found that there was an overall direct effect of media exposure on awareness of the case and on how much specific publicity people recognized. As noted, more media exposure led to more overall case awareness and (usually) to greater recognition of specific case-related pretrial publicity. However, media exposure alone did not lead directly to prejudgment. Instead, the greater tendency to prejudge a capital defendant's guilt appeared to depend on a respondent recognizing a greater amount of negative pretrial publicity pertaining to the crime or the defendant. Thus, the more information someone had gleaned from the media—information that was contained in pretrial publicity that tended to be negative—the more likely he or she was to convict the defendant in advance of his death penalty trial.

Our finding about the relationship between death penalty support and greater case recognition and knowledge of more items of case-related publicity also was important. In a system of death sentencing like ours, which selects jurors based in general on their support for the death penalty (something I address more systematically in chapter 5), this finding suggests that capital jurors on the whole may be more likely to have advance awareness of the death penalty case on which they eventually will sit, and to be more aware of potentially prejudicial case-related publicity long before the trial has begun.

Although Fukurai and I were primarily interested in the statistical relationships between exposure to publicity, case awareness, and prejudgment, it is also important to note that the *content* of the publicity that produced these results was often highly prejudicial—even inflammatory—in nature. In many instances, citizens, voters, and potential jurors were treated to sensationalized aspects of the case, inadmissible pieces of information about the crimes and the defendants, and highly incriminating forms of evidence that appeared in print or broadcast news stories well in advance of trial.

Nonetheless, I should note that despite the large amounts of prejudicial publicity (that often included legally inadmissible evidence), very high levels of community awareness, and significant prejudgment in the communities in question, judges in a number of these cases refused to change the venue of the trials. This meant that the capital defendants went to trial in communities where a very high percentage of potential jurors not only knew a great deal about the cases before any evidence was presented but also where many of them had reached the conclusion that the defendant in the case was probably or definitely guilty. Although I have much more to say about these issues in chapter 5, I briefly note some of their implications here.

In many jurisdictions, the legal standard that governs a change of venue is supposed to take the seriousness of the case explicitly into account. For example, the controlling change-of-venue standard in California lists "the nature and gravity of the offense" as one of the key criteria that courts are required to consider in deciding whether venue should be changed. That is, presumably because these kinds of cases are more likely to be brought into "the consciousness of the community," more sensational and legally serious crimes are supposed to weigh in favor of changing venue.[39] However, even in capital cases—where the great majority of change-of-venue motions are made—this consideration often is pro forma. Courts in general remain very resistant to venue changes.

When courts fail to change venue in capital cases, despite the high levels of potentially prejudicial publicity that typically surround them, they usually rely on other legal methods to limit or control the biasing effects of publicity. Yet the extensive research that has been done on these alternative approaches suggests that they often are ineffective. Among other things, this research has shown that although potential jurors may be cognizant of having been exposed to negative pretrial publicity (indeed, publicity that typically has led them to develop a prejudicial opinion of the defendant), they still tend to claim impartiality.[40] Moreover, even those persons who claim not to be influenced by negative pretrial publicity nonetheless are more likely to convict the defendant than those exposed to neutral publicity.[41] Research also indicates that despite attempts to ask jurors about the influence of pretrial publicity in voir dire, those who disclaim any bias are still more inclined to be punitive toward the defendant.[42] Finally, studies suggest that judicial instructions to ignore pretrial publicity generally fail to reduce its biasing effects.[43]

Combined with the results that Fukurai and I obtained in our sample of highly publicized capital cases, this research suggests that death sentencing may be facilitated by the legal standards and practices that govern change of venue. As these standards are commonly applied in highly publicized death penalty trials, they often fail to protect capital defendants from the very real prejudicial effects of the news coverage that surrounds their cases. As I have noted, these are precisely the kinds of cases in which change-of-venue motions are most likely to be brought, and in which relocating the trial to a more neutral jurisdiction unaffected by prejudicial pretrial publicity may be most needed. Thus, beyond the way in which case-related publicity in capital cases puts pressure on law enforcement and prosecutors to secure a conviction, media coverage also appears increase the likelihood that defendants in death penalty cases will face at least some jurors who have been biased against them well in advance of their trials.

Conclusion

The media's general handling of crime-related themes and its coverage of specific capital cases in local jurisdictions help to create a highly consistent, stereotypical, and narrow view of violent crime. Crime drama and news coverage tend to locate the causes of crime exclusively inside the persons who engage in it. Criminal defendants are depicted without context, typically portrayed in ways that "essentialize" and maximize their deviance. The heavy focus on the graphic and sometimes gruesome details of the crimes themselves omits any meaningful explanation or analysis of their criminal behavior. This kind of reporting typically leaves the emotionally engaged public with only one target against which to channel their fear and anger. In this sense, the newspaper coverage I discussed in this chapter is similar to the framework that media critic Jeffrey Scheuer found characterized television programming in general—a perspective that "reinforces an existential framework in which individuals, not systems or collectivities, are the locus of power and both the cause and the solution to social problems." As a result, Scheuer argued, television "is inept at showing more complex, long-term and institutional remedies" to social problems.[44] This perspective feeds directly into what commentator Austin Ranney has termed the "fast forward effect"—the public's demand that it be provided with "quick and final solutions to complex and intransigent problems."[45] The death penalty has precisely that feel, of a quick and final solution to a very complex problem. Other solutions to violent crime, of course, seem unduly complicated and delayed in their result.

Moreover, citizens, voters, and potential jurors are given little in the way of a legal framework for understanding the factors that must be brought to bear in rendering a verdict in an actual capital case. The news accounts of capital crimes and even press coverage of capital trials themselves lack meaningful discussions of the legal process by which death sentencing is supposed to occur. Moreover, the press ignores the kind of evidence that jurors must consider in deciding whether to spare a defendant's life or not. Indeed, in the more than 300 newspaper articles that Susan Greene and I analyzed, the term "mitigation" or "mitigating circumstances" was used exactly once, and it was immediately followed by a sentencing judge's assertion that the mitigation "failed to outweigh" what he termed "the revolting circumstances of the murders."[46]

Thus, the sentencing framework that governs the choice between life and death is virtually never mentioned and, perforce, never meaningfully explained. As a result, citizens, voters, and potential jurors lack basic knowledge about the kind of evidence that typically is presented at a capital penalty trial and that actual capital jurors are instructed to take into account. In this sense, at least as far as Greene and I could determine, the press did little or nothing to educate the public about the social contextual causes of crime, and even less to educate them about the broad set of factors that the law requires jurors to reflect on and be guided by in rendering fair and reliable sentencing verdicts in death penalty cases.

In a media context in which cases that result in death sentences are far more likely to be covered than those that result in life and where actual death verdicts are much more likely to be reported than life verdicts, death may become the public's expected outcome in capital cases. Moreover, when the press fails to explain the framework by which a principled capital jury could reach a life verdict, and only very rarely conveys the kind of mitigating facts and circumstances on which such a verdict could be based, life sentences are likely to appear irrational and lacking in any evidentiary basis. Members of the public may come to assume that such verdicts can only be rendered as a result of little more than mercy or sympathy that is ungrounded in logic or law. They have been given no other framework with which to understand how or why a jury might reach a decision for life.

None of this is meant to suggest that the media are implicated in some conspiratorial effort to promote or support the death penalty. Of course, they are not. However, their tendency sensationalize crime and demonize criminals is at odds with a balanced approach to the issues that ordinary citizens must resolve. Voters who help to decide on death penalty policies and jurors who render verdicts in capital cases operate in a culture that is saturated with one-sided, misleading, and fundamentally incorrect media messages and influences. To be sure, gruesome crime-related details and elaborate descriptions of depraved criminal traits are likely to pique interest, expand audiences, and generate revenue. Social contextual and social historical explanations, on the other hand, not only are dry and mundane by comparison but also are at odds with the dispositional themes the media have taught the public to regard as commonsensical. In the rare instances in which they appear at all, such explanations feel like far-fetched examples of excuse making, rather than scientifically grounded, accurate analyses.

In addition, the research Hiroshi Fukurai and I did on pretrial publicity in actual death penalty cases underscores the fact that extensive and sensational press coverage does have an effect on the citizens, voters, and potential jurors who are exposed to it. In addition to promoting a consistent and consistently damaging view of the capital defendants who, in turn, will be judged by the very members of the community that the media have taught to fear and despise them, press coverage helps to convince many of the most knowledgeable and informed members of the community that defendants in these cases are actually guilty.

The death-sentencing process is indirectly facilitated by case-specific media publicity that focuses on sensational aspects of the crime, relies very heavily on law enforcement and prosecutorial sources for most of its information, and helps to convince community residents that capital defendants are guilty. Yet stringent change-of-venue doctrines mean that capital cases almost always are tried in the jurisdiction in which the greatest amount of potentially prejudicial, case-specific publicity has been broadcast and printed. In this sense, the law does little to correct even the most basic of these publicity-created biases, ensuring that these particular potential threats to fair and impartial decision making go largely unaddressed.

Moreover, a broader media-related concern—coverage that consistently fails to explain or depict mitigation at the same time it repeatedly emphasizes aggravating facts and circumstances—is rarely acknowledged and never addressed at all. This issue—the way the media not only cover capital crime per se but also neglect to provide the public with complete or balanced information about how our system of capital punishment actually operates— may affect the beliefs that citizens have about prevailing death penalty practices. It is addressed in part in the next chapter.

4

The Fragile Consensus
Public Opinion and Death Penalty Policy

The [cruel and unusual punishment] clause of the Constitution, in the
opinion of the learned commentators, may be therefore progressive,
and is not fastened to the obsolete, but may acquire meaning as
public opinion becomes enlightened by a humane justice.
—*Weems v. United States* (1910)

I have found that [the American people] earnestly desire their
system of punishments to make sense in order that it can be a
morally justifiable system.
—Justice Thurgood Marshall (1972)

This chapter focuses on the nature of public opinion about capital punishment and its role in the administration of the death penalty in the United
States. As I noted in the last two chapters, economic and political forces have
helped to shape the media's depictions of crime and punishment. In addition
to the real dangers posed by the threat of violent crime, citizens' deepest fears
about victimization are intensified by repeated exposure to sensationalized
television images and story lines that demonize the perpetrators of crime.
Along with the often narrow, one-sided news coverage that surrounds individual capital cases, these factors help to increase the perceived need for harsh
punishments like the death penalty. This chapter examines some of the apparent attitudinal consequences of those threats, images, story lines, and
news coverage and the ways that they have helped to shape and maintain
public support for capital punishment.

Throughout the history of capital punishment, public opinion has played
a significant role in its administration. The death penalty has been the unique
focus of public debate in the United States, and American courts and legal
decision makers have taken stock of the attitudes of citizens concerning this
topic with an attentiveness reserved for no other legal sanction. In part, this
is because of the intense feelings that have been generated on both sides of
the issue. As Justice Brennan observed in *Furman*, "[f]rom the beginning of
our Nation, the punishment of death has stirred acute public controversy.
. . . The country has debated whether a society for which the dignity of the
individual is the supreme value can, without a fundamental inconsistency,
follow the practice of deliberately putting some of its members to death."[1]

Popular opinion has been cited in various legal decisions about the death penalty, ranging from the very existence of the penalty itself to the frequency and manner in which it has been imposed. Historian Peter Linebaugh observed that, when executions were carried out in town squares centuries ago, the public spectacle itself depended on "a rough agreement between those who wield the law and those ruled by it."[2] Although the spectacle of capital punishment has changed dramatically, the need for such "rough agreement" persists. As social psychologists Neil Vidmar and Phoebe Ellsworth noted, "[t]o some extent public opinion has always played a part in modern controversy about the death penalty."[3] The attitudes that people hold about capital punishment are *still* matters of considerable legal and political import.

Unfortunately, the fact that public opinion matters in this area of law as in few others has not elevated contemporary debates about the death penalty or ensured a particularly high level of rational, informed analysis. In fact, I will suggest that, especially in modern times, public support for capital punishment—which reached historic highs during the last quarter century and only recently began to return to previous levels—has depended on a *lack* of understanding about the how the death penalty actually operates in our society. The more people know about what really happens in the overall administration of capital punishment, the less inclined they are to support it. Thus, preserving our system of death sentencing depends in some ways on preserving the public's lack of accurate knowledge about how it actually functions.

Assessing the "Mood of the Onlookers": The Ebb and Flow of Death Penalty Support

Debates among lawmakers and judicial officials over the death penalty—in which explicit references to popular opinion have played a central role—have been recorded throughout history. Moreover, the assertion that the public does, or does not, "want" the death penalty has been a long and frequently cited justification for political action and legal change concerning capital punishment.[4] Thus, some discussion of the historical *context* of public opinion about the death penalty is useful in understanding the parameters of the contemporary debate.

Unlike, say, opinions about imprisonment or penal fines, public opinion about the death penalty—and popular reactions to its imposition—are part of the historical record in most nations. As Justice Brennan put it, "[t]here has been no national debate about punishment, in general or by imprisonment, comparable to the debate about the punishment of death. No other punishment has been so continuously restricted . . . nor has any State yet abolished prisons, as some have abolished this punishment."[5] Indeed, one historian referred to capital punishment as "the gold standard of community expression."[6]

Long before opinion polls or attitude surveys were available, evidence of the public's view of the death penalty came from a variety of indirect sources. They included public demonstrations by the crowds gathered around the gallows at Tyburn Hill in London, as well as the frequency of "jury nullifications" attributed to public distaste with the death penalty and the belief that it was too harsh a punishment to impose in many cases. In fact, the argument that the death penalty should be limited (if not abolished) in order to avoid jury nullifications played a role in abolitionist writing in both England and the United States. If Douglas Hay's observation that "[t]he rulers of eighteenth-century England cherished the death sentence" is correct, their affection was not always shared by the common folk.[7]

In the United States, historians gauged the level of public support for the death penalty by reference to the size and vehemence of the movements that were devoted to abolishing it. For example, the so-called antigallows movement in the first half of the 19th century "aroused violent debate" among ministers and religious leaders, social reformers, and legislators as well as members of the public.[8] The debate was largely suspended during the traumatic years of the Civil War, after which "men's finer sensibilities, which had once been revolted by the executions of a fellow being, seemed hardened and blunted."[9]

Opposition to the death penalty again gained momentum in the 1890s, as more "scientific" views of crime and criminals emerged. Increasingly, the notion that there were identifiable, external causes that helped to account for criminal behavior muted cries that the harshest possible penalties be imposed on wrongdoers. The movement to abolish capital punishment in the United States continued on an organized basis until just before the start of the World War I, and achieved some notable success—at least seven states abolished the death penalty during this period, presumably with the support (or, at least, acquiescence) of the public.[10] In the mid-1920s, a prominent death penalty expert opined that capital punishment would "finally pass away" sometime during the century, but his prediction obviously was mistaken.[11]

The Depression years, growing concerns about war, and then World War II itself preoccupied the American public over the next several decades. Support for the death penalty appeared to stabilize during this period and organized opposition to the death penalty gained little added momentum. In fact, some of the states that had abolished capital punishment reconsidered and reinstated it. By the late 1940s, death penalty opponents lamented the fact that the movement to abolish the death penalty appeared to have stalled in the United States, where "[n]o popular movement has questioned penal theory, least of all capital punishment."[12]

Of course, estimating the general level of public support for capital punishment on the basis of popular reactions to individual cases or the activities of organized interest groups overlooks the views of a very sizable number of people who are less directly involved with the issue. However, by the mid-

1930s the use of systematic public opinion polling had begun. From this point forward, historians and others would have a more precise record of overall trends in death penalty support on which to rely. For example, the Gallup polling organization conducted its first nationwide death penalty survey in 1936 and estimated that approximately 60% of the American public favored capital punishment for murder.

As figure 4.1 shows, public support for capital punishment has fluctuated since Gallup's initial poll. Although it is difficult to be certain (because Gallup did not poll consistently over these years), there is no evidence that public support varied much from the mid-1930s until the mid-1950s.[13] At that point the percentage of the public "in favor" of the death penalty began a modest but consistent decline. The lowest level of support occurred in 1966, when only 42% of the public supported capital punishment for persons convicted of murder. In fact, this was the only year in which Gallup estimated that the percentage expressing opposition to the death penalty (47%) exceeded those in favor. However, this trend also soon reversed itself. Reasonably steady increases in death penalty support occurred throughout the 1970s and 1980s. Gallup's estimates of death penalty support peaked in the early to mid-1990s, and began another modest decline after that.

What appears to be the most consistent and significant period of change—the 30-percentage-point increase in death penalty support between 1966 and 1994—coincided with general political campaigns to "get tough"

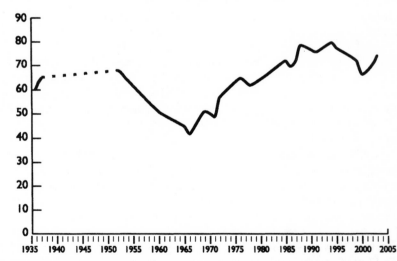

Figure 4.1 Gallup poll results: "Are you in favor of the death penalty for murder (or for persons convicted of murder)?" *Source:* Combined totals from www.pollingreport.com/crime.htm and H. Erskine, The Polls: Capital Punishment, 24 *Public Opinion Quarterly* 290–309 (1970). Calculations omit "no opinion/ undecided" respondents. The median of the 22 Gallup surveys taken over this 67-year period is 67% in favor, the mean 64%.

with criminals by increasing the harshness of the penalties they received. As two commentators put it at the start of this trend of increasing death penalty support: "Support for capital punishment seems to be strongly correlated with 'law and order' campaigns by local, state, and national politicians. It is one stark means a candidate has of displaying that he will 'do something about crime' if elected."[14]

Indeed, if anything, the high levels of measured support during these years may have understated somewhat the one-sidedness of the public and political consensus. Although upwards of 70–80% of the public endorsed the death penalty, actually fewer than one person in five typically was willing to state his or her explicit opposition (the balance of respondents expressing "no opinion" on the topic). From the early 1970s until well into the 1990s, very little visible, organized opposition or public debate about the death penalty occurred on a national level in the United States. Moreover, the death penalty continued to serve as an especially potent political symbol, leading one news commentator to quip at the start of the 1990s that "[t]he electric chair has replaced the American flag as your all-purpose campaign symbol."[15]

During these most recent decades, then, as law professor Samuel Gross accurately observed, a "new status quo" had been reached in which the death penalty was regarded as less controversial than at any time in the past. It had become simply "an accepted part of our criminal justice system." Indeed, capital punishment was an issue about which there was little public or political controversy or conflict in part because, as Gross put it in the late 1990s, "the sides are so severely mismatched."[16]

To the extent that "[p]eople learn about public opinion from media coverage, and particularly the coverage of public opinion polls,"[17] the American public learned a great deal about its own attitudes toward the death penalty during the 1980s and 1990s. These were times when headlines announcing the high levels of support for the death penalty were commonplace in newspapers across the country. Consider just these few: "Level of Public Support for Death Penalty at All-Time High—83%"; "The Times Poll: 75% Support the Death Penalty in California"; "79% of Americans Back Death Penalty"; "Death Penalty Support Hits Record High"; "Support Still Strong as Execution in California Nears, Poll Shows"; "Support Still Strong for Death Penalty: Poll Shows Virtually No Change Since Execution"; and "Poll: Support Strong for Death Penalty."[18]

However, despite the political and legal significance that is attached to the issue, the headlines and related news reports failed to make clear that most of the polls on which they were based asked only a single question about the death penalty, often as part of a longer series of questions concerning a variety of other issues. Thus, public support for the death penalty tended to be presented as unidimensional (i.e., people were depicted as "supporting" it or not),[19] and the potential complexity of people's views about capital punishment often was ignored. Among other things, news reports and the surveys on which they were based sometimes omitted discussion of the strength of support expressed by respondents and usually failed to examine the various *specific* circumstances under which persons thought the death penalty was warranted or not.

Failing to analyze the strength of respondents' support of the death penalty conveyed an "all or nothing" quality to public sentiments that may have masked significant, underlying ambivalence. Neglecting to specify the circumstances under which "public support" would translate into a recommendation that the death penalty actually be imposed conveyed an impression of broad, generalized support that may not have extended to all or even most cases.[20] Indeed, in spite of the apparent one-sidedness of public opinion, and perhaps, in an odd way, because of it, it was easy to miss the softness and complexity that characterized at least some people's support of capital punishment, features that were drowned out by all the apparent public enthusiasm and political promotion over the last several decades.

The softness in death penalty support seemed to come about as a result of the fact that a number of people said they were in favor of a system of punishment that, increasingly, they knew very little about. A lack of public discussion and debate limited the amount of accurate information that was readily available to most citizens. The hidden complexity in death penalty attitudes stemmed from the fact that, as noted previously, many surveys measured levels of public support by asking and reporting responses to only a single question—or a very limited set of questions—about capital punishment. Few pollsters probed any of the underlying nuances, perhaps assuming that the high levels of support meant that there were none.

Death Penalty Attitudes in Depth: Studying the Evolving Standards of an "Informed Citizenry"

In an attempt to explore some of these issues—at the very height of support for capital punishment in the United States—my colleagues Aida Hurtado and Luis Vega and I conducted a statewide survey of a representative sample of adult Californians, asking numerous specific questions about the respondents' death penalty attitudes and beliefs.[21] We wondered whether much public support for the death penalty was limited to certain kinds of cases that might not be representative of actual capital cases and defendants, and whether death penalty beliefs were dependent in some way on the lack of knowledge and amount of misinformation that seemed to be growing as death penalty support increased. To address these topics in-depth, we posed a lengthy series of questions about various aspects of the system of death sentencing, hoping to identify underlying patterns in the public's death penalty attitudes and to glean insights about the precise ways in which various factors influenced our respondents' beliefs about capital punishment.[22]

In our survey, a total of 498 adults were interviewed in what was likely the most detailed statewide survey of death penalty attitudes ever done in

California. Our survey was conducted by telephone, included some 40 death-penalty-related items, and employed modern sampling techniques designed to maximize the representativeness of the sample of respondents.[23] We attempted not only to go well beyond the limited, single-question approach to measuring general support but also to employ legally correct formulations of a series of interrelated death penalty questions. Among other things, we explained the overall legal procedures by which capital cases proceeded in California and most other states. Thus, within the limitations imposed by survey research methodology, we sought to have our respondents answer many of the death-penalty-related questions in the general legal context that they might be posed in court.[24]

More specifically, the survey itself was structured to address several major issues that are related to my main thesis about how our system of death sentencing is maintained. The issues included the underlying legal and psychological complexity of our respondents' death penalty attitudes; the degree to which general or abstract attitudes toward the death penalty varied as a function of particular facts about the crime and the person who committed it; whether death penalty attitudes were premised on erroneous or questionable assumptions about capital punishment (particularly, its administration and consequences); and whether support of the death penalty was in large part a function of the perceived absence of any effective alternative.

Not surprisingly, given the fact that the survey was conducted at the height of public support for the death penalty, close to 8 of 10 (79%) of our respondents said they were in favor of capital punishment. Moreover, fully half of them described themselves as "strongly in favor." As table 4.1 illustrates, these results were similar to those found in statewide polls conducted in other parts of the country at around the same time.

General Crime Control and Death Penalty Views

Previous research had documented the fact that death penalty attitudes were centrally related to people's beliefs about a wide variety of criminal justice matters. For this reason, we asked our respondents a series of eight criminal justice attitude items similar to those that had been used in a number of previous death penalty studies.[25] Their responses were generally consistent with results reported by others—particularly Phoebe Ellsworth and Robert Fitzgerald, in a study conducted in one large California county a decade earlier than ours.[26] Like them, we found that death penalty supporters were more likely to endorse what has been termed a "crime control" perspective concerning the criminal justice system while death penalty opponents were more likely to endorse an overall "due process" perspective.[27] For example, respondents who disagreed with the basic tenet of American jurisprudence that "it is better for society to let some guilty people go free than to risk convicting an innocent person" were significantly more likely to support the

Table 4.1
Abstract Support of Death Penalty at the
Height of Its Popularity

State	Support Level
California	79%
Florida	84%
Georgia	75%
Kentucky	69%
Maryland	64%
Nebraska	68%
New York	72%
Oklahoma	80%

The surveys were conducted in the mid- to late-1980s,
when death penalty support was at an all-time high. Specifically: California (12/89); Florida (5/86); Georgia (12/
86); Kentucky (12/89); Maryland (2/87); Nebraska (1/88);
New York (5/89); and Oklahoma (12/88).

death penalty, as were those who disagreed with the exclusionary rule and
believed that the insanity defense was little more than a "loophole" that
allowed too many guilty persons to go free.

In analyses of the increase in support for the death penalty that occurred
in the decades of the 1970s and 1980s, many commentators referred to the
broad shifts in the public's attitudes about the nature of crime control,
changes that Franklin Zimring and Gordon Hawkins have described this way:
"After a period of conflict about the proper role of crime control in America,
the decade since 1975 has witnessed an apparent law-and-order consensus
in public opinion."[28] A number of researchers have posited a connection
between support for the death penalty and a general belief in the use of
punishment as an appropriate—perhaps the only appropriate—response to
crime.[29]

Indeed, as previous research and common sense would lead us to expect,
there *were* large differences between death penalty supporters and opponents
on all measures of general attitudes toward punishment. Respondents who
believed that "criminals should be punished harshly to demonstrate that
society cares about the victims of crime" were significantly more likely to
support the death penalty, as were those who agreed that "it is more important that prisons punish criminals than rehabilitate them." On the other
hand, persons who disagreed that "even the worst criminal should be considered for mercy" were significantly more likely to support the death penalty,
as were those who disagreed that "harsher treatment of criminals is not the
solution to the crime problem."[30]

However, lest I create the impression that abstract support for the death

Table 4.2
Death Penalty Support and General Attitudes About Punishment

Agrees That:	Overall	Death Penalty Supporters	Death Penalty Opponents
Criminals should be punished harshly to show caring for victims	83.9	86.5	71
The worst criminals should not be considered for mercy	62.4	67.5	43
Harsh treatment is solution to crime problem	48.9	58	21.5
More important that prisons punish than rehabilitate	36.4	39.3	15.1

penalty reflected nothing more than an overall high level of punitiveness among our respondents, several other facts about the pattern of our punishment-related data should be noted. Most importantly, the survey results suggested that, despite strong abstract support for the death penalty, there was a fair amount of ambivalence and equivocation about the general use of harsh punishment in the criminal justice system. These feelings may help explain the complexity of the death penalty attitudes that I discuss in later in this chapter.

Although, on the one hand, there was widespread agreement among our respondents that "criminals should be punished harshly to demonstrate that society cares about victims of crime" (83.9% agreed strongly or somewhat), respondents did not on the whole believe that "it is more important that prisons punish criminals than rehabilitate them" (only 37.4% agreed strongly or somewhat, as compared to 56.3% who disagreed).[31] Moreover, nearly half of our respondents (45.8%) agreed that "harsher treatment of criminals is *not* the solution to the crime problem."[32]

It may be, as others have suggested, that many people support the death penalty for largely symbolic reasons, as a way of expressing their general concern about the seriousness of the crime problem and the plight of crime victims. Most people in our sample did not appear to be indiscriminately committed to punishment as the only solution to violent crime. Indeed, some were willing to consider limiting the use of harsh punishment even in the most extreme cases. Thus, although a majority disagreed that even the worst criminal should be considered for mercy, a sizable minority of our respondents (32.8%) thought mercy should be a consideration, even in the most extreme cases. This left open the possibility that, for crimes and criminals who were not literally "the worst," a higher percentage of our respondents favored mercy and would reject the use of the death penalty (even though they were strong supporters of capital punishment in the abstract).

Guided Discretion: Aggravating and Mitigating Factors

Recall that in the modern post-*Gregg* era, capital jurors are supposed to choose between life and death only *after* having considered certain specific factors that guide the discretion used in reaching their sentencing decision. Much legal significance thus is attached to having capital jurors assess the *specific* characteristics of crimes and defendants in capital cases. However, most surveys do not attempt to replicate this more nuanced decision-making process. As noted earlier, many surveys estimate the level of public support for the death penalty by relying on only a single question, or they pose their death penalty questions in terms of a single generic type of crime (usually "murder"). Researchers have suggested that posing such general or abstract questions encourages respondents to imagine a hypothetical defendant who is more deviant, powerful, and dangerous than the typical defendant who actually appears in court.[33]

Our survey tried to address these issues—that is, how potential jurors might respond to the realties of structured or guided capital penalty decision making and react to the introduction of some of the specific factors that often are present in the range of capital cases that actually go to trial. To do so, we asked respondents to evaluate a series of possible aggravating and mitigating circumstances that, under the statutory sentencing schemes of nearly all death penalty states, were like the ones that capital jurors would be instructed to consider in reaching their actual death penalty decisions.[34]

As a point of clarification, note that one aspect of modern death penalty law led us to include some items that were not specifically listed in the California statute or those of other states. Although aggravating factors are restricted by law to those things that are explicitly enumerated in death penalty sentencing instructions, mitigating factors are not. Thus, most death penalty statutes include a kind of "catchall" category that allows jurors to consider "anything else" that they find to be mitigating, in addition to whatever specific mitigating factors are listed in the sentencing instruction. Indeed, capital juries technically are required to at least *consider* any piece of mitigating evidence that the defendant does introduce.

To be sure, as I pointed out in chapter 1, many attorneys fail to make full and effective use of this important legal provision. Moreover, as I discuss in a subsequent chapter, jurors are often confused about what, exactly, constitutes "mitigation," so that they have a difficult time deciding whether and how evidence offered under the rubric of the catchall category should be considered. Nonetheless, it is likely that some of these not-otherwise-specified facts and circumstances would play an important role in a respondent's—or juror's—decision-making process. With that in mind, our survey included a number of examples of different types of mitigation that might be presented in a properly handled penalty trial.[35]

As table 4.3 illustrates, we found that there were a number of factors

Table 4.3
Capital Aggravation and Mitigation

Factors Making a Death Verdict More Likely		Factors Making a Life Verdict More Likely	
Factor Present in a Given Case	% Death-Qualified Californians Saying They'd Be More Likely to Vote for **Death**	Factor Present in a Given Case	% Death-Qualified Californians Saying They'd Be More Likely to Vote for **Life**
The murder was especially brutal, involving torture or extreme abuse.	84	Murder committed when the person was under extreme mental or emotional disturbance	57
Two or more victims were murdered	70	Until this crime, person had been hardworking and done good things for others	52
Convicted person showed no remorse	69	This crime was the only violent crime person had committed	50
The murder was committed in the course of a sexual assault or rape	60	Person institutionalized in past but never given help or treatment for his problems	42
Convicted person had committed at least one prior felony prior to the present crime	33	Person would be a hardworking, well-behaved inmate in prison	41
Murder was committed while person was under influence of drugs or alcohol	31	The murder was not premeditated but committed in robbery where victim resisted	43
		Person had been seriously abused as a child	41
		Murder was committed while person was under influence of drugs or alcohol	35
		The convicted person came from a background of extreme poverty	21
		Defendant under age 30	21

that, when present in a given case, would make potential jurors more likely to impose a death sentence. Several of these aggravators clearly reflected dimensions of heinousness in the crime itself—an especially brutal murder, or one with multiple victims, for example. Some of the potent aggravation also seemed to match up with the popular stereotype of demonized, violent criminality—a remorseless killer, or one who murdered in the course of a sexual assault. Not surprisingly, when any one of these factors was present in a case, a sizable majority of potential jurors perceived their aggravating significance and were more inclined to render death verdicts.

On the other hand, mitigating factors were somewhat more diffuse in their effect. Indeed, the one mitigator that was endorsed by the highest number of respondents—the fact that a murder was committed when the perpetrator was under extreme mental or emotional distress—ranked below all of the top four aggravators in its effect. Perhaps because, as I pointed out in chapter 3, mitigation is rarely depicted in the media, and members of the public are given no simple, uniform framework for knowing what is or should be considered mitigating, the potential jurors who participated in our survey varied more widely in how they perceived mitigation and whether they recognized it in any particular fact or specific scenario.

However, it certainly was not the case that mitigation was ignored or that mitigating factors lacked the power to influence respondents in the direction of a life sentence. Indeed, every potential mitigator in the survey was endorsed by a percentage of respondents that was the equivalent of at least two or more members of a 12-person jury (that is, 2 in 12, or 16.7%).[36] Thus, even among this group of otherwise very pro-death-penalty citizens, there were a variety of case-specific factors—ones that often are present in actual capital cases—that, in the limited context of a survey such as this, seemed to "humanize" the defendant and might result in nuanced decisions to sentence him to live rather than die.

In sum, the picture that emerged from the pattern of responses to these more detailed questions was much more complicated and textured than those typically reflected in unidimensional studies of death penalty attitudes. These jury-eligible respondents conceded that there were many factors that would incline them toward a life verdict, despite their abstract support for the death penalty. The factors included things like the fact that the person had never received treatment in the past for his problems, had been seriously abused as a child, and came from a background of extreme poverty.

Death Penalty Misconceptions:
Assessing the "Marshall Hypothesis"

In the landmark *Furman* case,[37] public opinion was mentioned and discussed explicitly in five of the Justices' nine separate opinions.[38] It formed an important part of the view expressed by Justices Brennan and Marshall that the death penalty had become a *per se* violation of the Eighth Amendment's ban on cruel and unusual punishment. For example, Justice Brennan included among the four principles he articulated for deciding whether a particular punishment violated the Eighth Amendment the requirement that the punishment "must not be unacceptable to contemporary society."[39] He made reference to the "continuing moral debate" over capital punishment and argued that the death penalty had "proved progressively more troublesome to the national conscience."[40]

Justice Marshall's *Furman* opinion focused even more directly on the question of public opinion. He argued that even a punishment that served a valid legislative purpose and was not excessive could violate the Eighth Amendment if "popular sentiment abhors it."[41] Although he conceded there were "no prior cases in this Court striking down a penalty on this ground,"[42] he reasoned that the very notion of evolving standards that reflected changing popular values required the Court to recognize such a principle. With precisely this principle in mind, he concluded that the death penalty violated the Eighth Amendment because it had become "morally unacceptable to the people of the United States at this time in their history."[43]

Indeed, Marshall thought that public opinion polls on death penalty opinion were of marginal value because too few people "were fully informed as to the purposes of the penalty and its liabilities."[44] He was not persuaded by the fact that numerous legislatures—presumably acting in accord with their constituents' wishes—repeatedly had enacted death penalty statutes throughout the nation's history. He thought that, at least in recent years, the "voice of the people" had been distorted by "indifference and ignorance," leading to a desire to preserve the status quo on capital punishment without much knowledge about whether doing so was really "desirable."[45]

Marshall countered that the best index of contemporary standards would be to "discern the probable opinion of an *informed* electorate."[46] In what has been termed the "Marshall hypothesis" by social scientists who have studied the issue subsequently,[47] he argued that if the general public were informed accurately about the workings of the death penalty and made aware of the evidence concerning its discriminatory imposition and ineffectiveness as a deterrent to murder, then "the great mass of citizens" would conclude it was "immoral."[48] In a sense, this is an argument about the way in which death penalty support depends on a low level of understanding about the death penalty itself. Obviously, one way to examine this hypothesis is to examine whether and how well citizens really are informed about the death penalty

Thus, our survey posed a series of questions about some of the most frequently asserted justifications for the death penalty and several widespread beliefs about how the system of capital punishment generally operates. This allowed a test of the contention not only that many citizens, voters, and potential jurors are misinformed about crime in general and capital punishment in particular but also that some of these myths and forms of misinformation are crucial to public support of the system of death sentencing. Several separate kinds of beliefs were addressed.

As a threshold issue, we attempted to determine whether citizens themselves believed that the way the system of capital punishment in the United States actually operated was an important consideration on which their support should be based. Some context for this question is in order. For most of the first half of the 20th century, public policy and sentiment seemed to have moved away from reliance on retributive justifications for punishment. In mid-century, for example, Justice Black summed up what seemed to be the consensus view: "Retribution is no longer the dominant objective of the criminal law. Reformation and rehabilitation of offenders have become important goals of criminal jurisprudence."[49]

In the early 1970s, however, a different perspective emerged. Buttressed by a movement among some social theorists and penologists to promote what was termed "just deserts" as the basis for punishment—the notion that criminals deserved to experience a specified measure of pain for each particular transgression—many politicians adopted the position that the state could and should punish for no other reason than to exact retribution from lawbreakers.[50] It was not long before many jurists and commentators suggested that the primary if not exclusive function of the death penalty was to further these interests in retribution. For example, Justice Stewart asserted in *Furman* that the "instinct for retribution is part of the nature of man,"[51] and again in his plurality opinion in *Gregg,* that the death penalty—as a unique vehicle for the expression of that instinct—could be seen as "essential in an ordered society. . . ."[52]

Indeed, some analysts argued that the renewed legitimacy of retribution accounted for the public's changing attitudes toward the death penalty over the last several decades. That is, the increased willingness on the part of citizens and politicians to embrace retributive motives as the rationale for criminal justice policy had become perhaps the most important reason for supporting the death penalty. As James Fox, Michael Radelet, and Julie Bonsteel suggested, "Americans now are unashamed, and perhaps even proud, to verbalize their desire for retribution,"[53] and their support of capital punishment gave voice to these newly legitimated desires.

We regarded retribution as a threshold question because, in a sense, it provided the context for all of the remaining questions about what the public really knew about and wanted from their system of death sentencing. After all, if most people did not really care about any other feature of the death penalty except its retributive capacity, then their lack of knowledge about what else it accomplished would be understandable. Whatever else can be said about the death penalty, it exacts the ultimate retributive price. In addition, if attitudes about the death penalty were based on purely retributive motives, most people would be unlikely to respond to new knowledge and more accurate information about the effectiveness of the system of death sentencing and its larger social consequences. Renewed public debate and greater access to social science data about how capital punishment was administered in the United States—of the sort I suggested in chapter 1 that the Supreme Court had shied away from admitting or acknowledging—would not likely affect popular sentiment.

However, we found that a majority of our respondents did *not* agree with the narrowly retributive view.[54] That is, 51% believed that retribution in itself was not a sufficient justification for the death penalty, and that, in evaluating death penalty policy, we should consider and take into account the broader social purposes and societal effects of the death penalty (and whether it does or does not achieve them). Only 35% expressed the view that retribution alone was a sufficient justification for the death penalty. This made our subsequent findings all the more surprising. Despite acknowledging the importance of what the death penalty accomplished and how it actually operated in our society—its broader social effects—large percentages of our respondents held misconceptions or erroneous assumptions about exactly those things. Each of these misconceptions is addressed in turn here.

The Proper Focus of Death Penalty Decision Making

As I pointed out in chapter 1, a major feature in the modern system of death sentencing is the opportunity to present information and testimony about the background and character of the defendant in the penalty phase of capital trials. This requirement was articulated explicitly in *Gregg*, elaborated on just a few years later,[55] and affirmed in several cases since then.[56] Indeed, it is one of the major reforms in the modern system of death sentencing. Thus, presenting information about the background and character of a capital defendant forms the core of virtually all effective defense trial strategies in capital penalty phases and is generally regarded as the only thing that can lead reliably to life rather than death sentences.[57] Yet recall that not only has the Supreme Court been reluctant to require attorneys to take advantage of this crucial provision, but the news media also has done virtually nothing to educate the public about the logic of this death-sentencing framework. Citizens are provided few if any details about background and social history factors in the lives of capital defendants, and press accounts given them virtually no guidance about how such things can and should play a role in understanding criminality or assessing culpability.

Perhaps not surprisingly, then, a majority (51%) of our respondents believed that the decision about whether or not to impose the death penalty should focus *only* on the characteristics of the crime for which the defendant was convicted (although a sizable minority—40%—acknowledged that the background and character of the defendant should be considered as well). As noted, a persistent, exclusive focus on the crime alone is contrary to the requirements of modern death penalty law. Yet it is an approach to death sentencing that seems to comport with the emphasis in fictional crime drama and the narrow crime-centered nature of media coverage in actual death penalty cases discussed in chapter 3.

Recall that a majority of our respondents believed that retribution alone was not a sufficient justification for capital punishment, and also that many of them regarded a number of noncrime factors and circumstances as mitigating when they were explicitly presented. However, it appeared that unless the potential mitigating significance of these various background factors was made very explicit and entirely clear, many respondents were inclined to shift their attention back to the crime alone. This narrow focus seems tailored to retributive concerns and little else in deciding whether or not a person actually should receive a death sentence.

The Deterrent Effect of Capital Punishment

Justice Marshall wrote in *Furman* that deterrence was "[t]he most hotly contested issue regarding capital punishment. . . ."[58] Despite being hotly contested, as I pointed out in chapter 1, it has not always been handled in a forthright manner by the courts and other legal decision makers. The empirical evidence on this question is quite straightforward.[59] Study after study consistently has shown that the death penalty does not measurably deter murder; it provides no incremental deterrent effect above the alternative of life imprisonment. Indeed, Zimring and Hawkins have summarized the overall results of existing research on the topic this way: "[T]he death penalty is about as relevant to controlling violent crime as rain-dancing is to controlling the weather."[60]

Yet the deterrent effect of capital punishment has been publicly touted by proponents of the death penalty as one of the primary reasons for its retention. For example, in 1981 the California State Attorney General's Office distributed a pamphlet to voters throughout the state that attempted to convince them that the state supreme court's failure to implement the death penalty was "a major reason" violent crime was on the rise. The state supreme court's "obstructionism" consisted of its refusal to approve a number of death sentences that had been handed down under statewide laws enacted just a few years earlier, ones that many legal scholars agreed were deeply flawed.[61] Nonetheless, the attorney general's "Special Report to the People" told Californians: "[T]he death penalty has been essentially nullified by the California Supreme Court even though it is considered to be the singularly most effective deterrent to murder available. . . . A major reason that murder and other violent crimes have reached intolerable levels is the historic unwillingness of the California Supreme Court to follow the will of the people."[62]

Perhaps because of their repeated exposure to this kind of misinformation about the deterrent effect of capital punishment—which erroneously characterized the death penalty as an essential weapon in the fight against serious violent crime—a very large number of our California respondents (74%) expressed the belief that it deterred murder. Notwithstanding the substantial empirical evidence to the contrary, this belief was widely held among our respondents irrespective of their gender, income level, or political affiliation.

The Comparative Costs of Life and Death Sentences

We also asked about an issue that, although it likely plays only a secondary role in shaping most people's views on capital punishment, is part of the general knowledge base from which people reason more broadly about capital punishment. It provides an additional index of how well informed the public in general is about the topic. Specifically, we asked respondents whether they believed the costs of death penalty imposition to exceed those of life imprisonment.

Some context for this question is in order as well. Hurtado, Vega, and I certainly were aware that the relative expense of the death penalty versus life in prison without possibility of parole played no formal role in the statutory scheme of any state. We also knew that few if any attorneys used it in an explicit way in capital trials as an argument to reach a life or a death sentence. Yet there was some reason to believe that it might influence public opinion concerning the death penalty and, perhaps, even the decision making of capital jurors.[63] That is, it was possible that the prospect of incurring the expense of a lifetime of incarceration for capital defendants—especially youthful ones with many years of imprisonment ahead of them—led some people to favor the death penalty.

Moreover, it has been suggested that "the execution of an individual in his or her 30s is less expensive than maintaining that person in prison for 30 or more years until a natural death occurs."[64] Such assertions about the comparative economic advantages of capital punishment fail to take into account the substantial legal costs involved death penalty trials and constitutionally mandated appeals. When capital trials are properly conducted by well-trained attorneys who utilize the full range of constitutional rights and procedures that modern death penalty doctrine allows, the added expense can be substantial. At the early stages of the case, this includes especially time-consuming pretrial investigation and complicated legal motions that are unique to death penalty cases. Because of the stakes involved, and the unusual practice of death qualification (discussed at length in the next chapter), jury selection in capital cases is more time-consuming than in other kinds of cases. In addition, a number of states as well as the federal government assign a second defense attorney to undertake some of the added legal tasks and responsibilities that a capital case entails. Additional time and expense are needed for investigators, attorneys, and experts to prepare for a whole separate phase of a capital case—the sentencing or penalty trial—and to conduct one if the client is found guilty in the first phase.

Although many jurisdictions may fall far short of providing truly effective, competent representation in capital cases, those that fall *too* far short

ıl by the appellate courts. When this happens, the costs of an entire
have to be absorbed. Moreover, the appeal process is more time-
ınd expensive in a capital case, as is the cost of higher-security
.ow confinement in many states. Indeed, virtually every study done
on this issue has concluded that the costs of the death penalty *exceed* those
of life imprisonment, and often by very substantial amounts.[65] Yet a majority
of our respondents (54%) endorsed the view that the death penalty was less
expensive than life in prison. This compared to only 26% who believed the
reverse, correct view—that the death penalty was, in fact, more expensive
than life imprisonment to administer.

The Meaning of Life Without Parole

Many commentators have speculated that the death penalty may be endorsed
by voters and jurors who are confused or skeptical about the legal alternatives
to capital punishment. For example, the public's concerns about the future
dangerousness of convicted murderers can only be allayed with accurate information about exactly what happens to those who are *not* sentenced to
death. Persons who believe that defendants who are sentenced to prison "for
life" actually might be released at some future point may favor the death
penalty for this reason alone. Indeed, at the time we did our survey, a number
of analysts already had suggested that "[p]rospective jurors often maintain
the common misconception that a life sentence is not, in reality, a *life* sentence."[66]

Such a misconception—potentially held by many citizens, voters, and
jurors—is rooted in past practices and easy to understand. For example,
jurors in a well-known California death penalty case that was tried in the
1960s, *McGautha v. California,*[67] interrupted their penalty deliberations to
ask the judge whether a life sentence meant the defendant would have no
chance of receiving parole. They were informed by the judge—who stated
the law correctly at the time—that the Adult Authority (California's equivalent of a parole board) was empowered "to determine if and when a prisoner
is to be paroled," no matter what his or her initial sentence.[68] Similar laws
were in effect in most states through the 1970s. Many citizens can recall
instances in which notorious prisoners responsible for especially heinous
crimes repeatedly were considered for parole and, in some cases, were released.

However, in the modern era of death sentencing most states enacted
laws that provided for a genuine life-without-parole alternative to the death
penalty. In many states, in fact, life without parole is the *only* other option
jurors can select in the sentencing phase of a capital trial. In a few other
states, they can choose from one or two other sentencing verdicts in addition
to life without parole or the death penalty.[69] Yet there has been relatively little
systematic education of the public about these significant changes in death-
sentencing laws. As a result, many members of the public are unaware of the

way the laws have been changed, are unclear about how the new sentencing statutes actually work, or remain skeptical about how they will be enforced in the future.

In fact, this was one of the most widespread and potentially influential misconceptions that our respondents held. Despite the fact that the sentence of life without possibility of parole was (and is) the *only* alternative available to capital juries in the penalty phase of death penalty trials in California, and that no capital defendant who received one of these life without parole sentences had ever been paroled from prison, many respondents simply did not understand—or believe—this. In our overall sample, fully 63.7% of the respondents endorsed the statement that "even people who are sentenced to life in prison without the possibility of parole manage to get out of prison at some point." Only 27% expressed the view that a life-without-parole sentence meant that a prisoner would never get out of prison, even though that had been the law in California for quite some time.[70]

Finally, we attempted to directly assess Justice Marshall's hypothesis about the influence of knowledge on support for the death penalty by comparing the death penalty attitudes of those persons who were more accurately informed about the death penalty with those who were less informed. Specifically, we used the answers to questions about the aforementioned four issues—the proper scope of death penalty decision making, whether the death penalty deterred murder, the relative costs of the death penalty versus life in prison without parole, and whether life without parole meant that a prisoner would not be released from prison—as indices of general death penalty knowledge. As table 4.4 A and B illustrate, those respondents who

Table 4.4
Death Penalty Support and Knowledge About Capital Punishment

A

	More Informed	Less Informed
In favor	20%	80%
Opposed	67%	33%

$\chi^2 = 80.4$, df (1), $p < .000$. Respondents were coded as "more informed" if they correctly answered 2 or more items, and "less informed" if 1 or none.

B

	Mean Correct Items
In favor	0.83
Opposed	1.88

$t = -9.8$, df (488), $p < .000$.

were more highly informed about the death penalty were much less likely to support it than those who had less accurate information. Analyzed somewhat differently, we found that the average number of correct answers given by death penalty supporters was less than half the average number of correct items by those who opposed the death penalty (.83 correct vs. 1.88). Persons strongly in favor were even less knowledgeable overall, getting only an average of .71 items correct.

Of course, these data do not prove that merely providing people with better or more accurate information about the death penalty would reduce their support. Indeed, for many people, support for capital punishment is a deeply embedded belief that will not yield easily, even to additional accurate facts. It is also possible that the relationship between support and knowledge reflects the tendency to seek out information that is consistent with one's beliefs and to ignore or overlook facts that contradict them. If true, this tendency may require death penalty supporters to continue to embrace misconceptions and ignore accurate information about the system of death sentencing.

Reversals of Death Penalty Support: Awareness of an Effective Alternative and the Perception of Systemic Flaws

If the fact that "the people cling to the death penalty" is to be used as a justification for its retention, as Raoul Berger and other death penalty advocates have argued,[71] then it is important to examine the question of why they cling to it. As several of the preceding analyses have suggested, those who appear to know the least about capital punishment support it most. The final section of this chapter addresses several aspects of this issue, including what happens to death penalty support when people are offered an effective alternative to capital punishment and whether becoming better informed about how the system of death sentencing really works changes the degree to which the public supports it.

When "Life Without Parole" Means Life Without Parole

If a significant number of people endorse the death penalty because they have reluctantly concluded that there is no other way to prevent convicted murderers from threatening free society, then their support may be based on a serious misconception about the state of the law and prevailing prison policies. To get a better grasp on this issue, we posed a final question to our respondents that asked them whether they would prefer the death penalty over life in prison without possibility of parole *if* the latter alternative really meant that the defendant would never be released from prison—as I noted, something that is current law in most death penalty jurisdictions—and that the prisoner would be required to work and to give part of his earnings to the family of his victim.

Under these circumstances, fully 67.3% of our total sample would have preferred life imprisonment over the death penalty. Put somewhat differently, the initial 79% level of support for the death penalty in the abstract fell to only 26% in favor when life without parole plus restitution was an option. These reversals—by people who initially chose the death penalty but switched to life plus restitution—were not limited to respondents who expressed only moderate support for the death penalty. We found that even among those persons who had initially stated that they were "strongly in favor" of the death penalty, *half* selected the life without parole plus restitution option when it was offered. There were no differences in the number of reversals on *any* of our measures of political affiliation or beliefs. Indeed, about two-thirds of the registered Republican, self-described "strongly Republican," and even self-described "conservative" respondents reversed their support of the death penalty when offered the alternative of life without parole plus restitution.[72]

Before leaving the topic of how the awareness of an effective alternative led to a reversal of death penalty support, it is worth noting that our California respondents were by no means unique in their willingness to support life without parole instead of capital punishment when it was offered to them. The same overall pattern that was obtained in California was reflected in the results of a nationwide public opinion poll conducted in 1985.[73] In addition, several separate surveys done in a number of individual states in the late 1980s—also at the very peak of general public support for the death penalty—reported the same kind of surprising outcome.[74] That is, although support for the death penalty in the abstract in these other states was also very high, a *majority* of people in most of the states surveyed nonetheless would have preferred the alternative of life in prison without possibility of parole plus restitution (and nearly as many in those states where restitution was not a part of the life without parole option offered in the survey).

Indeed, as table 4.5 shows, in every state in which this question was posed, support for the death penalty per se dropped to less than a majority. Thus, for example, New Yorkers, like their California counterparts, preferred life plus restitution over the death penalty by a 2 to 1 margin. This was true even in southern states, where support of the death penalty traditionally is the strongest and regarded as least susceptible to change.[75]

Heightened Concerns Over Wrongful Capital Convictions

A recent example of the media's impact on public opinion can be seen in the way another important death-penalty-related issue—concern over wrongful convictions—now is covered in the press. As death sentencing resumed in the United States in the late 1970s, death penalty opponents pointed to what

Table 4.5
Preference for Life Without Parole (Plus
Restitution) Over Death

State Polls	Death	Life
California	26%	67%
Florida	42%	49%
Georgia	43%	51%
Kentucky	36%	46%*
Nebraska	**	58%
New York	32%	62%
Oklahoma	48%	49%

*Alternative did not include restitution.
**Percent could not be determined from reported data.

they believed was the fallibility of the system itself and the possibility that innocent persons might be wrongfully convicted and sentenced to death. The finality and irrevocability of a death sentence led some to argue that this possibility alone was enough to justify its abolition. In the late 1980s, two such critics, Hugo Bedau and Michael Radelet, published the first of several scholarly analyses of the issue in which they concluded that there were many cases throughout history in which precisely this tragic scenario likely had occurred.[76] Yet, perhaps because there were relatively few well-known *recent* instances of this in the United States, the press gave the issue very limited coverage.

Indeed, the media's inattention to the issue throughout the 1980s may have contributed to the relatively low level of public concern about the risk of sentencing innocent persons to death, even as death rows began to fill with condemned prisoners and states began to accelerate the process of executing them. If anything, the media's coverage of death penalty law and procedure served indirectly to reassure citizens, voters, and potential jurors by suggesting that an *extra* measure of due process protection routinely was being afforded to death penalty defendants. In fact, the impression was created that the system of death sentencing was abundantly fair, elaborate, time-consuming to a fault, and, as a result, scrupulously accurate and reliable.[77]

Not surprisingly, then, when we asked our respondents in 1989 whether the risk of wrongful convictions in capital cases posed a significant concern for them, the great majority said it did not. Indeed, fully 63.7% of our overall sample believed that innocent persons were so rarely executed that it was an unimportant issue in the death penalty debate. Only 23% of our respondents told us that they thought that there was a possibility that innocent people were too often executed.

However, over the next decade or so the media focused unprecedented attention on the issue of wrongful convictions. Perhaps because these powerful human interest stories sometimes rival even the sensationalism of crime stories themselves, many dramatic, highly publicized cases captured the attention of reporters, news commentators, documentary filmmakers, and even playwrights.[78] The high level of public visibility that was brought to the issue of wrongful convictions in capital cases—in many instances, defendants who were definitively proven to be innocent through the use of DNA technology—and the surprisingly high number of exonerations of persons from death rows appear to have affected public opinion. Indeed, a number of states actually declared moratoria on executions until lawmakers could review the reliability of their death penalty procedures, and did so with apparent public assent.[79]

In fact, when Californians were surveyed more recently about how they now assessed the risks of wrongful convictions and the importance of this issue for death penalty policy, a surprisingly high percentage were concerned enough to endorse a total moratorium on executions in the state until the system of death sentencing could be studied and pronounced fair and reliable. Thus, just a decade after only 23% of our respondents saw the issue of wrongful convictions as an important concern in the administration of the death penalty, 73% of those surveyed said they were concerned enough about the risk of wrongful convictions that they were in favor of asking the governor to "halt all executions" until a study of the fairness of capital punishment in California could be completed.[80] Among other things, this illustrates the fluidity of public opinion about the death penalty, people's concern about the realities of death sentencing (in this case, the possibility of mistake and overreaching), and their responsiveness to additional, accurate information about how the system actually works.

Conclusion

Although strong, committed constituencies have formed on both sides of the issue, the overall level of public support for the death penalty in the United States has fluctuated throughout the nation's history. With the advent of scientific opinion polling, the ebb and flow of attitudes about the death penalty could be measured precisely. At one point in the recent history of the death penalty—the mid- to late-1960s—the public was more or less evenly divided on the question. But shortly after that, opinion began a significant and steady shift. Jan Gorecki has summed up the conventional explanation for the shift this way: "Casting about for a remedy against pervasive wrongdoing, the American public turned to the criminal justice system with demands for harshness and executions, and the system has been responsive to the public mood."[81] However, as I pointed out earlier, many scholars believe that the causal sequence appears to be much more complicated—"the system" to which Gorecki referred has been implicated in helping to create the mood of the public, perhaps as much or more than it has responded to it.

Public opinion was shaped in part by widespread media campaigns that forcefully promoted a broad political as well as criminal justice agenda. Capital punishment was an important component of both.

Although the death penalty was a hotly debated topic in the past, a very strong public and political consensus emerged in favor of the death penalty in the early 1970s. It literally quelled meaningful discussion and the presentation of thoughtful, alternative points of view. Thus, to the extent that there was any kind of mainstream public or political debate about capital punishment, it was limited primarily to differences of opinion about exactly how strongly (not whether) the death penalty should be advocated, or how widely or swiftly it could be implemented. For close to 25 years, the American public was exposed to very little fundamental questioning of the underlying rationale, purpose, or morality of the death penalty.

The survey research results discussed in some detail in this chapter illustrated several important things about the nature of this high level of death penalty support. For one, even at the peak of this support, most people were not indiscriminately punitive. Rather, when given the chance to make focused distinctions, people were able to differentiate between case features and the characteristics of defendants that made the death penalty seem either more or less appropriate. Thus, at a time when the percentage of persons favoring capital punishment was at an all-time high, particular aspects or features of reasonably typical capital cases led to slight increases and, in other instances, dramatic decreases in death penalty support.[82] For example, as different social historical factors were integrated into respondents' consideration of the appropriate punishment—something that, as I pointed out in chapter 3, the media almost never do in reporting about actual capital crimes, trials, and defendants—people responded with more nuanced views.

Indeed, it may well be that a level of "pluralistic ignorance" has been created over the last several decades by the way the press has represented the public's views in largely monolithic and unidimensional terms.[83] That is, those persons who hold thoughtful and complex views about the death penalty now may think of themselves as unique or among a very small minority of like-minded persons. Yet our survey and those conducted by several other researchers suggested that even strong death penalty supporters typically make nuanced judgments and, in fact, rarely express the kind of categorical pro-capital punishment views that are depicted in the press.

In addition, despite what has been portrayed as the increasing role of retribution as a major (perhaps the primary) political and legal justification for the death penalty, the research cited in this chapter suggests that most people feel that they need other reasons for supporting it. That is, a majority of people we surveyed believed that retribution alone was not enough justification, and that it was necessary to know what the death penalty accomplished in society in order to decide whether to support or oppose it. Ironically, despite this need to premise support on the basis of the other social purposes that capital punishment achieved, these same persons knew very little about those things. In fact, as I have said, the people who knew the least about how the system of death sentencing actually functioned in our society were the ones who supported it most.

Indeed, preserving the public's relative lack of knowledge about capital punishment may be crucial to keeping death penalty support high. Aspects of Justice Marshall's hypothesis—that if people knew how the system really worked then they would not support it—garnered some empirical support in our research. As I noted, many people appeared to express "support" for the death penalty without knowing exactly what it is they were endorsing. Yet, when they were given an opportunity to select a viable alternative to capital punishment, or were exposed to sustained media discussion of an aspect of the death-sentencing system previously hidden from public view (wrongful convictions), they were extremely responsive. Under these conditions, support for the death penalty falls below levels that—if they were sustained over a long period—likely would make continued operation of the system extremely problematic and perhaps impossible.

In some ways it is especially ironic that the lack of public debate and the erosion of popular knowledge about capital punishment should have occurred at a time in which so much more information existed about the death penalty than at any other period in history. Controversy over capital punishment may have been muted or nonexistent in public and political arenas over the last few decades, but, at the same time, extensive social science data were being accumulated that raised serious questions about the fairness of death penalty imposition, the existence of any deterrent effect, its comparative costs versus life in prison, and the possibility that seemingly elaborate death penalty procedures had failed to prevent erroneous convictions and mistaken death sentences from being rendered.

Even more troublesome, perhaps, is the fact that, as I discuss in the next chapter, as the system of death sentencing selects persons to participate in the all-important task of actually deciding whether someone lives or dies, it chooses them largely on the basis of their expressed support for the death penalty. The data presented in the present chapter suggest that such a screening process may have the effect of selecting some of the *least* well informed from among the pool of all potential jurors. Moreover, the system of death sentencing that depends so heavily on public support in order to remain viable may rely increasingly on popular misconceptions that, by design, go uncorrected. That is, as subsequent chapters also make clear, few if any of the misconceptions that prospective jurors bring to the courthouse are systematically corrected for them once they are selected and begin their service in actual death penalty cases. In fact, direct attempts to address many of the very misconceptions that were uncovered in our survey and others are explicitly prohibited by law.

5

A Tribunal Organized to Convict and Execute?

On the Nature of Jury Selection in Capital Cases

> [W]hen it is further considered that the issue of guilt or innocence
> in less important cases—the non-capital cases—is determined by a
> jury not similarly shorn of its most humanely disposed
> constituents, the result become even more ironic: the graver the
> charge, the less protection accorded the accused.
> —Walter Oberer, "Does Disqualification of Jurors for Scruples
> Against Capital Punishment Constitute Denial of Fair Trial on Issue
> of Guilt?" (1961)

The last several chapters have been devoted to the notion that citizens' beliefs about crime and punishment and their support for the death penalty are influenced in some significant ways by forces in the society at large. Among other things, highly politicized messages about crime and punishment; sensationalized media coverage of crime-related issues; and narrow, one-sided reporting about actual capital cases appear to have a real effect on the general public. These messages and images have an impact on the audiences exposed to them in ways that seem likely to influence the decisions that its members make as citizens, voters, and jurors. Exposure to partial and sometimes misleading information also may help to explain why the public's confusion about capital punishment is persistent and widespread. This confusion, as I showed in the last chapter, appears to be at the root of much death penalty support.

But, from this point forward, the legal system itself does a great deal to facilitate the process of death sentencing. Either by not effectively remedying some of the worst biases and misconceptions that have been created outside the courtroom or by actively intervening in ways that are likely to exacerbate them, a number of legal doctrines, practices, and procedures are directly implicated. This chapter examines the way the legal system handles several important issues that arise at the very outset of a capital case, when it comes time to select those persons who will serve as jurors during the trial. Jury selection or voir dire in death penalty cases presents special challenges, in part because of the serious and sometimes sensational nature of the crimes that give rise to them, and in part because of the persistent ambivalence about the death penalty that prospective jurors bring to the courthouse.[1] I suggest in this chapter that, from a psychological perspective, neither challenge appears to be met in entirely satisfactory ways.

Not surprisingly, many capital cases are very highly publicized. As I pointed out in chapter 3, there is reason to believe that much of this publicity has a real effect on persons who are exposed to it. However, the legal doctrines governing the most effective remedy for this threat to the fair trial rights of defendants—changing venue to jurisdictions less prejudiced by pretrial publicity—are very stringently applied. Relief is infrequently granted. The fact that the law disfavors venue changes has an especially serious impact on capital cases; it may result in capital jurors—more than the members of other kinds of juries—hearing evidence and rendering verdicts in cases in which they possess potentially prejudicial information and even have concluded, well in advance of the start of the trial, that the defendant likely is guilty.[2]

Moreover, the closer we get to the actual decisions that determine whether or not the death penalty will be imposed, the more direct, organized, and systematic many of the law's own biasing influences become. In fact, even though media misinformation and the lack of informed debate about capital punishment have operated to increase public support for it, the law still does not trust the administration of the death penalty to a truly representative group of citizens. Instead, the pool of eligible jurors is carefully screened so that the group judged "fit to serve" on capital cases consists entirely of those persons who have publicly stated that they actually can impose the death penalty.

This screening process—called death qualification—is controversial and has been carefully studied. The perceived need for death qualification is based in part on the fact that jurors in capital cases may be called on to perform a sentencing function (as well as to decide guilt or innocence), and also because moral and religious opposition to the death penalty in the United States has existed on a substantial and organized basis since colonial times. Thus, courts have chosen to "qualify" all prospective capital jurors by excluding by law those whose death penalty attitudes deem them "unfit."

Those who defend this process argue that death qualification represents a natural extension of the principle that persons who will not commit to following the law—here, by imposing the death penalty in the proper case—should never be permitted to serve as jurors. On the other hand, its critics call the practice an unfair anomaly that restricts capital jury service only to persons who are more likely to convict and, once having done so, to sentence a defendant to death. Despite its controversial status, death qualification is employed in literally every state in which the system of death sentencing operates.[3]

In this chapter, both important features of the way in which juries are selected in capital cases—the nature and consequence of stringent change-of-venue laws and practices, and the biasing effects of death qualification—are discussed.

The Limited Legal Response to Prejudicial Pretrial Publicity

As I have noted, because of their very serious and sometimes sensational nature, many capital cases receive special attention from the media. As the research discussed in chapter 3 showed, intense pretrial publicity can create prejudice that may bias the community or "venue" where the trial is scheduled to take place. In many such instances, potential jurors not only are aware of the particular case but have heard and can recall especially prejudicial facts long before any evidence actually is presented in court. Indeed, in many instances a majority of jury-eligible residents may have decided that the defendant is probably or definitely guilty, and they may have reached this conclusion well in advance of the start of the trial.

When there is a risk that the community from which the jury pool will be drawn has been tainted by prejudicial pretrial publicity, legal doctrines provide for a "change of venue" that moves the trial to a different geographical location. Although the decision of whether the venue of a trial will be changed depends on legal criteria that vary some from jurisdiction to jurisdiction, in most states, the site of a trial will be moved if it can be shown that pretrial publicity has created the "reasonable likelihood" that a fair and impartial jury cannot be impaneled there.[4] Thus, change-of-venue doctrine requires courts to assess various aspects of the case-related publicity, to estimate the reach or penetration of the publicity into the community, and to form a judgment about its potential to create prejudice in the jury-eligible persons who may have been exposed to it.[5]

For example, California courts generally use five criteria in deciding whether a change venue is warranted. The criteria include the gravity of the offense (more serious cases—such as capital cases—weigh in favor of changing venue); the nature and amount of publicity (more prejudicial publicity in greater amounts is worse); the status of the defendant (a community "outsider" or one from an especially derogated or disfavored group is thought to be more prejudiced by negative publicity); the status of the victim (publicity that depicts an especially revered or beloved victim or one who was particularly important to the community weighs in favor of changing venue); and the size of the community (prejudicial publicity is thought to have a more problematic impact on smaller communities than larger ones).

In theory, at least, such criteria appear to be straightforward, reasonably comprehensive, and capable of protecting the fair trial rights of criminal defendants. In practice, however, change-of-venue law suffers from several important limitations. For one, because of the added costs of conducting a trial away from the jurisdiction where most of the trial participants reside, changes of venue are expensive to undertake. This is especially true in capital cases, where the length and complexity of the trial itself tend to be much greater. The added expense of a change of venue means that judges are extremely reluctant to grant them and, because of the even greater expense, perhaps especially resistant to them in capital cases. Moreover, some analysts have pointed to the problematic fact that highly publicized capital cases often are highly politicized as well, placing "elected trial judges under considerable pressure not to . . . change venue."[6] Thus, in those cases in which community sentiments run highest—precisely the ones for which changes of venue are most needed—the political risks, especially to elected trial judges, are greatest.

Whatever the underlying reasons, even though the legal criteria that govern changes of venue seem reasonable and reasonably comprehensive, judges often raise the bar to a very high—sometimes seemingly insurmountable—level when it comes time actually to apply them. Thus, the threshold that many courts use to decide whether publicity is truly "prejudicial in nature," or "excessive in amount," is so stringent that even very highly publicized capital cases often cannot meet it. As one legal commentator correctly observed, among the possible remedies for potentially prejudicial pretrial publicity, "[c]hange of venue motions, above all others, are under-utilized by trial judges."[7]

As a result, many capital cases go to trial in communities that have been saturated with publicity that contains extremely prejudicial characterizations of defendants and damaging case-related information. Recall that in many of the cases whose data were analyzed in the Haney and Fukurai study in chapter 3, between 80 and 90% or more of prospective jurors had expressed awareness of the case, and half or more of those who were aware admitted that they had made up their mind that the defendant was guilty. Yet, despite this evidence of prejudice (created by extensive damaging pretrial publicity), in a number of these cases the capital defendant's request to change venue was not granted. In another one of the cases in that data set, a change of venue was granted, but apparently for the convenience of the court. That is, the trial was moved to the judge's home jurisdiction, a community where the awareness rate also was above 90% and more than three-quarters of the local respondents had prejudged the defendant to be guilty.

The reluctance to change venue certainly is not unique to the cases in our data set. In one notorious capital case in California that was not included in Fukurai's and my study, the media extensively reported graphic details of the crime that were contained in confessions that had been given by the defendant and his brother. Newspapers published editorials that referred to him as "subhuman" and a "recidivist psychopath" and called for the punishment in his murder trial to "nearly fit the crime." The press also ran a cartoon depicting the defendant as human sewage spilling out into the community and printed letters from readers demanding that the defendant be executed. Local stations conducted a television poll in which approximately 90% of the viewers opined that the death penalty should be imposed in the case. Despite these and numerous other prejudicial aspects to the pretrial publicity that surrounded the case well in advance of the trial, the judge denied the defendant's change-of-venue motion and the state supreme court upheld his decision.[8]

In other cases, defendants' otherwise inadmissible confessions formed part of an extensive barrage of case-related publicity—even an instance in which, ironically, as his change-of-venue hearing commenced, a defendant blurted out in court that "I am guilty."[9] Nonetheless, despite motions by these and other capital defendants to move their cases to less biased jurisdictions, trials in such cases typically are held in the communities in which extensive media coverage has occurred.

Studies suggest that the risks to the due process rights of defendants and the fairness of trials conducted in communities that have been saturated by this kind of media coverage are very real. In addition to Fukurai's and my study discussed at length in chapter 3, there is a strong consensus among social scientists that pretrial publicity does have biasing effects on the persons who are exposed to it and that, once created, those effects are extremely difficult to eliminate or neutralize. This is because persons tend to regard pretrial publicity as accurate and legitimate at the time they receive it. As a result, they store the information uncritically in memory. Once stored in this way, the information tends to be integrated into memory and judgment processes; its effects become difficult to isolate, disentangle, or reverse later on.[10]

Thus, people may be vaguely aware of having been exposed to the pretrial publicity but not necessarily aware of how much specific knowledge they have, how it has influenced or affected them, or how to go about controlling or resisting these media-based effects. Others who may have followed a case closely and know that they have been exposed to a great deal of potentially prejudicial information may believe unrealistically that they can somehow set it aside (even though this is likely a task that they have never been asked to perform before).

Indeed, one extensive literature review that statistically summarized the results of prior research concluded that data from many different kinds of studies converged on the robust conclusion that "pretrial publicity has a significant impact on juror decision making."[11] The same review concluded that these effects were greater in cases in which multiple items of negative information were contained in the publicity and the crimes depicted involved murder, sexual abuse, or drugs. Other research has shown that prejudicial effects can be created by publicity that is factual as well as sensationalistic.[12] Among the prejudicial effects that have been identified in various studies is the creation of a pro-prosecution orientation, an increase in the estimated strength of the prosecution's case, and a more consistently negative view of the defendant held by persons who have been exposed to pretrial publicity.[13] Not surprisingly, the cumulative impact of these various separate effects appears to influence the final verdicts that are rendered in the cases themselves.

Despite these empirically documented threats to jury impartiality, the judicial response to prejudicial publicity has been limited. As I noted, the legal threshold in change-of-venue motions is set quite high—so high that venue is changed rarely, even in very highly publicized cases. Despite the existence of judicial doctrines that focus the courts' attention on many of the key dimensions of pretrial publicity that would establish its potential prejudice, the decision whether to change venue in these cases typically comes down to something approximating actual prejudice. That is, for most judges: "The relevant question is . . . whether the jurors . . . had such fixed opinions that they could not judge impartially the guilt of the defendant."[14] As a result, many courts defer the decision about whether pretrial publicity has prejudiced the community until jury selection, when prospective jurors are asked not only about how much they have read and heard about the case but also whether they can "set aside" this knowledge and judge the case "based only on the evidence that is presented in court."

Unfortunately, this heavy reliance on jury selection overlooks the limitations of a process in which prospective jurors are queried publicly about their own biases. Prevailing federal constitutional law does not automatically entitle a capital defendant to inquire about the content of the publicity to which prospective jurors have been exposed. Instead, jurors often are asked only whether they think they can remain impartial in light of the information they already have about the case.[15] Whatever its legal rationale, this doctrine is based on several psychologically untenable assumptions. These assumptions include the notion that persons are aware of all of their biases, that they are willing to admit to them in open court and in front of authority figures who expect them to be unbiased, and that they are capable of predicting whether and how much those biases will affect their future decision making.

[T]he Pennsylvania Supreme Court has summarized this view succinctly: "Normally, what prospective jurors tell us about their ability to be impartial will be a reliable guide to whether the publicity is still so fresh in their minds that it has removed their ability to be objective."[16] To most psychologists, the opposite predictions seem much more defensible; that is, it is often the case that those who are most biased are least aware of their prejudices, least willing to admit to others that they have them, and are the least reliable judges of whether they can and will set them aside.[17]

Moreover, the courtroom setting itself is not particularly conducive to candor and self-disclosure, especially for prospective jurors who know they are supposed to appear fair and impartial.[18] Many social science studies have documented this fact. For example, in an observation and interview study that Cathy Johnson and I did, we found that jurors were able to survive the voir dire process and sit on felony juries even though they held opinions that were at odds with basic tenets of American jurisprudence (such as presumption of innocence) and had been asked about these very things during jury selection. Specifically, nearly half of the actual jurors in several felony cases said in posttrial interviews that they had *not* been able to "set aside" their personal opinions and beliefs even though they had agreed, during jury selection, to do so.[19] Another study that relied on posttrial interviews of persons who sat on criminal cases estimated that between a quarter to nearly a third of jurors were not candid and forthcoming in accurately and fully answering questions posed during the voir dire process.[20]

People who are placed in unfamiliar situations, like the courtroom, tend to be more sensitive and responsive to the social pressures of others.[21] They also may experience what has been termed "evaluation apprehension" when they feel they are being judged by persons in authority or high-status positions.[22] What prospective jurors learn about the expectations of others—particularly powerful others or authority figures—can influence the candor with which they express their own views.[23] Thus, it is not uncommon for jurors to adopt what is called a "social desirability response set"[24] in which they attempt to respond during voir dire in a socially appropriate manner instead of one that is entirely forthcoming or revealing. Although certain kinds of voir dire conditions and procedures can help to overcome the difficulties prospective jurors may have with candor—studies show that individual, sequestered voir dire (in which a single juror is questioned out of the presence of the others) is most effective—there is no jury selection process that can completely neutralize these psychological reactions and the way they limit the effectiveness of the jury selection process itself.[25]

Especially when prospective jurors sense that they may know something about the case that they are not supposed to know, they may engage in what Professor Edward Bronson has termed "minimization," by giving answers that understate the significance of or distance themselves from what they know. For example:

(By Defense Counsel) Q: Okay. The questionnaire asks for your opinions based on what you'd seen or heard about the publicity in the case, and you said, "I recall that he had confessed to the murders"?

A: Yeah. I *think* I've heard—heard it either on the radio or watching it on the news.

Q: Okay. Do you remember if you heard the details of the confession?

A: No, no.

Q: So, the only thing that kind of sticks in your mind is he's already confessed to the crime?

A: I *just* heard that he was arrested and confessed, and that was it.

Q: When you heard that or even today do you have any reason to doubt that he confessed? I mean, do you believe that he confessed?

A: Well, I'm sure he—not—no, I really don't. I—I don't know one way or the other because I really don't follow the news *all that much.*

Q: And it's okay if you have. We just need to know.

A: No. If the person confessed, they confessed. But I—I'm not judging one way or the other.[26]

To make matters worse, judges often inadvertently instruct prospective jurors on how they are supposed to think and act. After judges tell prospective jurors that they should not rely on publicity or be influenced by it, and even go so far as to suggest that this is an "obvious" principle of law, it is unlikely that many of them will candidly admit publicity-related prejudice. For example, as one judge instructed potential jurors:

> All right. If you were a juror in this case, *obviously,* you would have to decide the case based *solely and entirely* upon the evidence you see or hear in this courtroom, apply the law to the facts as you find them, and in that fashion attempt to reach a verdict. And *obviously* you could *not* be influenced one way or another by what you may have seen, read, or heard because *obviously* that's not evidence. Might not be accurate. Might not be true. But *we all know it's not evidence,* and it *could not be considered by you.* Do you understand that?[27]

Not surprisingly, then, studies report that although potential jurors may be cognizant of having been exposed to negative pretrial publicity, and even have developed a prejudicial opinion of the defendant, they still tend to claim impartiality.[28] In one study, after an extended voir dire process that focused on educating jurors, making them accountable, and directly asking them about the influence of pretrial publicity, those who had been exposed to such publicity still were more punitive toward defendants.[29] In other research, participants who claimed that they were not influenced by the negative pretrial publicity to which they had been exposed were nonetheless more likely to convict the defendant than those exposed to neutral publicity.[30] Studies also have shown that judicial instructions or admonitions to ignore pretrial publicity are ineffective at reducing its biasing effects.[31]

In fact, a number of reviews of the social science literature have concluded that the legal system tends to underestimate the strength of pretrial publicity effects, and that the other safeguards that courts use to limit or neutralize these effects, short of changing of venue, do not work very well.[32] Indeed, in addition to being ineffective, alternative remedies like judicial instructions in which judges tell jurors to "set aside" what they have learned from the media "sometimes produce a 'backfire effect,' resulting in jurors being more likely to rely on inadmissible information after they have been specifically instructed to disregard it."[33]

Of course, as I have already noted, the problems that stem from the law's reluctance to change venue are not unique to death penalty trials. However, because capital cases tend more often to be highly publicized, they are much more seriously affected by these legal shortcomings. The failure to implement truly effective remedies for the problem of pretrial prejudice means that capital defendants, especially, are in jeopardy of suffering its negative effects.

Eliminating "Scruples" From Death Penalty Decision Making

The remainder of this chapter is devoted to another critically important aspect of the jury selection process in death penalty cases. In the preceding section I argued that change-of-venue doctrines and the voir dire practices used to uncover publicity-related prejudice fell short of adequately protecting the fair trial rights of capital defendants in certain highly publicized cases. The legal problem that I addressed was one of omission—doctrines that failed to take the problem of pretrial prejudice seriously enough or remedies that did not address it effectively. The remaining sections of this chapter focus on a problem that is created or initiated by the law itself—an act of commission, if you will—that is structured into the system of death sentencing. Moreover, unlike the limitations of change-of-venue law and publicity-related voir dire, which compromise only certain death penalty cases, this problem threatens the fairness of all capital trials.

For nearly two centuries, prosecutors have sought to eliminate death penalty opponents from sitting as jurors on capital cases, and, for the same amount of time, attorneys representing capital defendants have objected to the practice. For example, in the first published opinion on death qualification, issued in 1820, Justice Joseph Story affirmed the death sentence of a man from whose jury two persons had been excluded, apparently because they "both appeared to be Quakers."[34] Story noted that "[i]t is well-known that Quakers entertain peculiar opinions on the subject of capital punishment," and asserted that Quakers in general "will not give a verdict for a conviction where the punishment is death unless the case be directly within the terms of the divine law." Because the jury that finally did sit in the case was "duly sworn and impaneled," Story decided that "[n]either the prisoner nor the government in such a case have suffered injury."[35]

Throughout the 19th century, large numbers of prospective jurors were disqualified from sitting on death penalty cases because of their opposition to the capital punishment—attitudes that were referred to as their "conscientious scruples" (or, simply, as "scruples"). In the days before systematic public opinion polling was available to accurately measure death penalty attitudes, death qualification itself provided commentators with a rough index of popular sentiment about capital punishment. Thus, Mackey reported that in the late 1840s, at the height of the movement to abolish the death penalty, "reformers made frequent mention of the difficulties involved in seating juries for capital cases. [Horace] Greeley exulted that a reported four-fifths of the people on a recent jury panel had stated their opposition to the gallows and had been dismissed" and another abolitionist claimed "that shortly it would be impossible to set a jury for a capital case anywhere in the northern states."[36] Greeley and other abolitionists apparently did not consider the effect of these widespread dismissals on the verdicts that were rendered by the jurors who remained.

In the intervening years, as death penalty support ebbed and flowed, most constitutional scholars and death penalty lawyers assumed that the U.S. Supreme Court would continue to support this long-standing practice. However, there were two broad trends under way—one legal and one attitudinal—that eventually brought the issue of death qualification to the Court in the late 1960s. The legal trend involved the gradual move by states toward the bifurcation of the capital trial into separate phases—guilt and penalty. Throughout much of the long period in which death qualification had been in use and authorized by the courts, the death penalty was mandatory once a jury convicted the defendant of a capital charge. Because the jury's guilty verdict was equivalent to returning a death sentence, it was reasonable to assume that a prospective juror's expressed unwillingness to impose the death penalty might prevent him or her from ever voting to convict. Death qualification in this context was aimed in part at making sure that a juror who was strongly opposed to the death penalty did not "nullify" the law by voting to acquit an otherwise guilty defendant.

Over the years, however, the jurors' decision-making task in capital cases was narrowed and differentiated. For example, California's death penalty law gradually evolved to reduce the scope of crimes for which the death penalty could be imposed. When the state's first penal code was enacted in 1850, the death penalty was mandatory upon a conviction of "murder." Six years later, California law distinguished degrees of murder, making the death penalty possible and mandatory only for first degree. By 1874, the legislature extended discretionary power to capital jurors by providing them with a choice between life in prison or the death penalty upon a conviction of first-degree murder.

Throughout the 20th century, there were similar changes in the statutory schemes under which death penalty laws were implemented elsewhere in the country. By 1949, the U.S. Supreme Court observed that "the belief no longer prevails that every offense in a like legal category calls for an identical punishment without regard to the past life and habits of a particular offender. This whole country has traveled far from the period in which the death sentence was an automatic and commonplace result of convictions. . . ."[37]

In 1957, California became the first state to bifurcate its capital trials, separating guilt determination from the decision of whether or not to impose the death penalty.[38] A few other states followed suit by adopting a fully bifurcated procedure. In some other jurisdictions, juries were given the opportunity to recommend a life sentence indirectly, by requesting "mercy" or "leniency" along with their guilty verdicts (and refraining from doing so when they wanted death to be imposed). The increased separation between determining guilt and deciding on an appropriate sentence made it possible for jurors who were opposed to the death penalty nonetheless to fairly discharge their guilt phase responsibilities.

The attitudinal trend that affected death qualification was one that I mentioned in the preceding chapter. Recall that in the late 1950s and early 1960s there was a gradual but consistent reduction in overall popular support for the death penalty. By the mid-1960s, public opinion was almost evenly divided on the question. Among other things, this meant that increasingly large numbers of persons were being excluded from capital jury service as a result of the opposition to the death penalty. The death penalty attitudes of the jurors who remained were, of course, increasingly unrepresentative of the population at large. The question whether this unusual practice of eliminating prospective jurors on the basis of an attitude that nearly half the population shared seemed ripe for the courts to revisit.

The implications of both trends—the changing nature of the capital jury's decision-making task and the extent of public opposition to the death penalty—were addressed in a landmark case decided in 1968. In *Witherspoon v. Illinois,*[39] the Supreme Court approved of the practice of death qualification but significantly limited its scope. Until *Witherspoon,* prosecutors had unlimited challenges to eliminate prospective jurors who voiced "conscientious scruples" against the death penalty—that is, anyone "who might hesitate to return a verdict imposing [death]."[40] In Witherspoon's own case, the prosecutor had managed to exclude roughly half of the prospective jurors. Indeed, the record reflected that the judge at Witherspoon's trial had dismissed some 47 potential jurors—in what the Supreme Court described as "rapid succession"—on the basis of their death penalty attitudes, prefacing his exclusions with the comment, "Let's get these conscientious objectors out of the way, without wasting any time on them."[41]

Obviously, the group that remained after the judge had completed this process was different from—and very probably much less sympathetic toward the defendant—than the one with which he had started. However, Witherspoon's appellate lawyer pressed another related point. He argued that the judge's elimination of every potential juror with the slightest second thought about capital punishment had left his client with a group that was predisposed to *convict* him.

It seemed clear that this issue posed one of those social fact questions that I discussed in chapter 1; it really could not be answered without some social science data. Either the behavior of death-qualified jurors convincingly showed that they were "conviction-prone" or not, and only systematic research could definitively answer such a question. Accordingly, Witherspoon's attorney offered what he described as "competent scientific evidence that death-qualified jurors are partial to the prosecution on the issue of guilt or innocence."[42]

In fact, however, the Supreme Court decided that the attorney's claim about the conviction-proneness of death-qualified juries was premature. The state of the evidence at the time Witherspoon's appellate lawyer raised the point was partial and still somewhat preliminary—indeed, the existing data were contained in only three research papers, none of which had been published. To be sure, Witherspoon's attorney *was* correct in asserting that competent scientific evidence was essential to address the claim of conviction proneness. At the Supreme Court level, however, the majority opinion in the case made only passing reference to the studies that the lawyer had offered to document some of the effects of death qualification. Properly, it would seem, the Justices questioned the unpublished status and limited scope of the research.[43]

However, although Justice Stewart's majority opinion concluded that the preliminary research that had been introduced represented evidence that was "too tentative and fragmentary" on which to premise a constitutional decision, he acknowledged that the Court was unable to completely resolve the conviction-proneness question "on the basis of the record now before us" and "[i]n light of presently available information."[44] In this way, he seemed to defer a final decision on the issue for a later time, perhaps in anticipation of better data. Indeed, he noted that a defendant "in some future case" might succeed in convincing the Court about the conviction-proneness of the capital jury.[45] In the meantime, the *Witherspoon* opinion did reduce the size of the group that could be excluded under death qualification—from anyone with "scruples" against capital punishment to *only* those persons who made it "unmistakably clear" that they could not vote to impose the death penalty under any circumstances.

Despite what some social scientists and legal scholars interpreted as an "invitation" from the *Witherspoon* Court to conduct research on the potentially biasing effects of death qualification, it remained a legally authorized and important part of the way juries were selected in capital cases for many years following the decision. In fact, nearly two decades later, rather than doing away with death qualification, the Court relaxed the standard by which prospective jurors could be excluded. In *Wainright v. Witt,*[46] the Court said that judges not only could exclude prospective jurors who said they were "unequivocally opposed" to the death penalty, but also those who felt their opposition to the death penalty would "prevent or substantially impair" them from performing their duties as jurors.[47]

Moreover, in the very next year the Court decided many of the questions that had been left open in *Witherspoon* (and ignored in *Witt*). The Justices responded to a direct constitutional challenge to death qualification that was premised on extensive social science data. Speaking as one of the researchers who conducted some of the research contained in that challenge, I can acknowledge that a number of those studies had been inspired by *Witherspoon* itself, and the implicit suggestion that more and better data would be received by an interested and open-minded Court.[48] However, this time the empirical data on the death qualification issue came to the Court long after *Gregg* had been decided; there were new, less sympathetic Justices and many of those who remained had become more hostile toward broad-based social scientific analyses (at least ones that focused on the systemic flaws in the death-sentencing process).

Thus, in *Lockhart v. McCree*,[49] the U.S. Supreme Court decisively rejected the claim that death qualification compromised the fair trial rights of capital defendants. Essentially applying a standard that no social scientific research could meet—namely, that controlled studies use "actual jurors sworn under oath to apply the law to the facts of an actual case involving the fate of an actual capital defendant"—Justice Rehnquist's majority opinion questioned the validity of all the data that had been adduced on the effects of death qualification.[50] In fact, he took the further step of ruling that, even if valid, such research did not resolve the constitutional issue that had been posed. This was because, as a majority of the Justices saw it, juries biased in the ways that death-qualified juries appeared to be could have arisen by chance. That is: "it is hard for us to understand the logic of the argument that a given jury is unconstitutionally partial when it results from a State-ordained process, yet impartial when exactly the same jury results from mere chance."[51]

Lockhart was a stunning defeat both for the lawyers who had challenged the fairness of the death-qualified jury and for social scientists who once again hoped to bring analyses of social fact questions before a Court that was receptive to their implications. As one commentator soberly concluded about the decision: "A more complete repudiation of social science research could hardly have been accomplished."[52] Its social science implications notwithstanding, *Lockhart* in effect guaranteed that death-sentencing decisions would be made by a carefully selected group of jurors, one very different from the kind of tribunals that are assembled to decide any other kind of criminal case. And, whatever the Court's intentions, this decision also helped not only to preserve but also to facilitate the death-sentencing process.

Death qualification creates an additional category of cause challenges in capital cases—directed at persons who are not allowed to sit as jurors because of their attitudes about the death penalty. As a result, the size of the group challenged for cause on this basis will vary as a function of death penalty attitudes in a given jurisdiction. That is, at any given time, in any given case, the number of prospective jurors excluded through death qualification will fluctuate according to the death penalty attitudes that are held by the jury-eligible members of the public. Despite these fluctuations, however, death qualification ensures that death sentencing itself will be facilitated, no matter the distribution of death penalty views among the general public. That is, when support for the death penalty wanes, more prospective jurors will be excluded at the outset of trial. As support increases, the size of the excluded group will become smaller, but death penalty supporters still will predominate among the persons who remain.

The psychological and legal implications of this fact have been carefully and clearly documented in a series of empirical studies done over the last several decades. The Supreme Court's opinion in *Lockhart* notwithstanding, we now know that the broad negative consequences of the procedure are at least twofold: Death qualification significantly skews the composition of the jury panel in ways that make it less balanced and fair, and the process itself has a biasing effect on those jurors who pass through it. Separately and in combination these effects appear to facilitate the conviction of capital defendants and the imposition of death sentences.

Composition Effects: Selecting Jurors More Likely to Convict and Sentence to Death

The composition effects of death qualification arise from the systematic way it distorts the outcome of the jury selection process in capital cases. Death qualification seeks to exclude jurors on the basis of only *one* of their attitudes—unequivocally strong beliefs about the death penalty. However, because people's attitudes about the death penalty are correlated with other things about them, the process of selection implicates beliefs and behaviors far beyond the intended scope. More specifically, because persons who strongly oppose the death penalty have many other characteristics and attitudes in common, any procedure that eliminates them also will disproportionately exclude those other characteristics from the jury pool. Critics of death qualification have argued that these effects are relatively stable and consistently prejudicial to the interests of capital defendants. More than 30 years of research on the subject provides much empirical support for their contentions.

One important way in which the composition of the capital jury is compromised by death qualification concerns the *representativeness* of the group of eligible, prospective jurors that it creates. In theory, at least, the capital jury is supposed to act as the conscience of the community, introducing community standards into the administration of the death penalty. Of course, to be its "conscience"—to decide a case the way the community would—the jury must fairly represent it. Precisely because attitudes toward the death penalty are not evenly distributed throughout the population, death qualification compromises the representativeness of the group of prospective jurors who survive its screening process.

For example, as figure 5.1 shows, the attitudes of women and, especially, blacks are consistently less favorable toward the death penalty than those of men and whites in general.[53] These differences are relatively large and have remained stable over time—over the last 30-year period averaging an approximately 11% differences in death penalty support between men and women and an over 28% difference between blacks and whites. As a result, a process that selects eligible jurors on the basis of death penalty support will exclude disproportionately greater numbers of women and blacks.[54] And, because blacks are already underrepresented on the jury lists in many parts of the country, death qualification may act to compound a preexisting prob-

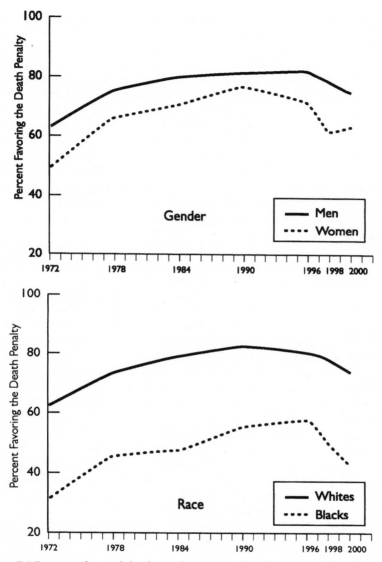

Figure 5.1 Race, gender, and death penalty support. Based on General Social Survey (GSS) national data, collected by the National Opinion Research Center. In 1972, the GSS posed its death penalty question as "Are you in favor of the death penalty for persons convicted of murder?" After that, the question was phrased as "Do you favor or oppose the death penalty for persons convicted of murder?"

lem.[55] In any event, the process insures that actual capital juries will be selected from a group of prospective jurors who are, by definition, unrepresentative of the community at large. Several social science studies have documented this basic effect.[56]

Another significant bias that death qualification appears to introduce into the composition of the capital jury is what some have termed "prosecution-proneness." Any process that systematically eliminates persons with strong feelings about the death penalty is likely to leave behind a group that differs on a host of other interrelated attitudes. For example, Robert Fitzgerald and Phoebe Ellsworth captured many of these differences in research that showed that death-qualified jurors were more likely to favor "crime control" perspectives on criminal justice issues, as opposed to persons excluded by the *Witherspoon* standard who tended to endorse a host of "due process"-related attitudes. Among the beliefs that the death-qualified respondents were significantly more likely to hold was that the failure of a defendant to testify at trial is indicative of guilt, the insanity plea is a loophole, and defense attorneys "need to be watched."[57] A group whose composition is systematically biased in these and other ways, merely as a result of having been death qualified, it would seem, violates the constitutional right to a jury that will judge case-related issues with fairness and impartiality. Among other things, by creating more "crime control"-oriented or "prosecution prone" juries, death qualification appears to undermine the "safeguard against the corrupt and overzealous prosecutor."[58]

The clear legal implications of some of the early death qualification studies were called into question by several changes in constitutional doctrine that occurred in the 1980s, and by shifts in the distribution of death penalty attitudes among the public at large. For example, recall that most scholars and researchers believed that the *Witt* standard[59] that was implemented in 1985 had increased the number of persons who were excluded by death qualification and that it further skewed the composition of the group of persons eligible to serve on capital juries. On the other hand, another Supreme Court opinion, *Morgan v. Illinois,*[60] required states to exclude potential jurors who said they would to *impose* the death penalty in every case. It was possible that the biasing effects of death qualification were neutralized or "balanced" by the exclusion of persons at both ends of the death penalty attitude spectrum.

Although the question of what should be done with "automatic death penalty jurors" had come up from time to time in the past, prior to *Morgan* most states did not answer it very clearly. Most scholars assumed that the group—composed, in essence, of persons who said that they would impose the death penalty in every case where the law allowed it—was small in number, but no one knew for sure. Few states conscientiously enforced any mandatory procedures for handling these jurors, and a number of them did not bother at all with what was termed "life qualification" (i.e., the elimination of prospective jurors who would not return a life sentence under any circumstances). In any event, the effects of excluding extreme death penalty proponents in the course of capital jury selection had not been studied systemically.[61]

In follow-up research on many of the same issues that Fitzgerald and Ellsworth examined, Aida Hurtado, Luis Vega, and I used our survey of jury-eligible Californians (discussed at length in the last chapter), to determine the impact of these post-*Witherspoon* changes in the legal doctrines governing death qualification. In general, we found that, no matter what legal standard was employed, the "modern" process of death qualification continued to significantly alter the composition of the capital jury pool in ways that tilted them against capital defendants.

Specifically, the fact that the group of "excludable" jury-eligible respondents (under *Morgan*) included those who were extreme death penalty supporters did reduce or eliminate a number of the differences between them and death-qualified respondents on general due process versus crime control attitudes. However, even though we posed the question in a way that was designed to maximize the number of pro-death supporters who were in the excludable group,[62] and despite measuring these attitudes at a time when death penalty support was at an all-time high (so that the group of death penalty opponents who were excluded was at its smallest, and the group of excluded death penalty supporters was at its largest), a host of other differences in perspective remained.

For one, as table 5.1 illustrates, modern death qualification produced a group of people—the *only* ones eligible to sit on capital juries—who were significantly less knowledgeable about the system of death sentencing itself. That is, the death-qualified group was significantly *more* likely to believe that penalty-phase decision making should focus only on the nature of the crime, and that the death penalty deterred murder. Death-qualified persons also were significantly *less* likely to believe that life without parole really meant that a prisoner would not be released from prison. Moreover, they had fewer concerns about other aspects of the system of death sentencing. Thus, they were less likely to believe that innocent people were too often convicted of capital crimes, or that the death penalty was unfair to minorities.[63]

One of the most legally troublesome effects of death qualification on the composition of the capital jury pertains to what researchers have termed "conviction proneness." By limiting capital jury participation to only those persons who share a pro-prosecution perspective and hold more favorable (but often erroneous) beliefs about how the system of death sentencing actually functions, death qualification ensures that the evidence presented at trial will be filtered through a particular set of juror predispositions. Surely, in some cases the weight of the evidence will completely determine the outcome of the case and no amount of bias or predisposition will alter the verdict. In other cases, however, even jurors who take seriously their responsibility to base decisions on the evidence and nothing else may be influenced in subtle ways by preexisting attitudes and expectations. We know that these

Table 5.1
Effects of "Modern" Death Qualification on General Beliefs About the
Death Penalty

Death Penalty Belief	Excludables (n = 95)	Death-Qualifieds (n = 403)
Focus only on crime, ignore background	45.3%	53.1%**
Death penalty deters murder	56.8%	76.2%***
LWOP means LWOP	41.1%	22.6%**
Too many innocent executed	35.8%	18.9%**
Death penalty unfair to minorities	53.7%	38%*

Level of statistically significant difference between excludables and death-qualifieds:
*p < .05, **p < .01, ***p < .001.
LWOP = life without possibility of parole.

things can influence the kind of information people choose to attend to, how that information is processed and stored, and the use to which it is put in subsequent decision making.[64] There is no reason to believe that the capital jury decision-making process is immune to these influences.

Thus, death-qualified jurors may literally "see" a case that is different from the one that would be seen by jurors who had not been selected by this process. They may be "perceptually ready"[65] to perceive incriminating evidence, they may grant greater credibility and weight to prosecution witnesses, and they may employ different standards of "reasonable doubt" and the "presumption of innocence" than jurors who are impartial. Their crime control orientation may make them more trusting of prosecution witnesses (such as police officers), and they may employ preexisting cognitive "scripts" that lead them to "fill in" facts and motives in ways that are especially unfavorable to defendants.[66] Ultimately, as the effects of these biases and predispositions accumulate throughout the trial, they will make their presence felt in changing the likelihood of conviction.[67]

Of course, defendants are not entitled to a procedure that yields any particular conviction rate. But a procedure that systematically elevates the percentage of guilty verdicts that are rendered presents a prima facie case of significant prejudice. Here, too, the data on the effects of death qualification are quite strong. Thus, numerous studies have documented the conviction proneness of the death-qualified jury.[68] For example, although it was an earlier study of the issue that employed the narrower *Witherspoon* standard of exclusion, the best and most elaborate research on conviction proneness was conducted by Claudia Cowan, William Thompson, and Phoebe Ellsworth. They used a realistic trial videotape, jury-eligible adult participants, and provided an opportunity for brief group deliberations (so the researchers could compare pre- and post-deliberation verdict measures).[69] Among other things, they found that death-qualified jurors were half as likely as those excluded by death qualification to vote "not guilty" (22.1% vs. 46.7%) on pre-deliberation ballots in response to a potential capital case scenario, and nearly a third as likely to acquit after deliberation had taken place (13.7% vs. 34.5%).

Other research has reached similar conclusions. In fact, a meta-analysis of all the studies done on this topic through the late 1990s concluded simply: "The results indicate that the more a person favors the death penalty, the more likely that person is to vote to convict a defendant."[70] Thus, to the extent that death qualification selects jurors on the basis of their willingness to impose the death penalty, it produces juries that are conviction prone.[71]

There is one final set of biasing effects that result from the way the death qualification process skews the composition of the group eligible to serve as jurors in capital cases. These particular effects are obvious—so obvious, in fact, that they often escape scholarly attention or analysis, even though they are central to the thesis of this book. Specifically, death qualification facilitates death sentencing by ensuring that the only jurors allowed to decide whether a capital defendant lives or dies have been selected on the basis of their willingness to impose the death penalty. Of course, a group selected on this basis is more likely to actually impose the death penalty than one selected through non-death-qualifying voir dire.[72]

However, there is a little more that can be said about the way these separate groups reach their sentencing verdicts. Again, relying on our state-wide study of death penalty attitudes, Hurtado, Vega, and I were able to document some of the differences in the considerations each group was likely to bring to bear in their decisions. As table 5.2 shows, death qualification selects for persons who are differentially responsive to certain mitigating and aggravating circumstances. That is, they are not only more in favor of the death penalty in the abstract but less likely to attend to certain mitigating facts about the defendant and more likely to react to certain aggravating facts about him or his crime. For example, compared to excludables, our death-qualified respondents were significantly *less* responsive to important, poten-tial mitigating factors (specifically, that the murder was not premeditated, the convicted person was over the age of 30, came from a background of extreme poverty, never received treatment for his preexisting problems, and had a loving family and friends who wanted him to live). On the other hand, they were significantly *more* responsive than excludables to most of the po-tentially aggravating factors (specifically, that the defendant was convicted of a brutal murder, killed more than one victim, committed the murder in the course of a sexual assault, had committed at least one prior felony, and had expressed no remorse for the present crime).

Similar results have been obtained in several different studies. For ex-ample, James Luginbuhl and Kathi Middendorf's study of several hundred persons serving on jury duty found that removing the so-called automatic death penalty jurors did "little to redress the biasing effect of eliminating death-scrupled jurors," and that, as a result, death-qualified jurors tended to accentuate the importance of the two common aggravating circumstances

Table 5.2
Effects of "Modern" Death Qualification on Perception of Mitigating and Aggravating Factors

	Excludables ($n = 95$)	Death-Qualifieds ($n = 403$)
Finds mitigating		
Felony murder not premeditated	54.7%	37.5%**
Defendant over age 30	33.7%	14.4%****
Convicted person from background of poverty	32.6%	17.6%***
Loving family and friends supportive	35.8%	15.6%****
Never received treatment	48.4%	38%*
Finds aggravating		
Especially brutal murder	67.4%	89.1%****
More than one murder victim	58.9%	72%****
Murder during sexual assault	49.5%	69.2%****
Prior violent felony	27.4%	35.5%***
Expressed no remorse	53.7%	72.5%****

$*p < .1$, $**p < .05$, $***p < .01$, $****p < .001$.

that are introduced in many capital cases (specifically, the defendant's past record of violent crime, and the heinous circumstances of the present crime). The jurors also minimized the importance of one of the most common mitigating circumstances (namely, that the defendant was under emotional distress at the time of the crime). Luginbuhl and Middendorf concluded that even under the modified doctrines that now govern the process, death-qualified juries "will thus be biased toward a penalty of death."[73]

Brooke Butler and Gary Moran reached similar conclusions in research conducted with a large sample of venirepersons in Florida. Using the broader *Witt* standard of exclusion, they showed that death-qualified jurors were more likely to endorse a long list of aggravating circumstances and less likely to endorse certain mitigators (such as a history of alcoholism, drug abuse, and having been abused as a child), in comparison to persons who would be excluded under prevailing legal doctrines.[74]

Together these studies suggest that death-qualified jurors not only start out more in favor of the death penalty but, because of their differential sensitivity to many different kinds of potential penalty-phase evidence, are less likely to be persuaded that life imprisonment is an appropriate sentence.

Conclusion

This chapter has focused on the way in which several of the unique aspects of jury selection in capital cases may undermine the fairness of death penalty trials and facilitate the process of death sentencing. The impartiality of the jury that is finally selected to decide guilt and possibly to choose between life and death in a capital case may be compromised by extensive, potentially prejudicial pretrial publicity. The inherent limitations of voir dire in those instances in which many prospective jurors are likely to be heavily influenced by such publicity underscores the importance of conducting trials in alternate, less biased venues. Yet the added expense of long and complex capital trials and the political pressure that judges may feel to weigh community sentiment more heavily than the constitutional rights of defendants help to explain the reluctance with which such motions are granted, even in high-profile, high-stakes death penalty cases.

Moreover, note that the definition of publicity-related bias in venue-related inquiries typically is shaped by concerns over guilt-phase impartiality—whether potential jurors can be "fair" in deciding if the defendant is guilty. Most change-of-venue analyses and publicity-related lines of voir dire questioning are focused on whether "[j]urors exposed to publicity which presents negative information about the defendant and crime are more likely to judge the defendant as guilty than are jurors exposed to limited [pretrial publicity]."[75] This narrow framing of the issue guides legal rulings, sets the parameters for publicity-related voir dire questioning, and is the focus of most of the research done on the topic (including my own). Yet this emphasis on guilt-phase prejudice, although understandable, addresses only one kind of publicity-related bias that can arise in a capital case. Thus, pretrial publicity may prejudice the *penalty-phase* decision making of jurors in a death penalty case, and this may represent a far more significant risk to the fairness of the proceeding. It is one that is not only often overlooked but also seems to defy meaningful and effective voir dire remedies.

If asked, these penalty-phase-related voir dire questions would have to address topics like these: Based on what you have read or heard, do you believe the defendant in this case is despicable or unworthy of mercy or compassion? Has the media convinced you that he is likely to be dangerous or uncontrollable in the future? Have you been so sensitized by the press to the consequences of the alleged crime for the surrounding community or for the victim's family that you would be more likely to condemn this defendant to death? Has the pretrial publicity in this case already convinced you that the defendant and his past life fit a media-created stereotype of depraved criminality to which you subscribe, so that his attorneys are unlikely ever to convince you that there are mitigating explanations for his behavior and positive traits that he possesses that would lead you to vote in favor of allowing him to live? No doubt these clumsily worded questions could be better phrased by more artful interrogators. Yet the issues themselves remain difficult to address in a meaningful way in voir dire, even though they touch on some of the most important prejudices that case-related publicity may instill in capital jurors.

Of course, citizens regarding a defendant who is depicted as "human sewage" by the local newspaper editor—a community opinion leader voicing what readers are likely to assume is a widely held view—may calibrate the defendant's worth as a human being and the appropriateness of the death penalty as a moral response to his crime very differently as a result. In some cases, *these* things and not the presumption of guilt are at the core of publicity-related prejudice. Yet, as I say, they are out of the reach of current venue law and beyond the capacity of voir dire practices to ferret out.

In addition, the fairness of capital juries is compromised by the legally mandated process of death qualification. As summarized in this chapter, numerous social science studies have documented the fact that death-qualified juries are very different from juries that were not selected in this way, and those differences extend far beyond the obvious ones in death penalty attitude. In general, such juries are composed of proportionately fewer blacks and women, contain more people whose attitudes favor the prosecution, and are more likely to convict a criminal defendant than are their non-death-qualified counterparts. Moreover, they are more likely to render death rather than life verdicts, in part because they find a number of aggravating factors more aggravating and mitigating factors less mitigating than do their non-death-qualified counterparts.

In these ways, death qualification "homogenizes" the jury by acting to reduce the diversity of opinion represented within it. The unanimity of perspective with which the death-qualified jury begins the trial, evaluates the evidence, and concludes its decision making—the kind of unanimity of perspective that the Supreme Court condemned in other contexts because it was likely to stifle vigorous deliberations—appears to make guilty verdicts more likely and to facilitate the decision to sentence someone to death.[76] Moreover, the fact that death qualification may produce juries composed of persons who are significantly less knowledgeable about the system of death sentencing than their non-death-qualified counterparts, creates an interesting irony. By virtue of this process, the only persons who can participate in death sentencing may be the ones who understand the least about it. These composition effects and this irony are intrinsic to the biased nature of the selection process itself.

6

Preparing for the Death Penalty in Advance of Trial
Process Effects in Death-Qualifying Capital Juries

Tendencies, no matter how slight, toward the selection of jurors
by any method other than a process which will insure a trial by a
representative group are undermining processes weakening the
institution of jury trial, and should be sturdily resisted.
—Justice Frank Murphy, *Glasser v. United States* (1942)

Attorneys and legal scholars often comment that trials—especially criminal
trials—are won and lost at the jury selection stage of the case. Public sentiments run strong on many of the issues that frame the context in which
decisions about crime and punishment are made in court and, depending on
the views and sentiments that are represented on the jury, one or another
outcome may be much more likely (if not actually foreordained). In most
kinds of cases this dictum about winning and losing in jury selection is a
cautionary tale about the importance of taking the process of picking a jury
seriously. Attorneys who are careless or indulge their unverified theories
about "ideal" jurors are likely to be disappointed when the jury's verdict
finally is returned. However, in capital cases, the winning and losing of the
trial at this early stage may come about in another way. Here there are structural issues that are brought to bear on the jury selection process that appear
to change the odds in these cases in ways that distinguish them from other
criminal trials.

As the studies reviewed in the last chapter illustrated, death qualification
significantly influences the composition of the jury that ultimately is selected
in capital cases. The group that remains once the process is complete tends
to be unrepresentative of juries in general and often does not reflect the
demographic makeup of the venue from which it is selected. Death-qualified
jurors also tend to favor the prosecution, are inclined toward conviction, and
tilt in favor of rendering death rather than life sentences. Of course, these
are the only kind of juries—ones composed exclusively of death-qualified
jurors—that the law permits to sit in capital cases. In addition, however,

these juries have something else in common. By definition, each member of a capital jury has experienced the *process* of death qualification—a sometimes lengthy procedure in which attorneys and judges question potential jurors about their death penalty attitudes and formally disqualify those whose views are most extreme.

In this chapter, I want to move from focusing on the characteristics of the people who are selected to participate as capital jurors and to look more closely at the process by which their selection is accomplished. Thus, I concentrate on what happens inside the courtroom and how that affects the way capital jurors think about and are likely to judge the issues that come before them. Because it is one of the first things that happens to prospective jurors in the initial stage of a capital case, death qualification is especially important in creating courtroom atmosphere and juror expectations. It is unusual because it represents an extended discussion of punishment—the death penalty—at the very outset of a criminal trial, before any evidence has been presented and, obviously, long before a guilt-phase verdict has been reached. It occurs in no other kind of case.

During this process, prospective jurors are asked specifically—sometimes repeatedly—whether they are so much opposed to, or in favor of, the death penalty that their views would interfere with their ability to function as fair and impartial jurors. In the case of death penalty opponents, the court and the attorneys want to know whether their opposition means that they could not return a death verdict in any case. Strong death penalty supporters are questioned about whether it is true that they would vote to impose the death penalty in every case in which it was a possibility. When death qualification is conducted with groups of jurors—typical in a number of jurisdictions nowadays—it ensures that persons who ultimately sit on capital juries have been exposed repeatedly to this kind of penalty-oriented questioning. Moreover, because the process entails excluding prospective jurors who express strong death penalty views, especially those who oppose capital punishment, jurors will have witnessed the dismissal of their peers on the basis of their unwillingness to support or endorse the death penalty.

It is possible that these experiences create certain expectations and preconceptions in the minds of the jurors about the legal case that is to follow, perhaps predisposing them to receive and interpret evidence in certain ways, and influencing the verdict and sentencing decisions they may be called on to make. Psychologists and lawyers are well aware of the degree to which the process of asking questions can impart as well as elicit information. In social science, this phenomenon represents a methodological concern that is reflected in terms such as "reactivity" (the possibility that people will react to and be changed by the questions they are asked) and "pretest sensitization" (the way in which the initial measurement of attitudes and beliefs can alter their subsequent expression).[1]

In law, too, certain limitations that are placed on the use of "leading" questions, and judicial displeasure directed at attorneys who use voir dire more to "educate" than inquire of jurors, reflect legal awareness of the phenomenon. Thus, judges have long been sensitive to the possibility that voir dire might be used to "condition" jurors to a particular point of view or set of expectations.[2] Legal commentators have expressed concerns about the role that trial consultants may play in this conditioning process, in part because they well understand that what gets said during voir dire may have a lasting effect on persons who are exposed to it.[3]

Moreover, many attorneys believe that the major goals of voir dire include educating jurors about the trial, preparing them for the kind of evidence they can expect to hear, and previewing the legal principles that they are to employ in evaluating the evidence. In fact, experienced, practicing trial lawyers advise others that "[v]oir dire is part of the conditioning process to achieve acceptance in the hearts and minds of the jurors of the law of your case."[4] Thus, under the guise of acquiring information during voir dire, attorneys may seek to communicate it as well. Lawyers on each side may make as little or as much of this opportunity as they choose, but they are all aware of the potential effects of the process.

In addition to the conditioning that may occur in voir dire, courts have recognized that another kind of learning may take place in the course of jury selection, especially when it is conducted in a group setting—that is, that there is a "danger that potential jurors would be prejudiced by comments made by other potential jurors during voir dire."[5] In addition, some research suggests that that prospective jurors may watch the way that certain kinds of responses that are given by others are received or reacted to by the judge or the trial attorneys. Once having learned from these exchanges, they may tailor their own answers accordingly.[6] Those who want to "contrive to be seated or excused" will know what to say in order to accomplish either goal.[7]

Thus, both in psychology and in law there is widespread recognition and concern that the process of posing questions may have an independent effect of its own—that the way the questions are asked may bias the responses that are given, that the process of asking itself may in some ways change the respondents who provide answers, and that the circumstances under which the dialogue transpires may impart as well as elicit information.

In death qualification, however, trial participants have little choice over many of these matters. As the last chapter underscored, long-standing legal doctrines provide that prospective jurors will be asked about their death penalty views in order to establish that they are qualified to serve. And, unless a court orders the process to take place under individual, sequestered conditions, the questioning will occur in the presence of other prospective jurors. In the following sections I provide some data and a psychological analysis of the likely effects of this process on capital jury decision making.

The "Process Effect": Conditioning the Jury to Death Sentencing

As a legally mandated procedure in which attorneys and judges discuss death penalty attitudes at length with many prospective jurors, the *process* of death qualification may have distinct psychological consequences that compound the other problems already associated with capital jury selection. An experiment that I conducted some years ago was designed to shed some light on this issue.[8] Because my interest was in measuring the consequences of mere exposure to death qualification—separate and distinct from the composition effects discussed in the last chapter—all the participants in the study were previously death qualified over the telephone.[9] Only jury-eligible adults were used, and they were randomly assigned to either experimental or control conditions. The key variable—exposure to death qualification or not—was contained in a videotape of a simulated voir dire. Videotaping was done in the moot courtroom of a law school, which provided a realistic setting. We used experienced trial attorneys in the roles of prosecutor, defense attorney, and judge, and the attorneys were instructed to conduct themselves as they would in an actual voir dire.

The videotapes were identical to each other except that the experimental tape included a 30-minute segment of death qualification. The experimental treatment thus consisted of a two-hour videotape of voir dire, including death qualification, in a criminal trial. The death qualification segment occurred near the beginning of the videotape, after the judge made some preliminary, explanatory remarks and addressed several panel questions to the veniremen. Two professional actors were included in the group and played the role of persons strongly opposed to the death penalty.[10] After initially expressing their opposition to the death penalty, they were questioned more extensively about their beliefs by both attorneys. Once it became clear that they could not consider imposing the death penalty in any case, the court dismissed them.

The remaining questioning was devoted to non-death-qualifying voir dire of each venireman by both attorneys. The standard criminal voir dire segment, present in both tapes, also contained a discussion by the judge of several relevant legal principles. His comments were modeled on the California Jury Instructions (CALJIC) and included a brief explanation of the presumption of innocence and reasonable doubt. He also explained that the mere fact that someone was being brought to trial for a crime was not evidence of his guilt. A control tape was created by editing the death-qualification portion out of the original tape; it contained only the judge's preliminary remarks and the remaining standard voir dire questioning by both attorneys. Except for the deletion, the control tape was identical to the experimental tape. Once participants in the study viewed either the experimental or control tape to which they had been randomly assigned, they all completed a questionnaire designed to assess their attitudes about the trial and the defendant.

As table 6.1 makes clear, the results of the study underscore the degree to which simple exposure to the death qualification process appears to change the mind-set of potential capital jurors. For example, the participants were asked to make their own estimates of the likelihood of the defendant's guilt and the likelihood that he would be convicted. In both cases, persons who were exposed to death qualification estimated significantly higher probabilities than those who were not. They also believed it was more likely that the defendant would be convicted of first-degree murder and would receive the death penalty.[11]

All of the prospective jurors also were asked to estimate the degree to which they thought the key trial participants believed the defendant was guilty. In each instance, exposure to death qualification increased their estimate of the prosecutor's, defense attorney's, and judge's belief in the defendant's guilt. It also led participants to perceive both the prosecutor and judge as more strongly in favor of the death penalty, and to believe that the law "disapproves of people who oppose the death penalty."

Of particular concern was whether exposure to the death qualification process directly facilitated death sentencing. Thus, the participants in the study also were asked to assume a set of facts in a hypothetical penalty phase (namely, that the defendant had been convicted of first-degree murder in

Table 6.1
Effects of Exposure to Death Qualification Process on Jury-Eligible Participants

	Exposed to Death Qualification	Not Exposed to Death Qualification	t	p
Likely defendant guilty of first-degree murder	46.7	36.2	2.12	.038
Likely defendant will be convicted and sentenced to death	39.6	24.5	3.00	.004
Estimate of trial participants' belief in defendant's guilt				
Defense attorney*	58.5	69.2	−2.38	.019
Prosecutor*	26.0	35.8	−2.09	.041
Judge*	42.1	51.6	−3.77	.0001
Estimate of judge's belief in death penalty	63.9	51.8	3.29	.002
Estimate that law disapproves of death penalty opposition	52.4	30.8	3.48	.001

All means are derived from a 100-point scale.
*Lower numbers indicate greater belief in guilt.

this case and, as a special circumstance, that he also had a prior conviction for the same offense) and then to indicate what they believed the appropriate penalty should be.[12] As table 6.2 indicates, persons exposed to death qualification were significantly more likely to select the death penalty than were those who had not been exposed to death qualification. These differences were by no means subtle: the verdict patterns in table 6.2 translate into a 57% rate of death sentencing by persons exposed to death qualification as compared to only 21.9% of those not exposed to death qualification who selected death as the appropriate punishment.

Overall, the results of this study indicated that potential jurors were strongly influenced by the process of death qualification itself and that they were likely to approach a death penalty trial in a frame of mind that differed significantly from that of participants who had not been exposed to the process. Of course, because both groups consisted only of persons who already held death-qualified attitudes or beliefs about the death penalty, the results documented a biasing effect that went beyond the composition effects discussed in the last chapter. This additional biasing effect stemmed from exposure to the death-qualifying questions and to the atmosphere that was created in the courtroom setting where discussions about the death penalty had taken place.

Moreover, as noted, there were several dimensions to the bias that resulted—potential jurors were rendered significantly more likely to believe that the defendant was guilty and that he would be convicted and receive the death penalty, as well as to believe that the attorneys and judge, in essence, shared their guilt-prone views. The process also appeared to create a pro-death-penalty atmosphere—prospective jurors were more likely to believe that the judge himself favored the death penalty and that the law disfavored those persons who did not. Most troublesome, perhaps, mere exposure to death qualification tilted the prospective jurors toward the death penalty, so that a significantly higher number of them thought that it was the appropriate punishment in a hypothetical case compared to those who had not been exposed.

In the sections that follow, I discuss some of the social psychological

Table 6.2
Effects of Exposure to Death Qualification on Verdict Choice

	Exposed to Death Qualification	Not Exposed to Death Qualification
Participants choosing:		
Life imprisonment without parole	15	25
Death penalty	20	7

$X = 8.95, p < .005.$

forces that may be at work as these changes in the mind-set of potential capital jurors take place.

Explaining the Process Effect: The Social Psychology of Death-Qualifying Voir Dire

The biasing effects of death qualification are social contextual in nature; that is, they come from exposure to a process and the surrounding atmosphere it creates (rather than residing in the characteristics of the persons who manifest the effects). Thus, they are best analyzed in social psychological terms. The first important component of the process involves the *implication of guilt* that occurs at the initial stage of a capital trial, stemming from the often protracted but otherwise anomalous discussion of penalty that death qualification requires. Jurors enter the courtroom in a state of some uncertainty about courtroom norms and the likelihood that the defendant is guilty. Of course, they know there is some likelihood of that he or she is responsible for the crime, otherwise there would be no trial. But death qualification appears to resolve much of this initial uncertainty in especially prejudicial ways. Like most persons placed in novel or unfamiliar situations, jurors are especially sensitive to cues from authority figures and apparently knowledgeable others. In the courtroom, the judge and attorneys are obvious candidates for such attention, and previous research suggests that jurors are, in fact, quite sensitive to the behavior of these major trial participants.[13]

By requiring the attorneys and judge to dwell on penalty at the very start of the trial, the death-qualification process implies a heightened level of belief in the guilt of the defendant on the part of these major trial participants. That is, jurors are likely to reason that if there was not a good chance that the defendant was guilty, then so much time would not be invested in discussing his postconviction fate. Even though jurors who draw this inference may not do so consciously, death qualification requires an initial discussion of penalty, and penalty implies guilt. This sequential inference is built into the very structure of the death-qualification process and, as I say, occurs in no other kind of case.

Judges who are sensitive to this issue may voice disclaimers to jurors to the effect that the penalty phase *may not* occur. Some judges are even conscientious enough to pose some of their death-qualifying questions in a contingent form (e.g., "*if* and only *if* you convict the defendant . . ."). However, several things limit the effectiveness of these disclaimers. The first is that, at best, they do no more than restate what, but for death qualification, should be obvious: The defendant *might* be found not guilty. When repeated, they often take on the quality of protesting too much.

Second, the disclaimers and contingent questions typically are confusing to prospective jurors, who do not always grasp their implications. To court personnel for whom capital trial proceedings are second nature, subtle variations in language may seem clear and able to convey a number of important distinctions. Yet even veniremen who have heard the capital trial process explained several times in the course of group voir dire may be uncertain about it. For prospective jurors who are unfamiliar with proceedings like these, the many legalistic explanations, the "only ifs" of these kinds of contingent explanations may add to their general confusion. The one thing that is likely to come through loud and clear is that the judge is asking them whether they can impose the death penalty later in this case.

Finally, despite an occasional disclaimer that the penalty phase might not occur, the voir dire questioners—the judge and attorneys—often behave precisely as though it will. That is, attempts to clarify the capital trial process may intensify the implication of guilt by inadvertently suggesting that the penalty phase *will*, rather than *may*, occur. For example:

> (By the Prosecutor) Q: All right. Mrs. Marshall, you know all that you are going to have to go through with the second phase?
>
> (By the Venireman) A: Yes.
>
> Q: To determine the death penalty. Do you feel that this would have any bearing on your deliberation with regard to the guilt or innocence of it, knowing that you are going to have to . . .
>
> A: Let me get this straight now.
>
> Q: There's two.
>
> A: Which, how I decide that, it was guilty of the crime, or not guilty, would this have anything to do with me deciding; no.
>
> Q: No. Even though that you are going to have to go through and consider this the second phase?[14]

A closely related social psychological factor is implicated when prospective jurors are encouraged in death qualification to reflect on how they will behave in the penalty phase that might occur. Even when questions are posed in scrupulously contingent terms, the very nature of this kind of inquiry invites veniremen to imagine themselves as jurors in the sentencing phase. Most courts interpret the *Witherspoon/Witt* standard to go beyond inquiring merely about abstract attitudes, so that jurors are called on to make behavioral predictions about themselves in order to assess their ability to impose the death penalty: Could you consider imposing the death penalty? Could you vote to impose it? Would you listen to penalty-phase evidence with an open mind and weigh considerations both for and against imposing it in a given case? Can you think of any case in which you would impose it? Would you automatically impose it in every case? These kind of questions are routinely posed in the death qualification process and they require prospective jurors to translate attitudes into speculation about what they might or would do under a set of future circumstances.

For example, consider the following discussion between a prospective juror in a highly publicized capital case who had indicated on her pretrial juror questionnaire that she thought anyone guilty of murder deserved the death penalty (an opinion that would qualify her as an "automatic death penalty juror"). Even though the judge had explained the process up to this point in carefully worded contingent terms, his questions soon set those contingencies aside:

(By the Judge) Q: Okay. Now, you made a statement [on the questionnaire], generally speaking, as follows: That you believe that the death penalty, quote, should apply, close quote, if the person is found guilty. By that what did you mean "should apply"? Do you recall answering that question?

A: Yes, I do. I'm trying to—

Q: What did you mean by that?

A: I just feel that if a person is found guilty—

Q: You don't get to a penalty phase unless they are found guilty.

A: I don't completely understand the—

Q: Do you understand it now?

A: Now I understand it, yes.

Q: Okay. You don't get to a penalty phase unless you made that finding, *maybe a month before you made a finding guilty of murder of the first degree, special circumstance true.* That's behind you. You've gone on to the next phase, and you found the person to be legally sane. That's behind you. Now the sole issue is penalty.

A: Penalty phase. Now I understand. It's clear to me.

Q: So what did you mean by that comment in the questionnaire if you found the person guilty, the death penalty "should apply" in a case like this?

A: I believe that if a person is mentally sane and he is found guilty of the counts that he is accused of, that the death penalty should be applied.

Q: When you say that, do you say that it should be applied automatically without consideration of the other penalty, which is life in prison without the possibility of parole?

A: Yes.

Q: So you would not—if I understand what you just told me, if you were in a penalty phase trial and you've made all these findings, don't forget a month before you found the defendant guilty of murder. You found the special circumstances true. You found him legally sane. That's all behind you. Now we are in the penalty phase, and the People are offering evidence why they believe the punishment should be death. The defense is offering evidence why they feel it should be life in prison without the possibility of parole. Is your state of mind such that you would automatically vote for death and not consider the evidence that might be presented to you as it bears upon life in prison without the possibility of parole?[15]

A different judge in an even higher-profile California case approached death qualification in much the same way—by having prospective jurors imagine that they had already convicted the defendant of the crime for which he was about to stand trial. For example:

> (By the Judge) Q: Okay. Now, I'm going to take you into this case just a little step further, a little deeper, okay? And this, again, I want to emphasize to you is a hypothetical question. Let me clear my throat.
>
> So, make-believe hypothetical question.
>
> We're talking about the guilt phase; you know, what happened in this case.
>
> Let's say you sit there with the other eleven jurors. You listen to what took place and you and the other eleven jurors are convinced beyond a reasonable doubt that this is what the defendant did:
>
> That he murdered his wife, Laci Peterson, who at the time was eight months pregnant; that also resulted in the death of the fetus, who would have been his minor child, Conner Peterson; then after he murdered his wife he transported her to the Berkeley Marina, put her on a boat, took her out into the middle of the Bay and then dumped her body into the Bay to cover up his crime.
>
> Let's assume that's what you find him guilty of.
>
> Now without hearing any other mitigating factors, nothing about that, just looking at the crime itself, is that crime all by itself so inflammatory to you, so repulsive to you that in your mind you've eliminated life without parole and you'd always pick the death penalty?
>
> A: Tough question.
> Q: I know.
> A: Yeah. It's a hideous crime.
> Q: Yeah. Sure.
> A: Unless there were circumstances, you know, that haven't been brought up yet.
> Q: Okay. Well, you go to take that on face value that this is what you find him guilty of.
> A: Okay. Well, then in that case it would seem, you know—it would seem that it would warrant the death penalty.[16]

Psychological research suggests that simply imagining or assuming that an event or outcome has occurred like this can *increase our subjective estimate* that it actually will take place. As social psychologist John Carroll put it some years ago, the "objective fact that some events are imaginary, hypothetical, inferred rather than observed, or even factually discredited is poorly coded or not properly used. Thus, the act of posing a problem or asking a question could itself change the beliefs of subjects."[17]

The phenomenon has been explained in several different ways. For one, early research has shown that once people generate a particular scenario their ability to generate alternative scenarios becomes more limited.[18] Moreover, once they have come up with a plausible cause for a particular outcome, they no longer think much about other possible causes.[19] More broadly, perhaps, this can be understood in terms of what cognitive theorists Amos Tversky and Daniel Kahneman have labeled the "availability heuristic."[20] They suggested that imagining an event made its cognitive category, as well as the necessary sequence of events that preceded it, more available and easier to mentally access. Once our mind has traversed a path, even in imagination, it seems easier and more likely to be traversed again. In addition, research suggests that this process is mediated by how easy the experience or event is to imagine in the first place. That is, if a particular event is already relatively easy to conjure, then thinking about its occurrence is likely to have an even greater effect.[21]

The implications of all of this for death qualification are obvious. By turning the attention and imagination of prospective jurors to the possible occurrence of a penalty phase, death-qualifying voir dire may increase their estimate that such an event will occur (as well as the sequence of events—including the defendant's conviction—that necessarily would precede it). Moreover, those jurors who already find this event easy to imagine (perhaps because pretrial publicity has prepared them for it) would be especially likely to be influenced by the act of imagining a penalty trial.

In fairness, many judges and attorneys regard this technique—asking prospective jurors to imagine themselves in the penalty phase—as the very best way to obtain an accurate estimate of a prospective juror's future penalty-phase behavior. In some sense, it may be. That is, getting prospective jurors to predict how they think they will behave in a future situation may be the best estimate that can be obtained at this early, preliminary stage. But the need to obtain this information in this precise a way is dictated by the death qualification process. It appears to have unintended negative consequences that may bias capital jurors in the guilt and penalty phases of the case.

Despite these negative psychological consequences, judges and attorneys often are persistent in encouraging veniremen to assume that the guilt phase of the trial has been completed and that a guilty verdict has been returned. For example, consider the following dialogue between a trial judge and a prospective juror who was initially reluctant to leave the guilt phase behind:

(By the Court) Q: All right, you wouldn't automatically vote for the death penalty in every case, would you, and never consider life without parole?

(By the Venireman) A: Well, no, because I understand, you know, the course and the person, you know—it goes like a step by step, you know? I cannot say he's guilty, you know, until, you know,

> I find the defendant, because I don't have facts, you know, what is the case.
>
> Q: All right. But let us assume that you've heard the evidence and you've been convinced beyond a reasonable doubt that [the defendant] is guilty of murder in the first degree. Just assume that to be true. Then there would be additional evidence introduced by both sides in this case as to which penalty should be imposed by the jury or not imposed, but which penalty should be the verdict of the jury, either death or life imprisonment.
>
> Could you consider both penalties?
>
> A: Yes . . . [22]

In practice, both of these effects—the structural implication of guilt and the way imagining the penalty phase makes it seem more likely to occur—often take place simultaneously. They are both difficult for even the most conscientious judges to avoid. For example, here is the death-qualifying preamble given by a trial judge who was about to question prospective jurors concerning their death penalty attitudes. As the transcript reveals, he was unusually mindful of the way that the mere mention of penalty may convey an unwanted message about the guilt of the defendant:

> (By the Court): The question of penalty happens in a separate trial, if it happens, and only after the jury has returned and we have recorded verdicts, finding, among other things, that somebody's guilty of special-circumstance, first-degree murder.
>
> So, you know, that may not happen. The problem doesn't arise. Nonetheless, we have to talk about it, and the fact that we talk about it says nothing about it, and the probabilities of its coming out. We'd have to talk about it even if there were only one chance in 10,000. We'd also talk about it if it were a virtual certainty. So the fact we talk about it doesn't tell you anything.[23]

However, after this thoughtful attempt to neutralize these biasing effects, he went on to discuss at length the following issues: the way in which the jury's task was one of "making a choice between two penalties that the law has laid down"; the fact that "if anybody dies, it will require the vote of all 12 jurors"; that a life without parole sentence means "the person leaves the prison in a casket"; that "nobody should have any doubt" that an execution will follow a death verdict; that although "the governor has the power to commute" sentences, from death or life without parole to something less but that, "in the real world in this day and age, it doesn't happen" so that the jurors should not assume "the governor will fix it if I get it wrong. It won't happen. You better not get it wrong"; that they should not attempt to decide the issue of penalty based on cost because "if you did, you'd probably get it wrong"; and that the jurors should "not decide the case on the theory that one penalty or the other would be more likely to deter people from committing crimes" because "[y]ou will have enough trouble trying this case without trying to solve the other problems of the world."[24]

Although each of these propositions is legally correct, none is necessarily objectionable, and all appear to be offered in the spirit of being informative, note that each one invites prospective jurors to think about various scenarios that imply that the defendant already has been found guilty. Moreover, once the judge's lengthy preamble was completed, he began the process of questioning prospective jurors about their death penalty beliefs this way:

> (By the Court) Q: Is there anyone who would not be able to make a separate impartial determination of penalty seriously considering both potential penalties no matter what the basis of the finding of guilt?[25]

Another social psychological aspect of the death qualification process that helps to explain its biasing effects is closely related to the first two. Imagining the penalty phase (and hearing other prospective jurors being asked to do the same) also exposes prospective jurors to the most profound issue that can be confronted in the courtroom—literally, life and death. Jurors must contemplate this issue early in the proceedings and, as a result, this may ease prospective jurors over an emotional hurdle that otherwise might have been more difficult to traverse later on. The psychological explanation for this phenomenon is straightforward. Clinical researchers have studied the way that thinking about and discussing a frightening event, under some circumstances, makes it less so. This is a basic assumption of what is termed "desensitization" therapy in which patients are placed in a state of relaxation and asked to imagine themselves in varying degrees of contact with a fear-arousing stimulus.

In this sense, because repeatedly exposing people to an aversive event accustoms them to it,[26] jurors who have confronted the daunting question of whether they could impose the death penalty, and have listened patiently while other prospective jurors have confronted the same question in voir dire, may be less anxious about and intimidated by it in the deliberation stage of the trial. In some instances, prosecutors go so far as to ask prospective jurors whether they could "look this defendant in the eye and say that death is your verdict?"[27] Obviously, thinking about and agreeing to cross such a steep emotional barrier well in advance of making the decisions that precede it may make those decisions less daunting later on. Thus, jurors who become desensitized to the prospect of voting to take someone's life may not only be willing to do that, if and when the time comes to make such a choice, but also may be less reluctant to decide guilt or find the special or aggravating circumstances that result in "death eligibility."

As noted previously, death-qualifying voir dire is conducted in open court in many jurisdictions, where other prospective jurors also are present.

Each venireman may hear these emotional issues referred to and discussed numerous times. Because death penalty supporters still significantly outnumber death penalty opponents, prospective jurors will listen to many of their peers publicly state their willingness to impose the penalty. A climate of death penalty support may be created as a result. If so, this apparent peer support and implied approval may ease otherwise reluctant jurors into the psychologically difficult decisions they may be called on to make later in the case. In such a climate, jurors who actually have second thoughts about the death penalty may hesitate to share them. Because no premium is placed on equivocation in this process, prospective jurors may feel that they should suppress their doubts. If and when this occurs, a false sense of certainty and unanimity is added to these collective endorsements of the death penalty. This, in turn, may create a level of pluralistic ignorance in which jurors with private reservations become convinced that no one else shares them.

The major trial participants—judge and attorneys—also may become desensitized to the emotional nature of the death-qualifying voir dire, inadvertently but outwardly treating death penalty imposition is a more or less routine or ordinary event. Because they repeat their prefaces and explanations again and again, as each new prospective juror or small group of veniremen appears, they may adopt a matter-of-factness in their questioning that influences jurors. For example, after asking a prospective juror to assume "that the evidence was overwhelming or beyond a reasonable doubt that (the defendant] was guilty of first-degree murder," one trial judge tried to explain the subtleties of the penalty phase this way:

> (By the Court) Q: If that happens, there will be a second hearing, and that hearing may take place right after the first hearing. It may be a week later. And at the second hearing, it's *a whole new ball game* with evidence being introduced and that type of thing. And at the second hearing the decision is *simply* whether she should receive life or death. *Just black or white type thing.* Would the fact that you can't make a decision taking life, would that prevent you in the first trial of finding her guilty of first-degree murder if the evidence was proven to you beyond a reasonable doubt?[28]

The process of death qualification also appears to *anchor* the instant case at the most extreme end of a continuum of heinousness. Prospective jurors learn that in the opinion of the trial participants who presumably have a much wider range of experience with such matters, the case about which they are being questioned falls in the small category of cases worthy of the most extreme punishment that the law permits:

> (By the Court) Q: ... Okay, having in mind the kind of case we have here, do you have any strong views or convictions or opinions concerning the death penalty so that regardless of what the evidence might be—this case, that you would automatically and

absolutely refuse under any circumstances to vote for or consider
the death penalty?[29]

In this instance the death qualification process has led the judge to inadvertently imply something prejudicial about the "kind of case we have
here," before any evidence has been presented about exactly what kind of
case it is. Thus, the process provides jurors with a legal yardstick that is
present in no other kind of case. It may create a set of expectations that
colors the way the jurors will perceive, weigh, and evaluate the evidence that
follows. By implying that the major trial participants—including the judge—
have concluded that the death penalty may be the appropriate punishment
here—in essence, that this is "a death penalty case"—a form of implied
labeling has been insinuated into the voir dire process. It provides jurors with
a legal gauge of the magnitude of the crime and the blameworthiness of the
defendant whose fate they are about to decide.

The North Carolina Supreme Court made a related observation some
50 years ago. A trial judge had made reference to two notorious and atrocious
killings in his questioning of two death-scrupled veniremen, ostensibly to
determine the limits of their opposition to capital punishment and to decide
whether they were "fit to serve" on the capital jury. Justice Ervin overturned
the conviction and death sentence, ordering a new trial based on his conclusion that "the questions (about the other, heinous crimes) had a logical
tendency to implant in the minds of the trial jurors the convictions that the
presiding judge believed that the prisoner had killed his wife in an atrocious
manner, that the prisoner was guilty of murder in the first-degree, and that
the prisoner ought to suffer death for his crime."[30] Although the trial judge
had informed the jury that he had not intended to compare the present case
with any others, Ervin observed that the "trial judge occupies an exalted
station, and jurors entertain a profound respect for his opinion," so that "it
is virtually impossible for the judge to remove the prejudicial impression
from the minds of the trial jurors by anything which he may afterwards say
to them by way of atonement or explanation."[31]

Just as in the North Carolina case, this aspect of the death-qualifying
voir dire may be intensified when judges or attorneys attempt to "rehabilitate" prospective jurors in an attempt to keep them in the jury pool. For
example, when defense attorneys question persons whose statements in opposition to the death penalty put them at risk of being excluded, they often
seek concessions from potential jurors to the effect that there are at least *some*
circumstances under which they might be able to impose the death penalty.
Usually, the only way to accomplish this is by suggesting examples of extreme
cases that the prospective juror might agree warrant the death penalty. But
these suggestions implicitly connect the present case to some of the worst
crimes that the prospective jurors can imagine, encouraging them to expect
the worst later on in the trial (or to interpret what they do hear later in the
trial as legally and morally comparable). For example:

(By the Defense Counsel) Q: Well, just so I understand, could you consider it even though you don't want to, would you refuse to consider the death penalty?

A: Yes.

Q: You would refuse to. Now, ma'am, you are aware that there has been some vicious crimes committed in our community over the years?

A: Yes.

Q: Thinking back on some of the ones in your mind that were perhaps the most brutal, the worst, are you saying even in that type of case you could not consider the death penalty because right now you don't have any evidence in this case to know where it would lie, as far as you are concerned, being brutal or whatever else, you don't know that, correct?

A: Yes.

Q: At this point. I am telling you to assume some of the facts from some of those terrible crimes you have heard about in the past. Are you saying that even in that instance you could not consider the death penalty in that type of case?

A: I might have considered it.

Q: In that type of case?

A: In some case, yes.

Q: Basically the Court will instruct you as to what the law is as relates to this case, you understand that?

A: Yes.

Q: And he will tell you what is necessary as far as the truth is concerned with respect to this case. If in the following instructions of the judge, following the guidelines that he gives you. If you felt that the death penalty was appropriate in this case, you could consider that, could you not, ma'am?[32]

In this way death qualification not only puts defense attorneys in the awkward position of implicitly comparing the present case to some of "the most brutal, the worst" but also of appearing to argue *for* death penalty imposition.[33]

Of course, persons with disqualifying death penalty attitudes are excluded from capital juries during death qualification. Depending on the way the voir dire is conducted and exactly how exclusions are handled, this may occur in front of other prospective jurors. If so, the process of exclusion is likely to imply legal or judicial *disapproval* of death penalty opposition. Indeed, eliminating death penalty opponents may appear to lend clear legal authority and legitimacy to death penalty supporters that would be lacking in the absence of this public demonstration. Among other things, it may help to convince jurors that the judge—as the person ultimately responsible for the exclusion of the offending jurors—personally favors the death penalty.

Jurors who identify with or wish to please this authority figure may be more likely to advocate what they believe to be the judge's pro-death-penalty view in deliberations. Moreover, some jurors may infer from watching the disqualification of those who balk at imposing the death penalty that the law disfavors any form of "timidity," and prefers hard line stands and the expressed willingness to readily consider imposing the most severe punishment.

Finally, in order to survive death qualification, jurors must *publicly affirm* their commitment to capital punishment by stating their willingness to impose it. Since the early demonstrations of Kurt Lewin more than a half century ago, social psychologists have collected evidence showing that the active, public advocacy of a position intensifies one's belief in it.[34] More recent research has corroborated Lewin's early insights—publicly committing to a particular position or belief tends to rigidify it, makes that position resistant to counterarguments, renders persons less likely to think about the potentially negative implications of the opinion itself, and sometimes increases the extremity with which the position itself is held.[35]

Thus, the public affirmation required by death qualification may increase a juror's initial support of the death penalty and his or her willingness to vote to impose it. Moreover, by taking a public stand to consider the death penalty and endorse it in the "proper" case, jurors may become invested in an image of toughness that will affect them in deliberation. That is, someone who has made a public commitment to death penalty imposition may be less likely to balk at other less drastic punishments like life imprisonment and the decisions that precede them.

In this way, beyond merely providing cues and implicit suggestions about the nature of the case that will follow, death qualification requires each juror to openly endorse the most extreme sanction that exists in law. It may be done in a way that seems to ask for a clear behavioral commitment. For example:

> (By the Prosecutor) Q: In an appropriate case, based upon the information that will be given to you, and the law that his Honor, Judge Matia, will give you, if you come to the conclusion that the imposition of capital punishment is the appropriate verdict at the second trial, do you feel that you could join with your fellow jurors and sign a verdict form indicating that?
>
> (By the Venireman) A: Yes.[36]

Not surprisingly, postverdict interviews with actual jurors have indicated that some of them erroneously believe that death qualification required them to promise the judge that they *would* impose the death penalty upon a conviction. Pro-life-sentence jurors who surface during penalty-phase deliberations may feel as though they are reneging improperly on this promise. In fact, one study concluded that one of the most effective techniques that pro-death-penalty jurors use in convincing "holdout" jurors who want to take more time to think about the sentencing decision is to "remind" them that "during jury selection, he or she had expressed a capacity to vote for the death penalty."[37] Of course, having the "capacity" to impose a death sentence is not the same thing as promising to do so in a particular case. Yet pro-death-penalty jurors may use this alleged promise, supposedly made in the course of death qualification, to argue to holdout jurors who favor life verdicts in deliberation that they have relinquished the right "to make a sentencing based on lingering feelings of opposition to the death penalty."[38]

"Modern" Death Qualification and the Process Effect: Life-Qualifying Voir Dire and Other Issues

There are several important caveats that should be appended to my summary of the various social psychological components of the "process effects" created by death qualification. The first is to note that the process effects documented in the first section of this chapter were based on only a single empirical study. I hasten to add that this study was regarded as highly realistic by the research participants (who rated its authenticity as very high) as well as by various judges who viewed the videotapes that were used and who ruled on the legal relevance and overall merits of the research. For example, Judge Thomas Eisele, a federal district judge who presided over an elaborate evidentiary hearing on death qualification in which he was called on to review and evaluate the study materials (and those of many of the studies on composition effects that were discussed in the last chapter), concluded that this particular piece of research "provid[ed] strong empirical support" for something that many trial lawyers and judges should already know, namely, that "regardless of the preconceptions which a juror might have before entering the courtroom, the questions and the answers and the dialogue pursued in the death qualification process have a clear tendency to suggest that the defendant is guilty."[39] Nonetheless, no matter how well done the research—and, perhaps to trial lawyers and judges, seemingly commonsensical its conclusions—only one controlled simulation study has documented this point.

Moreover, as I noted in the last chapter, since the process study was published in the mid-1980s, legal doctrines governing death qualification have changed somewhat. Although these new doctrines do not appear to have substantially altered the way death qualification biases the composition of the capital jury, as I discuss below, they *have* changed the way the process itself is conducted. For one, the new legal doctrines have introduced a fair amount of variation into capital jury selection practices. Under the earlier doctrines that were in effect at the time I conducted the process study, most courts approached death qualification in very similar ways. The ruling in *Witherspoon* had drawn what amounted to a bright line—unequivocal opposition to the death penalty—that resulted in the exclusion of prospective jurors who crossed it.[40] There was a more or less routine approach that courts employed in trying to determine whether a prospective juror's attitude about the death penalty had, in fact, crossed that line.

However, recall that the standard of exclusion changed in the mid-1980s, following *Wainright v. Witt*, from unequivocal opposition to whether one's death penalty attitude would "prevent or substantially impair" a juror in the performance of his or her duties.[41] Since then, the nature of the questioning and the decision rule that courts use to disqualify someone from participation have become more ambiguous. The Court in *Witt* announced its intention to stop attorneys and judges from conducting death qualification as "question-and-answer sessions which obtain results in the manner of a catechism."[42] As I noted in the last chapter, most researchers and practitioners believe that the new *Witt* standard expanded the category of exclusion. But the lack of precision in the standard itself has created more variation in the way the death qualification process typically unfolds.

The second change—perhaps in direct response to existing death qualification research—was that trial courts began to grant more regularly the defense requests to conduct at least this limited portion of the capital jury selection on an individual, sequestered basis. In fact, in a landmark California case, *Hovey v. Superior Court,* the state supreme court used the process study described earlier in this chapter as the basis for ordering that all death-qualifying voir dire to be conducted this way.[43] Even after this requirement was repealed later by the California legislature,[44] many courts in the state and elsewhere used their discretion to grant defense requests for this kind of voir dire.

These two changes—more variation in death qualification questioning to determine "substantial impairment" and the increased practice of asking death-qualifying questions out of the presence of other jurors—helps to explain the lack of systematic follow-up research on the important process effect issue. The way in which death qualification now is conducted has made the kind of simulation research design that was used in the original process study difficult if not impossible to repeat. Not only do variations in the questioning procedures themselves make it more difficult to capture a normative or "typical" death qualification, but the technique used in that study—varying *exposure* to the questioning of others rather than questioning participants directly—less accurately represents what now happens in those jurisdictions that use individual, sequestered voir dire.

A third and final change in the legal doctrines governing death qualification—introduced since the original process study was published in the mid-1980s—also is important to acknowledge and discuss. In 1980, Justice Byron White spoke for many legal experts and death penalty researchers when he suggested it was "undeniable" that jurors who believed in automatically imposing the death penalty were "few indeed as compared with those excluded because of scruples against capital punishment."[45] As I noted earlier, it was difficult to know the exact number of such persons—"automatic death penalty jurors" or "ADPs" as they came to be called—as most jurisdictions either failed to screen out jurors on the basis of their extreme death penalty support or were so unsystematic in doing so that it was impossible to reliably quantify how many of them there were.[46]

However, two developments raised the possibility that Justice White's consensus view, that ADPs were "few indeed," might need to be modified. For one, death penalty support continued to increase in the years after White's observation, and the size of the group of extreme death penalty supporters—persons so strongly in favor that they would always vote to impose the death penalty when the law gave them the opportunity—likely expanded. Second, in 1992 the Supreme Court explicitly required states to conduct what has been termed "life qualifying" voir dire in the selection of a capital jury. That is, as I noted in the last chapter, *Morgan v. Illinois*[47] held that persons who said that they automatically would vote to impose the death penalty now had to be excluded from participating on capital juries. As a result, courts everywhere began to inquire more regularly about this issue, and it has become clear that, although they generally do not match the numbers of death penalty opponents who are excluded, there are somewhat more ADPs than most experts previously suspected.

In theory, and depending on how the life qualifying questions are posed, the exclusion of this group of extreme pro-death-penalty supporters might serve to balance to some degree the exclusion of death penalty opponents. In actual practice, however, because of widespread variations in the way that life qualification is conducted, the impact of this doctrinal change is difficult to assess. In fact, there are several reasons to believe that life-qualifying voir dire does not nearly counteract or balance the effects of death qualification on the overall composition of the jury.

For one, as I pointed out in the last chapter, our study of death penalty attitudes in California indicated that many statistically significant differences remained in the composition of the death-qualified group versus those who had been excluded, even when the latter group was composed both of death penalty opponents *and* ADPs.[48] In addition, there are many anecdotal reports suggesting that life qualification typically is not conducted very effectively. Indeed, according to attorneys and researchers who have studied contemporary jury selection practices, "[t]he starkest failure of capital voir dire is the qualification of jurors who will automatically impose the death penalty ('ADP' jurors) regardless of the individual characteristics of the case."[49]

Among the various problems that plague capital jury selection, and which may help to explain concerns over the poor quality of life qualification, is the fact that judges typically do not explain the core concepts of aggravation and mitigation during jury selection, when prospective jurors are first likely to encounter them. Even when they attempt to do so in passing, mitigation tends to get short shrift, or is explained in a way that is not likely to match up to the testimony that jurors are likely to hear. For example:

(By the Judge): Okay. Would you be able to consider both penalties, listen to the evidence presented to you as it bears upon that issue, listen to what the People might offer by way of aggravation and—you know, aggravation means facts that might aggravate the crimes or might aggravate the defendant, make it worse, make him look badder, if that's proper, and listen to what the mitigation might be offered by the defense, things that might mitigate the offenses or mitigate the defendant, maybe good things about him. Do you follow what I'm saying?[50]

Of course, if the judge does not fully explain what mitigation means (including the fact that it includes background and social history information intended to explain the defendant's behavior in a way that lessens his culpability—as opposed to being limited to "good things about him"), then prospective jurors cannot honestly and accurately report whether they would take it into account.

Whatever the reason that ADP jurors are "slipping through" the voir dire process, the Capital Jury Project has presented data suggesting that there are quite a few of them. Indeed, in their interviews of persons who had actually served as capital jurors, nearly half or more said that the death penalty was "the only acceptable punishment" for most of the kinds of murder scenarios that the researchers posed to them.[51]

This issue is worth exploring in a bit more detail. In any given case, a prospective juror might self-identify as an ADP either because she believed that death was the only appropriate punishment for the crime (i.e., a crime like the one for which the defendant was on trial) or because he would refuse to consider the particular kind of mitigation that the defendant intended to offer as the basis for a sentence less than death. Thus, persons can be ADPs because they so strongly condemn certain aggravated behavior *or* because they categorically reject certain forms of mitigation. In either event, a death verdict would be automatic. Critics of the way current life qualification often is practiced suggest that trial judges fail to properly handle either kind of problematic death penalty attitude when it surfaces in jury selection.[52] Thus, both kinds of ADP jurors appear to survive the life qualification process.[53] Of course, adding life-qualifying questions to the overall capital jury process means that people are questioned about their willingness to return a life verdict in what they regard as the appropriate case. When this happens, the obvious one-sidedness of death qualification in which only extreme death penalty opponents are excluded (and, in group voir dire, excluded in front of other prospective jurors) has been addressed.

To be sure, there is no guarantee that there will be an equivalent amount of time spent on each kind of potential challenge or that the number of persons challenged for extreme death penalty opposition versus extreme death penalty support will be comparable. The numbers of people who surface at either end of the death penalty spectrum will vary as a function of the prevailing sentiment in the particular time and place where the death- and life-qualifying voir dire occurs as well as the manner and conditions under which the questions are posed.

However, some anecdotal evidence suggests that the process of asking death versus life qualifying questions in open court has a "differential effect" on prospective jurors such that those who strongly favor the death penalty may not as readily identify themselves as those who very strongly oppose. In several capital cases in California whose juries were selected at around the time that general attitudes toward the death penalty were at an all-time high, some 16.2% of several hundred prospective jurors said they were so strongly opposed to the death penalty that they might not be entirely fair, while only 1.7% indicated that they supported the death penalty so strongly that their fairness might be compromised.[54] But here, too—in light of changes in death penalty views and variations in the kinds of questions that are posed—it is difficult to know with actual certainty over time and across jurisdiction.

Modern Death Qualification Practices, on Balance

The various doctrinal changes that occurred since my original death quali- fication process study was completed include a *Witt*-based broadening of the standard of exclusion, a *Hovey*-inspired tendency to conduct death qualifi- cation under individual, sequestered conditions, and a *Morgan*-mandated requirement to life as well as death qualify the jury. What are their likely effects on the social psychological features of the process described earlier?

As table 6.3 suggests, it unfortunately does not appear that the process

Table 6.3
Process Effects and Current Legal Doctrines

Social Psychological Component	Negative Effect Reduced by:		
	Witt-Based Broadened Standard	*Hovey*-Type Sequestered Voir Dire	*Morgan*-Required Life Qualification
Implication of guilt	No	No	No
Effect of imagining an event	No	No	No
Desensitization effects	No	Some	No
Anchoring effects	No	No	No
Public affirmation	No	Some	Some
Legal disapproval of death penalty opposition	No	Some	Yes

effect is likely to be much affected. Except for one or two of the specific social psychological components described earlier in this chapter, the biasing effects are likely to remain or, in some instances, even increase. For example, *Witt*'s broadening of the standard of exclusion should not have any moderating influence on the process effect. In fact, if *Witt* voir dire is conducted in open court, in the presence of other veniremen, it might result in a longer period of repetitive questioning for a greater number of potential jurors. This, in turn, would likely intensify this aspect of the process effect.

Similarly, there is no reason to expect that conducting death-qualifying voir dire under individual, sequestered conditions would temper or reduce the various social psychological forces at work. In fact, although the repetitiveness of the questioning would be lessened (because jurors would not be present during the questioning of others), sequestered voir dire exposes every prospective juror to direct questioning about his or her death penalty attitude. For some jurors, this intense, personal focus might make an even more powerful impression of the implication of guilt and some of the other biasing effects.

Similarly, life qualification seems unlikely to significantly affect most aspects of the process effect. Here, too, the additional questioning required to identify ADPs represents additional time and attention devoted to the issue of punishment in advance of determining guilt, adding to and reinforcing most of the negative effects that are likely to result. On the other hand, the main positive effect of life qualification on the capital jury selection process is that prospective jurors are not necessarily exposed to the one-sided, apparent pro-death-penalty message that prevailed before this more balanced examination of both ends of the death penalty attitude spectrum was mandated.

Of course, this moderating effect depends on achieving a genuine balance in the nature and tenor of the questioning. Many critics of life-qualifying voir dire argue that capital jury selection still focuses on whether prospective jurors "are able to impose the death penalty" (rather than whether they *equally* "are able to impose life imprisonment"). If this criticism is accurate, it is unclear whether much moderating of this aspect of the process effect actually occurs. Similarly, the possibility that prospective jurors who might watch others excused on the basis of one or the other attitude toward the death penalty (implicitly suggesting a legal "preference" for one view) would have the effect "balanced" by life qualification depends on roughly comparable numbers of exclusions from the opposite ends of the attitude spectrum. Yet, as one attorney has observed, "although it certainly would help even the scales to have prospective jurors see others sent home for saying they could not consider life as an option," given the disparity in the numbers of each kind of exclusion in many jurisdictions, "potential jurors will often witness several death penalty opponents' excusals without ever witnessing a single life sentence opponent's similar excusal."[55]

Conclusion

The vast majority of persons currently on death rows across the country have been convicted and sentenced to die by specially selected death-qualified jurors. Thousands more have been tried, convicted, and given lesser sentences by the same kind of unique jury.[56] As this chapter and the preceding one have made clear, the inherent fairness of these verdicts is suspect. Indeed, the biasing effects of death qualification have been unusually well documented in a variety of social science studies. This research underscores that— at this crucial first stage of an actual capital trial—the group of potential jurors is significantly altered by the exclusion of those persons whose death penalty attitudes are deemed legally unacceptable. Moreover, as I have tried to show in this chapter, the screening process itself appears to significantly change the jurors who pass through it. Both kinds of effects operate in tandem to increase the probability that convictions and death sentences will result.

Although most analyses of the death qualification process have focused on its tendency to produce conviction-prone juries, there are additional dimensions to its biasing effects. Obviously, a jury composed only of persons who publicly state they *can* impose the death penalty is more likely to do so than a jury not selected with this capacity specifically in mind. Capital jury selection procedures that systematically exclude a disproportionate number of persons strongly opposed to the death penalty from any subsequent participation also convey the not-so-subtle message that the legitimate and favored position in the legal system is one supporting death penalty imposition.

Moreover, prospective jurors are often asked repeatedly whether they can "follow the law" by imposing the death penalty. Indeed, depending on how these death-qualifying questions are posed, some jurors may infer that the law actually requires them to reach death verdicts. Even though the requirement that courts pose life-qualifying questions is now in effect in these cases, the general tenor of the questioning seems to suggest that it is the jurors' ability to impose death that is at issue. In this way, death qualification may still resemble a conditioning process through which jurors subtly relinquish their power to deviate from the outcome they have inferred "the law" seems to favor.

In fact, given the critical role that individual attitudes generally appear to play in understanding certain kinds of social behavior (such as obedience to authority),[57] it is possible that the personal characteristics of death-qualified jurors render them especially receptive to arguments that they have made some implicit "promise" to the court by which their expressed willingness to impose death must be abided through deliberation and verdict.[58] If so, then, in at least some cases the death penalty may be meted out by persons who are unsure of its moral appropriateness in light of the particular facts of the case before them, but who believe that the legal process already has secured their commitment to render such a verdict.

It is sometimes suggested that the mere prospect of death penalty imposition will lead jurors to be more conscientious in their evaluation of the evidence in a capital case and more cautious in reaching their verdicts. There may be some merit to this suggestion. Other things being equal, we would certainly expect rational decision makers to proceed somewhat more carefully as the consequences of their decision became more serious. Yet, as applied to capital juries, both the composition and process effects of death qualification appear to undermine these otherwise natural tendencies. Death-qualified jurors begin with a crime-control rather than due process orientation that leads them to weigh the costs of harsh errors differently from others. Moreover, the process by which they are selected requires them to publicly affirm their willingness to impose the death penalty, and to do so in a legal atmosphere that seems to favor this view. Thus, death qualification undercuts the rational response of increased caution that we would expect to see manifested in the normative case by non-death-qualified juries.

Finally, no matter how these more subtle, social psychological processes actually play out among the members of any particular capital jury, note that death qualification facilitates death sentencing in this fundamental way: It ensures that the decision about whether any capital defendant lives or dies is made only by jurors who, in varying degrees, support capital punishment. In this sense, capital juries can only represent the conscience of one part of the community—the part that collectively tilts toward death. The fact that the legal system does not trust death penalty decision making to a group that reflects a broad and unbiased cross-section of the community says something unsettling yet important about the nature of the process in which it asks citizens to participate.

7

Structural Aggravation
Moral Disengagement in the
Capital Trial Process

[W]hat we want to cultivate is appropriate compassion based on reasonable judgments. . . . [W]e need to ask ourselves what the particular obstacles to appropriate compassion are in our society.
—Martha Nussbaum, *Upheavals of Thought: The Intelligence of Emotions* (2001)

In this chapter I examine some of the ways that the capital trial process itself helps to facilitate the death-sentencing process. Prospective jurors come to the courthouse already having been elaborately prepared to perform the lethal task that the state may ask them to undertake. Exposure to media misinformation, often frighteningly graphic images of stylized violence, and the narrow interpretive frames I discussed in chapters 2 and 3 have shaped many jurors' expectations long before any evidence has been presented. And, as the last two chapters have made clear, death qualification ensures that capital jurors have been carefully selected on the basis of a stated willingness to impose the death penalty in whatever case they believe it is appropriate.

Soon, however, they will be asked to contemplate doing something few if any civilians in our society are ever called on to do. Capital jury service involves more than merely supporting pro-death-penalty policies in the abstract, or voting for political candidates who give voice to the public's anger over violent crime or the desire for retribution in the case of an especially egregious case. Eventually, in the course of a capital trial, citizen-jurors may be asked to go beyond merely making a theoretical commitment to impose the death penalty in some hypothetical situation. Death penalty trials represent a rare moment in criminal jurisprudence in which jurors—not judges—bear the burden of making a sentencing decision that encompasses the stark and profound choice between life and death.

Thus, unlike most citizens, voters, and politicians for whom the death penalty remains a mere abstraction, capital jurors have more daunting psychological barriers to confront and, for some, to cross. Under *ordinary* circumstances, of course, a group of 12 normal, law-abiding persons would not be capable of calmly, rationally, and seriously discussing the killing of another. Such people would never be expected not only to decide that another person should, in fact, die, but then to take actions intended to bring that death about. Yet this is exactly what death penalty trials require of many capital jurors.

In this chapter I argue that, in order to facilitate the crossing of so many psychological barriers and prohibitions, an *extraordinary* set of conditions must obtain. As part of the system of death sentencing, additional steps of some kind must be taken to somehow "enable" the participation of ordinary people in this potentially deadly course of action. I discuss some of the legal and psychological mechanisms that are employed in death penalty law and in capital trial practice to bridge the gulf between the deep-seated inhibitions of capital jurors and state-sanctioned violence of the most profound sort.[1]

My discussion of the effects of these mechanisms is somewhat more speculative than the analysis of many of the other problematic features of death sentencing addressed elsewhere in this book. Quite frankly, there is less direct empirical research on this stage of the process than others. For obvious reasons, it is difficult if not impossible to simulate complex capital trials in ways that would allow the systematic study of all of their component parts. However, the nature and effect of the mechanisms that operate during the trial stage of death penalty cases are grounded in sound social psychological theory and confirmed in empirical research done in closely related contexts. Their cumulative influence on the death-sentencing process is worthy of comment and concern.

Mechanisms of Moral Disengagement in Death Penalty Trials

Writing about judges who participate in the act of death sentencing, Robert Cover commented on the "special measure of . . . reluctance and abhorrence" that they are required to overcome in order to do the "deed of capital punishment."[2] Capital *jurors,* of course, share none of a judge's prior socialization into the norms of well-coordinated legal violence, and they lack the judicial experience that would accustom them to its routine application. As a result, they must travel a greater psychological distance in order to overcome the special measure of reluctance and abhorrence with which the choice to impose a death sentence presents them. Yet the system of capital punishment depends on somehow overcoming these natural inhibitions and creating an atmosphere that facilitates the jurors' lethal behavior. The fact that each year several hundred juries in the United States, composed of otherwise normal, highly law-abiding, nonviolent citizens, are able to traverse the moral and psychological barriers against taking a life, and many times that number

seriously contemplate crossing these barriers, suggests that the soc
chological mechanisms in place to accomplish this task are surprising
fective.[3]

To explain how the legal system facilitates death sentencing in the im
mediate courtroom context, I rely on what have been called "mechanisms of
moral disengagement"[4]—psychologist Albert Bandura's term for the social
and cognitive processes that distance people from the moral implications of
their actions—as they function to facilitate the lethal behavior of capital
jurors. Thus, in addition to the components of the death-sentencing process
I have already discussed—ones that, except for death qualification, operate
primarily outside the courtroom—capital punishment depends further on
the implementation of various legal procedures within the trial process itself
that give lay decision makers even greater distance from the realities of their
decisions. These procedures and practices better enable capital jurors to sentence a defendant to die.

Mechanisms of moral disengagement serve to distort the human context
in which capital jurors operate. They reframe the decisions that jurors feel
they are being called upon to make, and do so in ways that remove much of
the moral tenor from the decisions themselves. These mechanisms also minimize jurors' sense of personal agency and awareness of the full range of
consequences that flow from their actions. Mechanisms of moral disengagement undermine the compassionate impulses that might otherwise be evoked
as human beings learn about the often profound challenges and struggles to
which many capital defendants have succumbed. In this sense, these mechanisms limit the effect of mitigating testimony that might influence jurors to
spare a capital defendant's life in capital penalty trials.

As I point out in the next chapter, "mitigation" and "aggravation"—the
two key terms that jurors in most jurisdictions are asked to "weigh" or balance in reaching their sentencing verdicts—are not well defined in jury instructions and are often poorly understood by jurors. For precisely this reason, the structure and tenor of the capital trial itself often plays an important
role in shaping how jurors come to understand these two key terms and
whether and how they apply them to the facts of the case at hand. In this
context, "mitigation" operates to undermine or overcome the tendency to
be punitive, and mitigating evidence is anything that in effect minimizes the
human response to punish harshly. Specifically, mitigation serves to neutralize, reduce, or eliminate the desire or need to react or respond to a capital
defendant by taking his life (through the imposition of a death sentence).

On the other hand, "aggravation" and aggravating evidence accomplish
the opposite effect, increasing the tendency to punish harshly. In this context,
aggravation makes capital jurors more likely to condemn a defendant to die.
Because the mechanisms of moral disengagement that I discuss in this chapter function to facilitate and intensify the punitive responses of jurors, they
represent what can be termed "structural aggravation." Although they appear

statute, these are the psychological factors that are
's of death sentencing, serving to make death verdicts

he following pages, the mechanisms of disengage-
f several different ways. Some of them come about
l structure and sequencing of evidence with which
l. Evidence and testimony that is likely to have a
on jurors occurs first and cannot be effectively
ated until the very last stage of the trial. Some of the moral
gagement derives from the formal, legalistic atmosphere of the trial
itself, and some from legal doctrines that prohibit jurors from learning about
certain issues that might balance the moral equation with which they are
working. And some of the disengagement comes about through omission—a
result of the fact that the law does not require attorneys to contextualize
capital defendants and their lives in ways that allow jurors to fully analyze
and weigh the issues of moral culpability that are supposed to guide their
decision making. As a result, in too many cases the opportunity is forgone,
and jurors render verdicts on the basis of limited and even inadequate information.

Dehumanization and Capital Violence

The first mechanism of moral disengagement that encourages jurors to overcome the prohibition against lethal violence is the *dehumanization* of the
capital defendant. It is a virtual truism among capital defense attorneys that
they must "bring the defendant to life so that the jury will want to let him
live." Law professor Joan Howarth has decried Supreme Court decisions that
act to limit what she termed the "real point" of the individualized capital
sentencing hearings, "which is to permit the jury to hear about humanizing
aspects of the defendant simply in order to be sure that the jury may see him
as a human being."[5] But why is this so important? The answer lies in the
comparative ease with which people are able to act destructively—even to
respond with deadly force—against targets that are not viewed as persons.
As Bandura put it, "[p]eople seldom condemn punitive conduct—in fact,
they create justifications for it—when they are directing their aggression at
persons who have been divested of their humanness."[6]

Social psychologists and others have documented many of the morally
disengaging aspects of dehumanization. Sociologists also have long known
that institutional mistreatment is facilitated by the dehumanization of patients and inmates. One of them termed the process of systematic institutional dehumanization a "degradation ceremony,"[7] while another described
it as a "mortification ritual"[8]—figuratively, the killing of the individual self
to be remade in the institutional image of something less than a full person.

Dehumanization operates to cognitively distance people from the moral

implications of their actions.[9] For example, as Tom Tyler noted, dehumanization "prevents the moral issues which are normally raised when harm is
being done to other human beings from being raised in a particular instance."[10] Perhaps this helps to explain why rituals of killing, whether state
sanctioned (as in executions or war) or on an individual level, almost always
involve the systematic dehumanizing of the victim, the stripping of human
qualities from the target of the lethal act. Indeed, preparations for war almost
always seem to include some form of dehumanization of the enemy.[11] As one
theorist put it, "it is justifiable . . . to kill those who are monsters or inhuman
because of their abominable traits, or those who are 'mere animals' (coons,
pigs, rats, lice, etc.), or those whose political views are unthinkably heinous
(Huns, communists, fascists, traitors)."[12]

Indeed, because "[c]apital punishment is warfare writ small,"[13] it is not
surprising to find this mechanism of moral disengagement at work in the
death-sentencing process. In fact, the history of the death penalty is replete
with examples of the ways in which dehumanization has facilitated state-
sanctioned killing. The tendency to extend mercy to those with whom we
feel kinship was recognized in Thomas Green's study of jury nullification by
13th- and 14th-century English juries. He observed that "[t]he leniency ac-
corded villagers by their neighbors may be put down to favoritism, but given
what jury behavior in homicide suggests, that may be just another way of
saying that jurors thought the rules too harsh when forced to apply them to
persons whom they knew well enough to identify with."[14]

However, capital trials help jurors to erect psychological barriers between
themselves and the defendant that facilitate dehumanization. Some of these
barriers derive from the distancing formality that attaches to legal language
and court proceedings generally. As one legal commentator has noted, "the
emotional, physical, and experiential aspects of being human have by and
large been banished from the better legal neighborhoods and from explicit
recognition in legal discourse. . . ."[15] Another acknowledged that the courtroom setting is "hardly intimate or otherwise conducive to 'knowing' someone"[16] and that anyone who advocates the empathetic understanding of a
defendant in a legal proceeding "must favor radical restructuring of court
procedures to make them more congenial" to such things.[17] Others have
argued that normative legal storytelling "disfigures" individuals[18] and "distorts" social arrangements and their descriptions.[19] And law professor Toni
Massaro has observed that, although trial procedures permit a limited
amount of personalizing storytelling, "all stories cannot dominate, and . . .
law often privileges the stories of the powerful and drowns out the voices of
the weak and marginal."[20]

Emotional distancing and the denaturing effects of legal formality are
especially damaging in death penalty cases because of the necessity that—to
be fair to the defendant whose life they hold in their hands—the capital jury
must experience him as a person. Yet, as Howarth wrote, like most other
areas of law, capital jurisprudence rigidly enforces a "rule-based, distanced,

and reasoned decisionmaking" that is always preferred over the "ever-present contextual, proximate, and emotional aspects of the decision to kill." Howarth argued that the more emotional elements of the death- sentencing process are "vehemently hidden and disowned" in death penalty procedure and doctrine.[21] Hiding and disowning the emotional content of a capital trial (the content that comes about as a result of grappling with the defendant's personhood) may morally disengage in ways that help facilitate death verdicts.[22]

In addition to the emotionally distant and decontextualized legal language by which the process proceeds, dehumanization is fostered by the structure of the capital trial itself. That is, it builds on the preexisting media stereotypes about the inhumanity of persons convicted of murder by delaying opportunities to humanize the capital defendant until the very last phase of the trial itself. As one lawyer put it: "While the state has often presented the evidence in the guilt phase that arguably makes the homicide especially heinous, the penalty phase is usually the defense's first opportunity to present to the factfinder the personal aspects of the defendant's life. . . . [I]t would be an unusual case where the defendant's family history and character were introduced in the guilt phase."[23] Until this point—days, weeks, or even months into the trial—most capital defendants have sat mute in the courtroom, each one a kind of criminological Rorschach card onto which jurors are invited to project their deepest fears and anger.

Thus, the dehumanization of the defendant comes about in part because of the prolonged period during which the jury has been encouraged both to regard him as less than a person and to perceive him as little more than an autonomous agent of violence, one who lacks a social context and, very often, a traumatic history that may help to account for that violence. By the time defense attorneys are afforded a formal opportunity to begin the process of humanization, there has been much time for these attitudes and impressions to crystallize and rigidify. Defense attorneys who hope to avoid the death penalty for their client somehow must undo the damage that this delay has done to the jury's view of the defendants and to their full understanding of the root causes of his violent behavior. Perhaps not surprisingly, at least one researcher found that at the conclusion of the guilt phase and before any penalty-phase testimony had been presented, twice as many capital jurors believed the defendant should be sentenced to death as believed life was the appropriate verdict.[24]

The ordering of the issues placed before the capital jury not only increases dehumanization but also creates an implicit contrast between the violence of the defendant and the violence that the jury is later invited to authorize. Research tells us generally that whenever events are compared in sequence, "the first one colors how the second one is perceived and judged." In capital trial contexts, the more flagrantly inhumane the acts that initially are judged, the more "one's own destructive conduct will appear trifling or even benevolent" later on.[25] In this way, capital jurors—especially those with qualms about the death penalty—can be morally disengaged from having to grapple with the human consequences of their sentencing verdict by virtue of the implicit and sequential comparison between the actions of the defendant and their own.[26]

There is one final way in which the capital trial may contribute to the dehumanization of the defendant and morally disengage jurors from the decision before them. An effective case in mitigation requires attorneys to genuinely humanize the defendant so that jurors may overcome preexisting stereotypes and expectations about the nature of violence, ones amplified by the aspects of the trial process to which I have referred. Yet experienced capital litigators have repeatedly warned that too many defense attorneys lack the kind of training and professional experience that is needed to find and develop "humanizing" testimony. In addition, far too many of them are denied the time and resources it would take to accomplish these tasks properly. As a result, little if any such testimony is effectively gathered, prepared, or presented in many penalty-phase cases.[27] Indeed, two legal commentators concluded that "it is commonplace in many states for trial counsel to fail to present *any* evidence or argument at all during the punishment phase of a capital trial."[28] Moreover, defense attorneys in many jurisdictions are overmatched and outspent by experienced prosecutors who have the state's considerable resources at their disposal.

The effect of the disparity in resources is amplified by the fact that the prosecution's implicit and overarching "theory" of the typical capital case generally comports with stereotypical beliefs about crime and punishment that are widely held by citizens and jurors. That is, the notion that the defendant's crime stems entirely from his evil makeup and that he therefore deserves to be judged and punished exclusively on the basis of his presumably free, morally blameworthy choices is rooted in a long-standing cultural ethos that capital jurors (like most citizens) have been conditioned to accept uncritically.[29] Moreover, it meshes perfectly with the well-documented tendency of people to commit what social psychologists call the "fundamental attribution error"—providing causal explanations for the behavior of others in largely dispositional or personal (as opposed to situational or contextual) terms.[30] As a result, the typical juror's preexisting framework for understanding behavior is highly compatible with the basic terms of the typical prosecutorial narrative.

This means that defense attorneys have a greater implicit burden to meet in capital penalty trials. They must, in essence, overcome what many jurors will regard as "commonsense." When they lack the training and resources to properly assemble all available mitigation, it is a burden they are not likely to meet. This means that many capital defendants will have their lives ended by juries that were never given a chance to truly understand them—juries that were morally disengaged from the humanity of the person on trial because they never received the information his attorney was unable—for lack of skill, effort, or resources—to present.

Violence Against the Deviant, Different, and Deficient

A second way that jurors are morally disengaged during the capital trial process is closely related to dehumanization. Philosopher Martha Nussbaum has observed that "compassion can be blocked by a sense of distance and unlikeness."[31] Beyond preventing compassion, the tendency to regard others as defective, foreign, deviant, or fundamentally different facilitates their punitive mistreatment. In wartime, in fact, the distinguishing characteristics of foreign enemies have been exaggerated in such a way as to emphasize their fundamental difference from the rest of us; it is not necessary to depict them as fully less than human in order to facilitate killing them.[32] Indeed, the "foreign menace" itself has been used in numerous political campaigns to create false unity among citizens that is founded on little more than common hatred of the different "other." Science and pseudoscience have been used to "prove" defect and deviance among groups targeted for cruel treatment and even extermination.[33]

Whether in wartime or not, there is much research documenting the tendency to derogate—diminish, reduce, belittle—those persons whom we intend to punish, or who already have been subjected to mistreatment.[34] As Samuel Pillsbury put it: "The more we can designate a person as fundamentally different from ourselves, the fewer moral doubts we have about condemning and hurting that person."[35] In the case of criminal defendants— many of whom come from preexisting derogated categories in our society— their perceived status as defective or fundamentally different makes them easier to punish.

In Martha Duncan's analysis of what she termed "metaphors of filth" in the criminal justice system (including some 34 appellate cases in which the prosecutor's reference to the defendant as "filth" was at issue), she highlighted various purposes served by portraying criminals as "dirty and slimy," including the way this kind of imagery cognitively reinforces the separation of "criminals" from the "noncriminals."[36] Duncan also astutely noted that attempts to bridge this divide between criminals and "normal" people posed a significant psychological threat to persons so intent on harshly punishing wrongdoers: "To appreciate the profundity of this challenge, one has only to remember Victor Hugo's character Javert in *Les Misérables*. Toward the end of the novel, forced to recognize the noble qualities in his criminal prey, Javert despairs of life's meaning and drowns himself."[37]

Of course, few capital jurors truly will ever know—by experience, identification, or intuition—the realities of the lives they are called on to judge in the way that Javert came to know Jean Valjean. But the structure of the capital trial does little to engender such human understanding. Traditional guilt-phase inquiries depict defendants as the agents of violence, never its victims, further distancing them from the rest of us. In addition to this focus in the guilt phase of the trial, the presentation of aggravating evidence—

including the aggravating features of the present crime, aspects of the defendant's past criminal history, and admissible "victim impact" testimony that underscores the human costs of those criminal acts—occurs at the outset of the penalty trial. Thus much of the trial itself is devoted to highlighting the defendant's criminality, absent a meaningful context in which it can be understood.

Just as with the process of dehumanization, the only real opportunity to prevent the "otherness" of a capital defendant (intensified by media-driven and culturally supported inferences about the internal causes of his criminality) from facilitating the jury's moral disengagement comes in the final stage of a capital penalty trial. Here is where the scope of potentially admissible evidence is significantly broadened, in theory allowing the defendant's often radically different behavior and lifestyle to be placed in a social context that permits the jury to understand it in human terms. However, by this time in the trial process capital jurors typically will have encountered—and been encouraged to dwell on—the nature and consequences of the defendant's capital crime and criminal history. Moreover, they will have done so long before they have learned anything about the larger context in which his actions occurred or the life history of the person who committed them (if, indeed, they learn about this context or history at all).

Although there are practical reasons for this sequencing, and it corresponds to the order of proof in other kinds of criminal cases, it may have especially morally disengaging consequences for capital cases. Because of the implicit emphasis on the otherness of the capital defendant until this crucial juncture late in the trial, the difficult challenge of bridging some of the psychological gap between defendants and those who judge them is made much greater. Thus, the ordering of the evidence that is built into the structure of the capital trial postpones (and may prevent entirely) the development of what law professor Lynn Henderson has called "empathetic narratives," those that involve, at least, "descriptions of concrete human situations and their meanings to the persons affected in the context of their lives."[38]

Capital jurors are entitled to hear this empathic narrative in order to engage in the "moral inquiry into the culpability of the defendant"[39] that modern death penalty doctrine requires them to conduct. If the jurors are to avoid the disengagement from defendants that comes from exaggerating the differences between them, then defendants must somehow be shown in settings or situations familiar to jurors. To be sure, "[t]he best way to draw the decision makers closer to the defendant is to tell them his story."[40] Attorneys have to present testimony about the larger context of their client's life that shows "the penalty jurors a portrait of their client that humanizes him: that is, makes connections between the client and the jurors."[41] Autobiographical[42] and ethnographic[43] accounts of the structural disadvantages of race and class underscore many of the difficulties that capital defendants and others like them have confronted as well as the prevalence of violence as a common adaptation under these circumstances.[44]

Thus, the otherness of the defendant to which most of the capital trial is devoted to establishing can only be overcome by providing an opportunity to understand the ways in which the defendant's destructive acts may be the culmination of a failed struggle against significant odds, or a lifetime of confronting and attempting to overcome formidable barriers, disadvantages, and (what proved to be) overwhelming circumstances. If jurors are not shown the ways in which lapses into lethal violence, outbursts of destructive anger, and even longer-term predatory habits often have compelling social histories and psychologically powerful social contexts associated with them that—although they certainly do not justify or legally excuse the actions—make them more understandable, they will proceed with their decision making distanced and alienated from the life they have been called on to judge.

Here, too, because legal doctrines have failed in the past to *require* that jurors be educated about these contexts, and many states correspondingly have failed to provide the resources with which to train attorneys and enable them to adequately explore these issues, death penalty trials often have served to de-emphasize any common human connections between jurors and defendants.[45] Instead, the proceedings serve to highlight the differences between them in ways that make the dissimilarities appear essential rather than situational. In many cases, they encourage jurors to understand the defendant's behavior in terms of his fundamental defectiveness.

Again, the failure of capital penalty trials to explicitly address the contextual explanations for the many individual differences between the defendant and the jurors—including differences in violent behavior—and the historical and situational patterns that help to explain (albeit not excuse) the defendant's conduct, gives capital jurors little choice but to morally disengage from him.[46] Once they do, prohibitions against lethal violence are relaxed, and the tendency to return death sentences increased.

Amplifying Dangerousness: Death Verdicts as Vicarious Self-Defense

People often react aggressively toward those who are perceived as frightening or are believed to pose a physical or psychological threat. Under these circumstances, we morally disengage from the potential consequences of our own violent behavior and regress to a more fundamental principle—self-preservation. In the extreme case, of course, this is the basis of the legal doctrine of self-defense, whose venerability reflects the law's recognition of the psychological power of fear to propel aggression.[47] Indeed, one of the most powerful emotional arguments that can be lodged in favor of the death penalty itself can be couched in precisely these terms—that we execute others out of the belief that this will protect ourselves and our community from future violence.

By highlighting and dwelling on the fearsomeness of the defendant—again, for the most part, absent a context and explanation—the capital trial process activates this mechanism of moral disengagement. To be sure, much of the fear that a capital jury experiences does not depend on a legal process of embellishment for its force and power. The basic facts of the typical capital murder case are themselves frightening and the jury's reaction is natural and inevitable. Yet, notwithstanding the universality of this emotional response, as Austin Sarat has noted, prosecutors put tremendous effort into "the graphic presentation and representation of the murder, as well as the technique used to bring about death and its consequences" in a capital trial and often will spare no expense "bring[ing] to life the violence outside law."[48]

Here, too, the structure of a capital trial ensures that the "weapons and wounds, instrumentalities and effects"[49] of the defendant's violence will always precede any acknowledgment of the humanity or personhood of the one responsible for it. Accordingly, many capital jurors will be frightened of the defendant and provoked to punitive and vengeful feelings, long before they are exposed to any other information about him. Similarly, note that the overall structure of the trial is replicated in the capital penalty phase where, as I have noted, the prosecution is first to present evidence of aggravating factors. Especially when this presentation includes testimony about prior crimes that the defendant may have committed (something that is considered an aggravating factor under virtually all capital statutes), this part of the trial may focus on the same types of frightening "weapons and wounds, instrumentalities and effects" that likely were at the core of the earlier guilt-phase trial.

Of course, defense attorneys are not permitted to present mitigation that moderates the jurors' fear of their client until the very final stage of the penalty trial; it is usually their first and only opportunity to humanize the defendant and explain his deviance in a way that links it to common human experience. Because the vast majority of the capital trial is devoted to dramatic renderings of the defendant's prior crimes and acts of individual violence, its structure helps to ensure that violence outside the law will be presented to the jurors without context, leaving them with little on which to rely for explanation but the misleading stereotypes and partial truths to which they have been exposed long before entering the courtroom.

Not surprisingly, perhaps, in postverdict interviews conducted by the Capital Jury Project and others, many capital jurors have reported being concerned about the defendant's future dangerousness whether or not that issue was raised explicitly at trial. For example, a South Carolina study found that capital jurors discussed this issue more than they discussed the defendant's criminal past, his background or social history, or any of his personal attributes (like intelligence or remorse). Moreover, despite having no special knowledge or expertise with which to analyze the question, approximately three-quarters of them concluded that the evidence presented at trial established that the defendant *would* be dangerous in the future.[50]

This conclusion is odds with what is known about the very low levels of violence not only among death- and life-sentenced prisoners but also among condemned prisoners who were subsequently released from prison. In fact, even in Texas, death-sentenced prisoners—who, by statute, have been judged explicitly by jurors to represent a risk of future dangerousness—are *not* a disproportionate threat to institutional order, to other inmates, or to custodial staff.[51] Nonetheless, the fear of future dangerousness persists among capital jurors there and in most jurisdictions. In this way, the structure of the capital trial and the focus on "weapons and wounds," among other things, appear to distort the jurors' views of the defendant, and facilitate their death-sentencing behavior.

The fear of capital defendants is intensified by another misconception that goes uncorrected in many capital trials—juror confusion over the alternatives to a death sentence. For example, the same South Carolina study referred to earlier found a significant difference between the amount of time life-sentencing jurors thought a defendant who did not get the death penalty would spend in prison compared to death-sentencing jurors, who believed the defendant would be released much earlier if they did not sentence him to die.[52] Similarly, another study found that three-quarters of those jurors who sentenced defendants to death believed he would spend less than 20 years in prison if he did not get the death penalty, and an equally high percentage of death sentencers reported being concerned about the possibility that "the defendant might return to society" if they let him live.[53]

Jurors voice these kinds of concerns even in states in which capital-sentencing statutes give them the option of sentencing to life without the possibility of parole as an alternative to the death penalty. For example, as I reported in chapter 4, my colleagues and I found that Californians in general did not believe that life without parole meant the defendant would never be released from prison. We also found that death-qualified respondents were significantly more likely to hold this mistaken belief.[54] Moreover, this widespread misconception gave rise to serious concerns voiced by actual capital jurors in California.[55]

As two researchers summarized: "Refusing to inform jurors about the statutorily mandated length of nondeath sentences appears to lead jurors to sentence to death when they would not do so if they were more fully informed of the law."[56] Of course, jurors who mistakenly believe that capital defendants will be released from prison may see themselves as defending the community against a threat—the threat of the defendant returning to live among them in the free world—that is nonexistent. Here, too, the failure to explicitly debunk commonly held misconceptions may facilitate their death-sentencing behavior.

There are several other ways that concerns over dangerousness may morally disengage capital jurors from their sentencing verdicts. Although it makes perfect sense to focus capital jurors on the defendant's violence, as I have noted, this typically occurs long before there is any real opportunity to contextualize the defendant's life. The fact that many capital juries are given only a *partial* understanding of the origins of this violence is likely to intensify the fear that is engendered. Jurors who learn that capital defendants were victims long before they became victimizers may be less likely to fear them, but this information is kept from jurors in many cases until long after it can do many defendants any good.

When jurors learn about the defendant's violence absent its context, they are deprived of any opportunity to connect his criminality to early experiences in settings or situations in which he was himself the fearful target of brutal mistreatment, chronic neglect, abandonment, and the like. In fact, however, most capital defendants have been both the victims *and* perpetrators of violence.[57] This is the tragic underlying logic of the aggression about which capital jurors ultimately must reach a judgment and factor into their decisions about blameworthiness. But this insight cannot be shared with jurors until the last part of the final stage of the trial.

Indeed, empirical research indicates that most habits of violence and aggressive demeanors have been learned *defensively*—usually in childhood and often in response to chronically abusive, harmful, or threatening circumstances that defendants certainly did not choose, and over which they had little or no control. We now know that abused children are much more likely to engage in violence as adults, giving rise to what some have called a "cycle of violence,"[58] and that there appears to be a relationship between the kind of abuse suffered as a child and the nature of the aggression manifested in adulthood.[59] Persons accused and convicted of capital murder are very often the victims of physical abuse and chronic neglect as children.[60] In addition, they often come from homes in which their mothers and other siblings also have been physically attacked in their presence. We now know that exposure to the abuse of others can be equally or even more psychologically damaging than direct victimization.[61]

Other social structural factors over which capital defendants have had no control also play an important role in the origins of their violent behavior. For example, we know that "poverty and lower-class status are marked by relatively punitive and coercive patterns of parenting,"[62] and that families undergoing economic pressure are prone to such critical events as unemployment and divorce, as well as child abuse.[63] In addition, poverty itself appears to create increased levels of depression, impulsivity, low self-esteem, and delinquency among children, in part because of its effects on parenting behavior.[64] Finally, poverty—especially persistent poverty—and its links to child maltreatment, are systematically related to race.[65] African American children are more likely not only to experience poverty per se but also to confront poverty that is "marked by its persistence and geographic concentration."[66]

All these factors may have played an important role in shaping the defendant's violent behavior. Testimony that addresses these factors can demonstrate to jurors that his fearsomeness as an adult may be rooted in his adaptations to the many threatening situations and circumstances to which he was forcibly exposed as a child or adolescent. Yet—because of the absence of any legal mandate to provide it, or the lack of resources with which to undertake the appropriately elaborate investigation to uncover it, or the failure to provide well-trained, competent attorneys and experts to assemble and present it—many capital jurors are denied access to the kind of broad-based contextualizing information that would help them to begin to understand the origins and limits of the defendant's violence. Of course, if capital jurors are never told these things, they have little choice but to attribute the defendant's violence to his evil nature or innate malevolence. Such attributions undoubtedly make defendants appear more frightening and dangerous, lead jurors to fear them even more, and make punitive sentencing responses more likely.

The morally disengaging effects of fear may be intensified by omitting other kinds of contextualizing information from capital trials. For example, jurors' understandable concerns about a defendant's potential future dangerousness would likely be moderated by learning that violent behavior in free society is frequently *not* predictive of violent behavior in prison (largely because the nature of the environments themselves differ so greatly).[67] At one time, perhaps, societies simply lacked the capacity to safely contain their most violent citizens short of drastic measures like execution. But jurors now make the choice between life and death in the face of a very different set of options. Legal doctrines that prevent detailed discussions of actual prison conditions and characteristically high levels of prison security during the penalty phase of capital trial, or attorneys who have the option but nonetheless fail to inform capital jurors about the ways in which sophisticated prison surveillance and other control devices effectively monitor and restrain the behavior of maximum security prisoners, allow capital jury decision making to be governed by misconceptions.

Whenever the capital trial process fails to disabuse jurors of their stereotypes about the origins of criminal violence or neglects to educate them about the ability of modern prisons to control and contain even unruly prisoners, it fosters sentencing decisions that are based on exaggerated concerns about future dangerousness. But decisions premised on unjustified fears may give jurors license to ignore the moral complexities of the choice between life and death. The law's failure to impose an affirmative duty on attorneys and courts to address these misconceptions appears to invite error and facilitate death sentencing.

Minimizing the Personal Consequences of Capital Punishment

People can be morally disengaged from the punishments they impose when the hurtful effects of those punishments are made to seem small, insignificant, or remote. Any course of action is easier to take if its potential negative consequences—to one's self or others—are minimized. Psychological research suggests that acts of obedience, even acts of obedient aggression, are facilitated by an organizational context in which behavior is "fragmented" (i.e., removed from its consequences).[68] The classic Milgram obedience studies provided some experimental evidence for this proposition.[69] Most of the experimental conditions in these studies were structured in ways that avoided bringing the participants face-to-face with the painful consequences that their actions had for others.[70] Indeed, Milgram demonstrated empirically that the participants' increased proximity to the victim reduced the likelihood that they would administer apparently painful and dangerous levels of shock. In this and similar research settings, persons who are forced to "get involved" and feel responsible for the targets of their actions will be more likely to behave in a socially responsible (not blindly obedient) manner.[71]

In a related vein, social psychologist Herbert Kelman demonstrated that "routinization"—the organization of human action in such a way that there is no opportunity and seemingly no reason to consider moral issues in the course of performing it—is an especially effective technique for undermining ethical restraints against violence.[72] In this regard, language itself can be used to distance persons from the true nature of the activities in which they engage, euphemistically blurring or masking many of the moral consequences of aggression, and making it easier to initiate and to repeat. Thus, social scientists have noted that language can "obscure, mystify, or otherwise redefine acts of violence," such as when the act of killing in wartime is termed "wasting," "zapping," or "liquidating" the enemy.[73]

The modern execution ritual itself provides a poignant and instructive example. Robert Johnson described the way in which each member of the execution team he studied was drilled in one specific and very small part of the overall killing process. This not only allowed members to become practiced and efficient at their tasks but also to distance themselves from the final consequence of their collective, coordinated actions.[74] Moreover, the more the drill was performed, the more routine it became, minimizing the execution team member's opportunity for thoughtful reflection on the true consequences of the activity. The tasks were described in terms that belied their overall lethal consequences, so that participants were encouraged to disengage from the deadly actions in which they played a part.

Similarly, aspects of the capital trial process may facilitate death sentencing by diffusing responsibility, reducing or removing the moral tenor from much of the decision making, and minimizing the costs of a death sentence by failing to emphasize what such a verdict actually means. Using the Milgram studies as a point of departure, Robert Weisberg's classic article on capital jury decision making posed an important empirical question— "whether jurors artificially distance themselves from choices by relying on legal formalities."[75] Research has confirmed his suspicions that they do. For example, one study of Indiana capital jurors uncovered not only "juror misperception of the responsibility for the death sentencing function"[76] but also

widespread difficulty among jurors in accepting responsibility for the defendant's fate, and even doubts about the propriety of jurors like them performing the capital sentencing task in the first place.[77]

Indeed, the issue of responsibility loomed so large for one jury in this
study that a lone holdout juror was able to sway the others by dramatically
underscoring the consequences of their decision: "I told them, put the kid
in the chair. Now would you go up there throw the switch yourself? They
said well that's not my job. I said you are doing your job now. If you say go
ahead, that's the same as you are doing it."[78] Perhaps not surprisingly, despite
fairly consistent national data about capital jurors' inability to accurately
comprehend and recall sentencing instructions, this study found that most
Indiana jurors "remember vividly the portion of the judge's instructions that
talked about the jury making only 'a recommendation.' "[79]

Capital trials, as Sarat has observed, present jurors with skewed narratives of violence. Indeed, as he put it, "[t]he state compels the juror to view
. . . graphic representations [of the defendant's violence] and to grasp the
death producing instrumentalities which are given special evidentiary value
in the state's case against the accused."[80] In addition, the Supreme Court has
sanctioned the use of so-called victim-impact testimony in capital penalty
trials, authorizing prosecutors to go even further and, essentially, to require
that capital jurors directly confront and consider the full range of terrible
consequences that the defendant's violence has wrought—regardless of
whether or not those consequences were intended or foreseeable—and to
explore the myriad dimensions of grief and loss and longing that a killing
invariably produces.[81]

The use of victim impact testimony is justified in the interests of maxi-
mizing the amount of information available to jurors in the course of making
their death-sentencing decision. But this information may impede the jurors'
response to key aspects of the defense penalty-phase case. Thus, Martha
Nussbaum has argued that the victim narratives that are introduced into
capital penalty phases discourage the jurors' exercise of compassion toward
the defendant because "they lead our minds to focus with sympathy on the
sufferings of people who are more like ourselves, when that suffering has
been caused by someone unlike." This sympathy may be so overpowering
that it thwarts the jurors' effort to understand the person who has caused
the suffering. As Nussbaum says, it can make the jurors "feel that they need
not do the imaginative work necessary to understand the defendant's history"
as a result.[82]

Moreover, there is an asymmetry to the knowledge that capital jurors
are permitted to receive that may increase levels of moral disengagement.
Specifically, although the viewing of the violence of the capital crime is made
mandatory, and learning of its myriad (even unintended) consequences is
now commonplace, the law systematically and explicitly prevents capital jurors from learning anything comparable about the execution that they are
being asked to authorize.

Legal doctrine is clear and unyielding on this point. For example, in one California case the state supreme court ruled unequivocally that "[e]vidence of how the death penalty will be performed, as well as the nature and quality of life for one imprisoned for life without he possibility of parole, is properly excluded" from the jury's consideration.[83] These assertions come without any underlying analysis or reasoning; they simply are part of a broader rule that the nature of the punishment itself is "not relevant to any issue material to the choice of penalty."[84]

Whatever their intent, it seems clear that this doctrine and the one announced in *Payne v. Tennessee* are simultaneously "pulling the victim closer [to the jury] while pushing the defendant and the execution away. . . ."[85] If, on the one hand, the pain that has been brought on the victims is emphasized in the penalty trial where jurors must decide between life and death, then the pain that will be inflicted on the defendant by the punishments the jury is contemplating also seems relevant to their decision. Without intending to oversimplify the difficult and sensitive task of striking the right balance—how much detail and in what form should it be presented—only an equitable opportunity to highlight both sets of harms, past and future, seems fair.

Instead, Sarat's description from the trial he studied applies to capital trials elsewhere: "Jurors were presented with no images of the scene of the prospective execution, of the violence of electrocution. No such images were admissible or available for the juror eager to understand what he is being asked to authorize."[86] Capital jurors are exposed to—indeed, they may be required to view—vivid narratives of the defendant's violence and are systematically excluded from any exposure to the violence that they are being invited to inflict, and the one-sided way in which the law makes one set of consequences salient and another invisible operates to disengage jurors from the full moral implications of their actions.

In fact, research with capital jurors also shows that not only are the details of the execution ritual systematically hidden from them but that most believe it is unlikely ever to occur. For example, in a study of capital jurors in California and Oregon, Lorelei Sontag, Sally Constanzo, and I found that "verdict skepticism"—disbelief that the sentencing decisions they reached actually would be imposed—pervaded the deliberation process. As one juror put it: "We talked about the fact that if you have a hard time voting for the death penalty, are you really not just voting for life imprisonment? Because there hasn't been an execution in over 20 years in California. And so, you know, is it really more a statement than it is an actuality?"[87]

These sentiments were not unique to California where, in fact, at the time of our study, no one had been executed for a long time. Thus, Sarat found that capital jurors in Georgia—where this was not the case—were equally skeptical about whether death actually meant death or: "[T]hey don't put you to death. You sit on death row and get old."[88]

Indeed, the treatment of capital jurors in this regard mirrors the way the public itself is systematically misinformed about many of these issues and kept from confronting the whole truth about the execution process that is conducted in their name. In a case that facilitated the televising of criminal trials, Chief Justice Burger contended that there was a "fundamental, natural yearning to see justice done," which meant that crucial aspects of the administration of justice should not function in the dark. He concluded that little or no essential "community catharsis" could take place if justice was done "in any covert manner.' "[89] Yet the courts have not only permitted but *insisted* on this darkness with respect to executions. In fact, one commentator has argued that the real purpose of so-called private execution laws that regulate who can attend executions may be to prevent members of the general public from hearing more directly about the details of the process by which the state kills its citizens, a point he believes "is reinforced by several state statutes, which provide that executions only be conducted during the middle of the night or that the details of executions not be published at all."[90]

The debate that took place in California over a decade ago about televising executions is instructive. In *KQED v. Vasquez*,[91] a local public television station sued in federal court to compel the state's department of corrections to permit the first execution in the state in some 25 years to be televised. The *KQED* suit implied that the governor and his appointed officials—who were all staunch death penalty supporters—were restricting access because of the effect that publicizing executions was likely to have on popular support for capital punishment. Although the state refused to concede this, its legal reply brief indirectly supported the contention by focusing on the reactions of certain members of the public who, the state's attorneys argued, would be incensed by exposure to the sight of an execution from which they would otherwise be prohibited. Thus, they claimed that prisoners would become enraged and uncontrollable at the sight of the execution, that some members of the public might want to take revenge on those prison staff members who participated directly in it, and even that some members of the press might attempt to use their videotape equipment to break the glass-enclosed gas chamber and halt the execution.[92] When a group of California legislators introduced a bill that would have allowed for televised executions, the leader of those opposing its passage argued: "There is a hidden agenda to this bill and that is to eliminate capital punishment as a law in California." The bill was defeated after "spirited debate."[93]

Whatever the legal or social merits of televising executions, the terms by which the issue is debated reveal a great deal about the dynamics of secrecy that surrounds state-sanctioned killing. Historian Thomas Laqueur argued that the state's increasing inability to effectively manage the "theater" of the execution—to control both the message of the gallows performance and the public's reaction to it—helped cause the move from public to private execution rituals: "As execution becomes ever more private and untheatrical it becomes ever more irrelevant. As it becomes public—if not on television then through the printed media—it becomes carnival which does not fit well with the culturally dominant view of the body politic."[94] So the modern state carefully regulates the private nature of the execution ritual to ensure that its citizens learn just enough (but not too much) about it. Moreover, those citizens who arguably have the greatest need to know the details of the process—capital jurors who are being asked to authorize it—may learn least of all.

As I noted previously, psychologists have observed more generally that people are "less willing to obey authoritarian orders to carry out injurious behavior when they see firsthand how they are hurting others."[95] The capital penalty trial's asymmetrical focus on the consequences of one kind of violence and not another also is furthered by failing to require that jurors get a firsthand look at the full *range* of this hurt. That is, the capital trial process does not require that jurors be sensitized to the fact that the defendant may have family, friends, and other people who care about him who will be victimized by his execution. Of course, there is no way that the defendant's family and loved ones can accurately conjure, in advance, the sadness and grief that they will experience upon the defendant's execution (what would be, in some sense, the equivalent of the kind of victim impact testimony that capital jurors do hear—only in this instance directed at the action the state is asking the jurors themselves to take). Nonetheless, if the penalty trial fails to inform jurors of the full range of psychic injuries that a death verdict is likely to bring about, then it may deny them the opportunity to weigh all of the potentially relevant moral considerations in reaching their verdict.

A related point concerns the way in which capital jurors in many jurisdictions are prevented from ever being fully informed about the alternative to the violence of a death sentence—life imprisonment. That is, caselaw in many jurisdictions prevents defense attorneys from presenting details about the pains of imprisonment and the severity of punishment it represents.[96] Capital jurors may manage to discount or dismiss the painful consequences of a life in prison as an alternative to death by harboring the belief that prison is a reasonably pleasant place or that, as noted earlier in this chapter, all life-sentenced prisoners will someday be released.[97]

Because the law denies capital jurors effective education about the nature of prison as punishment and the harshness and finality of a life sentence, many of them come too easily to conclude that it is not suffering enough. A death verdict becomes the only way they can express "their moral horror and revulsion at the violent and 'whimsical' killing"[98] with which they were confronted at trial. Thus, they vote to execute the defendant not because they have carefully made the moral decision that death is the uniquely appropriate punishment but because they mistakenly believe that its alternative is no punishment at all. Such jurors will be disengaged from the moral complexities of the choice before them whenever the law prevents them from understanding the real human consequences of the alternatives from which they must select.

Finally, capital jurors are distanced further from the moral complexities of their sentencing decision by the law's failure to educate them about a range of other consequences that attach to death penalty verdicts. There is no reason to believe that capital jurors are any different from citizens in general who, as I discussed in chapter 4, are filled with misinformation about the death penalty, many believing that it deters murder and is far less expensive than life imprisonment.[99] Unlike members of the general public, however, the misconceptions of capital jurors are acutely relevant to the life-and-death decision before them. Yet attorneys typically are prohibited from asking about those misconceptions in jury selection and are absolutely barred from addressing them systematically, through testimony, in the course of the trial.

Thus, the law not only does nothing on its own to disabuse jurors of their erroneous views about capital punishment and fails to proactively correct widespread misconceptions about what a death sentence is likely to accomplish but also precludes defense attorneys who would undertake these tasks (by, say, discussing the death penalty's lack of deterrent effect or its racially discriminatory features) from doing so. Many capital jurors leave their life-and-death deliberations quite skeptical of and unknowledgeable about the realities of *either* of the punishments they have chosen between, and quite confused about their real consequences. By passively encouraging capital juries to operate on the basis of inaccurate assumptions and common juror misconceptions, the legal system disengages them from the actual effects of their sentencing behavior in ways that may facilitate death verdicts.

Moreover, the skewed asymmetry of the narratives of violence that characterize capital trials helps render the entire process mystifying and morally disengaging. The consequences of the defendant's violence are made highly salient through the use of narrative devices that are so richly, comprehensively, and graphically detailed that they easily become the most compelling, wrenching part of the trial. On the other hand, the consequences of the state's violence—violence in which the capital jury is being asked to directly participate—are minimized, hidden from view, allowed to be misunderstood, or treated in such a way as to imply that others, later in the process, will be responsible for bringing them about.

Conclusion

Forms of structural aggravation—morally disengaging features of the capital trial process itself—help enable capital jurors to overcome the prohibitions against violence that must be traversed if normal, law-abiding citizens are to condemn their fellow citizens to death. Jurors are implicitly encouraged to dehumanize capital defendants, overemphasize and essentialize the differences between them, and interpret those differences in terms of fundamental defects and profound deficit. The death-sentencing process also acts to decontextualize the defendant's violence in ways that make it more frightening, thus amplifying the jurors' natural impulse toward self-protection and self-defense. In a variety of other ways, mechanisms of disengagement also serve to minimize the perceived personal responsibility and consequences of the legal violence in which the jurors are asked to participate. Under modern capital sentencing procedures, of course, jurors must choose between life and death. But many still do not believe death means death (or that life means life, for that matter). In fact, the law prohibits them from learning many of the details of either the kind of life *or* the kind of death that they are being asked to authorize.

To be seen and ultimately judged as a human being, a capital defendant must be given reality as person that extends beyond the typical juror's stereotypes of violent criminals and their understandably emotional reactions to his violent crime. Yet, as presently structured, the capital trial process does not require that this humanizing task be effectively accomplished. In many ways it actually may undermine the jury's ability to perform it. At many points, the complex capital sentencing calculus in which criminal behavior is weighed against the rest of the life and humanity of the person on trial is structurally and procedurally constricted, narrowed, and oversimplified. The moral grayness of the inquiry in capital trials thus is shaded back into a black-and-white drawing where, as Sarat has observed, "the force of law is represented as serving common purposes and aims as against the anomic savagery lurking just beyond law's boundaries."[100]

8

Misguided Discretion
Instructional Incomprehension in the System of Death Sentencing

[T]here are some contexts in which the risk that the jury will not,
or cannot, follow instructions is so great, and the consequences of
failure so vital to the defendant, that the practical and human
limitations of the jury system cannot be ignored.
—Justice William Brennan, *Bruton v. United States* (1968)

This chapter and the one that follows focus on some of the forces that more immediately influence the capital jury's crucial choice between life and death. To finally deliberate and render penalty-phase verdicts, jurors are required to perform a number of complex and emotionally charged tasks. To do so, they must bring to bear their diverse ideas about blameworthiness, culpability, and punishment. They also experience a range of natural human emotions in response to the tragic stories that often are told by both the prosecution and defense. In addition, as I have noted throughout this book, jurors must grapple with their own deep-seated inhibitions against violence. How the law purports to manage the complicated matrix of forces that are at work here is critically important to any fair and just resolution of a capital case. In a sense, what transpires at this stage of the process is the culmination of everything that has gone before.

The present chapter examines the primary legal vehicle used to regularize and control these forces in the hopes of making capital jury decision making reliable and fair—penalty-phase jury instructions. Recall that the pivotal portion of the *Furman* opinion that set the stage for the modern era of death sentencing was very much concerned with the "unbridled discretion" that had been afforded to capital juries in the past. Lacking appropriate guidance under the old system, it was thought, jurors had returned death sentences that were "wanton and freakish" and perhaps unlawfully discriminatory. The new death penalty statutes that were approved in *Gregg v. Georgia* attempted to strike a difficult balance between limiting the jury's discretion and, simultaneously, providing jurors with an opportunity to make individualized, case-by-case sentencing decisions.[1]

An especially important feature of the new laws—and the one to which this chapter is devoted—was the requirement that judges read a special set of instructions to jurors at the conclusion of the sentencing stage of the capital trial. Supposedly designed to guide and regulate the jury's discretion, these instructions were intended to eliminate the arbitrariness that had plagued death sentencing in past times. Indeed, according to the *Gregg* Court, the sentencing instructions were expected to "channel" the jurors' discretion, so that "[n]o longer can a jury wantonly and freakishly impose the death sentence; it is always circumscribed by the legislative guidelines."[2]

From the outset, however, this heavy reliance on sentencing instructions was based on a series of questionable assumptions. For one, it reflected a view that the capital jury's decision making should and could be guided by specific judgments that legislators had made—as embodied in the instructions themselves—about the characteristics that distinguished defendants who "deserved" the death penalty from those who did not. It also put faith in judges to adequately convey these judgments to jurors through instructions that told the jurors what to think about when they made their life-and-death decisions.

Psychologically, this approach assumed that jurors would be appropriately influenced by the instructions, and would use them in ways that made their decision-making process less arbitrary and more fair. Because it was the operation of extraneous factors (like race) that was thought to have produced the pattern of arbitrary and discriminatory death sentencing that the Supreme Court found unconstitutional in *Furman,* focusing the jury's attention elsewhere—that is, on a list of permissible factors—was supposed to reduce or eliminate their improper effect on capital verdicts.

In fact, however, the Supreme Court's decision to rely so heavily on jury instructions to correct the problems identified in *Furman* represented something of a judicial leap of faith. There was no empirical evidence to suggest that jury instructions could so significantly and reliably affect the behavior of jurors, and certainly none indicating that they could transform the way jurors went about performing such a complex and individualized decision-making task.[3] Nonetheless, Justice Stewart's plurality opinion in *Gregg* simply asserted, without any data to back it up, that the concerns expressed in *Furman* over the reliability of the capital jury's decision-making process "*can* be met by a carefully drafted statute" in which "the sentencing authority is apprised of the information relevant to the imposition of sentence and provided with standards to guide its use of the information."[4] Accordingly, *Gregg* approved the new Georgia death penalty statute because, as Stewart said, it would properly "focus the jury's attention on the particularized nature of the crime and the particularized characteristics of the individual defendant."[5]

These strong assertions about the power of judicial instructions to properly guide capital jurors in choosing between life and death were especially
surprising in light of the conclusion the Court had reached just five years
earlier. In a 1971 case, *McGautha v. California,* a majority had joined in
Justice Harlan's frank and pessimistic assessment of whether the complexity
of death penalty decision making lent itself to this form of judicial control.
Harlan concluded that the task of identifying in advance the factors that
called for the death penalty and expressing them "in language which can be
fairly understood and applied" by juries was one that appeared "beyond
present human ability."[6] Yet, in 1976, the Court authorized death-penalty
states to undertake exactly this task. Much of the rest of this chapter describes
how poor a job they have done in achieving it. In fact, there is much research
to suggest that the very instructions that were intended to properly guide the
jury deliberations at the final stage of a death penalty trial actually function
to undermine the reliability of penalty verdicts and to facilitate the death-
sentencing process.

The Psychology of Death Penalty Decision Making

The Court's heavy reliance on sentencing instructions to safeguard the constitutionality of capital punishment has focused much attention on the complex psychology of the capital jury. To be sure, as the Supreme Court has
acknowledged, "[a] capital sentencing jury is made up of individuals placed
in a very unfamiliar situation and called on to make a very difficult and
uncomfortable choice."[7] But the decision is more than "unfamiliar"—it is
unprecedented in human experience. Its difficulty is made greater by virtue
of the fact that no purely objective or factual analysis can compel a capital
juror to choose one alternative or the other in a capital sentencing trial. These
life-or-death verdicts are infused with much more value-laden subjectivity
than traditional guilt-phase decision making. Moreover, deciding whether
someone deserves to live or die is a profound moral assessment that very few
people ever are called on to make. Obviously, no one makes these decisions
with enough frequency to develop what might be considered "expertise," or
have absolute confidence that it has been done correctly. Yet capital juries—
composed only of ordinary men and women—are regularly enlisted to perform this extraordinary task.

In all the other kinds of decisions that jurors typically make, they function primarily as fact finders, reaching judgments about whether particular
acts were committed, by whom, and with what state of mind.[8] These judgments often are difficult and subtle, and they may require the jurors to analyze complex testimony that can lend itself to different, conflicting interpretations. Nonetheless, most guilt-phase decisions are reached by applying
a common set of basic assumptions about the physical and social world. In

most kinds of criminal cases, differences in the background experiences or values of jurors are unlikely to produce very significant differences in their understanding of basic causation in the physical universe or even psychological intuitions about the connection between thoughts and actions.[9]

Penalty-phase decision making is a different matter entirely. It requires capital jurors to engage in a constitutionally mandated inquiry into a defendant's "moral culpability." Unlike guilt-phase determinations, this one is grounded entirely in a moral and psychological universe. Jurors have to decide whether and how they understand the defendant's life and what value they will attach to it. They must answer the inherently "subjective question" of whether they believe life or death is warranted. Yet: "No scale is provided on which to weigh the evidence." Jurors not only lack a precise metric for weighing evidence but they also cannot assume any obvious or widely shared views about how to understand and to value a life. As a result, many jurors "look within themselves, reflect on all the reasons for each possible sentence, and then decide whether or not this defendant should die."[10]

But looking within themselves does not necessarily provide simple answers to the very complicated questions posed by the broad penalty-phase evidence to which they may have been exposed. Capital jurors may have to decide whether and how much to weigh an early history of child abuse, or exposure to chronic poverty, or lifelong societal discrimination. Should a defendant who has been damaged by years of prior abuse and neglect receive a jury's mercy or compassion because of the trauma he has been forced to endure, or do the scars of this mistreatment render him more likely to be dangerous in a future life of imprisonment? In other cases, jurors will have to ask themselves whether a long history of drug abuse makes a defendant more or less blameworthy for his violence. Or, they may be called on to determine whether someone who has been repeatedly institutionalized is less culpable because he is the product of institutional failure and neglect or actually more worthy of blame in light of numerous opportunities to change he was given by the best the system has to offer. A vast number of issues are potentially relevant to these kinds of inquiries, constrained only by the nature of the evidence and the complexity of the thinking brought to bear by the 12 persons who will deliberate the verdict.

Because of the range and the complexity of the questions, the broad scope of the evidence jurors may consider to answer them, and the absence of any obvious, common framework for resolving differences of opinion about the issues at hand, many capital jurors will look to the judge for guidance. Thus, the jury instructions take on greater importance than in other kinds of cases. In an ideal system, perhaps, these instructions *would* help jurors interpret and gauge the significance of the wide-ranging evidence introduced at the penalty trial and suggest how to use it in making the profound decision at hand. In theory, the instructions are *supposed* to do precisely this—to focus the jurors collectively on what is important, guide them as a group about which theories of moral assessment to use, identify precisely how certain factors or pieces of evidence should be taken into account, and instruct them on how to reach a consensus about this uniquely personal and deeply moral decision. Unfortunately, there is much empirical evidence to suggest that the capital sentencing instructions in which the Supreme Court placed so much faith and responsibility fall woefully short in accomplishing any of these critical tasks.

The California Comprehension Studies: Misguiding Discretion?

In order to examine some of the effects of capital penalty instructions on the death-sentencing process, my colleagues and I have conducted a number of empirical studies over the last several decades. Reasoning that jurors' discretion could not be guided properly by instructions that they did not understand—at least, not in ways that would increase the reliability of their decision making—we looked carefully at whether and how the instructions actually were comprehended. We found a number of problematic patterns that led us to troublesome conclusions about the process by which jurors choose between life and death.

In one of the first of these studies, Mona Lynch and I tried to determine how well the two core concepts—"aggravation" and "mitigation"—that jurors are supposed to use in reaching their penalty verdict actually were understood.[11] Recall that most state death penalty statutes ask jurors to take into consideration any aggravating circumstances (certain negative aspects of the crime, the defendant, or his past criminal behavior that would favor a death sentence) as well as any mitigating circumstances (any aspects of the crime, the defendant, or his past life that would favor a life sentence). The instructions also give jurors a list of specific aggravating and mitigating circumstances to look for and, if present, to consider in reaching their verdicts. In most states, the balancing of those factors that are supposed to weigh in favor of death and those that are supposed to weigh in favor of life serves to structure the decision-making process.

We chose to study these issues in California because, like most other states, its death penalty instruction does not clearly define these two key terms, "aggravating" and "mitigating." Unlike most states, however, California does not identify which of the factors in the sentencing template that the jury is to think about and consider are supposed to be aggravating and which are mitigating. As law professor Robert Weisberg noted, "[t]he California list of circumstances is unusual, because it blends aggravating and mitigating circumstances into a single list without distinguishing them. . . . Nevertheless, the jury instructions assume that the jurors can tell aggravating and mitigating factors apart."[12] Studying the California instruction allowed us to test this assumption as well.

Lynch and I collected data from nearly 500 upper-division undergraduate students, ranging in age from 19 to 36 years. Of course, we knew at the outset that these participants were not representative of the larger population from which capital jurors ordinarily are drawn. However, we reasoned that the most important way in which the students likely differed—their educational background—would tend to increase their comprehension of the instructions. Moreover, other research seemed to confirm our supposition that using college student participants in jury comprehension studies did not significantly compromise the generalizability of the results.[13]

The methodology we used was straightforward. After being given a general description of the capital trial process, our participants heard the standard California judicial instruction used in all capital cases tried within the state. This instruction consisted of a general section explaining the nature of the decision jurors would be asked to make followed by a listing of the template of specific factors that the jurors were told they should consider, take into account, and be guided by in reaching their verdict. The instruction ended with a brief description of the process that jurors are supposed to use in comparing factors in order to reach a penalty verdict.

Once the *entire* penalty instruction (including the template of factors) had been read aloud three times, Lynch and I asked our participants to define in writing the terms "aggravation" and "mitigation" as they were used in the context of the instruction. After they completed that task, they were told that they would be asked whether each specific factor was intended, in the context of the instruction, as aggravating or mitigating. Each of the specific factors was again read in sequence and then repeated. As each factor was read aloud for the final time, participants indicated whether the presence of that particular factor in a capital case should be considered either aggravating or mitigating.[14]

We then content-analyzed the participants' general definitions of aggravating and mitigating for overall accuracy.[15] Participants got partial credit for definitions that captured only a specific instance or individual example of something that could be considered either aggravating (e.g., "aggravating means to willfully or consciously commit a crime," or "the defendant intentionally tried to commit the crime with prior knowledge of the circumstances") or mitigating (e.g., "mitigating evidence would be if there is any way the defendant could in fact be innocent" or "to kill in self-defense or accidentally").

However, one of the continuing concerns about penalty-phase jury instructions is whether they are unduly restrictive. Specifically, legal commentators have worried that relevant mitigating evidence, especially, might be discarded or ignored because it did not fit neatly or comfortably into jurors' "commonsense" understanding of the term.[16] Thus, we counted as "legally correct" only those definitions that were sufficiently broad to encompass the notion that the terms "aggravating" and "mitigating" as used in this instruction referred to evidence whose effect, respectively, was to increase or decrease the level of punishment that would be imposed on a defendant in a capital trial. For example, as one of the rare participants who got both terms legally correct put it, "aggravating refers to factors with a negative social value, things that would lead you to favor the imposition of a harsher penalty, like the imposition of death rather than life without parole," while mitigating "means factors with a positive social value or that evoke sympathy, tending to favor the imposition of lesser punishment (like life without parole instead of death)."

Lynch and I found that a surprisingly high number of our college-educated participants were unable to comprehend the central terms of capital penalty-phase instruction. Moreover, far more confusion surrounded the concept of mitigation than aggravation. As table 8.1 indicates, comprehension was poor overall—only 8% could offer definitions of both terms that were legally correct, even after having heard the capital instructions read three times. This compared to 20% of the participants who were totally incorrect—provided answers that were either incomprehensible or entirely wrong—with respect to both aggravation and mitigation. Thus, there were more than twice as many participants in the study who had no idea what either term meant than could offer legally correct definitions for both terms.

In addition, we found that 64% of our sample provided partially correct definitions of aggravation, as compared to only 47% for mitigation. Participants often provided definitions of the term "aggravation" that related only to its commonly understood lay definition, as in "frustrated, in a state of emotion that is aggravated," or "to anger, to push, to irritate as a means of causing a reaction." Because the term "mitigation" is used primarily in legal contexts, there were fewer instances of subjects resorting to lay definitions. However, there were a higher number of incoherent or uninterpretable definitions of mitigation offered, as in "to deliberate, think over, outside the case," "a circumstance that is secondary to, not a result of the action," or "statements that can be argued either way."

As one measure of the special problems posed by the concept of mitigation, we found that 11% of the participants were unable to even guess at a definition of the term "mitigation" (i.e., offered no response whatsoever), as compared to only 3% of our participants who were unable to provide any definition of the term "aggravation." Thus, a total of 41% of our sample was either unable to respond when asked to define mitigation (11%) or provided

Table 8.1

Comprehension of Central Terms of Capital Decision Making

Concept	Legally Correct	Partially Correct	Totally Incorrect	Unable to Respond	Exclusively Crime-Related
"Aggravation"	15%	64%	18%	3%	70%
"Mitigation"	12%	47%	30%	11%	53%
Both	8%	46%	17%	3%	45%

definitions that were uninterpretable or totally incorrect (30%). With respect to the scope of the definitions provided, nearly half (45%) of our participants used exclusively *crime-related* definitions of both terms (even if they were incorrect). When we looked at only those who provided even partially correct definitions of each term, we found that 77% focused crime-related definitions of aggravation and 65% looked to the circumstances of the crime for definitions of mitigation.[17] This finding is particularly important in light of my earlier comment about concerns that the scope of mitigation that jurors think they can or should consider might be unduly constricted. Given the fact that most prosecutors emphasize the typically aggravated nature of capital crimes in their capital penalty-phase presentations, we found that three-quarters of our "accurate" participants understood aggravation in the way it was likely to be presented to them in the typical capital case. However, because most defense attorneys rely on *non-crime-related* mitigation, this compared to only a third of our "accurate" participants who comprehended mitigation in the way in which they would likely hear about it at trial.

As figure 8.1 indicates, when combined with the comprehension results, this further compounded the differences between the two terms—only about 20% of the participants understood mitigation in the non-crime-related way in which it is most often presented, as compared to 61% who understood aggravation in the crime-related way in which such evidence typically is introduced.

As noted previously, California's death penalty instruction is unique in that no labels are attached to the specific aggravating or mitigating factors that jurors are supposed to use in reaching their life-or-death verdicts. When we scored the accuracy with which participants categorized each of these

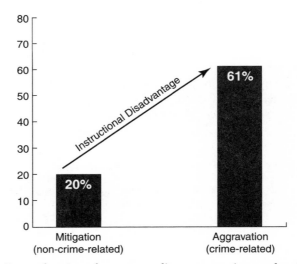

Figure 8.1 Comprehension of terms according to normative penalty-phase evidence.

specific factors (as aggravating or mitigating), however, we found a considerable amount of variation and a surprisingly amount of error.[18] As table 8.2 indicates, in the case of every single specific factor but two, 20% or more of our participants were incorrect in their judgments about whether a particular factor, if true or present in the case at hand, should be regarded as either aggravating or mitigating.[19] Even the seemingly straightforward factor that the defendant had committed prior acts of force or violence was misconstrued by almost one-fifth of our participants, as was the presence of prior felony conviction(s).[20] Thus, Lynch and I concluded that some of the confusion that people have with the core concepts of aggravation and mitigation clearly carries over to the template of factors that capital jurors in California are supposed to use in arriving at their sentencing verdicts.

Once again, when we examined the pattern of errors in categorizing mitigating factors more carefully, taking into account the kind of mitigation that is likely to be introduced in the typical death penalty trial, the results were even more problematic. Note that several of the specific mitigating circumstances (e.g., that the victim participated in or consented to the homicide, or that the defendant reasonably believed he had a moral justification for the murder) rarely, if ever, occur in any capital case. Yet, one of these— that the victim participated in or consented to his or her own homicide— was the best understood mitigating factor and the only one that was not misconstrued by at least a fifth of the participants in our study. On the other hand, the few potential mitigating factors in the California instruction that occur with some real frequency in capital cases were misunderstood by nearly

Table 8.2
Comprehension of Template of Capital Sentencing Factors

Factors	Participants Categorize as:	
	Aggravating	Mitigating
"a" (crime and special circumstances)	56**	44**
"b" (prior use of force or violence)	82	18*
"c" [prior felony conviction(s)]	79	21*
"d" (under influence of mental disturbance)	25*	75
"e" (victim participated in own homicide)	18*	82
"f" (moral justification for homicide)	23*	77
"g" (under duress or domination)	24*	76
"h" (impaired capacity to appreciate criminality)	23*	77
"i" (age at time of crime)	33**	67**
"j" (accomplice or minor participant)	25*	75
"k" (other extenuation of crime; character or record)	36*	64

*Indicates incorrect judgment.
**Because of statutory intent, wording, or judicial construction, either interpretation permissible.

a quarter of our participants actually to constitute *aggravation*. Thus, we found that fully 23% of the persons in the study actually thought that a defendant's impaired capacity to appreciate the criminality of his conduct should be regarded as aggravating, and 25% of them believed the same thing about the fact that the crime was committed while the defendant was under the influence of a mental or emotional disturbance.

In most capital penalty trials, by far the most important factor available to capital defendants as the basis for mitigation is the final one listed in the instruction—a "catchall" factor that includes anything else that would lessen the gravity of the crime and additional information about the background and character of the defendant that would lead jurors to favor a sentence less than death. In the typical case, it serves as the vehicle by which the defense presents broad mitigating evidence about the defendant that allows the jurors to see him as a human being and to understand the forces and influences that helped to shape his past behavior. It is the kind of mitigating evidence that is intended to encourage the jurors to show some compassion in sentencing the defendant to life rather than death. Yet, this factor actually was misunderstood by more than a third (36%) of our participants to constitute a form of aggravation. By contrast, then, note that one of the factors that rarely if ever occur in a capital case—that the victim consented in his or her own homicide—was the best understood form of mitigation while, as I say, the one most heavily relied on and typically the most important mitigating factor—the background and character of the defendant—was the least understood in the template.

Not long after Lynch and I had collected and analyzed the data from this initial study, the California Judicial Council revised the standard capital penalty-phase jury instruction. The new instruction presumably was intended to improve levels of juror comprehension[21] and included brief but explicit legal definitions of the terms "aggravation" and "mitigation." Obviously, in light of this change, it was important for us to assess the effects of the new and, we hoped, improved instruction. To do so, Lynch and I followed essentially the same procedure as in the first study. However, because the revised instruction included the term "extenuate"—something that ostensibly was inserted to help clarify the meaning of mitigation—we measured the participants' comprehension of this term as well.

Surprisingly, as table 8.3 illustrates, the inclusion of the "legal definitions" in the instruction made little difference in overall comprehension of the key capital sentencing terms.[22] If anything—perhaps because the especially confusing term "extenuating" was used to explicate it—mitigation was even *more* poorly understood than in the past, with nearly half (49%) of participants either offering totally incorrect definitions or unable to respond with a definition of any kind. Moreover, for 6 out of the 11 specific factors, the percentage of persons incorrectly categorizing the factor actually increased under the new instruction.

Table 8.3
Comparison of Comprehension: Old Versus New Instruction

Concept	Legally Correct	Partially Correct	Incorrect	Unable to Respond
Old Instruction (Without Definitions)*				
Aggravation	15%	64%	18%	3%
Mitigation	12%	47%	30%	11%
Both terms	8%	46%	17%	3%
New Instruction (With Definitions)**				
Aggravation	11%	60%	26%	3%
Mitigation	11%	40%	39%	10%
Both terms	7%	34%	15%	1%

*From Haney & Lynch (1994). $N = 491$.
**Current data; revised instructions. $N = 215$.

In this second study, Lynch and I also decided to assess whether prospective jurors understood the *decision rule* that the standard instruction gave jurors to follow in reaching their sentencing verdict—specifically, that "[t]o return a judgment of death, each of you must be persuaded that the aggravating circumstances are so substantial in comparison to the mitigating circumstances that it warrants death instead of life without parole." We posed some additional questions to determine how well participants comprehended this part of the instruction.

As table 8.4 shows, few of the participants properly comprehended the decision rule that they were supposed to follow. That is, only half understood that they were required to return a life verdict when mitigation outweighed aggravation, and although just a little more than a third (37%) understood that they could vote for either life or death if aggravation outweighed mitigation, 41% incorrectly believed that death was mandatory under those circumstances. Indeed, only one in six (15%) correctly understood that the law in California *required* a life verdict when aggravation and mitigation were judged to be equal, as opposed to 41% who believed, incorrectly, that they were permitted to choose either verdict under those circumstances. Here, too, not only was instructional comprehension very poor, but the errors were clustered in such a way that they clearly favored death over life sentences.

Despite what I said earlier about our expectation that college students would do better than average jurors on these comprehension tasks, their poor performance prompted my students and me to look at how well other groups of people—those more representative of typical capital jurors—might fare in understanding this critically important instruction. We also realized that the participants in these earlier studies were trying to understand the key instructional concepts absent any case-specific content. Perhaps knowing

Table 8.4
Comprehension of Weighing Process With Definitions

Scenario	Mandatory Life	Either Life or Death	Mandatory Death	Not Indicated by Instruction
If mitigation outweighs aggravation	50%*	27%	3%	20%
If mitigation equals aggravation	15%*	41%	2%	43%
If aggravation outweighs mitigation	5%	37%*	41%	17%

$N = 117$.
*Indicates correct response.

something about the actual case facts to which the instructions were to be applied would assist jurors in comprehending their meaning. To address both issues, in a study that we published in the mid-1990s, Lorelei Sontag, Sally Costanzo, and I analyzed the results of lengthy postverdict interviews conducted with 30 actual capital jurors who rendered verdicts in death penalty trials in California. They were selected from 10 different cases, equally balanced between life and death verdicts.[23]

Here, too, we were troubled by what we found. Even though they actually had served as jurors and rendered sentencing verdicts in capital cases, many interviewees reported being confused about the meaning of the sentencing instructions and admitted that they had not always understood how they were supposed to apply them to the evidence that had been presented during the penalty trial to chose between life and death. For example, although they were acutely sensitive to the life histories of capital defendants in each of the cases, the instructions did not clarify how those histories were supposed to be factored into their decision. Unless the attorneys in the case had clearly emphasized the relevance of the information for their verdict, it appeared as though the evidence was likely to be shunted aside or ignored.

The interviews revealed that fewer than half of the California jurors (13 of 30) had even a reasonably accurate understanding of the terms "aggravation" and "mitigation," despite having heard evidence, arguments, and instructions presented in penalty-phase trials in which they deliberated and rendered sentencing verdicts.[24] They were especially unclear about the proper scope of the mitigation. Indeed, jurors in 8 of the 10 capital juries we studied reported that they had dismissed non-crime-related mitigating evidence (such as testimony about the defendant's background and character) if they did not believe it directly lessened his responsibility for the offense itself.[25]

In fact, many jurors operated with what amounted to a presumption for death. Thus, about a third of the sample not only focused their entire penalty-phase inquiry squarely on the nature of the crime itself but also did so in a way that essentially dictated a death verdict. For example, one of them con-fused the penalty-phase decision with a judgment about the defendant's san-ity—an issue that necessarily would (or should) have been resolved much earlier in the trial: "I think the bottom line was, at the time he was commit-ting [the crimes], did he know what he was doing? Did he know right from wrong? That's the whole thing."[26] Of course, a defendant who did not know right from wrong at the time of the crime would not be facing the death penalty at all. Other jurors also ignored everything that was presented in the penalty trial and focused only on the crime. Because they dismissed the mit-igation that the defendant presented, they invariably imposed the death pen-alty. As one member of a jury that returned a death verdict said: "[The defendant] brought all these witnesses in who attested to his character, and what a good person he was and how he had been, you know. And it was, all that was pretty much not—we didn't use that too heavily at all. It was in-teresting, but it had no bearing on the case. There is just—his whole life boils down to this one incident [the crime]."

The presumption for death also came about when these actual jurors—much like the student participants in our comprehension study—failed to understand the decision rules in the instructions that they were supposed to follow. Thus, one-third of the jurors who were interviewed reported that they had incorrectly understood of the weighing process in such a way that death was the only possible sentencing verdict they could have reached given the evidence that was presented in the cases on which they sat. This was true despite the fact that, as I noted previously, California law does not mandate death under any circumstances and, in fact, actually *requires* a life verdict unless aggravation substantially outweighs mitigation.

Finally, the very low levels of comprehension among actual California capital jurors led several of my graduate students and me to study several other interrelated issues. Carmel Benson, Amy Smith, and I wondered whether the lack of comprehension among actual capital jurors might have something to do with an issue that I discussed in chapter 6—the way that death-qualifying voir dire selects jurors on the basis of their death penalty support. Thus, we did several simulation studies to explore relationship be-tween attitudes toward the death penalty, comprehension of instructions, and recollection of closing arguments by one or the other side of a capital case. The pattern that emerged raised additional concerns about whether sentenc-ing instructions actually were comprehended by the persons who were ex-pected to follow them.

In particular, in a study of over 400 student participants, we found that death penalty attitudes were significantly but negatively related to instruc-tional comprehension. Although the unusual nature of our college student sample made it difficult for us to properly "death qualify" them—about an equal number reported themselves opposed to capital punishment as in fa-vor—it was clear that a procedure that selected participants on the basis of their death penalty support would increase the number of instructional errors

Table 8.5
Comprehension of Central Terms by Death Penalty Attitude

	Legally/Partially Correct	Incorrect/Unable to Respond
Death Penalty Attitude: **"Aggravation"**		
Support	58.2%	41.8%
Oppose	64.8%	35.2%
Death Penalty Attitude: **"Mitigation"**		
Support	45.6%	54.4%
Oppose	56.4%	43.6%
Death Penalty Attitude: **"Extenuation"**		
Support	12.2%	87.7%
Oppose	21.9%	78.1%

among the persons who were chosen. As table 8.5 illustrates, participants who favored capital punishment tended to comprehend the key terms of the death penalty instruction more poorly than those who were opposed.

In an additional study, with a smaller sample of participants, we found not only that death penalty attitude affected the level of comprehension but also that death penalty supporters were more likely to inaccurately recall closing arguments made by prosecution and defense. In addition, they were more likely overall to recall closing argument themes that were crime-oriented in nature. This suggests that, to the extent that jury selection in death penalty cases tends to select jurors on the basis of their support for capital punishment, the practice may result in juries that not only are especially prone to error in recalling closing arguments but also tend to focus disproportionately on crime-oriented themes. Combined with the earlier finding that persons tend to comprehend death penalty instructions in terms of crime-oriented aggravation, this potential bias among death penalty supporters may be significant.

Thus, Smith, Benson, and I speculated preliminarily that in actual practice, death-qualified juries that lean heavily in favor of the death penalty may be more likely to make mistakes in comprehending instructions and in accurately recalling closing argument themes and to naturally favor crime-oriented themes likely to be offered by the prosecution in capital cases. Of course, more research is needed on these issues before any firm conclusions can be reached.

Miscomprehension Elsewhere: More Evidence of Confusion-Related Prejudice

The high levels of confusion we found in the aforementioned studies are not unique to California. Indeed, the inability of jurors to accurately comprehend and apply capital sentencing instructions has been well documented in many other jurisdictions. In addition to finding that comprehension is poor overall, other researchers have identified the same troublesome clustering of comprehension errors that we did—jurors elsewhere have more difficulty understanding mitigation than aggravation, they tend to improperly and unnecessarily restrict the scope of mitigation that they believe the instructions authorize them to take into account, and they misunderstand decision rules in ways that increase in the number of death sentences that they render.

For example, an Ohio study found that a high percentage of jury-eligible citizens were unable to comprehend and correctly apply the mitigation-related sections of each state's capital instructions but not the components dealing with aggravation.[27] Similar patterns have been found with college student participants. For example, sociologist Michael Radelet found that the majority of college students to whom Florida's capital penalty instructions were read aloud erred on a series of comprehension questions, especially those that pertained to the concept of mitigation. He concluded that the pattern of comprehension errors created an overall bias in favor of death verdicts.[28]

Many other researchers have found that prospective jurors inappropriately restrict the scope of mitigating evidence that should be relevant to their penalty-phase decision making. For example, when Professor Hans Zeisel examined the comprehension of the Illinois capital sentencing instruction among jury-eligible citizens, he found that approximately one-third of them incorrectly answered basic questions about the use of mitigation in a capital penalty trial, and a substantial number of them failed to understand that they were supposed to consider *any* mitigating factor offered.[29] Similarly, researchers in Tennessee concluded that the majority of their jury-eligible participants "failed to understand the concept of nonenumerated mitigating circumstances" that was contained in the state's capital instruction.[30]

Attempts to correct these errors by rewriting the instructions have met with only modest success (and, of course, the results reflect the comprehension of instructions that have not yet been used in any actual case). Thus, in a follow-up study to Zeisel's research, psychologist Shari Diamond and psycholinguist Judith Levi used instructions that were written in more accessible, understandable language in order to improve the extent to which death-qualified, jury-eligible participants understood the scope of allowable mitigation. Nonetheless, close to half (42%) of their participants were confused by even the revised, improved instructions.[31]

Similarly, in a series of carefully conducted studies by Richard Wiener and his colleagues, a pattern of comprehension errors was identified that led Missouri jurors to undervalue the role of mitigation in the death penalty decision-making process. When Wiener created a version of the instruction that was designed to increase clarity, he achieved only moderate, mixed improvements. Wiener's studies also suggested that jurors were especially confused about how they were supposed to balance aggravation and mitigation in order to reach a sentencing verdict, and that those persons who understood the instructions least well were the ones most certain that defendants should be sentenced to death.[32]

Wiener's findings that jurors are confused about how they should combine and compare aggravating and mitigating circumstances to reach a sentencing verdict are corroborated by our California research and by other studies. Simply put, jurors in many states do not understand the mechanics of the weighing process that they are required to use in arriving at a sentencing decision. For example, most of the respondents in the separate studies done by Zeisel and by Diamond and Levi did not understand which side had the burden of proof under the Illinois instruction.[33] Similarly, a majority of the participants in Michael Radelet's Florida study erroneously believed that a capital jury was required to impose a sentence of death if the mitigators had not been proved by the defense.[34] And, although the majority of the participants in the Tennessee sentencing instruction study correctly understood the burden of proof that was required to find aggravators, they generally did not understand that state law provided for a lower standard of proof for finding mitigation.[35]

Interviews with actual capital jurors from many different jurisdictions confirm that confusion and misunderstanding plague the penalty-phase decision-making process in death penalty trials. For instance, Theodore Eisenberg and Martin Wells interviewed South Carolina jurors about their capital trial experiences and found, among other things, that they were very confused about the standards of proof that related to mitigating factors (which the South Carolina statute indicated needed to be found only by a preponderance of evidence rather than "beyond a reasonable doubt"). The overall level of confusion was so substantial that the researchers concluded that death had become "[t]he default sentence in a capital case." That is, as they put it: "[T]he tilt towards death suggests that a defendant with a confused jury may receive a death sentence by default, without having a chance to benefit from legal standards designed to give him a chance for life."[36]

A similar study by social psychologists James Luginbuhl and Julie Howe documented the poor comprehension of penalty instructions among capital jurors in North Carolina. The problems were serious overall—Luginbuhl and Howe found that less than 50% of the jurors interviewed were correct in answering more than half of the questions they were asked about the operation of the sentencing statute. But the lack of comprehension was asymmetrical; it pushed the jurors toward death and away from life verdicts. Thus, about half of them mistakenly believed that the judicial instructions authorized them to rely on *any* aggravating circumstance, whether or not it was enumerated in the statute, and to rely on a mitigating circumstance *only* when there was unanimous agreement that it had been proven beyond a reasonable doubt.[37]

The death-tilting effect of the state's instruction was further underscored by the answers to another set of questions that Luginbuhl and Howe posed: "[R]oughly a fourth of the jurors felt that death was mandatory when it was not and approximately one-half of the jurors failed to appreciate those situations which mandated life." The authors concluded that although the North Carolina capital sentencing instruction was comprehended poorly overall, "comprehension appears worse when mitigating factors are considered."[38]

In fact, most of the interview data that have been collected by the Capital Jury Project—an ambitious 14-state study in which intensive interviews have been conducted with persons who actually have served on capital juries—confirm this asymmetry: Jurors operate with serious misconceptions about what they are supposed to be doing and the resulting confusion produces a distinct bias in favor of death verdicts.[39] Indeed, as two Capital Jury Project researchers concluded, the overall pattern that emerged from the numerous interviews indicates that the typical capital jury decision-making process "appears to violate constitutional principles established for this momentous of decisions," including the failure "to understand, consider, and give effect to mitigating factors."[40]

Just Following Orders, More or Less

Finally, in addition to this level of outright confusion, the sentencing instructions may adversely affect the jury decision-making process in other ways. For one, the instructions appear to serve as a form of "authorization" for death sentencing. That is, they allow some people to believe that they are merely following a legal formula or complying with a set of rote instructions rather than making a personal and discretionary decision whether to sentence someone to death. Of course, people are more likely to reach punitive decisions, even to act violently, when they feel they have been placed in situations in which standard moral principles do not apply—such as when they feel they have been authorized by powerful others to act outside the boundaries of normative moral codes. Social scientists have written extensively about so-called crimes of obedience—harmful actions taken not as a result of considered personal choice or individual preference but rather out of compliance with coercive norms imposed by powerful political and legal forces that seem to compel certain kinds of behavior.[41]

The Milgram obedience experiments are the classic social psychological demonstration of this phenomenon. Milgram's participants delivered what they were led to believe could be lethal doses of electric shock to another person simply because they had been "ordered" to do so by a legitimate-appearing authority figure.[42] Other social psychologists have broadened the analysis of the psychology of obedience, emphasizing the importance of "authorization"—taking actions that appear to be sanctioned authorized by persons who appear to be in legitimate positions of authority. Under these circumstances, "lower-level actors need not deny their moral values, simply their applicability to the situation,"[43] because their actions have been have condoned, encouraged, or ordered by higher authorities.

Robert Cover and others have written about the way that the discomfort a person may feel in the face of a difficult moral choice "will be reduced insofar as he can view himself as a mechanical instrument of the will of others."[44] Many capital jurors appear to appreciate this fact at an intuitive level and report relying heavily on the sentencing instructions to reach their penalty verdicts. Given how poorly the instructions themselves are comprehended, this is, to say the least, ironic. But it also raises the possibility that the instructions are not comprehended well enough to properly structure the jury's decision making yet provide enough apparent authorization to enable jurors to avoid a sense of personal responsibility for the decisions that they make. Some capital jurors readily acknowledge that, as a member of a jury that sentenced a defendant to die put it: "You need guidelines. You know, that takes it off of how you feel."[45]

Indeed, some jurors come to believe that they are not personally choosing to have someone put to death but, rather, are just following the legal orders they have been given—whether in the form of "*just* weighing the factors" provided in the kind of instructions in use in most death penalty states or "*just* answering the questions"[46] of the sort that are posed in special-issues states like Texas and Oregon (where statutes specify several questions that capital jurors must answer in order to reach their sentencing verdict). As one member of a California jury who voted to impose a death verdict put it: "My justification of the whole thing is, it's not really my decision, it's the law's decision. They told me to just look at this in the penalty phase, mitigating, aggravating. I've done it."[47]

Similarly, a number of the capital jurors whom law professor Joseph Hoffman interviewed in Indiana believed that the judge's sentencing instructions defined "a legally 'correct' capital sentencing outcome." Indeed, as he put it, "[t]hey interpreted the judge's instructions as eliminating most of their own personal moral responsibility for choosing life or death for the defendants. . . ."[48] Of course, if capital jurors are not clearly and explicitly informed that legal authorities do not require death verdicts in *any* case, this sense that "the-law-made-me-do-it" may come to influence their decision-making process. This possibility is made more likely by the formal language that characterizes the standard sentencing instructions that serve as the primary source of legal authorization. Because the instructions are not designed to highlight the moral and human elements of the death-sentencing decision, jurors may overlook or ignore them.

The sense of responsibility that capital jurors feel for the ultimate consequences of their decision may be diffused in another, closely related way. As I have suggested, psychological research has demonstrated that "[p]eople behave in injurious ways they normally repudiate if a legitimate authority accepts responsibility for the consequences of their conduct."[49] Not surprisingly, perhaps, although jurors in capital cases are charged with the extraordinary personal responsibility of making a life-or-death sentencing decision, as one commentator has put it, "individual jurors are relieved to share the decision with other jurors."[50]

Indeed, the natural tendency to share responsibility with others may be intensified in capital cases, where many jurors have come to believe that *someone else*—typically appellate judges—have the *ultimate* responsibility to decide the life-or-death question that has been posed to them. Standard capital penalty instructions do little or nothing to disabuse them of this widespread misconception. Moreover, the Supreme Court has taken an increasingly broad view of how far prosecutors can go in giving the impression that jurors are just contributing to—rather than actually making—the life-or-death decision.[51] Ironically, the very judges on whom capital jurors may be relying to review and "correct" any erroneous sentencing decision, in turn, may defer to and rely on the *jury's* earlier decision to insulate themselves from the moral issues posed by death verdicts. Thus, in the words of one legal observer, the sense of collectivity that surrounds the decision making in a capital case—the notion that, because there is the perception that so many people are involved, no one individual feels entirely accountable—can be viewed as a paradigm of "diffusion of and thus escape from responsibility."[52]

Lethal Fictions: Preserving Confusion and Unreliability in Death Sentencing

A little more than a decade after the *Gregg* decision had placed a heavy burden on capital sentencing instructions to guide juror discretion, the U.S. Supreme Court seemed to reaffirm their importance. In *Mills v. Maryland*,[53] the Justices underscored the need to ensure juror comprehension and ruled that the mere possibility that a single "reasonable juror" was confused or misinformed about the meaning of the judge's instruction would raise questions about whether a capital jury "conducted its task improperly." Emphasizing the "high requirement of reliability on the determination that death is the appropriate penalty," the Justices returned the case to the trial court for resentencing.[54] The *Mills* Court noted that even though there had been no "extrinsic evidence" addressing the key psychological question—"what the jury in this case actually thought"[55]—the *possibility* that a single confused juror might block consideration of all of the mitigating evidence that was presented "is one we dare not risk."[56]

However, *Mills* was decided by a closely divided Court, one that subsequently retreated from what appeared to be a strong statement about the importance of instructional comprehension. Ironically, this retreat occurred as social science evidence mounted showing that jurors in many jurisdictions were extremely confused by the instructions, so much so that many likely conducted their most important task—choosing between life and death—improperly. Yet, in a number of subsequent cases—including some where extrinsic evidence of juror confusion did surface—the Court seemed to turn a blind eye to these important concerns.

The Court's problematic post-*Mills* jurisprudence is illustrated in *Boyde v. California,*[57] where some of the very aspects of the California instruction that Lynch and I studied were at issue. Despite the heavy crime focus that is written into the California instruction itself (where 9 of 11 factors deal explicitly with crime-related issues), and the way its most important mitigating factor is phrased simply as "any other circumstance which extentuates the gravity of the crime," the Justices were confident that California jurors somehow knew that they were supposed to reach beyond the facts of the crime and consider evidence of the defendant's background and character as mitigation.[58] Of course, much of the research reviewed earlier in this chapter documented the degree to which this confidence was misplaced.

In a later case, *Buchanan v. Angelone,*[59] the Court went even farther in making unjustified assumptions about how (and how well) jurors were likely to interpret capital sentencing instructions. Thus, a majority of the Court decided that Virginia jurors somehow inferred or intuited that they had been authorized to take mitigation into account, although the instruction they were given failed even to use—let alone define—the term "mitigation."[60] To reach this conclusion the Court ignored research showing that the sentencing instructions in general—and the term "mitigation" in particular—were extremely difficult to understand. Instead, the Justices provided their own interpretation of the Virginia instruction. This interpretation included the contention that the clauses in the instruction "clearly condition the choices that follow," that the disputed meaning of a key paragraph nonetheless was "clearly" conveyed, and that any claim that the instruction likely had been misunderstood "could *only* result from a strained parsing of [its] language." Moreover, even if the majority of Justices entertained "some doubt as to the clarity of the instruction," they were confident that the jurors somehow had divined the meaning of mitigation and managed to figure out the proper way to apply the concept from the "entire context in which the instructions were given."[61]

The Court was not moved to a different view two years later when, despite its earlier assertions in *Buchanan* that the meaning of the Virginia instruction had been perfectly clear, the Court considered a Virginia capital case in which the jurors actually sent a note to the trial judge expressing confusion and asking, "What is the rule? Please clarify?" The judge refused to answer their question and sent back a note directing the jurors to the very instruction that had provoked the confusion in the first place. Notwithstanding the jury's expressed confusion, and the judge's refusal to help them resolve it, Chief Justice Rehnquist's majority opinion concluded there was only a "slight possibility" that they had remained confused about the instruction, and this possibility was "insufficient to prove a constitutional violation. . . . "[62]

Indeed, instead of grappling in a meaningful way with the potentially confusing nature of capital sentencing instructions, the Court has continued to rely on a series of outmoded legal doctrines that ignore much of what social scientists now know about the difficulties jurors have in comprehending jury instructions in general and the penalty-phase instructions in particular. Thus, the opinions regularly assert that there is a presumption that jury members understand and follow the instructions they receive[63] and also that they understand whatever answers—however unhelpful—the trial judge gives to the questions they may pose.[64] In fact, the Court has gone so far as to assert that "[t]o presume otherwise would require reversal every time a jury inquires about a matter of constitutional significance, regardless of the judge's answer."[65]

Yet there is a fairer and more reasonable solution to this problem. That is, rather than presuming comprehension (that may not exist) or automatically requiring reversals (in a practice that would be impossible to sustain), the Court could examine the issue on a case-by-case basis but within the larger context of the social science literature on comprehension. Looking to the relevant circumstances in order to determine whether jurors in any case might have been confused (either by poorly worded jury instructions or by a judge's unhelpful answer to their questions) simply would necessitate a careful and honest assessment of the instructions and the context in which jurors tried to understand them.

Indeed, the Court has said that capital sentencing instructions are constitutionally defective if there is a "reasonable likelihood" that they have misled a jury into condemning a defendant to death.[66] In a case decided in the same term as *Mills*, the Court established a standard—"what a reasonable juror could have understood"—that seemed to acknowledge the relevance of social science data on the issue of comprehension.[67] These kind of inherently empirical questions can be answered intelligently only in the larger context of what is now known about the widespread lack of instructional comprehension. However, as I have suggested, it became clear in subsequent cases that a majority of the Justices were not interested in examining existing empirical evidence. Instead, they speculated on their own about what reasonable jurors did and did not understand while, at the same time, ignoring social science studies that suggested otherwise.

Thus, despite extensive research to the contrary, law-trained judges often opine that "it is difficult to see what is confusing about [the] instructions" to the lay jurors who are called on to interpret them.[68] There are numerous examples at the Supreme Court level and below in which judges offer testimonials about the "ease" with which the "commonly accepted and ordinary meaning" of key terms in the sentencing instructions can be discerned by persons "of ordinary intelligence" (despite, in some instances, jurors' direct statements to the contrary).[69]

Taking their lead from the Supreme Court, other appellate courts often focus only on the narrow question of whether the capital sentencing instructions that have been given by the trial judge are "accurate," or legally correct.[70] But this begs an equally important question that typically yields more troublesome answers: whether the accurately stated instructions have been understood correctly by the jurors who must apply them. As with the Supreme Court itself, lower appellate judges who lack any data of their own, and who explicitly reject or tacitly ignore empirical evidence to the contrary, continue to assert that "reasonable jurors would not have been under [a] misapprehension" created by the instructions. They sometimes do so even when the trial judge verbally misstated the instructions at the time he or she provided them to the jury.[71]

This is particularly unfortunate because, in fact, many trial judges pointedly refuse to provide clarification beyond the instructions themselves, even when jurors make it clear that they are confused and need guidance concerning the key terms on which they are supposed to rely.[72] Some judges have been openly blasé and dismissive about the nature of the problem: "For as long as the United States has been a nation, judges have been using legalese in instructing juries, with an inevitable adverse effect on the jury's comprehension. We do not think that traditional forms of jury instruction are now, and always have been, unconstitutional because of this."[73]

Even Justice Stanley Mosk, one of the California Supreme Court's most thoughtful justices, fell prey to the legal conceit that the cumbersome language in which the state's capital sentencing instructions are couched was comprehensible to average jurors. Although Mosk conceded that definitions of the key terms "aggravation" and "mitigation" would be helpful and therefore should be given in the future "to foster rational decisionmaking," he also endorsed the proposition that " '[a]ggravation' and 'mitigation' are commonly understood terms. A trial court is not required to instruct on the meaning of terms that are commonly understood."[74] Moreover, he elaborated that "[a] jury should be able to identify the specified circumstances as 'aggravating' or 'mitigating' by itself. This is because their nature is 'self-evident.' "[75]

Consistent with long-standing and well-justified doctrine, courts also refuse juror requests to research the meaning of the key terms on their own. However, combined with the judges' refusal to provide clarification, capital jurors are left in a quandary. In one Missouri case, for example, a capital jury sent a note to the judge asking, "What is the legal definition of mitigating (as in mitigating circumstances)?" The trial court responded: "Any legal terms in the instructions that have a 'legal' meaning would have been defined for you. Therefore, any terms that you have not had defined for you should be given their ordinary meaning." The jury followed up with another note that asked: "Can we have a dictionary?" to which the trial judge responded, "No, I'm not permitted to give you one."[76]

On direct appeal, the Missouri Supreme Court unanimously found that "despite the fact that one or more jurors may have been confused" about the meaning of mitigation, the trial judge was correct in refusing to provide a dictionary for the jurors and also correct in refusing to define the term for them. The court said that jurors must "rely solely upon the evidence and the court's instruction." The jury's inability to understand the instruction apparently was not taken as an impediment to relying on it.

In the same opinion, the Missouri justices also were presented with the results of previously discussed research that psychology professor Richard Wiener had conducted on the incomprehensibility of the Missouri instructions. However, they dismissed the studies because Wiener's participants "did not act as jurors . . . were given hypothetical facts . . . did not hear the testimony of witnesses . . . or deliberate with eleven other jurors."[77] Not only would these criticisms preclude the use of most forms of social science research, but they also ignored the results of research that had been done with actual jurors by the Capital Jury Project and others who found many of the same problems as Wiener. In place of a substantial empirical record to the contrary, the Missouri court substituted its own view: that, in the context of the sentencing instructions, "no reasonable person could fail to understand that 'mitigating' is the opposite of 'aggravating.' "[78]

It is worth noting that most researchers study the comprehension of the sentencing instructions at an individual level. Thus, for largely practical reasons, few studies provide direct tests of whether the jury's *collective* understanding would improve in the course of deliberation. However, several things suggest that it would not. For one, there is nothing in the instructions that requires capital juries to reach consensus about the meaning of the key terms themselves. The verdict forms do not require them to agree on the factors that led them to their verdict and this is made explicit in the instructions that are used in a number of states. Moreover, the extent of the errors in comprehension is so great that the collective wisdom of most capital juries still would produce a group whose overall understanding was quite low.

Indeed, based on the data in the first California study that Mona Lynch and I conducted, the likelihood of a capital defendant's life-or-death verdict being decided by a jury in which at least one member was completely inaccurate in his or her definition of either aggravation or mitigation, and incorrect as to at least two specific factors that are in the capital sentencing template in California, was much greater (19% of our sample) than the likelihood of such a jury containing a juror who was legally correct on both terms and completely accurate as to the sentencing template (.04% of our sample). Thus, jurors who were inaccurate on many key issues would almost always significantly outnumber the accurate ones.

Although it is unclear how differences of opinion about the meaning of the instructions would be resolved in any particular jury, there is no reason to believe that the accurate jurors would be more likely to prevail. In addition, Professor Phoebe Ellsworth's research on the general issue of whether "twelve heads are better than one" in improving jury comprehension of instructions indicated that while some errors of instructional interpretation were corrected in deliberation, about an equal number of correct interpretations were relinquished in favor of incorrect ones.[79] Note also that the postverdict interview data from the study that Sontag, Costanzo, and I did, as well as the extensive Capital Jury Project data based on interviews conducted in numerous other states, confirm that many errors persist through deliberation and verdict in actual cases in which juries deliberated as a group.

Thus, it does not seem reasonable for appellate courts to assume that instructions that are incomprehensible on their face will be rendered more understandable through some other means. Even attorney arguments—sometimes pointed to as a means of enhancing instructional comprehension in real cases—often fall far short of this goal. When Mona Lynch and I content-analyzed actual closing penalty-phase arguments given by both prosecuting and defense attorneys we found that even when attorneys got the meaning of the instructions right (which was by no means all the time), jurors were still left to sift through what were usually diametrically opposed explanations of the key concepts.

Specifically, when we examined the arguments given at the conclusion of a sample of 20 California capital cases (selected so that they were evenly divided between cases that had resulted in life and death verdicts), we found that attorneys spent surprisingly little time attempting to clarify the penalty-phase jury instructions. In fact, the key terms or concepts—"aggravating" and "mitigating"—were both defined in some manner by at least one of the attorneys in fewer than one-third of the 20 cases. However, when one or the other lawyer did undertake this task, he or she often was either incorrect or incomplete in the definitions provided. When both opposing lawyers undertook the task, perhaps not surprisingly, they most often worked at cross-purposes with each other. That is, prosecutors and defense attorneys offered jurors fundamentally different interpretations of the meaning of the two core sentencing concepts. As would be expected, perhaps, they also gave opposing accounts of whether either kind of evidence had been presented in the penalty trial and how much weight the jurors should give it. As a result, little or no clarity emerged from the exchanges.[80]

Thus, denied a balanced and comprehensible instruction from the judge—something the appellate courts simply have been unwilling to order—many capital jurors also appear to get little or no help from attorneys on either side. Indeed, they are left to their own devices to somehow divine the clear meaning of the sentencing instructions or, perhaps more likely, proceed without any.

Conclusion

The key provisions of the capital sentencing instructions in use throughout the United States are difficult if not impossible for many jurors to understand. The instructions fail to clearly explain the crucial concepts of "aggravation" and "mitigation." As a result, they leave many jurors at the mercy of preconceptions that they may have brought into the courtroom and feelings that may have been stirred in the course of what are often emotionally wrenching trials. Moreover, comprehension errors are not evenly distributed; rather, in virtually every study done on the issue, jurors have a much more difficult time correctly understanding what is meant by mitigation. For example, as I described previously, after having heard the sentencing instruction read to them three times, less than half of our California participants could provide even a partially correct definition for mitigation, almost a third provided definitions that were uninterpretable or incoherent, and slightly more than 1 subject in 10 was so mystified by the concept that he or she was unable to venture a guess about its meaning. Equally problematic is the fact that many jurors have special difficulties comprehending mitigation in ways that are broad enough to encompass the kind of evidence that typically is introduced to save a capital defendant's life.

Several troublesome consequences likely follow from this widespread lack of basic comprehension. The first is that that many jurors simply may disregard the parts of the sentencing instruction that they do not understand. Social psychologists have underscored the obvious importance of clarity and accessibility in the processing of verbal information—that words must be correctly understood before people can be properly influenced by them.[81] Capital jurors who are confused about the basic concepts that are supposed to be employed in capital decision making, misunderstand which factors in the sentencing template should lead them toward one verdict or the other, and are mistaken about the rules that govern the process by which they are to reach a sentencing decision have not been "guided" to more reliable and fair outcomes. Lacking guidance and left to their own devices, jurors may resort to deep-seated stereotypes and other improper considerations—the kind of impermissible factors whose effects were supposed to be reduced or eliminated by the instructions and perhaps the same ones responsible for the patterns of arbitrary and discriminatory death sentencing identified and condemned in *Furman*. Indeed, at this final stage, jurors' life-and-death decisions may be especially susceptible to many of the social psychological forces that I discussed in previous chapters.

The research reviewed in the preceding pages also suggests that the sentencing instructions focus capital jurors on the crime itself, often to the exclusion of any other legally relevant and potentially persuasive mitigation. In part because few people have prior experience applying the concept of mitigation in settings outside the courtroom—and thus have no store of knowledge other than the legal instructions from which to divine its meaning—it seems likely that mitigating evidence will be discounted or ignored in the jury's decision-making process. Put bluntly, absent strong and perhaps repeated clarifying explanations by the court and the attorneys, the half or so of the jurors who do not really know what mitigation means may be inclined to ignore it.

Moreover, uninterpretable or misconstrued instructions are likely to morally disengage capital jurors from the task at hand. Psychologists know generally that "[t]hrough convoluted verbiage, destructive conduct is made benign and people who engage in it are relieved of a sense of personal agency."[82] The convoluted verbiage in the standard capital jury instructions distances jurors from the realities of the decision they are being called on to make. As one scholar observed: "Under the pre-*Furman* system, the jury rendered a moral decision; it reached into its gut to decide whether death was the appropriate punishment for the defendant. Now, however, the jury is sometimes torn between rendering a moral decision and applying a legal formula they don't quite understand."[83]

Finally, it is important to note that, contrary to the beliefs of many citizens, not all of the jury-related biases (and the sentencing errors to which they give rise) are corrected in the appellate reviews that follow. Although it is certainly true that, as James Liebman, Jeffrey Fagan, and Valerie West have shown, the reversal rate in capital cases is high,[84] appellate judges—perhaps because they share many of the same views of the sentencing instructions as their trial court counterparts—do not focus heavily on the comprehension-related issues I have discussed in this chapter nor necessarily perceive them as problematic. Despite the frequency of reversals in capital cases, state and federal courts are loath to disturb jury verdicts because of a lack of instructional comprehension, rarely reaching very deeply under the veneer of rationality with which the jury's decision-making processes are cloaked.

Justice Stewart's plurality opinion in one of the key 1976 cases that reinstated capital punishment in the United States characterized the new sentencing instruction-based death penalty laws—ones that many states had passed and which the Court then approved—as ensuring "an informed, focused, guided, and objective inquiry into the question of whether [a defendant] should be sentenced to death."[85] Unfortunately, the research discussed in this chapter indicates that they often do nothing of the sort.

9

Condemning the Other

Race, Mitigation and the "Empathic Divide"

It is tempting to pretend that minorities on death row share a fate
in no way connected to our own, that our treatment of them
sounds no echoes beyond the chambers in which they die. Such
an illusion is ultimately corrosive, for the reverberations of injustice
are not so easily confined.
—Justice William Brennan, *McCleskey v. Kemp* (1987)

At the start of this book I noted that the various social psychological influences and effects that facilitated the death-sentencing process were cumulative—that is, that together they represented a procedural whole that was
larger and more powerful than the sum of its individual parts. In this chapter
I want to examine some of the ways in which those forces come together to
affect whether a capital defendant is condemned to death. Although the social
psychological processes that I have discussed to this point apply to death
penalty trials in general, here I want to discuss an important subset of capital
cases—ones in which defendants are African American. These cases have
special historical significance, as I note later, and they illustrate the way in
which the capital trial process can be further compromised by the pernicious
influence of race-based animus.

One mechanism of moral disengagement that I discussed at some length
in chapter 7—the tendency to create, highlight, or exaggerate difference and
transform it into defect and deficiency—helps to explain the chronic racism
that has plagued the criminal justice system throughout our nation's history,[1]
including, of course, the legacy of discriminatory death sentencing.[2] As Samuel Pillsbury observed: "In a society such as ours, where race is an obvious
and deeply-rooted source of social differences, race presents the most serious
otherness problem."[3] I argue in this chapter that aspects of the death-
sentencing process serve to preserve this sense of race-based otherness and
amplify its effects on the capital jury's choice between life and death.

Finding and Presenting Mitigation: Flaws at the Heart of the System

In the typical capital trial, prosecutors encourage jurors to make their ultimate sentencing decision on the basis of what are often isolated—albeit tragic and horrible—moments of aggression that, in the absence of any other information, are used to represent the entire life and the whole of the person. The strategy is to appear to have captured the essence of the defendant in the snapshot that has been taken of his violence. From this perspective, the full measure of the life and the worth of the person are restricted to this field of isolated violent acts.[4] It is an understandable and effective way to seek and to obtain death sentences.

On the other hand, as I have noted, the Constitution requires that capital jurors also be permitted to consider a broader evidentiary base on which to premise their life-and-death decision. Thus, they must at least consider testimony about the background and character of the defendant in those cases in which it is presented. The existence of a separate penalty trial allows the capital jury to focus intensely on the defendant and his life. Similarly, the rule that capital-sentencing instructions should not explicitly narrow or preclude the scope of mitigating evidence that jurors are told they may rely on in their decision-making process reflects a bedrock constitutional principle— the choice between life and death should *not* be premised on a consideration of the crime alone.[5] Unfortunately, there is much evidence that, in practice, little is done to ensure that the spirit of this broadening principle is upheld in all or even most cases.

As I noted in the last chapter, the capital-sentencing instructions do not clearly articulate the scope of the penalty-phase decision-making process so that capital jurors understand the breadth of information that is relevant to their moral inquiry into the defendant's culpability. As the research I discussed in the last chapter indicates, the instructions appear to contribute to the jurors' narrow crime focus by failing to make clear *what else* (like the background and character of the defendant) should be taken into account in choosing between life and death. In so doing, the instructions themselves seem to assist or encourage jurors to ignore the defendant's personhood, further disengaging them from the moral implications of their decision.

Recall also that attorneys appear to spend surprisingly little time attempting to clarify the penalty-phase jury instructions. When they do undertake this task, as Lynch and I found, they often are either incorrect or incomplete in the definitions they provide. Moreover, prosecutors and defense attorneys are likely to offer jurors fundamentally different interpretations of the meaning of the concepts and opposing accounts of whether such evidence has been presented in the penalty trial and how much weight it should be given. Jurors typically have to sift through diametrically opposed explanations of the key concepts, precisely the ones that a defined in the instructions themselves.[6]

There is another way in which defense attorneys m respect to the critically important concept of mitigation. scholar Welsh White described it: "Because defense couns derstand the dynamics of the penalty trial, there has been a number of cases in which defendants have been executed af presented little or no mitigating evidence at their penalty trials. . . . But even attorneys who understand the dynamics of a capital trial may be ill equipped to assume the role demanded of them in that setting."[7] Thus, capital jurors may have to decide the defendant's fate lacking any real understanding of the concept of mitigation—the only concept in the sentencing instructions that can lead them to a life verdict—and without the benefit of having had the case presented by a defense attorney who had effectively assembled the evidence to fully embody it.

Failing to assist jurors in understanding the causes of the capital crime and the various forces that may have influenced the defendant and affected his level of culpability does lay decision makers a disservice. But, especially in highly publicized cases in which the general public has become invested, it does citizens at large a disservice as well. That is, absent a meaningful discussion of the defendant's life and an explanation of his criminality that includes context and history, jurors are left with a sense that crime is random, unpredictable, and unpreventable. Confronted with inexplicable violence, capital jurors certainly are more likely to impose the death penalty. But a society confronted with similarly incomplete narratives also is more likely to become fearful and punitive.

Putting the defendant's life in a human context, situating his actions within a personal history, and appreciating the set of connections he has to other lives are among the only ways a capital jury can be led to a life rather than a death sentence. As I noted in chapter 7, the opportunity to present this kind of information and encourage the jurors to engage in these kinds of analyses and to make these connections is withheld until the final stage of the trial, when it may be too late. Moreover, because of the instructional incomprehension discussed in chapter 8, the information itself may be received by the jurors without any coherent, clarifying, and legitimizing message from the judge about its importance to the decision at hand. Precisely because they often start at a significant penalty-phase disadvantage, defense attorneys who fail to undertake these challenges in essence concede a death verdict for their clients.

The poor timing of the defense case in mitigation, the fact that it would require most jurors to perform the difficult work of in essence changing their minds about the defendant, the heavy crime focus of the penalty instructions that follow, and the poor performance of many defense attorneys who lack the training and resources to overcome these obstacles may help to explain hy the Capital Jury Project found that the penalty phase (i.e., "evidence about the defendant's punishment") was the *least* well remembered stage of the entire trial process for capital jurors,[8] and that half of the jurors had actually made up their minds (were "absolutely convinced" or "pretty sure") about the appropriate penalty once they had convicted the defendant of the guilt-phase crime.[9] It is also not surprising, in this context, that 40% of the capital jurors believed the heinousness of the crime *compelled* a sentence of death.[10]

In this chapter I suggest that various aspects of the death-sentencing process that accumulate and interact with one another to facilitate death verdicts overall operate with special force and effect in the case of African American defendants. The racial dynamics that are added to this already deadly mix of social psychological forces may help to explain the high rates at which African Americans continue to be sentenced to death at high rates by largely white juries, especially in those cases in which their victims also are white. I address these issues in some greater detail in the sections that follow.[11]

Biographical Racism and Discriminatory Death Sentencing

The practice of capital punishment and the social evil of racism have certain things in common. They are both forged from many of the same human emotions, including anger, hatred, and fear. They are both facilitated when their adherents treat people as though they were not human. They both focus our attention only on certain isolated, odious characteristics—observed, inferred, assumed, or simply attributed—which then are taken as emblematic, to the exclusion of all others, and that facilitate our condemnation of their targets.[12] The death penalty and racism depend on a form of "psychological secrecy"—the refusal to deal with the painful emotional dilemmas that would be generated and the moral ambiguities we would be forced to confront if we looked closely and honestly at what we are doing and why.[13] Instead, in the case of the death penalty, the public is given access to only superficial and schematic details of the lives of capital defendants that facilitate their dehumanization and enhance what historians have called the civil ordering function of the execution ritual. Much as racism requires us to ignore the truth about those it victimizes and diminishes, and insists that we keep a distance from the persons that it targets lest we learn the truth about the cruel falsehoods racism perpetuates, capital punishment, as I tried to show in several previous chapters, thrives under circumstances that push us away from truly understanding those on whom it is inflicted and how.

Of course, there are differences between lawfully condemning someone to die and prejudicially condemning someone to the margins of social existence. In addition to the difference between literal and social death is the fact that someone who is condemned to die almost always has done something truly horrible in order to become eligible for execution, while the victims of racism have done nothing to precipitate their invidious mistreatment. Yet there are similarities in the psychology by which both proceed, and those similarities have forged an empirical connection between capital punishment and racist times and places. Throughout the history of American criminal justice, African Americans have received death sentences disproportionate to their numbers in the general population. These disproportions have been more shocking in some jurisdictions than others, and for some crimes more than others (rape, in particular), but the variations have rarely been so great as to mask the overall differences in treatment.

Louis Masur's historical study of capital punishment in the 18th and 19th centuries noted that even then, "those whom the state hanged tended to be young, black, or foreign."[14] More recent statistics suggest that the racial dimension to this pattern persisted. For example, between 1930 and 1982, African Americans comprised 10–12% of the United States population but 53% of those executed.[15] In presumably more enlightened times, only modest reductions in these disparities have been brought about. For example, in 1995, a year in which 56 persons were executed in the United States, over 40% were persons of color (25 of 56), almost all of whom were African American (22 of 56, or 39% of the total).[16] In addition to disparities in rates of execution, the overrepresentation of African Americans on death rows also persists. For example, in 1987 they comprised 41% of the prisoners condemned to death in the United States, about 3.5 times their number in the general population.[17] Even more recent statistics show little change, and certainly no decrease in overall percentages. Thus, blacks were 39% of all persons on death rows throughout the country in 1991, and 43% in 2001.[18]

Of course, these gross racial disparities do not account for the higher rates at which African Americans are arrested for murder in the United States. Yet even though they are not necessarily probative of "discrimination" in criminal justice system decision making, unadjusted statistics—the percentages of African Americans sent to death row or executed—are nonetheless relevant to discussions of racial fairness. Unless one is prepared to defend the indefensible proposition that African Americans have an innate predisposition to homicidal violence, these persistent disparities indirectly reflect the continued exposure of African Americans to powerful criminogenic conditions, something I discuss later in this chapter.

Moreover, even much more sophisticated statistical analyses of patterns of death penalty decision making that do control for rates of arrest, and sometimes for many other variables, generally find that the race of the defendant as well as, certainly, the race of the victim have an important effect on whether suspected murderers are charged with death-eligible crimes and whether juries vote to impose the death penalty in their cases.[19] Despite some variation in the outcomes of the studies, racial discrimination in the act of sentencing someone to death persists, sometimes strikingly so, as when an African American capital defendant has been convicted of a potentially capital murder in which his victim was white. The extent to which we overpunish African American defendants is masked somewhat by the fact that most homicide is intra-racial, the apparent tendency of criminal justice decision makers to undervalue African American victims, and the smaller number of cases in which African American defendants are charged with killing white victims.

However, the point at which calculations begin in many of the studies of sentencing discrimination occurs long *after* some of the most potent and destructive racialized forces at work in our society have already taken their life-altering toll. Research that focuses on the lives of capital defendants of all racial and ethnic backgrounds underscores the extent to which they have been exposed to powerful criminogenic (or "crime producing") factors and other traumatizing events and experiences long before their capital crimes were committed. This is especially—perhaps uniquely—true in the case of African American capital defendants who, because of the continued significance of race in American society, face more severe criminogenic factors, more often, and for longer periods of time.

These experiences represent a form of "biographical racism"—the accumulation of race-based obstacles, indignities, and criminogenic influences that characterizes the life histories of so many African American capital defendants. As these experiences accumulate over the life span, they exercise such profound influence over the life course and social histories of those exposed to them that they literally shape their biographies. These experiences are structural and are built into the very social contexts and life circumstances that have surrounded many African American capital defendants at key developmental stages of their lives. These life-shaping forces are psychologically central to understanding the "background and character" of a defendant and, as a result, should be uniquely legally relevant to the decision of whether or not he lives or dies. Yet, as I discuss in the remainder of this chapter, too often this information is either not presented to or not appreciated by the capital jury that should rely on it.

Some Structural Components of Biographical Racism

Terrible, traumatizing, and criminogenic social histories are not the unique province of minority capital defendants.[20] Indeed, the lives of *many* capital defendants are filled with what psychologists have termed "risk factors," potentially harmful experiences that greatly increase the likelihood that persons will engage in troubled, problematic behavior in the future.[21] However, because of the continued correlation of race with so many other painful and potentially damaging experiences in our society, the life histories of African American defendants are often replete with such risk factors, in ways that are distinctive and distinctly mitigating. In this section I briefly touch on just some of the components of the biographical racism from which many African American capital defendants have suffered.[22]

For example, we know that poverty forces family members to adapt to scarcity in ways that affect interpersonal relationships and, in turn, child development. One ethnographer studying children growing up in a poor urban neighborhood acknowledged their impressive resourcefulness in coping with poverty but nonetheless was forced to conclude that these admirable adaptive skills were still "no match for the physical toll of poverty and its constant frustrations and humiliations."[23] African American children, particularly, are more likely to live under conditions of *chronic* poverty,[24] the kind most likely to produce dysfunctional long-term adaptations.[25] Many researchers have documented the ways in which chronic economic hardships produce family disruption and psychological distress for both parents and children. This distress undermines parents' ability to provide nurturing care and increases tendencies toward inconsistent discipline that are, correspondingly, associated with increased depression, drug use, and delinquency among their adolescent children.[26]

We also know that persistent poverty is predictive of severe and recurrent child abuse. That is, parental "[v]iolence does occur at all income levels but it is more often repeated among the persistently poor."[27] Thus, even though they suffer disproportionately from "virtually every form of stress affecting full and healthy development," including being denied proper medical care and deprived of adequate food, clothing, and housing, "[n]one of these stressors is more threatening to the healthy development of black children and to the stability of their families than intrafamilial child abuse."[28] Among other things, exposure to violent, abusive parenting is *criminogenic*. That is, it shapes and influences young lives in ways that make subsequent criminal behavior more likely and significantly increases the chances of juvenile justice system intervention later on.

Of course, not every family adapts to the pressures of chronic poverty in the same way, and certainly not all African American capital defendants have experienced abusive parenting. But there are many other aspects to biographical racism that many have endured. For example, significant numbers of African American children "still encounter expressions of racial hatred, live in racially segregated neighborhoods, and endure the suspicion widespread among many people in positions of authority."[29] Many of them grow up in communities torn by violence, so that they are at risk of victimization in their own neighborhoods, where they lack physical and psychological safe havens.

If it is true, as sociologists teach us, that "[t]o understand the biography of an individual . . . we must understand the institutions of which [he is] a part,"[30] then understanding the biographical racism to which African Americans are exposed requires special attention to the nature of the institutions into which they are disproportionately drawn. Indeed, the lives of African American children are more often shaped and redirected by harsh forms of direct state intervention in ways that increase the likelihood that they will be placed in juvenile justice institutions and, at later ages, incarcerated in the adult criminal justice system.[31] There are many factors that contribute to this funneling effect.

Thus, African American children, especially—either because of different levels of need or differential processing at the hands of agency decision makers, or both—more often become wards of the so-called child welfare system in the United States, and are subjected to its often painful and potentially criminogenic influences. Although African Americans comprise 17% of the nation's children, they account for 42% of all children in foster care in the United States.[32] In some communities the disparities are even more dramatic. For example, African American children constitute 95% of all those in foster care in city of Chicago.[33] Moreover, once they are in the child welfare system, African American children are less likely to receive in-home social services, or mental health care, and they are more likely to be institutionalized for their emotional problems.[34]

Other patterns in the treatment of African American children are likely to have differential criminogenic effects. For example, they appear to be singled out disproportionately for school discipline and are more likely to be punished for nebulous infractions (such as "excessive noise" and "disrespect"). The differentials are large—one study found that, even after controlling for socioeconomic differences, African American children in middle school were more than twice as likely to be sent to the principal's office or suspended, and four times as likely to be expelled than their white counterparts.[35]

Some social scientists have theorized about various ways that public schools help to construct "bad boys" out of young African American male students.[36] For example, differences in "manners, style, body language, and oral expressiveness" may subtly but systematically influence the way in which teachers apply school rules and label African American students, ultimately placing them "at the bottom rung of the social order."[37] Moreover, as Anne Ferguson has put it, "[i]n the case of African American boys, misbehavior is likely to be interpreted as symptomatic of ominous criminal proclivities"[38] and the long-term consequence of this interpretation may be to "substantially increase one's chance of ending up in jail."[39]

There is also evidence of racial inequality in the assignment of African American children to special education classes. Nationwide statistics indicate that they are three times more likely to be labeled developmentally disabled and twice as likely to be labeled emotionally disturbed as their white counterparts.[40] Once diagnosed, they are more likely than white students to be separated from mainstream classrooms, and are more often relegated to underfunded and poorly designed programs that provide them with marginal educational experiences and minimal employment skills. At least one study of this problem concluded that its long-term effects contributed to higher rates of unemployment and incarceration among young African American adults.[41]

As adolescents, African Americans are more likely to be exposed to violence in their neighborhoods and in their schools, experiences that not only predispose them to higher rates of posttraumatic stress disorder (PTSD)[42] but also serve as risk factors for subsequent emotional problems, drug use, delinquency, and criminality. One critically important consequence of the way these and other risk factors combine in the lives of African American children and adolescents is the *much* higher rate of juvenile justice system intervention to which they have been subjected.

In fact, the overrepresentation of minority youth in these institutions is so widespread that juvenile justice researchers and policy makers refer to it by its acronym—"DMC" (for "disproportionate minority confinement"). African American and Latino children are overrepresented at literally every stage of juvenile justice system processing—in arrests, referrals to juvenile court, and among those who are held in detention awaiting the disposition of their case. They also are more likely to be formally charged in juvenile court, more likely to have their case waived from juvenile to adult court, and more likely to receive a disposition that requires an out-of-home placement (such as a commitment to a locked institution).[43]

Indeed, minority youth represent the *majority* of children held in juvenile facilities. For example, although they comprised 34% of the U.S. population in 1997, they represented 62% of children who were incarcerated that year. The disparities are especially large for African American youth. For example, African American children with no prior admissions to the juvenile justice system were six times more likely to be incarcerated in a public facility than white children with the same background who were charged with the same offense. African American children who had one or two prior admissions were *seven* times more likely to be incarcerated than whites with the same background history. Moreover, African American youth who were held in custody remained an average of 61 days longer than did whites. And the disparity in length of confinement was particularly pronounced for drug offenses, for which African American juveniles were confined an average of 90 days longer than their white counterparts.[44]

As recently as the late 1990s, after decades of supposed reform, the American Bar Association and the U.S. Justice Department issued a joint report that was highly critical of many of the nation's juvenile justice institutions. Echoing the concerns expressed in previous nationwide studies, the report acknowledged that the facilities were "increasingly overcrowded," "significantly deficient," and held a disproportionate number of minority young offenders incarcerated for property and drug-related crimes. The authors expressed concern over the "[w]ell documented deficiencies" in conditions of confinement, and the nature and poor quality of treatment and educational services, security, and suicide prevention. As they noted, "[s]ubjecting youth to abusive and unlawful conditions of confinement serves only to increase rates of violence and recidivism and to propel children into the adult criminal justice system."[45]

"Disproportionate minority confinement" means that these harmful consequences necessarily fall more heavily on African American children than on others. Along with other minority children, they will be placed at even greater risk of subsequent incarceration as a result of this form of early state intervention. In fact, analysts like Barry Feld have argued persuasively that the increasingly punitive juvenile justice policies that "impose harsh sanctions disproportionately on minority youths" have, in turn, transformed the very nature of the juvenile court system in the United States, blurring the differences in procedures and substantive goals between it and the adult criminal courts.[46] In part because "the segregation of blacks living in concentrated poverty in urban America coalesced and influenced patterns of youth crime,"[47] it was easier for predominately white policy makers deciding how to handle "someone else's kids"—usually African American kids—to implement increasingly severe punishments. Softer and more benign methods, once justified by the increasingly defunct rehabilitative ideal, fell into disfavor.

Many African American children are further "propelled" toward the adult criminal justice system by an additional set of factors that compounds whatever painful and damaging experiences they may have suffered in juvenile institutions. For adults as well as juveniles, crime is shaped by its social ecology—the characteristics of the neighborhoods in which it occurs. Like many other people returning from juvenile and adult institutions, many African Americans are consigned to inner-city environments filled with criminogenic risks and threats.[48] The difference is that, in many minority communities, there are so many more of them enmeshed in a cycle of incarceration and reentry. Lacking any social and economic cushion with which to absorb returning and displaced residents, these places hover at the "tipping point," beyond which insurmountable levels of personal and neighborhood disorganization and chaos may occur.[49]

In many of these areas, the lives of African American residents are much affected by what researchers have termed "criminal embeddedness"—immersion in a network of interpersonal relationships that increase their exposure to crime-prone role models.[50] Neighborhoods characterized by criminal embeddedness are highly criminogenic and also extremely difficult to survive. Recent statistics indicate that African Americans are about nine times more likely than whites to be murdered with firearms.[51] Not surprisingly, as social scientists Michelle Fine and Lois Weiss found in their study of the urban inner-city, residents of both genders and all races and ethnicities were very concerned about street crime and violence. However, despite the high rates at which they were victimized by street crime, African American and Latino men were more likely to voice fears about "*state-initiated* violence, detailing incidents of police harassment, the systemic flight of jobs and capital from poor communities of color, the over-arrest of men of color, and the revived construction of prisons."[52]

Other researchers have used the term "neighborhood disadvantage" to describe the nexus or cluster of interrelated factors that often accompany poverty in minority communities and amplify its negative effects on individual development as well as on adult behavior.[53] The impact of these factors disrupts the social organization of the neighborhood, undermines the development of shared community norms, and weakens families and their ability to socialize children in positive ways. Not surprisingly, many of these neighborhood disadvantages are criminogenic in nature. For example, high rates of unemployment and the prevalence of single-parent families in neighborhoods can minimize the amount of time that children spend with positive role models. Disadvantaged neighborhoods also tend to suffer extreme levels of transience and mobility, which contribute to an overall sense of impermanence and disorganization. The development of stable, consistent, and consensual community norms against crime and violence is undermined as a result.

Indeed, many autobiographical and ethnographic accounts of the lives of African Americans have underscored precisely these disadvantages, ones that many African American capital defendants have confronted throughout their lives.[54] They are the result of powerful sociopolitical and economic forces that adversely affect the choices of individual actors, choices that are often less a product of rational or conscious decision-making processes than attempts to struggle with "[f]eelings of sheer humiliation and embarrassment, disappointment and frustration, grief and loneliness, and fear and anxiety (especially concerning suspicion, rejection, and abandonment)."[55]

Race continues to shape the biographies of African American capital defendants well into adulthood. For example, the racial dimension to poverty in the United States in some ways deepens the stigma, renders its consequences more chronic for adults as well as children.[56] In some areas of the country the structural disadvantage and economic marginality are staggering. For example, Neeta Fogg reported in 2003 that 45% of black men in Chicago between the ages of 20 and 24 were out of work and out of school.[57] Similarly, nearly half of all African American men between the ages of 16 and 64 in New York City were unemployed in 2003.[58] In the face of such severe deprivation and disadvantage, race seems to heighten the sense of injustice and intensify the righteous outrage that develops among people who have been confined in what one commentator has termed a "subculture of exasperation."[59]

In addition to these sociological and economic consequences, racism also has an impact on the biographies of African Americans in ways that are more psychological in nature, exposing them to significantly higher levels and unique forms of interpersonal and "environmental" stress.[60] For example, they may be subjected to what have been termed "microaggressions"—the "subtle, stunning, often automatic, and non-verbal exchanges which are 'put downs' of blacks" by whites who may employ them "unintentionally" but nonetheless persistently.[61] The cumulative impact of these microaggressions "has the potential to be the straw that breaks the camel's back due to the relentless nature of the racialized bombardment and the difficulty of attributing racial animus, that hostility which is thought to indicate intention."[62]

Although as a rule African Americans are subjected to a greater number of such provocations, they do not have the same leeway as others to respond. Indeed, the greater amount of criminal justice system surveillance, monitoring, and intense policing of African Americans, disparities in the prosecution and punishment of African Americans for similar crimes that are treated very differently (perhaps as a function of the race of the defendants likely to commit them),[63] and the multitude of other criminogenic criminal justice interventions to which they are exposed (such as higher rates of "three strikes" prosecutions[64]) help to account for the drastic levels of over-incarceration of African American adult men—rates that exceed those of blacks in South Africa.[65] Prison itself, the difficulties of postprison adjustment, and the fact that probation and parole now function as an agencies of social control rather than providers of reintegrative services[66] all combine in potentially destructive ways to more adversely affect the lives of African Americans than others.

This brief cataloguing of the structural and other obstacles faced by African Americans has addressed only some of the factors that distinguish their lives from those of nearly everyone else in this society. These components of biographical racism go a long way toward explaining—at a broad level with sobering implications—the continuing disproportion of African Americans in our nation's prisons and on its death rows. Anyone who has worked extensively with capital defendants knows firsthand about the wages of this kind of racism, the way it interacts with criminal justice system decision making and inflicts additive effects on the lives of young minority men that become the dominant framework around which their social histories have been structured.

Structural Mitigation in the Social Histories of Capital Defendants

On a case-by-case basis, biographical racism also represents a form of what might be called "structural mitigation"—mitigation that is structured into the lives of African American defendants by the continued importance and pernicious consequences of race in American society. In precisely the degree to which African American capital defendants have undergone these unique and potentially criminogenic experiences in our society, they approach their capital trials with social histories that include a built-in store of significant mitigation that capital juries are required to consider in deciding their fates.

To be sure, this kind of mitigation is not categorical—it does not, on its face, preclude the imposition of the death penalty (as the Supreme Court now has ruled that, say, age and developmental disability do).[67] Nor is this an argument to the effect that African Americans are not "capable" of committing a capital crime or that they are not "responsible" for what they do.[68] Rather, it is a statement about the special store of mitigation—considerations that weigh heavily in favor of granting life rather than death verdicts—that has been inscribed into their social histories by the very nature of the experiences to which, as a result of their race, African American defendants have been exposed and subjected.

To develop this notion a little more, let me briefly discuss the concept of mitigation and how it is supposed to operate in capital trials. Legal commentators have helped to refine the concept of mitigation by reminding defense attorneys that they must show jurors that the defendant's actions were "humanly understandable in light of his past history and the unique circumstances affecting his formative development."[69] Thus, a mitigating social historical analysis of a defendant's life that highlights the role of factors such as poverty and abuse does not excuse serious violent crime, but it renders past criminal behavior "more understandable and evokes at least partial forgiveness." It is a framework that must be brought to bear in a capital penalty trial in order "to spark in the sentencer the perspective or compassion conducive to mercy."[70]

In 1987, Justice O'Connor articulated what she characterized as a "long-held" societal belief that "defendants who commit criminal acts that are attributable to a disadvantaged background, or to emotional and mental problems, may be less culpable than defendants who have no such excuse."[71] She summarized the significance of this belief for "the individualized assessment of the appropriateness of the death penalty," noting that the process of understanding the role that someone's disadvantaged background or emotional or mental problems have played in his or her life course and past criminal behavior is central to the constitutionally required "moral inquiry into the culpability of the defendant."[72] And, just a few terms ago, O'Connor authored an opinion that finally imposed a *duty* upon defense attorneys to assist jurors with this inquiry by developing mitigation through a detailed social historical analysis of the capital defendant's life.[73]

These legal notions about the basis of mitigation are grounded in sound psychological theory. The theoretical basis for a model of mitigation begins with what social psychologists know as "attribution theory," the proposition that people regularly make causal attributions about the behavior that they witness other people engaging in.[74] Depending on whether they attribute the causes of the behavior in question to the internal dispositions and willful choices of the actor or to external circumstances and conditions over which the actor has less control, the behavior and the actor are judged very differently. That is, the nature of the causal attribution affects judgments about the moral quality of the act and the moral culpability of the actor.

It is well established in the application of attribution theory to legal settings that jurors engage in a process of analyzing the causes of a defendant's behavior, his intentions in the course of that behavior, and the outcome of the behavior itself in the course of attributing blame, gauging blameworthiness, and assessing culpability.[75] When the perceived cause of a criminal act is internal and volitional—stemming from personal traits and choices—increased levels of culpability are assigned and higher levels of punishment are perceived as warranted. Reversing or moderating the attributional process by which higher levels of culpability are assigned—by providing alternative causal explanations for actions or for an entire life course—is the essence of mitigation in a capital-sentencing context. Thus, in terms of the "moral inquiry into the culpability of the defendant" that is essential to the capital jury's choice between life and death, anything that shifts the ultimate causal attribution (in part or in whole) from the defendant to some external cause or condition not under the control of the defendant has a mitigating effect or consequence.

Because of the well-documented general tendency for people to attribute actions to the actor, not to the situation or to other background factors—committing what social psychologists call the "fundamental attribution error"[76]—the task of shifting the attributional frame or schema in this way can be extremely difficult. Moreover, all other things being equal, the greater the harm that the particular behavior brings about, the more likely that it will be attributed to internal causes (i.e., to the perpetrator of the act).[77] In addition, the less similar the persons whose behavior is being judged to the persons making the judgment, the greater the tendency to perceive internal causes for their behavior, to hold them more responsible and culpable for their actions, and to punish them more harshly.[78]

In the case of capital jurors, who typically are called on not just to evaluate a single act but an entire life—indeed, to assess the moral worth and overall culpability of the person who is on trial in a death penalty case—the process of understanding the attributional causes of the course of the defendant's life requires a narrative understanding of who the defendant is and how and why he has done the things he has. As one commentator has summarized it, "[i]n compiling evidence of mitigating circumstances, attorneys and social workers investigate not only a client's present mental state, but his childhood, family life, and the community in which he was raised."[79] In other words, in a capital penalty trial, the inquiry into moral culpability is broadened in a way that provides the jury with insights into how and why the defendant made certain life-altering choices and, as a result, what level of blameworthiness attaches to the defendant overall.

Thus, evidence that provides a humanizing narrative account of the defendant's life and prior actions is essential to a case in mitigation because it helps capital jurors understand how forces beyond the defendant's control shaped the direction of his life and the adaptive nature of many of the actions in which he engaged. A narrative that allows the jury to see the defendant as a person, rather than, for example, as a "monster," shifts the attributional framework and thereby lessens his level of moral culpability.[80]

The opportunity to render compassionate justice requires that jurors be given the guidance to walk the "delicate line" that philosopher Martha Nussbaum describes: "We are to acknowledge that life's miseries strike deep, striking to the heart of human agency itself. And yet we are also to insist that they do not remove humanity, that the capacity for goodness remains when all else has been removed."[81] Of course, like all capital defendants who are more than the sum total of the risk factors to which they have been exposed, African American defendants are, and must be depicted as, whole persons whose humanity transcends the biographical racism to which they have been subjected and the structural mitigation offered on their behalf.

Crossing the Empathic Divide: The Need to Transcend "Otherness"

A meaningful moral inquiry into the culpability of the individual defendant requires capital jurors to cross an "empathic divide"—a cognitive and emotional distance between them that acts as a psychological barrier, making genuine understanding and insight into the role of social history and context in shaping a capital defendant's life course difficult to acquire. The recognition of basic human commonality, an opportunity for capital jurors to connect themselves to the defendant through familiar experiences, common moral dilemmas, and recognizable human tragedies, is the starting point for compassionate justice. But the empathic divide stands in the way of that kind of understanding. Its roots are deep but not difficult to trace.

In a capital penalty trial, precisely because the harm for which the defendant is responsible is so great, and the typical capital defendant is perceived as so dissimilar to the jurors (by virtue of his behavior if nothing else), the challenge of overcoming basic attributional bias is always significant. This challenge is made greater by many of the social psychological forces I described at length in preceding chapters, and it can be met only through the most conscientious efforts. These efforts include painstaking investigation, the organization of diverse life facts into a meaningful narrative with coherent mitigating themes, and an effective, honest, humanizing presentation to jurors that places the defendant's behavior in a larger context that will allow them to better understand him.

However, in the case of African American capital defendants, the empathic divide unfortunately is much wider. This is in part because of an even more extreme attribution error that whites tend to commit when they interpret and judge the behavior of minority group members. Indeed, this tendency to attribute the causes of the behavior of African Americans to their negative internal traits has been termed the "*ultimate* attribution error."[82] Whether the error is ultimate or merely fundamental, its consequences are truly significant. As Anthony Amsterdam and Jerome Bruner have observed, racism involves the opportunistic use of race: "To disempower the group constructed as 'other' in order to empower *our group* by contrast to 'them.'

This requires the creation and maintenance of an *essentialist*, 'natural kinds' category scheme that imbues the 'others' with intrinsic, immutable qualities making them different from us."[83]

Attributing deeper and more negative traits and motives to minority group members in our society—traits and motives that are represented and perceived as natural, intrinsic, and immutable—makes it even more difficult for whites to appreciate the role of social history and present circumstances in shaping the life course of African Americans. In capital cases, it interferes with the ability of jurors to take structural mitigation into account as they assess the culpability of individual African American defendants. Thus, the empathic divide that separates jurors from capital defendants in general grows wider as a result of the psychological distance between whites and African Americans. If the psychological distance between white jurors and African American defendants is even greater than usual—for example, if the jurors themselves are racially prejudiced—then the problem is likely to be much worse.[84]

Moreover, there is some evidence that it may be intensified by certain aspects of the capital trial process itself. For one, as I pointed out in chapter 5, the legally-mandated practice of death qualification means that the already considerable racial and corresponding experiential and attitudinal divisions that separate defendants from jurors in criminal trials will be significantly widened in capital cases. Put differently, death-qualified juries are even less likely than most to share any status characteristics or common life experiences with capital defendants that would allow them to bridge the vast differences in behavior that the trial is designed to highlight. If "[d]ifferences in group membership between punisher and punished increase the risk of nonmoral judgment," then death qualification increases the likelihood that these kinds of judgments will be made in capital trials.[85]

Laura Sweeney, Mona Lynch, and I have conducted several studies on the nature of the death-sentencing process in which this concept—the empathic divide—appears to have played a role. For example, in a meta-analysis of experimental studies of race and sentencing that included some of our own research on death penalty imposition, Sweeney and I found that jurors sentenced differently as a function of the racial characteristics of the case. Thus, in the 14 individual studies that we analyzed, there *were* overall racial discriminatory effects for both race of defendant and race of victim.[86] The statistically significant discriminatory effects were larger when the studies were well controlled and when the race of the jurors was taken into account. Specifically, we concluded that "racial bias in criminal sentencing is a very precise, specific phenomenon," more likely to be manifested when race of juror and victim, in addition to defendant, were taken into account.[87]

Because the results suggested that special decision-making processes might be at work when jurors and defendants were of different races, Sweeney and I followed the meta-analysis with a direct simulation study of the death-sentencing process in which we systematically varied the race of the defendant and victim. We hoped to determine how jurors thought about sentencing issues in general and whether they thought differently about them when the defendant was a member of another racial group. We found first of all that there were large differences, across different types of capital crimes, for race of defendant and race of victim. That is, our student-jurors discriminated against African Americans both as defendants and as victims. Participants who considered exactly the same case facts and "evidence," presented in exactly the same way, rendered significantly more death sentences if the defendant was African American and if his victim was white.

When we tried to determine how and why this occurred by asking participants in each condition to explain their sentencing decisions, we found that found that white participants interpreted aggravating and mitigating circumstances differently as a function of the racial characteristics of the case. In particular, they tended to weigh aggravating circumstances more heavily when the defendant was African American. Similarly, they were reluctant to attach much significance at all to mitigating circumstances when they were offered on behalf of an African American defendant. The participants also mentioned "stereotype-consistent" reasons for their sentencing verdicts (i.e., negative qualities of the African American defendants), and they appeared less able or willing to empathize with or enter the world of African American defendants (as manifested by the tendency to write significantly less overall in explaining their sentencing decision, and significantly less about the black defendant in specific).

In the late 1990s, Mona Lynch and I studied some of these same issues, but in conjunction with the research we had done on the comprehension of capital sentencing instructions that I described in the last chapter. This time, however, we used death-qualified, jury-eligible participants from the surrounding community rather than students. Our experimental study was designed to examine what role if any the jurors' difficulty in understanding and correctly applying capital sentencing instructions might play in racially discriminatory death sentencing.[88] Among other things, Lynch and I found that our white jurors sentenced African American defendants to death more often than they did whites. There was about a 10-percentage-point overall difference that was determined by race—white defendants were given death sentences a little more than 40% of the time, African American defendants a little more than 50%. The harshest sentencing occurred in the black defendant/white victim condition, where death sentences were rendered by 54% of the participants.

However, when we looked only at those participants who had a difficult time correctly understanding the sentencing instructions—the bottom half of our group of participants in terms of instructional comprehension—the margin of overall discriminatory death sentencing doubled from a 10- to a 20-percentage-point difference. That is, African American defendants were sentenced to die 60% of the time, to life by 40% of the participants; exactly the reverse was true in the case of white defendants—they got life sentences

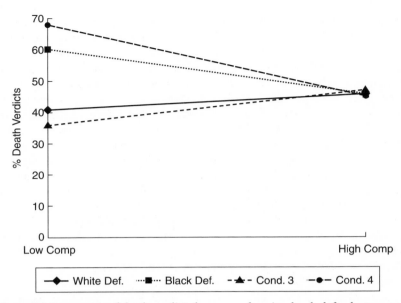

Figure 9.1 Percentage of death verdicts by comprehension level: defendant race and cross-racial conditions.

about 60% of the time and death sentences 40%. As figure 9.1 illustrates, being confused about the instructions seemed to allow a greater amount of prejudice to come into play in the death-sentencing process, while high levels of comprehension appear to reduce or eliminate its effect.

Keep in mind that the case facts—including all the facts that were presented at the penalty trial—were identical; race was the *only* thing that varied. Thus, we also were surprised to find that our jurors regarded exactly the same mitigating and aggravating evidence very differently depending on whether it was offered in a case in which the defendant was white as opposed to one in which he was African American. As table 9.1 indicates, these differences were marginal in the case of aggravation—although in each instance the same aggravating factors were regarded as slightly more aggravating for African American than for white defendants—none of the differences was statistically significant. However, in the case of three of the four mitigating factors we introduced—that the defendant suffered abuse as a child, had psychological difficulties that had gone untreated, and suffered from drug abuse problems—jurors found the testimony significantly more mitigating for white defendants than it was for African Americans. Only one mitigator— that the defendant had a loving family that did not want to see him die— was interpreted the same way for African American and white defendants.

In addition, not only were jurors likely to underuse mitigation for African American defendants, but many of them were more likely actually to *misuse* it. That is, as table 9.2 illustrates, some jurors inappropriately con-

Table 9.1
Mean Weighting of Penalty Phase Evidence By Race of Defendant

	Race of Defendant		t-Value for Mean Difference
	Black	White	
Specific mitigating evidence			
Child abuse	3.16	2.64	3.26*
Psych. problems	3.48	3.06	2.95*
Drug abuse	3.90	3.49	2.94*
Loved by family	3.25	3.09	1.16 (n.s.)
Specific aggravating evidence			
Murder facts	5.65	5.52	0.80 (n.s.)
Victim impact	4.60	4.40	1.24 (n.s.)
Murder photos	5.20	5.10	0.72 (n.s.)
Lack of remorse	5.11	5.09	0.13 (n.s.)

Means based on seven-point scale in which higher number indicates evidence was seen as supporting a death sentence, lower means indicate evidence was seen as supporting a life sentence.
*$p < .004$.

verted some of the mitigating factors into aggravating factors (by indicating that their presence in the case inclined them toward a death rather than life sentence). In the case of two important mitigating factors—that the defendant was abused as a child and that the defendant suffered from psychological problems that had gone untreated—jurors were about twice as likely to do this when the defendant was black as when he was white.

These data help to confirm, as I have suggested, that white jurors, in particular, are either less able or less willing to empathize with and appreciate the mitigating significance of key background factors in the lives of African American defendants in making assessments of blameworthiness and moral culpability. This failure to hear and acknowledge the impact of race in the lives of African American defendants brought about by the empathic divide is reminiscent of what Peggy Davis wrote about the Supreme Court's handling of the *McCleskey* case, discussed at length in chapter 1, but here writ small in the minds of capital jurors whose "cognitive habit[s], history, and culture" sometimes leaves them "unable to hear the range of relevant voices and grapple with what reasonably might be said in the voice of discrimination's victims."[89] But that barrier—the built-in barrier against hearing, understanding, taking into account, and integrating into compassionate decision making—can only be overcome in the present system by attorneys who

Table 9.2
Use and Misuse of Mitigation By Race of Defendant

	White Defendant			Black Defendant		
	Weighed Toward Life	No Wt. in Decision	Weighed Toward Death	Weighed Toward Life	No Wt. in Decision	Weighed Toward Death
Mitigating evidence						
Child abuse**	72%	20%	9%	54%	29%	17%
Drug abuse*	44%	38%	18%	29%	48%	23%
Psych. problems**	61%	30%	9%	45%	38%	18%
Loved by family*	51%	46%	3%	43%	48%	9%

Chi-square tests of significance: $^*p < .05$, $^{**}p < .01$.

work with the utmost effectiveness on behalf of their death penalty clients. The failure to meet this high standard would seem to virtually guarantee death rather than life verdicts for most African American capital defendants.

There are a few final points to be made about how these issues can combine to affect the outcome in any given case. For the most part, our current system of death sentencing fails to recognize the existence of this empathic divide—for death penalty defendants in general or African American defendants in particular. It does little or nothing to require that defense attorneys make every effort to cross the divide for jurors and has refused to mandate that judges assist them in doing so (by, at least, using sentencing instructions that the jury can comprehend). Moreover, in conjunction with the mechanisms of moral disengagement I discussed in chapter 7 and the psychological consequences of the death-qualification process, the capital trial process seems to operate in ways that intensify the effects of this divide. With respect to death qualification, recall that this unique feature of death penalty voir dire renders the jury pool less representative of the community in general and less likely to include African American members in particular. In addition, it helps to identify prospective jurors of all races who may be uncertain or ambivalent about the death penalty. They, in turn, are then more likely to be targeted for prosecutorial peremptory challenges.[90]

Thus, death qualification helps to ensure that African American defendants are more likely to be judged by white jurors and by those in favor of the death penalty. But, by selecting for death penalty supporters, it also helps to guarantee that those jurors who serve are less likely to accurately comprehend the capital sentencing instructions than if death qualification had not occurred. Recall the study described in chapter 8, that Amy Smith, Carmel Benson, and I conducted in which we found that death penalty support was highly correlated with poor instructional comprehension. This suggests that, ironically, the jury selection process that is used at the outset of a capital trial helps to ensure that fewer jurors will understand the crucial instructions that are supposed to govern their behavior at its final stage.[91] Poorer levels of instructional comprehension, as Lynch and I showed, further disadvantage African American capital defendants in this process.

Conclusion

This chapter addressed some of the ways in which the various social psychological components of our system of death sentencing can accumulate and interact over the course of a capital prosecution to diminish the constitutional right to have a capital jury consider the full range of available mitigation in deciding between life and death. By taking one historically important example—the fate of African American defendants in this process—I have tried to illustrate the way in which the reality of death penalty trials may fall short of the image of fairness that surrounds them. Because of the operation of various social psychological forces and mechanisms—created by practices and procedures that are built into the system of death sentencing—defendants may receive a diminished rather than enhanced brand of justice. Instead of correcting the problematic effects of the biases introduced into this process at earlier stages, our system of death sentencing either ignores or proactively compounds them at subsequent stages. In the end, less reliable and less fair outcomes are the predictable result.

It could be argued that the courts have an affirmative duty in all death penalty cases—but certainly ones involving African American defendants—to proactively seek to overcome the effects of what I have termed an "empathic divide" between capital jurors and defendants. It is a divide that is widened in the case of African Americans who are on trial for their lives, especially in cases where both the jurors and victims are white. Requiring jurors to grapple seriously with the nature of those structural forces outside the courtroom that help to account for the defendant's behavior and life course—especially when the racial dynamics of the case are likely to amplify already punitive tendencies—might begin to ensure that death sentencing is always the product of genuinely engaged and fully informed inquiries into the moral culpability of defendants. Absent an explicit, concerted attempt to make social history, structural disadvantage, and biographical racism a central focus of jury decision making in these kinds of cases, the social psychological forces I have discussed in this chapter are likely to amplify already substantial obstacles to fairness and distort the outcomes of capital trials.

10

No Longer Tinkering With the
Machinery of Death
Proposals for Systemic Reform

[T]he penalty of death is qualitatively different from a sentence of
imprisonment, however long. . . . Because of that qualitative
difference, there is a corresponding difference in the need for
reliability in the determination that death is the appropriate
punishment.
—Justice Potter Stewart, *Woodson v. North Carolina* (1976)

Historian Stuart Banner has observed that there has always been "a tension
between the general and the particular, between the approval of death as a
punishment and a strong reluctance to carry out the distasteful steps necessary to put that punishment into practice."[1] He suggested that this tension
led, among other things, to the abolition of public executions. In this book
I have suggested that the tension persists and is managed—although not
entirely resolved—through the various social psychological mechanisms and
legal procedures discussed in the preceding chapters.

In the course of this discussion I often have referred generically to "the
law" and "the system of capital punishment." At times, these references may
have seemed to imply that the system functioned in uniform ways, perhaps
even with a conscious or conspiratorial design. I intended to impute none
of these qualities. Instead, I believe that over time these procedures and legal
structures have evolved as a function of accumulated decisions made by
numerous legislators, judges, and others who, because of their implicit support for the death penalty, have chosen, preferred, and approved policies and
practices that they understood—usually at an intuitive level—ensured the
viability of capital punishment. In some sense, of course, conscious intention
is not essential to the process I have described; as long as decision makers
assume that the system of death sentencing is likely to persist as part of the
established legal order, many of them are likely to make decisions and support policies that implicitly facilitate its preservation.

Collectively, as I have suggested, those policies and practices operate to
morally distance citizens, voters, and jurors from the otherwise impossibly

difficult psychological challenges with which death sentencing presents them. By talking about the "system" and "design" of capital punishment, then, I mean only—but at least—that there is an interconnectedness to the parts of the death-sentencing process in the United States. As the process unfolds, it is experienced as the sum of all of its interlocking parts, and those parts operate in tandem to help facilitate the actual imposition of the death penalty. In fact, I have argued further that there is a distinct "death tilt" to the way we go about death sentencing that is best grasped by examining the social psychological effects produced by the interlocking parts of this system as they fit together and function as a whole.

Thus, in addition to the "law on the books" aspects of capital punishment, there are complicated, critically important "law in reality" components that must be understood. Here is where the death penalty functions as a complex social psychological network that creates a special set of reactions in those persons who are exposed to and influenced by it. Those reactions are what make the operation of the system possible and, in the final analysis, facilitate the imposition of the death penalty. Here is also where I propose that many systemic reforms must be directed if capital punishment is to become truly fair and reliable in actual practice. These reforms stem directly from the many research-related concerns raised in each of the previous chapters.

Using Social Psychological Data as the Basis for Systemic Death Penalty Reforms

The research I described and discussed in the preceding chapters speaks to many systemic problems. However, despite their depth and scope, few of these problems are truly insurmountable. The law's inherent conservatism certainly impedes meaningful reform of the entrenched practices and the policies that have evolved to protect the death penalty status quo. But these kind of legal barriers impede most forms of law reform. "Law and lawyers," Karl Llewellyn once famously remarked, often "struggle for what is old, for what may be outworn, against the claims of anything that may be new."[2] Nothing—except, perhaps, for politics—makes these barriers any more insurmountable in the case of capital punishment. Indeed, the real obstacle to meaningful reform of this system appears to be the politically expedient use—at times, even exploitation—of the death penalty. It is a potent weapon that has proven to be extremely difficult for politicians and politically minded jurists to relinquish.

Because I have written these chapters from the standpoint of a research psychologist rather than a judge or politician, I have the luxury of discussing what is possible rather than what is legally practical or politically feasible. And I propose to do exactly that—to proceed unencumbered by having to navigate around or through all the legal precedents that have been interposed to prevent meaningful reform, or to convince politicians to talk to citizens and voters honestly about the problems that continue to plague the system of death sentencing and acknowledge the insignificant impact it has on violent crime rates. Setting aside the looming, overarching question—what is for many death penalty opponents the only important question—of whether capital punishment is ever morally justified, I propose to discuss instead how the system of death sentencing would need to be reformed, legally and psychologically, if it is ever to be considered fair and reliable in its administration. Of course, this chapter is intended to start, or help further, that conversation, not to end it.

As I mentioned at the very start of this book, I have done research on the death penalty for more than 25 years. When I first began to study different aspects of capital punishment, I was convinced that the flaws in death-sentencing practices and procedures that I and other researchers uncovered could be fixed through "tinkering" with one or another "broken" component.[3] Accordingly, in each of the empirical studies that my graduate students, colleagues, and I did, we focused on a single, specific aspect of the death-sentencing process. But the closer I came to the realities of death sentencing and the more knowledge I acquired about how the system of capital punishment actually functioned, the more I appreciated how deep-rooted and interconnected the various problems were. Although anyone who works for very long on the task of legal change comes to appreciate the value of incremental progress, I began to doubt whether piecemeal solutions would make a significant difference in the reliability of the death verdicts and the quality of the justice with which they were delivered.

I know that claims that one or another area of law is flawed because it is, in essence, "not perfect" may ring hollow in an imperfect legal world where human beings necessarily make mistakes and occasionally reach incorrect decisions. But the flaws in the system of death sentencing that I have analyzed in the preceding pages are structured into the system itself. Indeed, most of the issues I have discussed pertain to the normative rather than atypical death penalty case in the United States. I have addressed primarily those problems that appear when the system is operating more or less as it is supposed to operate. Thus, I have not used the most egregious examples of how a death penalty case can go wrong or restricted my discussion narrowly to those states or regions of the country where practices and procedures fall woefully short of what even most courts in most places would agree is required to produce a fair result.

Of course, there are instances in which judges and attorneys do manage to correct some of the worst problems that plague the system of death sentencing by going well beyond what is narrowly required and overcoming many of these structural flaws. I know firsthand that there are many cases in which capital defendants are afforded a fair result. Yet these things often occur in spite of the psychological mechanisms and entrenched practices and procedures I have described and analyzed here, not because of them. The opposite point is also true—namely, that underfunded, undertrained, and inexperienced attorneys can and often do function in ways that amplify rather than overcome the flaws in the system. Thus, no number of legal reforms—including the structural changes that are proposed in the following pages—can succeed without the presence of competent lawyers who have the resources, skill, and opportunity to take proper advantage of them.[4]

The question of whether a defendant "deserves" the death penalty poses profoundly complex legal and moral issues. Even in an ideal system, it would present attorneys, judges, and jurors with many psychological and intellectual challenges. Yet aspects of the system of death sentencing that I have discussed in this book have made it difficult to address those challenges in honest and authentic ways. Because of the way it is structured—its overall design—the many parts of this system have become impediments to fair and reliable decision making and, in many instances, facilitate death-over-life verdicts. The fact that these overarching problems are structural and systemic and that they operate cumulatively and in tandem means that they must be addressed in kind (i.e., through a set of interlocking reforms designed to remedy the entire system of death sentencing rather than one or another faulty component).

Resetting the Parameters of the Debate

The initial set of problems that I analyzed focused on a flow of misinformation—misinformation about the way the system of death sentencing actually operates in our society and about who commits capital crime and why. This misinformation shapes the perspective of many citizens, voters, and jurors who may be called on to make important decisions about capital punishment. As a result, they often are left with a limited, narrow, and even inaccurate base of knowledge from which to reason and decide about whether and when the ultimate punishment may be justified. Because the misinformation comes from diffuse yet powerful sources and reflects varied motives and entrenched interests at work, this problematic feature of the system of death sentencing will be especially difficult to correct.

Social Science and Constitutional Decision Making

In the opening chapter of this book I discussed the Supreme Court's post-*Furman* tendency to ignore overarching analyses of many of the worst aspects of our system of death sentencing, leaving many citizens, voters, and jurors with an inaccurate view of how and how well (or poorly) capital punishment actually works. From a social science perspective, at least, the Court has seriously mishandled several of the most crucial challenges that have been lodged against the death penalty in the post-*Furman* era. Indeed, the primary shortcoming has been the way the Court minimized or ignored the social fact data that had been collected on many of the issues that were in contention in these cases.[5] Irrespective of the constitutional merits of the results and the legal logic by which they were reached, the Court's insistence on ignoring the social facts of capital punishment meant that its death penalty jurisprudence was founded on a flawed empirical record. It also has compromised the public's understanding of the nature and consequences of the system of death sentencing.

Some legal scholars have attributed the Court's general reluctance to incorporate social science knowledge into constitutional decision making to the backlash that followed its brief reference to psychological research in *Brown v. Board of Education.*[6] I do not believe that tells the whole story. If it did, the Court would never have relied so heavily on social science in *Furman*—as chapter 1 in this volume made clear, much more extensively than in *Brown*. Instead, it was as though the Justices who formed the majority in the many post-*Furman* death penalty cases in which social science was ignored or dismissed took to heart Justice Marshall's prediction about the consequences of an "informed citizenry." That is, that if the public was "better informed" and possessed more accurate knowledge about the social facts of capital punishment, then more of its members would judge its morality more critically; indeed, they might, as Marshall put it, "consider it shocking, unjust, and unacceptable."[7]

In *Gregg* and subsequent death penalty cases, many Justices have avoided these potentially critical judgments by ignoring or dismissing the social science evidence that might produce them. In fact, the Supreme Court's refusal to grapple with many death-penalty-related problems—indeed, not even to acknowledge many of them in a forthright manner—appears to be in direct proportion to the scope and magnitude of the problems themselves. To preserve the overall system of death sentencing, the key elements of the system on which its viability depended had to survive constitutional scrutiny relatively unscathed, no matter the number and scope of well-documented social realities that had to be denied or ignored along the way. *Furman*'s apparent willingness to subject the entire system of capital punishment to careful and sustained social science scrutiny seemed to have opened a Pandora's box that the Court has been trying to close ever since.

This unwillingness to acknowledge and respond to the growing body of scholarship in social science and law certainly has hurt the Court's credibility with scholars and even some jurists who see judicial decision making as a broad and serious intellectual undertaking whose mandate includes grounding opinions in the best available knowledge. In addition, continued insistence on ignoring social realities that are becoming much more widely and publicly known and accepted may even jeopardize the Court's broader standing. Especially in light of the heightened public scrutiny that has been brought about as a result of well-publicized miscarriages of justice—dramatic death row exonerations and the like—many citizens are beginning to question the presumed procedural infallibility of the process that many of the Justices have endorsed.

More recently, however, at least some Justices appear to have reconsidered and even reversed the post-*Furman* reluctance to acknowledge and incorporate social science data into constitutional decision making in general and in death penalty jurisprudence in particular. Indeed, some recent cases certainly suggest that such a shift in perspective and approach may be under way.[8] It also may be that despite the Court's best efforts—when all the facts are in and the data fully analyzed and carefully considered—there is no way to adequately remedy all the flaws that plague the system of death sentencing and ensure its constitutional operation. But continuing to treat the social facts and empirical data that document systemic failures in death penalty imposition as somehow irrelevant to constitutional decision making seems increasingly indefensible.

Reframing the parameters of the Supreme Court's analysis of death-penalty-related issues (and thereby broadening the terms of the public debate as well) would require the Justices to rely more fully and responsibly on social science data. Professor Michael Dorf has made a series of useful suggestions about how this could be done generally, and many of them apply with special force to death penalty litigation. For example, Dorf has suggested that the Court "rely to a greater extent on empirical and policy analysis in its written opinions"; that the Justices can "encourage lead counsel and amici to include more such material in the own presentations to the Court"; and that their opinions might not only cite more empirical data submitted in these briefs but also take a less passive role in the proceedings by directing the proceedings by "invit[ing] counsel to address specific factual questions" much as they often request that counsel address and argue specific legal issues or questions; and that the Court rely more heavily on "adjunct fact gatherers" such as special masters or experts "to assist with the complex factual questions" that often arise.[9] These procedural innovations would provide much needed opportunities for the social realities of capital punishment to become more central to the Court's death penalty jurisprudence.

Correcting the Effects of Media Bias and Misinformation

Of course, narrowly framed and dismissive Supreme Court opinions are merely one component in the flow of misinformation about the system of death sentencing. To be sure, most citizens, voters, and jurors are much more likely to be influenced by the mass media. Exposure to the individualizing and sensationalized images of criminality that the media project heightens the audience's fear of crime and shapes its perspectives on punishment. As I noted in chapters 2 and 3, the media tend to locate the causes of violent crime exclusively within those persons who perpetrate it. In addition, the risk of victimization is exaggerated and the social contextual roots of criminality typically are ignored.

It is tempting to discuss the media as a singular undifferentiated whole. Yet the word "media" is plural and there are many forms of media.[10] I tried in chapters 2 and 3 to make distinctions between types of media as they seemed important. However, with respect to crime and crime-related coverage, the media often *do* function in much the same way. All forms now seem to converge on some version of "infotainment" wherein so-called hard news meshes imperceptibly into drama and vice versa. Indeed, the major television networks regularly compete with one another over a newly popular dramatic form—the "police procedural" in which minute details of police investigation fill out the story lines of weekly crime dramas. As most readers know, a television program named *C.S.I.* (for "crime scene investigation") became so popular in the United States that it spun off several variations of itself that, in turn, each ranked on the list of highest-rated prime-time shows.[11] And before *C.S.I.*, there was (and is) *Law and Order*, characterized as "already the most ubiquitous show on television" even before "it spun off not one but two thematically connected series."[12]

Unfortunately, citizens, voters, and capital jurors who rely primarily on the media for the information about crime and punishment are miseducated by what they see and hear. The media effectively set crime-control agendas and provide the public with frameworks of understanding crime that draw heavily on subsidized news operations. At best, they reflect a law enforcement perspective on issues that individualizes the nature of the crime problem and tends to demonize defendants. Further, media coverage of individual capital cases often reinforces these general biases. Here too the stories tend to be focused on the nature of the crime, provide little or no balanced coverage of the defendant's background or social history, and depict aggravation far more extensively than mitigation. In addition, there is evidence that the nature of the coverage makes a difference, and that persons who have been exposed to prejudicial pretrial publicity are actually more likely to be aware of individual capital cases and also to believe that the defendants in them are guilty. Omnipresent and powerful, the media matter.

The challenge of correcting media-related biases is daunting. However, there are some mechanisms that could be implemented to broaden media perspectives and render their crime news reporting more accurate. Media critics have called on citizens to apply "critical thinking" to media messages and develop what Jeffrey Scheuer termed "media literacy" in which the audience attempts to correct for the built-in biases, motives, and slanted or incomplete narratives contained in print and broadcast materials as they are received.[13] As a death-penalty-related reform, this would require, among other things, that citizens better understand the central importance of many of the penalty-phase issues that the media now systematically overlook—for example, that readers and listeners essentially "decode" the media messages they receive, implicitly correct for individualizing biases, and search for information about background and context that otherwise might be deemphasized.

An informed audience also might apply pressure to the media directly in its coverage of crime and punishment in general and death penalty cases in particular, demanding meaningful analyses that address the origins of the defendant's violence. Law professor Susan Bandes observed that meaningful and informative news coverage in capital cases would require reporters and news commentators to appreciate the fact that a particular capital defendant "may have committed a crime worthy of punishment, but not of a death sentence." But she also conceded that this represented one of the greatest hurdles to the fair and balanced reporting of death penalty trials because such a story line is "too nuanced to fit any recognizable dramatic category."[14] Yet, under pressure, the media might overcome the tendency to sacrifice otherwise important components of trial-related coverage to simplistic and sensationalistic approaches.

Other media analysts have recommended that journalists expand their sources beyond the law enforcement agencies from which they receive so much of their subsidized news. Specifically, social agencies and community residents can help surface "information about neighborhood life pertinent to crime stories," and crime stories can be put "in a larger context." Critics also have recommended that news media conduct audits of the content of their communications, asking themselves, "if the only information our readers and viewers got was from our news, what would they know about violence?"[15]

The media's fixation on criminal violence and the distorting lens through which it is depicted—the sensationalizing of crime and demonizing of its perpetrators—penetrates the communities from which capital jurors are drawn. As the research discussed in chapter 3 showed, certain kinds of media exposure also may introduce serious case-specific bias into a capital trial and threaten impartial decision making. In addition to whatever can be done to correct media bias in general, and to balance and broaden the perspectives that news outlets depict, the effects of extensive case-specific pretrial publicity on the fair trial rights of capital defendants should be addressed directly.

Thus, because of what research tells us about the way exposure to extensive pretrial publicity can bias the jury pool, the change-of-venue criteria that judges apply in capital cases need to be liberalized and the prejudice thresholds they apply lowered. Capital cases, especially, should not go to trial in jurisdictions in which prospective jurors have been saturated with prejudicial publicity and, as a result, may hold beliefs and have formed conclusions that will compromise their ability to fairly decide the case. Indeed, a rebuttable legal presumption might be created *in favor* of a change of venue in capital cases that have generated a certain quantity of publicity, and for those in which community surveys empirically document specified high levels of pretrial case awareness and prejudgment.

Creating an "Informed Citizenry"

Public opinion about capital punishment has been shaped in large part by these previously discussed sources—the Supreme Court's unwillingness to acknowledge persistent problems in the administration of the death penalty, general media coverage of crime and punishment issues that sensationalizes and distorts the issues, and case-specific news stories that create a narrow and often biased understanding of both capital defendants and the process by which their cases are adjudicated. As chapter 4 made clear, general and abstract death penalty support tends to be high. However, despite certain case-related factors that can push it even higher, for most people, support tends to erode quickly once respondents are provided humanizing details about defendants and meaningful alternatives to capital punishment from which to chose.

Moreover, even abstract death penalty support tends to depend heavily on a lack of knowledge or understanding about how the system of capital punishment actually operates. In fact, as the study I discussed earlier showed, the people who know the least about how the system of death sentencing actually functions appear to be the ones who support it most. Thus, preserving the public's relative lack of knowledge about capital punishment may be crucial to keeping death penalty support high. Yet it is difficult to defend any legal and public policy that depends so much on widespread ignorance, especially when it is a policy that places individual lives in jeopardy. The continued collection and analysis of accurate information about the system of death sentencing by social science researchers and the increasingly widespread public dissemination of these findings both represent natural remedies to this problem.

Here, too, the mechanisms by which these systemic flaws can be addressed are easier to identify than the strategies by which courts, government agencies, and the media can be persuaded to implement them. Nonetheless, campaigns of public education that examine and discuss the realities of death sentencing can enhance the general level of debate over whether and how capital punishment should be modified, abandoned, or preserved. More informed debates over capital punishment may result in both the benefits and the burdens of the death penalty being taken honestly and accurately into account in public policy initiatives. Indeed, a kind of "truth in advertising" law might be put into place and applied to politicians who persist in presenting factually inaccurate information in their discussion of these and related issues. To the extent to which there is continued public support for the death penalty, it should at least be predicated on accurate views of the way the system actually functions.

Reforming the Pretrial Process in Capital Cases

Several recent Supreme Court cases have emphasized the centrality of jury decision making in criminal cases by requiring that juries decide all questions that affect the severity of the conviction and the level of punishment.[16] These cases bring increased attention to the capital jury itself—including the way in which its members are selected, the mind-set with which they approach the critically important tasks with which they are entrusted, the rules by which the jurors operate, the extent to which they are able to understand and properly apply the instructions that are supposed to govern their decision making, and whether and how they are provided with the kind of information they need to engage in a constitutionally mandated inquiry into the moral culpability of the defendant on which their sentencing verdict must turn.

Reducing Publicity-Related Prejudice

In part because of the high levels of publicity that surround them, capital cases present a special set of jury selection problems. As I have noted, most citizens get most of their information about the death penalty from the media. Given the media's primary concern about increasing the size of the audiences they attract rather than the quality of the public education they provide, few capital cases are likely to be depicted in fair-minded ways that fully inform citizens and potential jurors about the complexities of the issues that will have to be decided. In addition to media-related reforms that may reduce the amount of misinformation that is disseminated, and change-of-venue reforms that may make it easier for capital defendants to be tried in less prejudiced jurisdictions, jury selection can play an important role in enhancing the fairness of the capital trial process. Hence, the overall quality of the voir dire that is permitted and practiced in capital cases will have to be improved so that it is more able to ferret out potentially prejudiced jurors.

As Courtney Mullen accurately describes the process that often transpires in highly publicized cases, a number of potential jurors typically admit to having heard or read about the specific case in question and some even may acknowledge having discussed it with their friends and family. However, if and when the veniremen concede having formed an opinion about the defendant's likely guilt, trial judges typically intervene. Prospective jurors are asked—sometimes in rapid succession and often in a manner that implies the appropriate answer—whether they can set aside their opinions, listen to the evidence presented in court, do their duty as jurors, follow the law, and render a decision fairly and impartially based only on what they have heard and seen presented in court. Few people want to admit to being closed minded, unwilling to listen, or reluctant to follow orders from a judge. Fewer still will depict themselves as persons inclined to render unfair and biased verdicts. In response to the overtly leading questions that often are posed, then, "most jurors straighten their bodies, look the judge straight in the eye and respond, 'Yes, sir!' "[17]

A legal system that is serious about ensuring the fair trial rights of capital defendants would address these problems by providing expanded, attorney-conducted voir dire as a matter of law. It also would require that trial judges in death penalty cases apply especially lenient standards of exclusion for cause on the basis of exposure to prejudicial pretrial publicity. Moreover, it would end the practice of allowing potentially prejudiced jurors to serve as essentially their own guarantors of fairness (by having their retention turn largely on their own willingness to disclaim or minimize the effects of publicity on their future impartiality).

I have already noted the importance of changing the legal threshold for change-of-venue motions in capital cases. This is not the first time this recommendation has been made. Justices Brennan and Marshall once argued that there should be special presumptions in change-of-venue motions whenever they are filed in death penalty cases. They argued that the additional and vitally important *sentencing* responsibility that capital jurors may be called on to assume in such cases heightens the concern over a different kind of publicity-related prejudice. The comparatively narrow focus of a noncapital change-of-venue inquiry—whether prospective jurors have prejudged the defendant's guilt—stops short of addressing crucial capital penalty trial issues. Thus:

> There may be little reason to doubt the testimony of such jurors at *voir dire* that they could put aside their knowledge of the consequences of the crime in order to establish the facts of its commission. But the jury wears an altogether different hat when it sits as sentencer. It must make a moral decision whether a defendant already found guilty deserves to die for his crime. As we have previously recognized, the function of the sentencing jury is to "express the conscience of the community on the ultimate question of life or death."[18]

Prospective jurors who are familiar with the consequences of the crime for the larger community, or who may know legally inadmissible details about the defendant's past life, or have heard other persons express opinions about his moral turpitude or unsavory behavior are biased in ways that could prove fatal to a capital defendant. These risks are difficult to address meaningfully in voir dire and do not threaten fundamental fairness in this way in any other kind of criminal case.[19] They help to justify the use of a different approach in balancing of fair trial rights of capital defendants against other interests in deciding whether a death penalty trial should be moved from a venue in which extensive publicity has occurred.[20]

Note also that the decision whether to change venue focuses exclusively on case-specific bias. That is, legal scrutiny is conditioned by case-related publicity that has risen above the already steady stream of damaging and sometimes legally inadmissible crime-related information, images, and story lines to which the public is regularly exposed. Only publicity that has become distinctive, memorable, or, at least, recognizable, on its own terms— publicity that stands out from the din of general media misinformation—

can serve as the basis for a change of venue. Similarly, voir dire in which prospective jurors are queried about what they may have read or heard about this particular case does not surface information about the influence of *general* media-created biases and prejudices.

Getting at this kind of prejudice would prove difficult if not impossible. ("Do you feel that you have been so immersed in crime and punishment-related media story lines that you cannot fairly judge a real, as opposed to fictional, criminal case?" "Have your fears about violent crime been raised to such a high level by the media that you are eager to punish a guilty person with the maximum possible punishment?") In this sense, although they are important reforms, liberalizing change-of-venue doctrines and granting attorneys broad latitude in the scope of jury selection represent modest remedies for the narrowest, most pointed form of a much larger and more diffuse problem. The general influence of media-based bias and misinformation on death penalty decision making remains. But this suggests at least that the kind of case-specific publicity for which there is a remedy should be taken much more seriously.

Addressing the Damage of Death Qualification

Death qualification is an anomalous feature of the capital trial process that requires penalty to be discussed long before penalty is relevant. The attention of prospective jurors is drawn away from the presumption of innocence and onto post-conviction events. As I noted in chapters 5 and 6, this anomaly is structural and is built into the very nature of the process. If a guilt-phase jury is to be death-qualified, certain psychological imperatives attach to this stage of the proceedings. Thus, the problems that are created are not a simple matter of language, unfortunate phrasing, or the injudicious choice of words by the judge or the attorneys during the voir dire. As one commentator put it: "Death qualification as currently practiced tilts the jury first towards guilt and then towards death, both by removing too many of certain kinds of people from the pool, and by affecting the expectations and perceptions of those who remain."[21]

Because the negative effects of death qualification flow from its structurally anomalous position in the jury selection process, they can be remedied only by addressing that fact—by somehow eliminating the death qualification of the guilt-phase jury. This would require a jury to be death qualified and empowered to proceed with sentencing if and only if the defendant was convicted of a death-eligible crime. The procedure might entail the subsequent death qualification of the original guilt-phase jury (augmented by additional alternate jurors, selected at the time that the guilt-phase jury is impaneled and substituted as needed for original jurors who are not death qualified). Or, it might entail a process of bifurcation in which a completely separate penalty-phase jury is impaneled. This second jury might be selected and seated at the outset of the guilt-phase trial and assume full responsibilities only after a penalty trial became necessary. Alternatively, such a second jury might be selected and impaneled from a new pool of prospective jurors drawn if and when the defendant was convicted.

These are admittedly elaborate and as yet untested procedural modifications. But a legal system that is fully committed to insuring a capital defendant's Sixth Amendment right to be tried by an impartial jury would undertake the task of implementing and systematically evaluating them to determine which alternative best achieves this goal. Moreover, suggestions to radically reform and perhaps eliminate the practice of death qualification have been made in the past. In *Witherspoon* itself, Justice Douglas concurred in the result but argued that a person accused of a capital crime should have the benefit of the "controlling principle of mercy in the community," if, indeed, the community was merciful. Yet he noted that the practice of death qualification "results in weeding out those members of the community most likely to recommend mercy and to leave in those most likely not to recommend mercy." He thought this improper and recommended that the practice be abandoned entirely.[22]

More recently, from time to time, thoughtful jurists have considered the biasing effects of death qualification, reviewed the extensive and consistent social science data on the issue, and concluded that the process must be eliminated or radically altered. For example, New Jersey State Supreme Court Justices Handler and O'Hern reached this conclusion in the late 1980s, after the U.S. Supreme Court decision in *Lockhart* had ruled the practice constitutional. As Justice Handler noted, "While no one insists that procedure can be made perfect, in no other context has this Court accepted the proposition that mere prosecutorial convenience—or *any* state interest—justifies procedures that render the jury 'somewhat more' conviction prone."[23]

Another aspect of the capital jury selection process that would be addressed in a program of systematic reform concerns what, as I noted in chapter 6, has been termed "life qualification." Requiring capital jurors to be capable of imposing life as well as death sentences has been mandated since the early 1990s, when the Supreme Court decided *Morgan v. Illinois*.[24] But there are a number of nonobvious components to this seemingly straightforward requirement. For example, as John Blume and his colleagues have noted, it means that "voir dire should ensure that the venire members seated on the jury are empowered to react to mitigating evidence in accordance with the dictates of their conscience, even in the face of adverse reactions from other jurors."[25] However, in order to get to this point, the life qualification process must be improved in several ways. That is, it should require that prospective jurors receive an accurate explanation of the nature of mitigation and that attorneys have an opportunity to question veniremen to determine whether they are willing to at least consider it in their penalty-phase decision making.

Part of the problem is that death penalty opposition and support are not just opposite ends of the same spectrum; they are rooted in different considerations. In the case of unequivocal opposition, persons are opposed to the punishment itself. That is, to a true death penalty opponent, the individual defendant and the particular crime are irrelevant to their opposition; the person opposes capital punishment. On the other hand, automatic death penalty advocacy is less a rejection of the punishment of life imprisonment as it is a statement that, once a certain threshold of heinousness in the crime or level of culpability in the defendant has been crossed, the only appropriate penalty automatically becomes death. For the most part, then, the process of death-qualifying jurors requires that they be asked about the punishment of death and little else. Most jurors either know beforehand or are able to determine quickly for themselves how they feel about the death penalty, especially if they are unequivocally opposed. However, there are exceedingly few if any people who are so enamored of the death penalty that they would automatically reject life imprisonment for any defendant and for any crime, choosing—every time—to impose the death penalty as long as the law authorized them to do so. Instead, they have a threshold above which they feel only death will suffice. Admittedly, for some people the threshold may be set quite low, but there usually is one. Thus, the real task in life qualifying a strongly pro-death penalty juror is figuring out where his or her threshold of heinousness and culpability is set. This cannot be done without extensive questioning about the nature of the case and defendant, including the type of mitigation that might be presented at trial.

Thus, prospective jurors who know at the outset that they would not consider certain forms of mitigating evidence that might be introduced into a capital trial (or know that they are likely to regard it as aggravating) should not be permitted to serve in such a case. Generic and abstract questioning in which persons are asked only whether they would "consider the mitigating factors as provided by the court" are inadequate in light of what is known about the high level of confusion that surrounds the concept of mitigation. To be sure, prospective jurors should be able to understand and be willing to apply aggravating evidence as well. However, research suggests that this is a much less problematic issue. Thus, for as long as death qualification continues to be a part of capital jury selection—until the dual jury reforms suggested previously are implemented—it should not only include a thoughtful and probing discussion of mitigation in which prospective jurors learn what this important legal concept actually means but also should properly screen out those jurors who cannot accept or apply it to the case at hand.[26]

One final death qualification-related reform stems from the social science data that I have previously cited. It pertains to the Supreme Court's continued use of the sentencing behavior of capital juries as an index of public attitudes about the death penalty.[27] This approach seems misguided for several reasons. Capital juries are *by definition* unrepresentative on this issue: It is the one consistent and systematic dimension on which they have been pre-selected. The death qualification process overtly and intentionally restricts participation on capital juries only to those persons who are unusually in favor of the death penalty. As I noted in chapter 5, research continues to underscore the many ways in which death-qualified juries are unrepresentative of the larger communities from which they are drawn, not just on the basis of their death penalty beliefs but also on the basis of a wide range of additional demographic and attitudinal dimensions. Whatever else can be said about the process of death qualification, it seems difficult to contend that the death-sentencing behavior of death-qualified juries tells us anything representative about the "conscience of the community" from which they were selected.

Moreover, the public opinion research I cited in chapter 4 indicated that death penalty support appears to be highest among persons who understand the least about the operation of the system itself. Thus, although capital jurors certainly will know more than others about specific details of death penalty cases on which they have served, they may be less well informed than other citizens about capital punishment in general and may lack the kind of broad-based knowledge that should guide public policy choices.

There are even more reasons to question the sentencing behavior of capital juries as an index of any national consensus on the death penalty. Capital jury behavior is the product of many of the social psychological forces I have addressed at length in the preceding pages. It is hardly an objective index of people's unencumbered feelings and views about this complicated social, political, and moral issue. Moreover, the behavior of capital juries is explicitly constrained by the very decision makers whose laws the Court must evaluate. That is, capital jury behavior takes place in a legislatively created context, in response to legislatively determined decision-making rules. It is shaped, conditioned, and constrained by the very statutory schemes the Court is called on to scrutinize. In addition, as I already have discussed in some detail, jurors typically find that some parts of these statutory schemes—the sentencing instructions, in particular—are difficult for them to interpret or comprehend. This, too, distorts the meaning of the actions that jurors may take in response to directions that they do not entirely understand.[28]

Finally, many critical commentaries have documented the widespread inadequacies that plague the quality of capital representation in many parts of the country. These continuing problems raise serious questions about the nature and quality of the evidence (particularly mitigating evidence) and the effectiveness of the lawyering on which many jury verdicts are based. Obviously, if capital juries render verdicts that are based on inadequate, poorly developed, or ineffectively presented evidence, then their decisions hardly provide an objective index or accurate reflection of community sentiment or public support about the death penalty.

Morally Engaging Capital Jurors in the Course of the Trial

In chapter 7, I suggested that the structure and sequencing of evidence in the capital trial process contributed to the moral disengagement of capital jurors. The morally distancing features I discussed included the virtually exclusive focus on crime-related evidence and the correspondingly minimal attention given to the personhood of the defendant in the guilt phase of the trial, followed by exclusively crime-related evidence in the penalty phase and, only then, the presentation of contextualizing, social historical information. I concede that these structural aspects of the capital trial process are not easily modified or reformed.

That said, there *are* some special modifications might be made in capital trial procedures to address these order effects, out of recognition that death is different and to acknowledge the significance that our society attaches to the sanctity of life (including the life the jury is being asked to take). For example, capital trials might broaden the scope of permissible guilt-phase testimony by the defense that humanizes the defendant and give the defense the option to request that evidence in the penalty trial be presented in a more chronological sequence, so that the defense could open as well as (perhaps) close the penalty trial.

Moreover, acknowledging the problematic structural imperatives in the capital trial process underscores the importance of effectively addressing those mechanisms of moral disengagement that *can* be remedied. In this context, consider Capital Jury Project data that show that capital jurors from a number of states perceived prosecutors to be significantly better than defense attorneys in communicating, preparing, and appearing committed to their case, as well as fighting harder at *both* the guilt and punishment stages of the trial.[29] It is difficult to account for these findings except as a partial function of the disparity of resources that characterizes death penalty cases.[30]

The effects of this objective disparity are likely to be intensified by a subjective factor at work in many of these cases. Most often, the prosecution's implicit and overarching "theory" of the case is that the defendant's crime stemmed largely if not entirely from his evil makeup. Jurors are told that he deserves to be judged and punished solely on the basis of his presumably completely free, morally blameworthy choices. It is a theory that generally comports with stereotypical beliefs about crime and punishment that are rooted in a long-standing cultural ethos that capital jurors (like most citizens) have been conditioned to accept uncritically.[31]

Add to this the well-documented tendency of most people to provide causal explanations for the behavior of others in largely dispositional or personal (as opposed to situational or contextual) terms—what, as I noted in previous chapters, social psychologists call the "fundamental attribution error"[32]—and the compatibility of the typical juror's preexisting framework for understanding behavior with the basic assumptions that appear in the typical prosecutorial narrative becomes apparent. In conventional social psychological terms, the defense penalty-phase presentation must somehow correct and reverse the fundamental attribution error and educate jurors about the historical, contextual, and situational influences on the defendant's behavior. On the other hand, the prosecution's approach is to embrace and build on this error.

Most prosecutors, then, speak the "commonsense" language of most capital jurors. Defense attorneys, on the other hand, must work much harder to overcome preexisting beliefs, to encourage jurors to think in unfamiliar ways about the nature of fair and just punishment, and to educate them about why and how to do so. As Lynne Henderson put it: "While the defense will seek to have the jury empathize with the defendant, the defense narrative—unattached to legal form—is a difficult one to convey, and the legalistic formula can provide sanctuary from moral anxiety."[33] Samuel Pillsbury has concluded much the same thing: "The prosecution will tell a story designed to provoke anger; the defense will respond with one to evoke sympathy. The sentencer must choose between or among them. As the law now stands, this gives the prosecution a significant advantage at the punishment stage. The law's sanction of retribution and the fact of criminal conviction, give weight and legitimacy to the prosecution's angry appeal. The defense needs a similar, legally authorized, emotional appeal to check that anger, to keep the debate within moral bounds."[34]

Thus, the objective disparity in resources worsens an already disadvantaged position. Defense attorneys have a steeper hill to climb and fewer resources with which to do so. To be sure, data collected directly from capital jurors pointing to prosecutorial effectiveness indicate that defense attorneys have much to learn about using whatever resources they do have to humanize defendants and keep the sentencing debate within moral bounds. In the absence of a legally authorized, defense-oriented emotional appeal to match the law's "sanction of retribution"—an appeal that the current instructions clearly fail to provide—defense attorneys must labor mightily to reach persuasive parity with prosecutors. But many of them also need additional training and trial-related resources to assist them in the task of morally engaging capital jurors.

In addition, although our capital jurisprudence occasionally pays homage to the importance of compassion, typically, it does nothing to ensure that compassion is engendered in sentencing decisions. One way that compassionate justice might be created and maintained in capital jury decision making would be to permit or require judges to employ a "preinstruction" at the outset of a capital penalty trial that highlighted the importance of compassion and underscored the value that the law requires jurors to attach to the defendant's personhood. Such a preinstruction, designed to help the jury members properly frame many of the issues that will be presented in the penalty trial that will follow, might take the following form:

Ladies and Gentlemen of the Jury:

We are a society that values life over death. Indeed, it is only in the name of that value that the death penalty can be justified under our law. Thus, we will proceed in this stage of the trial under a presumption that *life* without possibility of parole is the preferred sentence, and also that the *life* of the defendant will be the focus of the attorneys' presentations and your decision making.

The defendant in this case is entitled to a presumption of personhood. Despite what you have convicted him of doing, and whatever else you may decide he is guilty of having done, he is a member of the human community. You should not reach a decision to take his life unless you decide that, based on everything you have heard presented, you are completely convinced that he is among "the worst of the worst" and has forfeited the right to continue to live, even in prison. It is a decision that you should reach only in the most extreme cases and with the utmost seriousness and reluctance.

Out of a belief that past experience helps to shape present and future conduct, we are permitting the defendant's attorneys to present evidence and testimony about his life history. We know that factors such as childhood maltreatment—abuse and neglect— poor parenting, poverty, racism, and so on, can significantly influence the direction of someone's life. If offered by counsel, these factors are all relevant for you to consider and take into account in your decision. These formative factors are not offered as excuses on the defendant's behalf because the issue of excusing his conduct is not part of your decision-making process in this stage of the trial. Rather, this evidence is offered in the way of explanation for his conduct—helping you to understand the course of his life, both good and bad, and, to the extent that it is applicable, also to understand the first degree murder of which you have convicted him.

Why, you might ask, does the law go to the trouble of having you try to understand the defendant's life and behavior? Your job now is to assess what the law calls "culpability"—how much is the defendant and the defendant alone to be blamed for what he has done. The prosecution will talk to you about bad things the defendant has done, and the defense will seek to explain these things, to put them in context. This is because, in our society and under our law, people whose lives and actions have been shaped and influenced by harmful treatment and conditions beyond their control are regarded as less blameworthy—less culpable—than others. They therefore may deserve less punishment.

Because of the special responsibility that the state assumes when it intervenes in the life of a juvenile or adult offender, any evidence of what is sometimes called "institutional failure" and, certainly, institutional abuse earlier in the defendant's life takes on special importance in understanding the rest of his life course. If you find evidence of institutional failure or mistreatment, that too should be given serious consideration by you in assessing the defendant's personal moral culpability because it is that very same state that now seeks to take the defendant's life, a life that it may have had a significant hand in shaping.

Similarly, because a defendant's life is made up of bad things he has done, as well as bad things that have happened to him and shaped who he became, the prosecutor has every right to present evidence of certain kinds of past bad conduct on the part of the defendant that you should also consider and take into account in your decision. Moreover, we know that a human being is more than the sum total of the bad things he has done. Thus, the defense will have an opportunity to talk to you about the good things the defendant has done as well. You should take all of these dimensions into account in making your assessment of the value or worth of the defendant and whether there are aspects or qualities in him that you believe should be preserved by allowing him to live in prison, as well as things that he may have done that you condemn.

You have convicted the defendant of first-degree murder, the gravest offense of which someone can be convicted. However, by no means are all first-degree murders punishable by death. In fact, in the United States, over the 30 or so years since the death penalty was reinstituted, only a small percentage of first-degree murder convictions have resulted in death sentences. Something more must be shown before a person convicted of first-degree murder can be considered for the death penalty. You have found special circumstances in this case and that is what qualifies this defendant for a possible death sentence. But relatively few special circumstances cases result in a death sentence, so much more generally must be shown before you can decide to impose the ultimate punishment. The prosecutor is entitled to present these additional factors, and has the burden of proving beyond a reasonable doubt, both that these additional factors—aggravating circumstances— have been proven to all of you, and that you believe that this means the defendant deserves to be executed as a result.

More specifically, in the guilt phase of this trial, the law permitted the prosecutor to present evidence concerning the circumstances of the murder that you have found was committed by the defendant. As I said, however, the prosecutor is entitled in this second phase of the trial to present further evidence of the circumstances of the crime, if s/he elects to do so, and you will be instructed, and both sides may argue, that you should consider these circumstances in rendering your verdict. As part of the consideration of the circumstances of the crime, you may also hear testimony about the consequences of the crime, what is sometimes called "victim impact" testimony. That, too, is appropriate, because the profound seriousness of the decision you are being called upon to make requires us to provide as much information as possible that you might find relevant or useful in making your decision.

Similarly, in this part of the proceeding, we will present evidence about the two punishments that you will be asked to select between—life in prison without parole, and the death penalty. This is not done to inflame your passions or to in any way prejudice your decision making but, as in the guilt phase, to inform you fully about the consequences of one's actions, in this case, *your* actions. We recognize that it is not reasonable or fair for the legal system to ask you to choose between two punishments, electing one as appropriate and the other not, without providing at least some information about the nature of those punishments. So both sides will be entitled to present you with testimony about life without parole in our state's maximum security prisons, and detailed information about the procedures that are used to execute a prisoner under our state law.

Moreover, just as you may hear testimony about the consequences of the defendant's criminal acts, the impact of his behavior on his victims, you may also hear testimony about the consequences of the two alternatives we are asking you to select between, the consequences of a life and a death sentence not only for the defendant but also for relatives of the defendant and other persons who care about him. These people can rightly be viewed as interested parties in the outcome of this case and, in whatever sense you find appropriate, you may wish to consider the consequences for them of either verdict that you choose to render.

Because our society so values life over death, and because taking the life of another person in the name of the state is the most awesome duty that government entrusts to its citizens, certain of the principles I instructed you to use in the guilt phase of this trial have been modified and made more stringent in this second phase, where you are being called upon to make a life or death decision. When I instructed you in that first phase that, in order to find the defendant guilty of the crime(s) with which he was charged you must find that the prosecutor had proven each element of that crime "beyond a reasonable doubt," it is not inappropriate in this phase of the trial for you to operate with an even higher standard of proof. Some capital jurors like yourselves realize that, although they found guilt phase evidence sufficient beyond a reasonable doubt, they still harbored some possible doubt, what is sometimes referred to as "lingering doubt." It is not inappropriate for you, if you should have such lingering doubt about decisions made earlier in the case, to take it into account in deciding upon penalty.

Although it was essential during jury selection for me to question you about your feelings toward the death penalty and life imprisonment, and to make sure that you could both consider and, where appropriate, vote to impose either punishment, you have not and should not consider yourself as having made a promise of any kind to this court or anyone else that you will impose one or another punishment—only that you will follow the law that I have and am now instructing you on, and that you will consider both punishments, keeping in mind that, as I said at the outset of this instruction, out of the profound respect that we hold for human life, our society always privileges life over death. The decision is yours to make, based on what you will hear and see in this portion of the trial, and nothing else. No one can question or dispute the legitimacy of whatever decision you make.

Further, you must presume in your deliberations that life means life without parole (that is, that the defendant will never get out of prison), and that death means death (that is, that the defendant will be executed). Although there is the possibility of legal appeals, in this or any criminal case, you should know that with respect to this stage of the proceedings only a death sentence can be appealed, and that the ultimate reversals of jury decisions because of juror error or impropriety are very rare. Thus, you should assume that your verdict with respect to sentencing this defendant will be carried out. Out of the respect and legitimacy that the law attaches to the collective wisdom of the capital jury, it rests the primary responsibility for the fate of this defendant with you and no one else.

Critics of an approach to structuring capital jury decision making in this way—one that emphasizes empathic concerns and seeks to overcome some of the morally disengaging aspects of the trial process to this degree—may worry that it will elevate a "more individualized justice" above the generalized principles that characterize the rule of law.[35] Yet individualized, compassionate justice is supposed to be the touchstone of constitutional decision making in a capital penalty trial. As one legal commentator has concluded: "The question of what punishment an offender deserves requires a complex factual and moral evaluation. . . . [I]f accuracy in desert evaluation is paramount, as it is in the capital context, we must adopt a broad view of culpability that defies encapsulation in rules."[36] Although, in general terms, "[l]egal decisions and lawmaking frequently have nothing to do with understanding human experiences, affect, suffering—how people *do* live,"[37] the failure to overcome this bias in capital penalty trials can and regularly does have fatal consequences.

Indeed, capital jurors also are disengaged from the moral consequences of their penalty decisions by being encouraged to ignore another cost that attaches to executions—the value of the person whose life they are being asked to take. In response, Pillsbury has argued that capital trials should discharge what he calls an "empathy obligation."[38] Because an empathic perspective highly "values and seeks to find the good in the offender's character," the capital jury "should be informed of the obligation to care about the offender as a morally worthy creature and should be given the opportunity to hear about his good deeds, his capacity for and desire to do good,"[39] just as they are and should be reminded about the importance of their caring for the victims of his actions.

At present, of course, the law does nothing to require that capital juries contemplate the defendant's good qualities—qualities that will die with him if he is executed—and nothing in the capital sentencing instructions mandates them to factor the loss of these qualities, or future contributions the defendant might make in the course of his life in prison, into account. For example—and the list varies from case to case—no existing capital penalty procedures or instructions require jurors to consider the possibility that a death sentence means that a future life of meaning in prison may be foregone, that someone who might make useful contributions in the form of needed prison labor or represent a calming influence on younger, less experienced prisoners will be lost, that continuing relationships on which loved ones have come to depend and from which they draw support will end, that the use of creative talent that gives pleasure to others will expire, or that the exercise of a religious commitment and dedication to a life of redemption will be terminated by a death verdict.

To be sure, none of these things necessarily will prove decisive in a final sentencing decision—some capital jurors may decide that many of them are trifling matters when compared to the deeds for which the defendant has been convicted. Yet they form the other side of the balance sheet of death to which capital jurors should at least be reminded to cast a glance and reflect on before they proceed to decide the defendant's fate. Unfortunately, these issues are not always addressed by defense attorneys through penalty-phase testimony or in defense penalty-phase closing arguments. Even in the normative case, death sentencing proceeds in a lopsided way—with much of the intuitive pull of the case leaning the capital jury toward state-sanctioned capital violence by minimizing its potential costs. For this reason, as well as others I have mentioned, the legal fiction that the fate of a capital defendant may be safely entrusted to an attorney who is presumed to be competent but who may leave many of these crucial issues untouched should be challenged and corrected.

In this regard, philosopher Jean Hampton has highlighted the way in which what she terms "moral hatred" can blind others to potentially good aspects of a wrongdoer's character and lead them to ignore the circumstances that may place his actions in a less blameworthy light.[40] Similarly, mechanisms of moral disengagement that operate in capital trials may make the good aspects of a defendant's character more difficult to perceive, blind jurors to circumstances that might lessen his blameworthiness, and ensure that moral hatred rather than forgiveness prevails. Hampton conceded that forgiveness—which she argued has potentially beneficial effects on both victim and perpetrator—can and should be forgone when "too much of the perpetrator is 'morally dead.' "[41] But constricting the range of information that jurors are given about a capital defendant can result in his being presented in precisely that light. To counteract this tendency, jurors should learn that violent criminal acts are typically the *joint* product of personal characteristics and unique situational forces that are often unlikely to recur.[42]

In addition, capital defendants should be entitled to have juries view photographs or documentary representations of the execution chamber, death row, cells in the prisons where a death- or life-sentenced prisoner is likely to be kept. This kind of realism is especially important to bring to bear in cases in which prosecutors are permitted to argue that prison is not punishment enough (or that the defendant would be "impervious to suffering in prison"). Earlier I commented about the asymmetry of current death penalty law in which prosecutors may routinely introduce gruesome photographs at the guilt trial and again at the penalty phase. Courts regularly find that such crime-scene photographs are not "unduly prejudicial." Yet, at the same time, they often hold that "evidence regarding the facilities on death row and the manner of carrying out the death penalty [are] irrelevant to our capital sentencing scheme."[43] A legal system genuinely committed to giving capital jurors all of the information they would need to intelligently choose between sentencing alternatives would broaden the scope of evidence that is admissible on these issues.

Regularizing the Capital Jury Decision-Making Process

As I noted in chapter 8, the Supreme Court confidently endorsed statutory reforms that relied heavily on judicial instructions to regularize and rationalize a death-sentencing process that had been plagued in the past by bias and unreliability. The basic notion, as expressed in these early, landmark cases was that the previously "unbridled" discretion of jurors could be brought under control by having judges provide them with a list of factors or issues to think about, consider, and to use in certain specified ways in making the choice between life and death.

As I discussed at length, there is now much reason to believe that this "guided discretion" model was advanced with far too much optimism. Indeed, courts quickly seized on these instructions as the solution to a host of interrelated constitutional problems, and they did so long before their effects were well understood. A number of studies dating back to the mid-1970s and appearing continuously since then have demonstrated that many of the very same problems that had plagued the previously unconstitutional schemes of death penalty imposition are still present long *after* the implementation of these new sentencing models.

As the research my colleagues and I conducted in California suggested, and as much the same kind of data collected by other researchers in other jurisdictions indicated as well, the standard-instructions are so difficult for average people to understand and apply that many jurors simply are unable to comprehend their most basic features. This instructional confusion begins with the question of what the concepts of aggravation and, especially, mitigation actually mean and extends to uncertainty about which of the specific factors should tip the scales in the direction of life or death. The errors are fundamental, they are made frequently, and there is no evidence that they are corrected in the course of jury deliberation. As a result, there is no assurance that the process routinely results in reliable verdicts being rendered.

Moreover, as I also have noted, there is a significant one-sidedness to the jurors' confusion. On the one hand, the kind of evidence that typically makes up the bulk of a case in aggravation—the facts of the crime, prior criminal acts, victim accounts of impact and loss—are things that tend to be socially agreed on as increasing the severity of whatever punishment is deserved. On the other hand, the kind of evidence that makes up the typical case in mitigation is undermined not only by the jurors' inability to understand the concept itself but also by the tendency to believe that it pertains primarily to a set of crime-related factors that rarely are presented by the defense in a capital penalty phase.

Further, to many jurors who lack a framework for comparing things as horrible as types of murder or placing a defendant along a continuum of persons who have killed another human being, the particular capital crime and its individual perpetrator are likely to represent the "worst of the worst." Thus, the typical juror's individual "blameworthiness scale" is not likely to be calibrated in a way that accounts for the full range of capital cases. Yet capital sentencing laws contemplate precisely these kinds of comparative judgments. This, too, likely tips the scale in favor of death rather than life verdicts in some cases.

In addition, by couching the jury's life-and-death decision in terms that imply that some kind of legal formula is driving the sentencing verdict, the instructions may remove or undermine the jurors' collective and individual sense of moral responsibility. Thus, at this very final stage, the process leaves some jurors with a feeling that they are being compelled to reach a decision that does not reflect their personal views. This, in turn, can disengage critical ethical concerns and deep moral considerations. The old system of capital jury sentencing in which little or no guidance was provided to jurors who were trying to choose between life and death did lead to verdicts that were unpredictable and, as the Supreme Court reasonably concluded in *Furman,* were seemingly unreliable. Yet it, as law professor Joseph Hoffman pointed out, it had an advantage over the modern system because it emphasized that the "verdict must express the individual opinion of each juror," based on that juror's judgment and conscience.[44] Formulaic death sentencing and instructions that appear to allow or even encourage jurors to relinquish personal responsibility provide a strong argument in favor of revised instructions that both guide discretion *and* emphasize the individual responsibility of each juror.

These problems of instructional incomprehension and concerns over the integrity of the message the instructions convey strike at the fairness and reliability of the system of capital punishment. In fact, the Supreme Court's unwillingness to address these issues in a forthright manner may stem in large part from its recognition of precisely this—that to acknowledge the magnitude of the problem would call into question the entire enterprise to which the Court has given its blessing since the mid-1970s. As Ursula Bentele and William Bowers have put it, the Court continues to assume that the *Furman*-inspired reforms—primarily the heavy reliance on sentencing instructions—have succeeded in guiding the jury's discretion, and "indeed, it is on that assumption that death sentences continue to be imposed and affirmed."[45] But we know now that the assumption is faulty.

I noted in chapter 8 that the Supreme Court has rejected challenges based on evidence that capital jury instructions are difficult to comprehend and the contention that jurors cannot follow them properly. It has done so largely by relying on the presumption that jury members adequately understand and correctly follow the law that they receive from the judge. Yet even the case that the Court typically cites as precedent for this proposition also acknowledged the following: "The rule that juries are presumed to follow their instructions is a pragmatic one, rooted less in the absolute certitude that the presumption is true than in the belief that it represents a reasonable practical accommodation of the interests of the state and the defendant in the criminal justice process."[46]

Effectively addressing these instructions-related problems will require a change in judicial perspective. Many judges still believe that the practice of studiously avoiding any inquiry into the jury's decision-making process— including ignoring clear evidence that its members were confused or misguided—represents a great strength of our legal system. As a panel of the Seventh Circuit put it: "One enduring element of the jury system, no less vital today than two centuries ago, is insulation from questions about how juries actually decide. Jurors who volunteered that they did not understand their instructions would not be permitted to address the court, and a defendant could not upset a verdict against him even if all of the jurors signed affidavits describing chaotic and uninformed deliberations."[47]

Many courts also continue to maintain that a trial judge's most appropriate response to clear indications that jurors do not understand capital instructions is simply to repeat them. Thus, during oral argument in *Weeks v. Angelone*,[48] a relatively recent case in which the Supreme Court once again affirmed the right of capital jurors to be confused in rendering their life-and-death verdicts, one Justice declared the instruction "perfectly sound," even though the jurors indicated by their question that they could not understand it. The Court rejected the suggestion that a judge should try to answer jurors' questions by doing more than referring them back to the very instruction that they said had confused them by calling it "an extraordinary doctrine." As I say, implementing remedies to the problem of instructional incomprehension will require long-standing judicial views to be challenged and changed.

However, research that Amy Smith and I recently conducted shows that it *is* possible to correct and improve some of the most problematic features of the capital jury sentencing instructions. A relatively straightforward modification in the standard California instruction—the use of linguistically improved instructions that simplified some of the most cumbersome and confusing language, and the inclusion of "pinpoint" instructions that provided case-related examples of key terms (i.e., specific pieces of evidence that could be interpreted as aggravation and others that could be interpreted as mitigation) significantly improved our jury-eligible adult participants' understanding of the concepts overall.[49] Although this is only an initial study on this important question, and much more research is warranted, these encouraging results suggest that there are ways to address the problem of instructional incomprehension that will result in a more reliable jury decision-making process overall.

In addition to addressing the general confusion that is created by incomprehensible instructions, I believe that courts that are serious about increasing the reliability and fairness of capital jury decision making will need to consider including comprehensible instructions that address widespread misconceptions that research tells us are likely to be held by the typical capital juror. For example, only a small minority of states explicitly instruct capital juries about parole-related issues.[50] Yet, as Steiner, Bowers, and Sarat have demonstrated, "folk knowledge" about the early release of life-sentenced prisoners, although incorrect, provides a persuasive argument in favor of death verdicts in certain jurisdictions.[51] There is no reason why jurors should not be told the truth about the sentencing options that they are choosing between. Social science research has challenged the notion that jurors will not think about otherwise relevant things simply because the law does not discuss or address them. In capital cases, there is a strong argument for judges to acknowledge many of the common myths and patiently debunk them, perhaps, both in the form of a preinstruction as the penalty trial begins and a standard jury instruction just before deliberations commence.

Reforming the Capital Penalty Trial

In creating the modern capital jurisprudence that now governs death penalty trials, the Supreme Court broadened the scope of penalty-phase evidence in important ways. Among other things, of course, capital juries are permitted to consider the background and character of the defendant whose fate they decide. The critical legal concerns here are fairness and reliability—ensuring that only those truly deserving of the death penalty receive it. This important doctrinal requirement in capital cases broadens the discourse and debate about the lives of capital defendants. It also has the potential to generate real knowledge and insight about the social historical roots and contextual determinants of violence at a time when more is known than ever before about them.

Yet the law does not yet clearly *require* attorneys to present all of this kind of information to capital jurors in every case in which it may be useful. More importantly, perhaps, many states still fail to provide the resources needed to ensure that the information can be properly gathered and analyzed. In addition, as I have discussed at length, the courts have done little to ensure that capital jurors truly understand the judicial instructions that are supposed to legitimate its use. Instead, many capital defendants watch their cases decided by jurors who have not learned the full truth about the social historical and contextual factors that helped to shape their life and influence their criminal behavior. And many capital jurors are allowed to muddle through this life-and-death decision-making process mired in faulty media-based stereotypes and confused about what if any relevance mitigating evidence has to the issues at hand.

Moreover, it is important to note that, if capital jurors do not "get it right" here, there are no guarantees that there will be legal correctives consistently applied *later* in the death-sentencing process to reverse inaccurate or misguided decision making once the jurors' work is done. Indeed, legal commentators have decried the much greater distance that higher courts have from the realities of these life-and-death decisions than the juries that render them, even terming appellate judges in capital cases "the epitome of distanced, clean, bureaucratic executioners" who engage in "sentencing as paperwork."[52] And, as if to complete the moral distancing that the system of capital punishment maintains to keep us from taking responsibility for what we do, subsequent decision makers use each of the preceding stages of legal authorization as the justification for leaving well enough alone: "[J]udicial imprimatur serves to absolve other governmental actors from responsibility for independently evaluating death decisions."[53]

In light of the importance of the quality of the penalty-phase presentation to a fair outcome in a capital case, what is to be done? Some commentators have argued that the defense case in mitigation is so critical to the fair administration of the death penalty that courts should *appoint* attorneys especially to develop and present it in certain cases,[54] while others have suggested that courts should apply heightened standards of ineffective assistance in the appellate review of this portion of the capital trial.[55] As I noted in chapter 1, a little more than 25 years after ruling that capital defendants could not be precluded from presenting such testimony, the Supreme Court finally made explicit what had been understood among competent and conscientious death penalty attorneys for many years—that a careful and complete social history investigation must be conducted in every case and that potentially mitigating testimony must be effectively presented during a defendant's capital penalty trial.[56] Thus, capital attorneys are now required to conscientiously investigate and present such evidence to the jury in the capital penalty trial. To be sure, this ruling is an important, commendable step in the right direction. But a number of questions remain unresolved (including the fate of capital defendants in states that still fail to provide attorneys with the training and resources to do a competent job in investigating, analyzing, and presenting such evidence, and cases in which attorneys present some mitigation, but nowhere near all that is available or enough to be persuasive with the jury).[57]

Given the importance of this kind of testimony in deciding the fate of a capital defendant, it is not unreasonable to *require* that a complete mitigation case be presented in *all* cases before the jury is permitted to reach a death verdict. In many jurisdictions, judges cannot sentence a criminal defendant to prison—even for a modest term of confinement—without having considered a comprehensive and presumably carefully prepared "presentence report" that routinely is submitted to them. Yet capital juries in these same jurisdictions may be called on to sentence a defendant to death with less information at their disposal.

Indeed, for capital defendants to be treated fairly in the capital sentencing process, a way has to be found to reliably bridge what I termed in the last chapter an "empathic divide" that separates them from jurors. As I suggested in that chapter, the divide is greater in cases in which white jurors sit in judgment of African American defendants. In fact, there are many possible specific remedies to this kind of racial discrimination in the application of the death penalty. From a psychological perspective, in addition to the importance of overcoming the empathic divide through the effective presentation of social history and other forms of mitigation (whose value and relevance in a particular case would need to be made clear by virtue of improved capital sentencing instructions that specifically acknowledge and legitimize their mitigating significance), efforts to ensure racially diverse capital juries and to restrict the use of the death qualification process to purge them of minority group members seem particularly important.[58] So, too, do reforms such as the proposed Racial Justice Act that would allow statistical evidence of systemic discrimination to be presented as the basis for precluding death sentences from being sought or imposed.[59]

Of course, the empathic divide exists in every capital case, no matter the race or ethnicities of the defendants and jurors. Although there is no simple formula by which the empathic divide can be bridged, there are some basic approaches to this critically important task. Bridging this divide can be accomplished only through an extremely conscientious effort by defense team members who must engage in painstakingly in-depth and elaborate investigation, the organization of diverse life facts into a meaningful narratives with coherent mitigating themes and an effective, honest, humanizing presentation to jurors that places the defendant's behavior in a larger context that will allow them to better understand him. In all capital penalty trials, "the goal is . . . to reach conclusions about how someone who has had certain life experiences, been treated in particular ways, and experienced certain kinds of psychologically-important events has been shaped and influenced by them."[60]

To accomplish this goal, lawyers, investigators, and experts must be given all of the training, time, and resources necessary for them to uncover, analyze, integrate, and present the important race-related and other facts and circumstances that make the defendant's life understandable. In addition, judges must employ comprehensible instructions that acknowledge the mitigating significance of social history testimony and authorize jurors to rely on it. Otherwise, the empathic divide—kept in place by many of the practices and procedures I have analyzed and reviewed in the preceding pages—may remain, and many jurors will proceed psychologically and morally distanced from the task at hand.

Conclusion

A democratically administered system of capital punishment requires citizens, voters, and capital jurors to endorse policies, vote in favor of laws, and even render verdicts designed to bring about the death of another person. Under normal circumstances, the psychological barrier against taking a life is exceedingly difficult for most people to cross. The preceding chapters have analyzed the various social psychological mechanisms that help to create the extraordinary conditions that enable widespread public participation in this otherwise prohibited activity. Together, these mechanisms operate cumulatively and in tandem to form the larger system of death sentencing.

In this chapter, I have argued that because the various parts of this system operate as a whole, truly significant improvements in the reliability and fairness of the decision-making process will require overarching reforms. Justice Harry Blackmun, writing in dissent in a California death penalty case, raised the same point about the importance of transcending piecemeal approaches to the evaluation and reform of this system: "[T]he Court isolates one part of a complex scheme and says that, assuming that all the other parts are doing their job, this one passes muster. But the crucial question, and one the Court will need to face, is how the parts are working together to determine with rationality and fairness who is exposed to the death penalty and who receives it."[61] I have suggested that, when we analyze "how the parts are working together," in psychological as well as legal terms, the rationality and fairness of the system is called increasingly into question.

In order to facilitate the death-sentencing behavior of ordinary people, many of the legal values and principles on which our system is based often are compromised or sacrificed. Indeed, the first important component of the system that I analyzed that facilitates death sentencing was the tendency of courts and legislatures to refuse to look honestly and accurately at the overall social context in which capital punishment operates. Many legislators still prefer political sloganeering to thoughtful analyses or careful empirical assessments of the complicated questions that the death penalty presents. The judiciary—especially the U.S. Supreme Court—has adopted a jurisprudence that, in many respects, continues to ignore social science data. To do otherwise, I believe, would place the continued viability of the present system of capital punishment in grave jeopardy. Opening up the system to legally relevant study and analysis, and allowing social science data to play a role in the resolution of social fact-based constitutional issues, would make many of the previously mentioned reforms inevitable. Indeed, the reforms I have suggested here are derived directly from the social psychological theory and research discussed in the preceding chapters.

Moreover, by suggesting that these problems are structural and normative—rather than the product of individual malfeasance, ill will, or incompetence—I have tried to focus intensely on systemic issues. Although many of the problems I have described can and often are made worse by woefully inadequate funding for death penalty cases, poorly trained, inexperienced, and underpaid attorneys, and local legal cultures that render death sentences more or less routine, the overarching system of death sentencing itself tilts in this troublesome direction.

At the same time, I recognize that there are many especially well-trained, highly motivated, adequately funded attorneys who labor mightily to overcome the effects of this social psychological death-oriented framework, and who succeed more often than they fail. But the law still does too little to ensure or require that this level of effective representation is provided as a matter of course. Although observers applaud it when it occurs, it still too often does not. And, of course, the nation has done very little to restructure the system to guarantee that these kind of heroics are not necessary in order to bring about a fair result. This chapter has outlined some of the restructuring that would be necessary to achieve that end.

Concluding Thoughts
Death Is Different

Those whom we would banish from society or from the human community itself often speak in too faint a voice to be heard above society's demand for punishment.
—Justice William Brennan, *McCleskey v. Kemp* (1987)

The death penalty stands as a symbol of crime and punishment in our society, one onto which many Americans project their fears of criminal victimization, their attitudes about fairness and justice, and their beliefs about the nature of evil and the possibility of moral redemption. Social science researchers know that a person's attitude toward capital punishment is pivotal—it is the one attitude that tells us the most about someone's general beliefs on a broad array of other criminal justice issues.

To political philosophers, however, the death penalty is more than a symbolic statement about crime control. It also expresses something important about the relationship of citizens to the state and the enormous power that some societies have entrusted to government officials. Indeed, near the end of the 17th century John Locke actually defined political power itself as "a right of making laws with penalties of death."[1] Throughout history, the death penalty has been at the center of many partisan debates, and, in modern times, it has retained much of its political cache. In fact, capital punishment remained the mainstay of many elected officials who struggled to find an emotional issue with which to excite and galvanize supporters.

Like the violent encounters that give rise to them, capital trials often are dramatic, tragic, and compelling. These human dramas are part of what command the public's attention in death penalty cases—a horrible crime has been committed and the life of the accused hangs in the balance. Even though these dramas touch only a comparatively few persons in a direct or personal way—of the thousands upon thousands of persons who pass through the criminal justice system, very few are tried for capital crimes and fewer still are condemned to death—their significance far overshadows their comparatively small numbers.

Despite their infrequency, capital cases also garner more than their share of social scientific and legal attention. In part this is because they represent the standard or benchmark against which fair process and the justness of our system can be gauged or measured; if we are willing to tolerate unfairness and injustice in cases in which a person's life is in jeopardy, then confrontations with the apparatus of the state in criminal cases where the stakes are less profound are likely to be less well scrutinized or carefully examined. Put differently, if we do not demand justice here, what kind of claim can we or will we make elsewhere?

To many citizens, the elaborate legal scaffolding that surrounds death sentencing is the most visible part of the system, and perhaps rightfully so. As I say, it is critically important to any claim we might have of being a fair and a just society in which the rights of criminal defendants are scrupulously protected. But it is only one side of a complicated story. Although they are important and significant, the many special legal procedures and protections that govern death penalty cases belie the psychological forces at work to enable and facilitate death verdicts.

Thus, when we examine whether and how well many of these seemingly elaborate procedures work in practice—an examination that requires careful social scientific analysis—we often come to very different conclusions about the supposed fairness of the system of death sentencing. In this book I have argued that, when viewed in its entirety, our system of capital punishment often falls short of dispensing the fair, consistent, and impartial brand of justice that our Constitution and core political and moral values would seem to require. Many other legal analysts, commentators, and social science researchers have reached much the same conclusion, in gathering numbers, in recent years.[2]

In summary form, here is what the social science research I have cited and discussed in the previous chapters tells us about the normative capital case that passes through the American criminal justice system: A capital defendant is likely to go to trial in a community saturated with media misinformation that individualizes the causes of crime, sensationalizes its graphic details, and demonizes its perpetrators. In all likelihood, members of the community (including some potential jurors) will have been exposed to varying degrees of case-specific prejudicial publicity, perhaps a significant amount of which will bias them about the case, provide them with little or no social history or other mitigating context for the crime or defendant, and, among other things, convince many of them in advance of trial that the defendant is guilty. Whether contaminated by prejudicial pretrial publicity or not, the community in which the case will be tried is likely to be populated by large numbers of people who support the death penalty, but whose pro-death-penalty views are founded on a number of misconceptions about what capital punishment can accomplish, and how the system of death penalty imposition actually functions.

The actual jury that is impaneled to decide the defendant's guilt and, perhaps, the question of whether he will live or die, will be different from, and less sympathetic than, juries that sit in any other kind of criminal case. Specifically, death qualification ensures that it will be missing a higher percentage of women and minorities, as well as a higher number of persons who endorse "due process" orientations toward the criminal justice system. Moreover, as a group, the death-qualified jurors are likely to have a lower threshold of conviction; that is, they generally are more likely to convict on the basis of the same set of facts and circumstances. In addition, their mere exposure to the process of death qualification adds to many of these biases (by, among other things, increasing the jurors' estimate that the defendant is guilty and that death is the appropriate punishment).

Once the capital trial itself begins, jurors will be exposed to structural aggravation, in the form of morally disengaging aspects of standard courtroom practice and procedure that distance them from the psychologically daunting decisions they are being called on to make. In a number of jurisdictions, they will be expected to render life-and-death verdicts after having heard only part—often only a small part—of the mitigating social history and other testimony that would help to contextualize the defendant's life course, render his actions more understandable, and, therefore, perhaps, make him less culpable and not deserving of the death penalty. In addition, many of the jurors will find that the key penalty-phase instructions that are supposed to guide their decision-making process are virtually incomprehensible. Jurors assertive enough to request clarification will learn that judges are reluctant to help, and they are forced to return to the very legal formulations that confused them in the first place. Among other things, the confusion that is sown by these instructions appears to widen the empathic divide that separates capital defendants from the persons who must judge them, all the more so when they are separated by race as well as lifestyle and general background experiences.

Many of the reactions that this network of social psychological forces engenders in citizens, voters, and jurors are unique to the system of death sentencing. This, in turn, raises real questions about the fairness and reliability of the outcomes that are produced. In the case of capital punishment, of course, the price of *any* unfairness, injustice, or error renders these shortcomings qualitatively different from those in other areas of law. This is the basis of the often-repeated assertion in capital jurisprudence and trial practice—the one so disdained by Justice Scalia and other supporters of capital punishment—that "death is different."[3] Death is unarguably different from all other criminal punishments and, I have suggested, the death penalty has an unmistakably different effect on persons who debate, advocate, oppose, and litigate capital punishment.

Even as recently as the 19th century, when penal institutions were poorly run and notoriously porous, many concerned communities were at a loss to know how to protect themselves against violent criminals. It was possible then to think of the death penalty as furthering a policy of collective social protection—self-defense writ large, so to speak. To many thoughtful, informed, and caring people capital punishment seemed like a reasonable last resort in the effort to stem a rising tide of crime. In addition, in times when public executions were the norm, deterrence seemed like a likely, defensible rationale for capital punishment. Although the accounts of pickpockets working the crowd as the hangings took place at Tyburn Hill should have given death penalty advocates pause, it was easy to assume that the harshest possible punishment would create the most effective deterrent to crime.

But the logic of neither justification has survived into the modern world. Contemporary society is now kept safe by use of the most sophisticated, elaborate, and secure prison systems imaginable. We have built places from which virtually no one escapes, in which prisoners can be kept under nearly constant surveillance, and where even the most seemingly intractable behavior is brought forcefully under control. Even though attempts still are sometimes made to establish the legitimacy of capital punishment by reference to its historical—even biblical—acceptance, they ignore the fact that the earlier widespread use of the death penalty occurred in societies that did not have these modern prisons at their disposal.[4]

In addition, our crime-control policies are now informed by carefully collected social science data that disprove the existence of *any* significant deterrent effect for the death penalty. Whatever effective approaches remain to be implemented to reduce violent crime, there is no evidence that the death penalty is one of them. In short, the most rational justifications—societal protection and deterrence—no longer obtain. In this context, capital punishment seems increasingly gratuitous, and the death penalty has lost much of its luster as a result.

The only remaining purpose ostensibly served by the modern death penalty—retribution—is impervious to new empirical data or much rational debate. Persons either believe in retribution and feel that it is a necessary and correct moral principle or they do not. But even many persons who endorse the general notion of retribution find that it entails what has become an increasingly complex moral inquiry in the case of capital punishment. Thoughtful retributivists certainly should be troubled by evidence that race and a lottery-like system (by which, for example, lawyers of widely varying degrees of competence and commitment are assigned to death penalty cases) continue to play important roles in determining which capital defendants live or die. Many death penalty supporters also are given pause by the fact that there is now much reason to question the reliability of the procedures used to assign and calibrate the culpability—the "death-worthiness"—of individual defendants. Others are concerned to learn that the choice to impose the death penalty or not is by no means free and unencumbered by prior conditioning and long-term exposure to a steady diet of misleading information. Far from a dispassionate decision based on a purely reasoned and careful assessment of all the relevant information, research tells us that it is still too often a stereotype-driven outcome based on partial and inaccurate beliefs that are widely disseminated and supported by society in general and by the legal system in particular.

This book has examined some aspects of the process by which these troublesome things are accomplished, and suggested a number of the elaborate legal reforms needed to address them in a meaningful and hopefully effective way.

Notes

Chapter 1

1. D. Hay, Property, Authority, and the Criminal Law, in Douglas Hay, Peter Linebaugh, J. Rule, E. Thompson, and C. Winslow (Eds.), *Albion's Fatal Tree: Crime and Society in Eighteenth-Century England* (pp. 17–63), New York: Pantheon Books (1975), p. 28.

2. The U.S. Supreme Court has ruled that mentally ill prisoners may be executed as long as they are not legally "insane" or "incompetent to be executed"—a standard that requires merely that they understand the nature of the death penalty and why it is being imposed on them. See Ford v. Wainwright, 477 U.S. 399 (1986). With respect to children, the Justices previously decided that persons who were as young as 16 years old at the time of their crime may be given the death sentence. See Stanford v. Kentucky, 492 U.S. 361 (1989). However, just this year, the Court reversed itself in a narrow 5–4 decision that banned the death penalty for juveniles under the age of 18. See Roper v. Simmons, 125 S.Ct. 1183 (2005). Similarly, after ruling in 1989 that the Constitution did not prohibit the execution of developmentally disabled capital defendants [Penry v. Lynaugh, 492 U.S. 302 (1989)], the Court decided 13 years later, in Atkins v. Virginia, 536 U.S. 304 (2002), that a new national consensus now rendered the practice unconstitutional.

3. Simmons v. South Carolina, 512 U.S. 154, 183 (1994) (Scalia, J., dissenting). At other times, Justice Scalia has called capital jurisprudence the product of a "fog of confusion" [Morgan v. Illinois, 504 U.S. 719 (1992) (dissenting), at 751] and a "blow against the People" (at 752).

4. H. Bedau and M. Radelet, Miscarriages of Justice in Potentially Capital Cases, 40 *Stanford Law Review* 21, 83 (1987). Bedau and Radelet identified some 350 cases in which a factually innocent person was convicted of a potentially capital crime. They were able to attribute these erroneous convictions to a number of systemic

factors including, in descending order of importance, perjury by prosecution witnesses, the pressure of community outrage, mistaken eyewitness identification, coerced or other false confession, an inadequate consideration of alibi evidence, and the prosecutor's suppression of exculpatory evidence.

5. The Death Penalty Information Center keeps a running tally of these exonerations. See http://www.deathpenaltyinfo.org/article.php?scid=6&did=109 (last visited April 12, 2005). Although death penalty supporters have challenged what, exactly, constitutes an "exoneration," this is hardly the record of infallibility that many citizens thought had been achieved.

6. Only a handful of states in the United States have even implemented minimal standards for death penalty representation. Of them, only one—New York—has a statewide standard that meets the American Bar Association's recommendation that any death penalty lead counsel have had at least nine prior jury trials, including three murder trials and one death penalty trial as well as familiarity with psychiatric and forensic evidence and completion of a death penalty training program.

7. M. Radin, Cruel Punishment and Respect for Persons: Super Due Process for Death, 53 *Southern California Law Review* 1143 (1980).

8. According to Professor Liebman and his colleagues, between 1973 and 1995, appellate courts found reversible error in 68% of all capital sentences nationwide. In addition, in 82% of the cases that were retried after reversal, a sentence of less than death was rendered. In fact, in 7% of the retrials, the defendant actually was acquitted of the capital crime. See J. Liebman et al., A Broken System: Error Rates in Capital Cases 1973–1995 (2000), available at http://www.law.columbia.edu/instructional services/liebman/liebman_final.pdf (last visited Dec. 3, 2001).

9. Roland Barthes, Dominici, or the Triumph of Literature, in *Mythologies,* New York: Hill and Wang (1972), p. 46.

10. C. Haney, The Fourteenth Amendment and Symbolic Legality: Let Them Eat Due Process, 15 *Law and Human Behavior* 183–204 (1991), p. 183. Two researchers have empirically documented the degree to which most citizens endorse the Court's legitimacy. See T. Tyler and G. Mitchell, Legitimacy and the Empowerment of Discretionary Legal Authority: The United States Supreme Court and Abortion Rights, 43 *Duke Law Journal* 703 (1994). I believe this is one of the reasons that many people from both ends of the political spectrum were so dismayed over the obvious partisanship that seemed to guide the outcome of Bush v. Gore, 531 U.S. 1046 (2000). For example, see discussions in Bruce Ackerman (Ed.), *Bush v. Gore: The Question of Legitimacy,* New Haven, CT: Yale University Press (2002). Concern persists that this case has jeopardized the Court's ability to have the same broad moralizing influence in the future.

11. S. Levinson, "The Constitution" in American Civil Religion, 1979 *Supreme Court Review* 123 (1980); S. Levinson, Pledging Faith in the Civil Religion: Or, Would You Sign the Constitution? 29 *William and Mary Law Review* 113 (1987). See also Hans Kohn's description of the Constitution as "unlike any other: it represents the lifeblood of the American nation, its supreme symbol and manifestation. It is so intimately welded with the national existence itself that the two have become inseparable." Hans Kohn, *American Nationalism: An Interpretive Essay,* New York: Macmillan (1957), p. 8.

12. Note the self-consciousness that some Justices have about the way in which the Court's institutional legitimacy depends in some sense on the public's perception of its principled decision making. For example, in Planned Parenthood of South-

eastern Pennsylvania v. Casey, 505 U.S. 833 (1992): "The Court must take care to speak and act in ways that allow people to accept its decisions on the terms the Court claims for them, as grounded truly in principle, not as compromises with social and political pressures having, as such, no bearing on the principled choices that the Court is obliged to make. Thus, the Court's legitimacy depends on making legally principled decisions under circumstances in which their principled character is sufficiently plausible to be accepted by the Nation . . ." Id. at 865–866. I am suggesting the reverse: that the Court's institutional legitimacy lends much credence to the practices it approves.

13. For more detailed discussions of this and related issues, see several articles of mine: C. Haney, Psychology and Legal Change: On the Limits of a Factual Jurisprudence, 6 *Law and Human Behavior* 191 (1980); C. Haney, Social Factfinding and Legal Decisions: Judicial Reform and the Use of Social Science, in D. Muller, D. Blackman, and A. Chapman (Eds.), *Perspectives in Psychology and Law* (pp. 43–54), New York: Wiley (1984); and C. Haney, Psychology and Legal Change: The Impact of a Decade, 17 *Law and Human Behavior* 371 (1993).

14. Legal realism had its roots in an even more explicitly social science-oriented jurisprudential movement, Roscoe Pound's so-called sociological jurisprudence. See R. Pound, The Scope and Purpose of Sociological Jurisprudence (pts. 1–3), 24 *Harvard Law Review* 591 (1911); 25 *Harvard Law Review* 140 (1912).

15. M. Dorf, Foreword: The Limits of Socratic Deliberation, 112 *Harvard Law Review* 4–83 (1998), p. 45. For the complex history of realism and social science, see John Schlegel, *American Legal Realism and Empirical Social Science*, Chapel Hill: University of North Carolina Press (1995).

16. William Twining, *Karl Llewellyn and the Realist Movement*, London: Weidenfeld and Nicolson (1973), p. 382. Of course, it is a bit of an exaggeration to say that we are *all* realists. Justices Antonin Scalia and Clarence Thomas, for example, are self-described "originalists" who advocate interpreting constitutional provisions exactly as the Framers originally understood them. For example, see A. Scalia, Originalism: The Lesser Evil, 57 *University of Cincinnati Law Review* 849 (1989).

17. J. Monahan and L. Walker, Social Authority: Obtaining, Evaluating, and Establishing Social Science in Law, 134 *University of Pennsylvania Law Review* 477 (1986).

18. Brown v. Board of Education, 347 U.S. 483 (1954).

19. *Brown* contained one footnote—footnote 11—that cited seven published social science studies or texts. See 347 U.S. 483 at 495. But the role of social science and the contributions of social science experts to the litigation strategy that preceded the *Brown* decision had been extensive. See Mark Tushnet, *The NAACP's Legal Strategy Against Segregated Education, 1925–1950*, Chapel Hill: University of North Carolina Press (1987).

20. 347 U.S. at 495.

21. Michael Meltsner, *Cruel and Unusual: The Supreme Court and Capital Punishment*, New York: Random House (1973).

22. Furman v. Georgia, 408 U.S. 238 (1972).

23. Id. at 313 (White, J., concurring).

24. A series of state death penalty statutes passed in the aftermath of *Furman* were evaluated in opinions issued simultaneously by the Court in its 1976 term. The lead case, Gregg v. Georgia, 428 U.S. 153 (1976), approved of Georgia's new death penalty statute in which a judge or jury was required to find at least one aggravating

circumstance beyond a reasonable doubt and then to consider other aggravating and mitigating circumstances before sentencing a defendant to death. In Proffitt v. Florida, 428 U.S. 242 (1976), the Court similarly approved the new Florida death penalty statute in which, following a jury's "advisory" verdict, a judge was required to weigh aggravating against mitigating factors to determine whether the death penalty should be imposed. The Court approved a very different kind of death penalty statute in Jurek v. Texas, 428 U.S. 262 (1976), examining the new Texas death penalty statute that required capital jurors to answer three questions affirmatively—whether the defendant's homicidal act was intentional, was not a reasonable response to provocation, and whether the defendant was likely to commit future acts of violence constituting a continuing threat to society—before sentencing him to death. However, in Woodson v. North Carolina, 428 U.S. 280 (1976), and, similarly, in Roberts v. Louisiana, 428 U.S. 325 (1976), the Court rejected new death penalty statutes that made the death penalty mandatory upon a conviction of first-degree murder.

25. *Gregg*, 428 U.S. at 169.

26. Id. at 173.

27. Id. at 179.

28. Id. at 183.

29. Id. at 185.

30. Contiguous state and other comparisons dating back many years had shown that homicide rates had risen more rapidly for states with a death penalty than for those without. For example: Raymond Bye, *Capital Punishment in the United States*, Philadelphia: The Committee of Philanthropic Labor of Philadelphia Yearly Meeting of Friends (1919); G. Vold, Can the Death Penalty Prevent Crime? 12 *Prison Journal* 3 (1932); K. Schuessler, The Deterrent Effect of the Death Penalty, 284 *The Annals* 54 (1952); G. Vold, Extent and Trend of Capital Crimes in the United States, 284 *The Annals* 1 (1952); Thorsten Sellin, *The Death Penalty*, Philadelphia: American Law Institute (1959); W. Reckless, The Use of the Death Penalty, 15 *Crime and Delinquency* 43 (1969). Some time series studies that examined the effect of execution risk on homicide rates actually have found more positive than negative relationships—more executions appear to be followed by increases in homicide rates in some jurisdictions during some time periods. A number of these studies were published long before *Gregg* was decided, and many more have appeared in the years since. As William Bowers summarized the data: "Most investigators set out to test for deterrent effects and rejected the deterrence hypothesis. A few claimed to find deterrent effects, but have since had their findings discredited, even reversed. Our review indicates that the failure to find deterrence in study after study may add up to more than the absence of deterrence." W. Bowers, The Effect of Executions Is Brutalization, Not Deterrence, in K. Haas and J. Incardi (Eds.), *Challenging Capital Punishment: Legal and Social Science Approaches* (pp. 49–98), Newbury Park, CA: Sage (1988), p. 65. Data on the more immediate or short-term effect of executions reach similar counter-deterrence conclusions. For example, see W. Bowers and G. Pierce, Deterrence or Brutalization: What Is the Effect of Executions? 26 *Crime and Delinquency* 453 (1980). See also W. Graves, A Doctor Looks at Capital Punishment, 10 *Journal of the Loma Linda University School of Medicine* 137 (1956) [reprinted in Hugo Bedau, *The Death Penalty in America*, New York: Anchor Press (1967)]. These overall results appear to be consistent with international data showing the lack of any deterrent effect of the death penalty. For example, see Dane Archer and Rosemary Gartner, *Violence and Crime in Cross-National Perspective*, New Haven, CT: Yale University Press (1984).

31. *Gregg*, 428 U.S. at 186. In the more than 25 years since this sentence was written, I know of no single legislature that has undertaken an empirical study of the deterrent effectiveness of the death penalty and none that has based death penalty legislation on a careful reading of statistical studies about deterrent effects, local or otherwise.

32. Id. at 226 (White, J., concurring).

33. Stuart Banner, *The Death Penalty: An American History,* Cambridge, MA: Harvard University Press (2002), p. 8.

34. U.S. Department of Justice, National Prisoner Statistics, No. 45, *Capital Punishment, 1930–1968* (August 1969), p. 7. The same report noted that a total of 3,859 persons had been executed over this period, 2,066 of whom were African American.

35. 408 U.S. at 389.

36. Id. at 449.

37. Maxwell v. Bishop, 398 F.2d 138, 147 (8th Cir. 1968). William Maxwell was an African American sentenced to death in Arkansas after being convicted of raping a white woman. As part of his evidentiary hearing on the issue of discriminatory imposition, he submitted the results of an analysis of Arkansas death-sentencing patterns for the crime of rape covering the years 1945–1965. The Arkansas study was part of a larger, 12-state study conducted in the summer of 1965, examining patterns of discriminatory death sentencing throughout the South. The expert who testified at Maxwell's hearing, Professor Marvin Wolfgang, presented data showing that blacks convicted of raping white victims were disproportionately sentenced to death. Among other things, the Arkansas study showed that a black man who raped a white woman had about a 50% chance of receiving the death penalty, compared to a 14% chance when the perpetrator and victim were of the same race. See id. at 141–144. Although Blackmun found the argument "interesting," and perhaps valuable "as an instrument of social concern," he concluded that "the statistical argument does nothing to destroy the integrity of Maxwell's trial." Id. at 147. Blackmun went further: "We can understand and appreciate the disappointment and seeming frustration which Maxwell's counsel must feel in again failing to prevail on a still more sophisticated statistical approach. They will ask themselves just how far they are required to go in order to prevail. We are not certain that, for Maxwell, statistics will ever be his redemption." Id. at 148. That was in part because Blackmun felt that such statistical analyses "are necessarily general" and, therefore, he simply could not or would not accept that they "have valid application to Maxwell" or, apparently, to any other individual defendant. Ibid.

38. *Maxwell,* 398 F.2d at 148.

39. *Furman,* 408 U.S. at 450.

40. McCleskey v. Kemp, 481 U.S. 279 (1987).

41. Id. at 332 (Brennan, J., dissenting).

42. For example, see W. Bowers and G. Pierce, Arbitrariness and Discrimination under post-*Furman* Capital Statutes, 26 *Crime and Delinquency* 563 (1980); R. Lempert, Desert and Deterrence: Assessing the Moral Bases of the Case for Capital Punishment, 79 *Michigan Law Review* 1177 (1981); M. Radelet, Racial Characteristics and the Imposition of the Death Penalty, 46 *American Sociological Review* 918 (1981); and H. Zeisel, Race Bias in the Administration of the Death Penalty: The Florida Experience, 95 *Harvard Law Review* 456 (1981).

43. Samuel Gross and Robert Mauro, *Death and Discrimination: Racial Dispar-*

ities in Capital Sentencing, Boston: Northeastern University Press (1989), at p. 55. Their statistical analyses were based on data from Georgia, Florida, and Illinois.

44. For a conceptual discussion of this issue, see Charles Black, *Capital Punishment: The Inevitability of Caprice and Mistake,* New York: Norton (1981). For a summary of some of the empirical research that had been done to that point, and some additional data of their own, see M. Radelet and G. Pierce, Race and Prosecutorial Discretion in Homicide Cases, 19 *Law and Society Review* 587 (1985).

45. This research is published in D. Baldus, G. Woodworth, and C. Pulaski, Comparative Review of Death Sentences: An Empirical Study of the Georgia Experience, 74 *Journal of Criminal Law and Criminology* 661 (1983); David Baldus, George Woodworth, and Charles Pulaski, *Equal Justice and the Death Penalty: A Legal Empirical Analysis,* Boston: Northeastern University Press (1990).

46. Many of the important variables statistically controlled for in archival studies co-occur with race in the real world. Indeed, this is one way to conceptualize the full effect of racism—that other disadvantaging variables, over which individuals have little or no control, are correlated with race in our society. They can be parceled out in a statistical sense, but rarely if ever in real life.

47. *McCleskey,* 481 U.S. at 297.

48. See, for example, Bowers and Pierce, *supra* note 42; Gross and Mauro, *supra* note 43; M. Radelet and G. Pierce, Choosing Those Who Will Die: Race and the Death Penalty in Florida, 43 *Florida Law Review* 1 (1991); and Zeisel, *supra* note 42.

49. Because the Court of Appeals below had found the study to be valid, Justice Powell was constrained to assume this to be the case. He did not seem very enthusiastic about this assumption.

50. *McCleskey,* 481 U.S. at 292, footnote (emphasis added).

51. Id. at 292. Justice Blackmun, whom Powell had cited in raising these kinds of concerns about systemic patterns of discrimination versus the proof of prejudice affecting an individual case in *Furman,* disagreed with his analysis in *McCleskey.* Blackmun wrote in dissent that the sophistication with which the data were structured and analyzed "convinc[ed] me of the significance of the Baldus study." Id. at 354.

52. Id. at 292.

53. Id. at 297.

54. It essentially required a prosecutor to come forward to admit that, "Yes, we asked for the death penalty because the defendant in this case was black," or a juror to acknowledge that, say, "My fellow jurors and I would have given the defendant a life sentence but he killed a white victim."

55. *McCleskey,* 481 U.S. at 302.

56. Id. at 302–303, quoting Coley v. State, 231 Ga. 829, 834, 204 S.E.2d 612, 615 (1974)].

57. Id. at 303, quoting *Gregg,* 428 U.S. at 167. Yet earlier in the opinion the Court had acknowledged that jurors "cannot be called . . . to testify to the motives and influences that led to their verdict." The Court's later reassurance that the Georgia death penalty law required the state supreme court to "review each sentence to determine whether it was imposed under the influence of passion or prejudice" did not clarify how this could be done effectively if jurors could not be required to testify about their motives and influences. See *McCleskey,* 481 U.S. at 302.

58. Id. at 309–320.

59. Id. at 310–311.

60. Id. at 313, internal citations omitted, emphasis added.

61. Id. at 309, quoting Batson v. Kentucky, 476 U.S. 79, 85 (1986).

62. See generally S. Bright, Counsel for the Poor: The Death Sentence Not for the Worst Crime but for the Worst Lawyer, 103 *Yale Law Journal* 1835 (1994).

63. For example, see Wainwright v. Sykes, 433 U.S. 72 (1977).

64. Welsh White, *The Death Penalty in the Eighties: An Examination of the Modern System of Capital Punishment,* Ann Arbor: University of Michigan Press (1987), p. 54. See generally White's chapters 3 and 4.

65. In an important case decided in its 2003 term, the Supreme Court finally placed an obligation on defense counsel to find and, where appropriate, present this kind of mitigating testimony. Unfortunately, thousands of capital defendants had their cases decided before the Court expressed this important requirement. See Wiggins v. Smith, 539 U.S. 510 (2003). It remains to be seen how *Wiggins* will be implemented and enforced, especially in states that still fail to provide attorneys with adequate resources with which to accomplish the difficult and time-consuming task of finding, analyzing, and presenting effective mitigation.

66. *Furman,* 408 U.S. at 295. Although his attorney presented no evidence in Furman's defense, for some reason he did allow his client to admit in open court that he was guilty of the crime. Furman gave his version of the killing: "They got me charged with murder and I admit, I admit going to these folks' home and they did caught me in there and I was coming back out, backing up and there was a wire down there on the floor. I was coming out backwards and fell back and I didn't intend to kill nobody. I didn't know they was behind the door. The gun went off and I didn't know nothing about no murder until they arrested me, and when the gun went off I was down on the floor and I got up and ran. That's all to it." Id. at 295 (app. 54–55).

67. *McCleskey,* 481 U.S. at 295 (emphasis in original).

68. Id. at 302 (emphases added). Returning to the same issue a few pages later, Powell emphasized how important it was that capital juries could not "be precluded from considering, *as a mitigating factor,* any aspect of a defendant's character or record" that he offered as the basis for a sentence less than death. This was because "[a]ny exclusion of the 'compassionate or mitigating factors stemming from the diverse frailties of humankind' that are relevant to the sentencer's decision" were unacceptable under the Court's modern capital jurisprudence." Id. at 304. And just a few pages after that, the opinion continued to emphasize that state statutes and trial judges "cannot limit the sentencer's consideration of any relevant circumstance that could cause it to decline to impose the penalty." Id. at 306.

69. Id. at 308, quoting *Gregg,* 428 U.S. at 207. Again, a few pages later, Powell reiterated the constitutional requirement "that juries be allowed to consider 'any relevant mitigating factor,' " because the "discretion to evaluate and weigh the circumstances relevant to the particular defendant and the crime he committed is essential." *McCleskey,* 481 U.S. at 313.

70. D. Dorin, Far Right of the Mainstream: Racism, Rights, and Remedies from the Perspective of Justice Antonin Scalia's *McCleskey* Memorandum, 45 *Mercer Law Review* 1035–1088 (1994), p. 1043.

71. The record in the federal court below showed how little McCleskey's attorney actually had done to prepare for his case. For example, he did not interview a number of potentially important *guilt-phase* witnesses. In addition, he appeared to

have done almost nothing to prepare for his client's all important penalty trial. With the exception of asking McCleskey for names of persons "who would be willing to testify for him," and perhaps posing the same vague question to his sister (who denied that he ever did), the lawyer interviewed no penalty-phase mitigation witnesses and did no independent mitigation investigation at all. See McCleskey v. Zant, 580 F. Supp. 338 (D. Ga. 1980). Of course, when it came time to try to save his client's life, he had nothing to present.

72. Banner, *supra* note 33, at 279.

73. Among others, Stephen Bright has written persuasively about and documented many of these flaws. See Bright, *supra* note 62. One recently decided case illustrates the problems that still plagued this system in many parts of the country well into the 1990s. An attorney hired to represent a death penalty defendant accused of killing five people presented little or no effective mitigation at the penalty phase of his client's trial. He later explained his poor performance this way: "I mean, I had a caseload that I had to work with. I wasn't getting any money . . . out of this case. . . . I was in over my head at that point. . . . [It was] something that I had never deal with before." Indeed, he had been paid "somewhere in the neighborhood of $1500 to $2,000" to work for more than a year on the case, one that was complicated enough to have generated 10 volumes of trial testimony. See Smith v. Mullin, F.3d 919, 939 (10th Cir. Okla. 2004). Some would argue that reversals like this show that the system eventually corrects it most egregious mistakes. But there are many instances in which these mistakes go uncorrected. For example, in In re Andrews, 124 Cal. Rptr. 2d 473 (2002), the trial attorneys did even less than in Smith's penalty phase, choosing not to call a single witness in the case in mitigation. This, even though a subsequent postconviction proceeding showed that the potential mitigation in the case was so extensive that more than 50 witnesses were called in a hearing that took weeks to complete. The California Supreme Court nonetheless dismissed the significance of the trial attorneys' negligence and inaction, and affirmed the defendant's death sentence. Several *New York Times* articles on the system of death sentencing also indicate that many of the worst abuses—the appointment of inexperienced or incompetent attorneys and the underfunding of capital defense in general—persist in present times. For example, see D. Johnson, Shoddy Defense by Lawyers Puts Innocents on Death Row, *New York Times,* Feb. 5, 2000, p. A1, and S. Rimer, Questions of Death Row Justice for Poor People in Alabama, *New York Times,* March 1, 2000, p. A1. In addition, the latest American Bar Association Guidelines on effective representation in capital cases include this observation: "The commentary to the first edition of this Guideline noted that 'many indigent capital defendants are not receiving the assistance of a lawyer sufficiently skilled in practice to render quality assistance' and supported the statement with numerous examples. The situation is not better today." American Bar Association Guidelines for the Appointment and Performance of Defense Counsel in Death Penalty Cases, 31 *Hofstra Law Review* 914, 928 (2003).

74. With the exception of those very few issues where the Court simply could not ignore social science data because they formed the entire basis of claims that the justices were obliged to resolve—the issue of racial discrimination addressed so unsatisfactorily in *McCleskey,* and death qualification, which, as I discuss in chapter 5, was addressed in a similar way—the Justices have simply sidestepped inconvenient social facts about the way in which capital punishment is often administered in the United States. This harsh conclusion—that the Court has mishandled social science data (when the Justices have deigned to acknowledge them at all) is shared by other

scholars. For example, James Acker thoughtfully reviewed some 28 Supreme Court death penalty decisions that were decided between 1986 and 1989 and concluded that "[S]ocial science evidence had little influence on the Court's death penalty decisions. Lead opinions brushed aside convincing empirical evidence . . . and refused to consider social-scientific evidence relevant to capital punishment." J. Acker, A Different Agenda: The Supreme Court, Empirical Research Evidence, and Capital Punishment Decisions, 1986–1989, 27 *Law and Society Review* 65, 82 (1993). More recently, several commentators reached essentially the same conclusion: "Supreme Court Justices rarely take into account empirical research when making decisions, and they seem particularly opposed to incorporating social-scientific scrutiny of the death penalty." A. Clarke, A. Lambert, and L. Whitt, Executing the Innocent: The Next Step in the Marshall Hypothesis. 26 *New York Review of Law and Social Change* 309, 309 (2000–2001).

75. *McCleskey*, 481 U.S. at 302.

76. Although the Court had said on several prior occasions that states could not prevent capital defendants from introducing mitigation—to do so would have defeated the logic of the sentencing formulas that the Court had earlier embraced and left defendants with no basis for defending themselves in the specialized sentencing hearings—it took the Court nearly 30 years—a period in which some ten thousand death sentences were rendered in the United States, and nearly 900 executions were performed—before it actually *required* attorneys to attempt to develop critically important social history and other mitigating information.

Chapter 2

1. I have written several articles that in some ways address the media stereotypes that systematically misinform the public about the causes of violent crime and the characteristics of the persons who commit them. For example, see, C. Haney and J. Manzolati, Television Criminology: Network Illusions of Criminal Justice Realities, in E. Aronson (Ed.), *Readings on the Social Animal* (pp. 125–136), San Francisco: Freeman (1980); C. Haney, The Social Context of Capital Murder: Social Histories and the Logic of Mitigation, 35 *Santa Clara Law Review* 547 (1995); C. Haney, Riding the Punishment Wave: On the Origins of Our Devolving Standards of Decency, 9 *Hastings Women's Law Journal* 27 (1998). Portions of this chapter draw heavily on some of that earlier writing.

2. F. Cook and W. Skogan, Agenda Setting and the Rise and Fall of Policy Issues, in David Protess and Maxwell McCombs (Eds.), *Agenda Setting: Readings on Media, Public Opinion, and Policymaking* (pp. 189–209), Hillsdale, NJ: Erlbaum (1991), p. 205.

3. Ray Surette, *Media, Crime and Criminal Justice: Images and Realities* (2nd ed.) (1998), p. 24. Consider, also, Richard Sparks's observation that the "massive development of television and its associated industries has historically coincided with a period of chronic, and sporadically acute anxiety about crime and policing." Richard Sparks, *Television and the Drama of Crime: Moral Tales and the Place of Crime in Public Life*, Philadelphia: Open University Press (1992), p. 16.

4. A. Stanley, TV Weekend: Moody Loners vs. Bad Guys, *New York Times*, Sept. 26, 2003, p. E1, col. 1: "There are more than two dozen crime shows on prime time this season, and fewer than half are satellites of 'CSI' and 'Law and Order.' "

5. Center for Media and Public Affairs, The Media at the Millennium: The Networks' Top Topics, Trends, and Joke Targets of the 1990s, 14(4) *Media Monitor* (2000).

6. Martin William, *Television: The Casual Art*, Oxford: Oxford University Press (1982), p. 121.

7. E.g., Mark Fishman, *Manufacturing the News*, Austin: University of Texas Press (1980).

8. C. Jencks, Is Violent Crime Rising? *American Prospect* 98 (Winter 1991).

9. Id. at 99.

10. F. Butterfield, Crime Panel Fears New Wave of Violence, *San Francisco Chronicle*, Jan. 6, 1996, p. A7.

11. For example, see M. E. McCombs and D. Shaw, The Agenda Setting Function of the Mass Media, 36 *Public Opinion Quarterly* 176 (1972); David L. Protess and Maxwell E. McCombs (Eds.), *Agenda Setting: Readings on Media, Public Opinion, and Policymaking*, Hillsdale, NJ: Erlbaum (1991).

12. Walter Lippmann, *Public Opinion*, New York: Macmillan (1922).

13. For example, see G. Funkhouser, The Issues of the Sixties: An Exploratory Study in the Dynamics of Public Opinion, 37 *Public Opinion Quarterly* 62 (1973); S. Iyengar, M. Peters, and D. Kinder, Experimental Demonstrations of the "Not-So-Minimal" Consequences of Television News Programs, 76 *American Political Science Review* 848 (1982); K. Smith, Newspaper Coverage and Public Concern About Community Issues, *Journalism Monographs* (#101) (1987).

14. E. Atwood, A. Sohn, and H. Sohn, Daily Newspaper Contributions to Community Discussion, 55 *Journalism Quarterly* 570 (1978).

15. See D. Hill, Viewer Characteristics and Agenda-Setting by Television News, 49 *Public Opinion Quarterly* 340–350 (1985).

16. Compare V. Hans and J. Dee, Media Coverage of Law, 35 *American Behavioral Scientist* 136 (1991): "Those who lack firsthand experience with the legal system will probably construct their mental images of it from the media's disproportionate coverage of violent and sensational crimes and its focus on law enforcement rather than the trial and due process." Id. at 140.

17. See Surette, *supra* note 3.

18. M. Barlow, D. Barlow and T. Chiricos, Mobilizing Support for Social Control in a Declining Economy: Exploring Ideologies of Crime Within Crime News, 41 *Crime and Delinquency* 191 (1995); J. Ditton and J. Duffy, Bias in the Reporting of Crime News, 23 *British Journal of Criminology* 159 (1983); M. Fishman, Crime Waves as Ideology, 25 *Social Problems* 531 (1978); R. J. Gebotys, J. V. Roberts, and B. DasGupta, News Media Use and Public Perceptions of Crime Seriousness, 30 *Canadian Journal of Criminology* 3 (1988); S. Gorelick, "Join Our War": The Construction of Ideology in a Newspaper Crimefighting Campaign, 35 *Crime and Delinquency* 421 (1989); E. Greene, Media Effects on Jurors, 14 *Law and Human Behavior* 439 (1990); and R. I. Mawby and J. Brown, Newspaper Images of the Victim: A British Study, 9 *Victimology* 82 (1984).

19. For example, see Barlow et al., Ditton and Duffey, and Greene, *supra* note 18.

20. Cook and Skogan, *supra* note 2, at 205–206.

21. M. Gordon and L. Heath, The News Business, Crime, and Fear, in Protess and McCombs, *supra* note 11, at 72.

22. R. Vitelli and N. S. Endler, Psychological Determinants of Fear of Crime: A Comparison of General and Situational Prediction Models, 14 *Personality and Indi-*

vidual Differences 77 (1993), p. 83. See also Gebotys et al., who reported that "in all three cities [that were surveyed], readers of the newspaper that devotes the largest proportion of its newshole to crime exhibit higher levels of fear of crime than do readers of other papers in those cities." *Supra* note 18, at 246.

23. Vitelli and Endler, *supra* note 22, at 83.

24. See Gebotys et al., *supra* note 18.

25. R. Surette and A. Richard, Public Information Officers: A Descriptive Study of Crime News Gatekeepers, 23 *Journal of Criminal Justice* 325, 326 (1995).

26. For example, see Fishman, *supra* note 7; M. Gordon and L. Heath, Reactions to Crime: Institutions React: The News Business, Crime, and Fear, 16 *Sage Criminal Justice System Annuals* 227 (1981); Gorelick, *supra* note 18; Richard Surette, *Media, Crime, and Criminal Justice,* Belmont, CA: Wadsworth (1998); and Surette and Richard, *supra* note 25.

27. C. Whitney, M. Fritzler, S. Jones, S. Mazzarella, and L. Rakow, Source and Geographic Bias in Television News 1982–4, 33 *Journal of Electronic Broadcasting and Electronic Media* 159 (1989).

28. J. Turk, Public Relations' Influence on the News, 7 *Newspaper Research Journal* 15 (1986).

29. Turk, *supra* note 28.

30. Richard V. Ericson, Patricia M. Baranek, and Janet B. L. Chan, *Negotiating Control: A Study of News Sources,* Toronto: University of Toronto Press (1989), p. 93.

31. Surette, *supra* note 26, at 58.

32. Quoted in M. Hallett and D. Powell, Backstage With "Cops": The Dramaturgical Reification of Police Subculture in American Crime "Info-Tainment," 24 *American Journal of Police* 101, 125 (1995).

33. Katherine Beckett, *Making Crime Pay: Law and Order in Contemporary American Politics,* New York: Oxford University Press (1997), ch. 5.

34. For example, see C. Edwin Baker, *Advertising and a Democratic Press,* Princeton, NJ: Princeton University Press (1994).

35. E.g., Barlow et al., *supra* note 18; D. Humphries, Serious Crime, News Coverage, and Ideology: A Content Analysis of Crime Coverage in a Metropolitan Paper, 27 *Crime and Delinquency* 191 (1981).

36. E. Rogers and J. Dearing, Agenda-Setting Research: Where Has It Been, Where Is It Going? in J. Anderson (Ed.), *Communication Yearbook* II (pp. 555–594), Newbury Park, CA: Sage (1988), p. 579. See also Donald Shaw and Maxwell E. McCombs (Eds.), *The Emergence of American Political Issues: The Agenda-Setting Function of the Press,* St. Paul, MN: West (1977); R. Cook, T. Tyler, E. Goetz, M. Gordon, D. Protess, D. Leff, and H. Molotch, Media and Agenda Setting: Effects on the Public, Interest Group Leaders, Policy Makers, and Policy, 47 *Public Opinion Quarterly* 16 (1983); Cook and Skogan, *supra* note 2.

37. Beckett, *supra* note 33.

38. Id. at 27.

39. J. Roberts and A. Doob, News Media Influences on Public Views of Sentencing, 14 *Law and Human Behavior* 451 (1990).

40. J. Roberts and D. Edwards, Contextual Effects in Judgments of Crimes, Criminals, and the Purposes of Sentencing, 19 *Journal of Applied Social Psychology* 902 (1989).

41. Hans and Dee, *supra* note 16, at 142.

42. C. Morton, Accent on Living, *Atlantic Monthly* (Sept. 1951), p. 87.

43. See S. Stark, Perry Mason Meets Sonny Crockett: The History of Lawyers and the Police as Television Heroes, 42 *University of Miami Law Review* 229, 268 (1987).

44. For example, using a slightly different time frame, one estimate based on Gallup poll and National Opinion Research Center (NORC) General Social Survey data indicated that support for punitive criminal justice sanctions increased steadily during the 1970s, so that there was a 14-percentage-point increase from 1972 to 1980 in the number of persons desiring harsher punishments of criminals in the United States. C. Silver and R. Shapiro, Public Opinion and the Federal Judiciary: Crime, Punishment, and Demographic Constraints, 3 *Population Research and Policy Review* 255 (1984). As I discuss in greater detail in chapter 4, public opinion shifted from less than 50% in favor of the death penalty in the mid-1960s to nearly 80% in favor by the end of the 1980s.

45. Stark, *supra* note 43, at 260.

46. Id. at 269.

47. Sparks, *supra* note 3, at 27, referencing Erik Barnouw, *Tube of Plenty*, Oxford: Oxford University Press (1975), and Todd Gitlin, *Inside Prime Time*, New York: Pantheon (1985).

48. Harry Castleman and Walter Podrazik, *Watching TV: Four Decades of American Television*, New York: McGraw-Hill (1982), p. 246.

49. C. Haney and J. Manzolati, Television Criminology: Network Illusions of Criminal Justice Realities, in E. Aronson (Ed.), *Readings on the Social Animal* (pp. 125–136), San Francisco: Freeman (1977).

50. James Carlson, *Prime-Time Law Enforcement: Crime Show Viewing and Attitudes Toward the Criminal Justice System*, New York: Praeger (1985), p. 189.

51. In this context, it is important to note that depictions of "crazy" or psychologically disturbed criminals in television crime drama were devoid of the sympathetic or disabling features of mental illness. That is, television criminals typically were viciously, frighteningly, and diabolically mad, something that may help to account for the fact that, as I note near later in this chapter, heavy television viewers were not willing to reduce or mitigate the responsibility of "crazy" criminals by endorsing the insanity defense.

52. A methodological problem plagued this and all similar studies that divide people into categories of "heavy" and "light" viewers. Because the participants in these studies are not randomly assigned to conditions, the causes of differences between them cannot be unambiguously identified. Our "heavy viewers" may have had attitudes consistent with television criminology *before* they began watching TV. The pervasiveness of the media stereotypes and the relative absence of alternative sources of information about crime in this culture appeared to us to implicate television as a causal agent. But without elaborate cross-lag correlational designs that were beyond the scope of our study, we could not be absolutely sure.

53. R. Young, Race, Conception of Crime and Justice, and Support for the Death Penalty, 54 *Social Psychology Quarterly* 67, 68 (1991).

54. John Sloop, *The Cultural Prison: Discourse, Prisoners, and Punishment*, Tuscaloosa: University of Alabama Press (1996), p. 142.

55. S. Pillsbury, Emotional Justice: Moralizing the Passions of Criminal Punishment, 74 *Cornell Law Review* 655 (1989). See also Kathryn Gaubatz, *Crime in the Public Mind*, Ann Arbor: University of Michigan Press (1995), who argued that the punitive consensus that came to dominate public attitudes toward crime and pun-

ishment by the mid-1990s could be explained in large part by an inability to empathize or to perceive commonalities with persons who had committed crimes and to view them instead as having moved "beyond the pale." Gaubatz, at 163.

56. G. Gerbner, Violence and Terror in and by the Media, in Mark Raboy and Bernard Dagenais (Eds.), *Media Crisis and Democracy: Mass Communications and the Disruption of the Social Order* (pp. 94–107), London: Sage (1992), p. 96.

57. Barnouw, *supra* note 47, at 214.

58. Erik Fromm, *The Sane Society,* London: Routledge & Kegan Paul (1956), p. 142.

59. D. Giles, A Structural Analysis of the Police Story, in S. Kaminsky (Ed.), *American Television Genres* (pp. 67–84), Chicago: Nelson-Hall (1985), p. 81.

60. Thomas Harris's book *The Silence of the Lambs* (New York: St. Martin's Press, 1988) was made into a film by Orion Pictures in 1991.

61. There was, of course, another "bad guy" in this movie. Here is how one literary critic described him: "Buffalo Bill is dirty, inarticulate, artisanal (as opposed to artistic), vulgar, faggy, misogynistic, violent, perverted, tattooed, and mutilated; he listens to heavy metal, he drives a van, he lives in the suburbs, he owns a toy poodle named Precious, he is a Vietnam veteran. In short, he is an unformed, shadowy, vaguely working-class, gay composite non-character, a study in suburban Gothic, an appalling stereotype of class and erotic loathsomeness." A. Donald, Working for Oneself: Labor and Love in *The Silence of the Lambs,* 31 *Michigan Quarterly Review* 346 (1992). There are exceptions to this role. In the film *Monster,* released in 2003 by Newmarket Films, writer-director Patty Jenkins effectively contextualized the life and violence of Aileen Wuornos, who was convicted of several murders and executed the year before the film was released.

62. *Natural Born Killers* (1994), Warner Brothers Films. The screenplay was adapted from an original story by Quentin Tarantino, whom one reviewer dubbed "the new guru of gore." S. Kauffmann, Natural Born Killers, 211 *New Republic* 26 (Oct. 3, 1994).

63. For example, see P. J. NcNulty, Natural Born Killers: Preventing the Coming Explosion of Teenage Crime, 71 *Policy Review* 84 (1995).

64. Nancy Rosenberg, *Mitigating Circumstances,* New York: Dutton (1993), p. 3. The title provided an interesting twist on a badly misunderstood topic. As I discuss in detail in chapter 8, despite its absolute centrality to any attempt at fairly implementing the modern death penalty, "mitigation" is probably the least understood concept in current capital sentencing formulas.

65. Rosenberg, *supra* note 64, at 3.

66. Id. at 355.

67. *Newsweek,* Jan. 18, 1993, pp. 48–50.

68. *Newsweek,* Aug. 2, 1993, p. 40.

69. *New Age Journal,* Feb. 1993.

70. T. Maeder, Chicago's Jack the Ripper (reviewing H. Schechter, *Depraved: The Shocking True Story of America's First Serial Killer,* 1994), *New York Times Book Review,* Nov. 27, 1994, p. 25.

71. For example, see Haney, The Social Context of Capital Murder, *supra* note 1, for a discussion.

72. Sparks, *supra* note 3, at p. 12.

73. Stark, *supra* note 43, at 246. For the related thesis that the economic structure of the media constrains the messages it disseminates and subverts its editorial

content to reflect only a homogenized view of reality that is most comforting and attractive to affluent readers and viewers, see Baker, *supra* note 34. See also Gerbner, *supra* note 56.

74. J. Caputi, The Sexual Politics of Murder, 3 *Gender and Society* 437, 444 (1989).

75. For an especially thoughtful discussion of this issue, especially in the context of social histories and capital mitigation, see G. Watson, Responsibility and the Limits of Evil: Variations on a Strawsonian Theme, in Ferdinand Schoeman (Ed.), *Responsibility, Character, and the Emotions: New Essays in Moral Psychology* (pp. 256–286), New York: Cambridge University Press (1987).

76. R. Williams, Legitimate and Illegitimate Uses of Violence: A Review of Ideas and Evidence, in William Gaylin, Ruth Macklin, and Tabitha Powledge (Eds.), *Violence and the Politics of Research* (pp. 23–45), New York: Plenum Press (1981), p. 34.

77. As one media critic has put it: "For the most part, the media present myths and symbolic narratives which distort and obscure the realities of social violence, taking agency and responsibility away from the social structure that actually benefits from it and projecting it onto other kinds of symbolic beings—monsters, demons, cabals of futuristic conspirators." E. Rapping, The Uses of Violence, 55 *The Progressive* 36 (Aug. 1991).

Chapter 3

1. Kai Erikson, *Wayward Puritans: A Study in the Sociology of Deviance*, New York: Wiley (1966), p. 12.

2. Steven Box, *Deviance, Reality and Society*, London: Holt, Rinehart, and Winston (1971), p. 40. Of course, nowadays moral instruction of this sort comes from television as well. As two communications scholars put it, "the amount of crime news on local television exceeds the amount found in newspapers and on national television newscasts." Jeremy Lipschultz and Michael Hilt, *Crime and Local Television News: Dramatic, Breaking, and Live From the Scene*, Mahwah, NJ: Erlbaum (2002), p. 15.

3. C. Russell, True Crime, 17 *American Demographics* 22 (1995).

4. A. Clarke, A. Lambert, and L. Whitt, Executing the Innocent: The Next Step in the Marshall Hypothesis, 26 *New York Review of Law and Social Change* 309, 345 (2000–2001).

5. C. Haney and S. Greene, Capital Constructions: Newspaper Reporting in Death Penalty Cases, 4 *Analyses of Social Issues and Public Policy (ASAP)* 1 (2004).

6. For example, see S. Sherizen, Social Creation of Crime News: All the News Fitted to Print, in Charles Winick (Ed.), *Deviance and Mass Media* (pp. 203–224), Beverly Hills: Sage (1978).

7. Statistics on life-versus-death verdicts come from a variety of sources. According to one estimate, 84% of first-degree murders are "death penalty-eligible" in California but only 9.6% actually receive the death penalty. See S. Shatz, The California Death Penalty Scheme: Requiem for *Furman*? 72 *New York University Law Review* 1283 (1997). Of course, not all of those death-eligible cases were tried as capital and not all of those that were went to a penalty phase. However, it is clear that a death verdict is the exception rather than the rule among those cases that technically are eligible to receive it. This fact is not often conveyed in the media.

8. For example, see J. S. Carroll, N. L. Kerr, J. J. Alfini, F. M. Weaver, R. J. MacCoun, and V. Feldman, Free Press and Fair Trial: The Role of Behavioral Research, 10 *Law and Human Behavior* 187 (1986); M. Fishman, Crime Waves as Ideology, 25 *Social Problems* 531 (1978); M. T. Gordon and L. Heath, Reactions to Crime: Institutions React: The News Business, Crime, and Fear, 16 *Sage Criminal Justice System Annuals* 227 (1981); S. Gorelick, "Join Our War": The Construction of Ideology in a Newspaper Crimefighting Campaign, 35 *Crime and Delinquency* 421 (1989); D. J. Imrich, J. Dorothy, C. Mullin, and D. Linz, Measuring the Extent of Prejudicial Pretrial Publicity in Major American Newspapers: A Content Analysis, 45(3) *Journal of Communication* 94 (1995); P. J. Lavrakas, D. P. Rosenbaum, and A. J. Lurigio, in Ray Surette (Ed.), *The Media and Criminal Justice Policy: Recent Research and Social Effects* (pp. 225–240), Springfield, IL: Charles C. Thomas (1990).

9. T. Perry, Street-Smart Escapee Knows Tricks of Eluding Team of Pursuing Lawmen, *Los Angeles Times*, Oct. 9, 1992.

10. M. Pinsky, Yorba Linda Suspect Is Captured, *Los Angeles Times*, March 8, 1995.

11. Killer's Sentence in Hands of Jury: Prison or Death a Troubled Man or "Predatory Beast"? *Sacramento Bee*, Oct. 7, 1997, p. B3.

12. Penalty-Phase Arguments Begin for Redd, *Los Angeles Times*, Oct. 31, 1996, p. B5.

13. H. G. Reya, Deadly Carjacking Raises Questions and Fears, *Los Angeles Times*, Oct. 8, 1992.

14. J. Moran, Jury Recommends Death for Killer, *Los Angeles Times*, July 11, 1995.

15. Man Sentenced to Die for Killing Two Japanese Students, *The Fresno Bee*, July 30, 1996, p. A3.

16. "Gone Bad" Cop Wanted for Killing at Grocery Store, *San Francisco Examiner*, Aug. 21, 1994, p. C3.

17. M. R. Sandys and C. M. Chermak, A Journey Into the Unknown: Pretrial Publicity and Capital Cases, 1 *Communication, Law and Policy* 533 (1996).

18. Murder Suspect Arrested After a Traffic Stop, *Los Angeles Times*, March 8, 1995, p. A3.

19. Moran, *supra* note 14, at B3.

20. Sherizen, *supra* note 6, at 207.

21. Stuart Banner, *The Death Penalty: An American History*, Cambridge, MA: Harvard University Press (2002), p. 164.

22. Katherine Beckett, *Making Crime Pay: Law and Order in Contemporary American Politics*, New York: Oxford University Press (1997); R. Surette and A. Richard, Public Information Officers: A Descriptive Study of Crime News Gatekeepers, 23 *Journal of Criminal Justice* 325 (1995).

23. Beckett, *supra* note 22, at 211.

24. Gary LaFree, *Rape and Criminal Justice: The Social Construction of Sexual Assault*, Belmont, CA: Wadsworth (1989), p. 236.

25. See generally C. Haney, The Social Context of Capital Murder: Social Histories and the Logic of Capital Mitigation, 35 *Santa Clara Law Review* 547, 547 (1995).

26. A. Furillo, San Joaquin Fugitive Linked to Capital Killing Arrested, *Sacramento Bee*, June 22, 1993.

27. Santa Ana Man Confesses to Slaying of Wife, in Law, *Los Angeles Times*, July 8, 1994, p. 1A.

28. "Gone Bad" Cop Wanted in Killing at Grocery Store, *supra* note 16, at C3.

29. C. Haney and H. Fukurai, Indifferent as They Stand Unsworn?: Pretrial Publicity, Fairness, and the Capital Jury, unpublished manuscript, University of California, Santa Cruz (2004).

30. N. M. Steblay, J. Besirevic, S. M. Fulero, and B. Jimenez-Lorente, The Effects of Pretrial Publicity on Juror Verdicts: A Meta-Analytic Review, 23 *Law and Human Behavior* 219 (1999).

31. For example, see E. Constantini and J. King, The Partial Juror: Correlates and Causes of Prejudgment, 15 *Law and Society Review* 9 (1980); J. L. Freedman and T. M. Burke, The Effect of Pretrial Publicity: The *Bernaldo* Case, 38 *Canadian Journal of Criminology*, 253 (1996); G. Moran and B. L. Cutler, The Prejudicial Impact of Pretrial Publicity, 21 *Journal of Applied Social Psychology* 345 (1991); R. J. Simon and T. Eimermann, The Jury Finds Not Guilty: Another Look at Media Influence on the Jury, 48 *Journalism Quarterly* 343 (1971).

32. For example, see A. L. Otto, S. Penrod, and H. R. Dexter, The Biasing Effects of Pretrial Publicity on Juror Judgments, 18 *Law and Human Behavior* 453 (1994); S. Sue, R. Smith, and R. Gilbert, Biasing Effects of Pretrial Publicity on Judicial Decisions, 2 *Journal of Criminal Justice* 163 (1974).

33. For example, see H. R. Dexter, B. L. Cutler, and G. Moran, A Test of Voir Dire as a Remedy for the Prejudicial Effects of Pretrial Publicity, 22 *Journal of Applied Social Psychology* 819 (1992).

34. For an excellent review and integration of these studies, see C. Studebaker and S. Penrod, Pretrial Publicity: The Media, Law, and Commonsense, 3 *Psychology, Public Policy and Law* 428 (1997).

35. On the use of survey research techniques generally, see Schuman and Kalton, Survey Methods, in G. Lindzey and E. Aronson (Eds.), *The Handbook of Social Psychology*, Volume I (3rd ed.), New York: Random House (1985), pp. 635–697; and Earl Babbie, *Survey Research Methods*, Belmont, CA: Wadsworth, 1990. Since the 1970s, when the percentage of U.S. households with telephones exceeded 90%, interviews by telephone became "the most popular form of data gathering in survey research." James Frey, *Survey Research by Telephone*, Newbury Park, CA: Sage (1989), p. 23.

36. Random digit dialing, or RDD, is a telephone survey technique in which computer-generated digits are assigned to existing telephone prefixes within the target sample area. The advantage of this technique is that it "theoretically provide[s] an equal probability of reaching a household with a telephone access line (i.e., a unique telephone number that rings in that household only) regardless of whether its telephone number is published or listed." Paul Lavrakas, *Telephone Survey Methods: Sampling, Selection, and Supervision*, Newbury Park, CA: Sage (1987), p. 33.

37. The format of this survey was originally developed by the first author and members of the National Jury Project. I am grateful to the National Jury Project, particularly to Beth Bonora, Lois Heaney, Joie Hubbert, and Terri Waller for their close collaboration and assistance in the design of the questionnaires and framing of the key change of venue concepts and issues. I am also grateful for the contributions of Professor Edward Bronson who served with me as an expert consultant in the design, implementation, and interpretation of the data in many of the individual change of venue cases that Professor Fukurai and I analyzed.

38. Social scientists typically report the significance of statistical relationships in terms of p values—the probability that an obtained relationship between variables

or difference between groups could have arisen by chance. A relationship or differ-ence generally is not reported as "statistically significant" unless the p value is less than .05 (or, one chance in twenty that it could have arise by chance); p values of less than .05 reflect stronger relationships (ones even less likely to have arisen by chance). This convention is followed in table 3.5 and for all of the statistical rela-tionships reported in this book.

39. Specifically, the California Supreme Court ruled that the "nature and gravity of the offense" was a strong consideration in favor of changing venue. The Court further clarified: "The peculiar facts or aspects of a crime which make it sensational, or otherwise bring it to the consciousness of the community, define its '*nature*'; the term '*gravity*' of a crime refers to its seriousness in the law and to the possible consequences to an accused in the event of a guilty verdict" (emphasis added). Mar-tinez v. Superior Court, 29 Cal. 3d 574, 582 (1981). By this criteria, of course, capital crimes generally would be the most sensational and the consequences certainly the most grave.

40. Moran and Cutler, *supra* note 31.

41. For example, see N. L. Kerr, G. P. Kramer, J. S. Carroll, and J. J. Alfini, On the Effectiveness of Voir Dire in Criminal Cases With Prejudicial Pretrial Publicity: An Empirical Study, 40 *American University Law Review* 665 (1991); Sue et al., *supra* note 32; S. Sue, R. Smith, and G. Pedrozza, Authoritarianism, Pretrial Publicity and Awareness of Bias in Simulated Jurors, 37 *Psychological Reports* 1299 (1975); and W. C. Thompson, G. T. Fong, and D. C. Rosenhan, Inadmissible Evidence and Juror Verdicts, 40 *Journal of Personality and Social Psychology* 453 (1981).

42. See Dexter et al., *supra* note 33.

43. For example, see S. Fein, A. L. McCloskey, and T. M. Tomlinson, Can the Jury Disregard That Information? The Use of Suspicion to Reduce the Prejudicial Effects of Pretrial Publicity and Inadmissible Testimony, 23 *Personality and Social Psychology Bulletin* 1215 (1997); G. P. Kramer, N. L. Kerr, and J. S. Carroll, Pretrial Publicity, Judicial Remedies, and Jury Bias, 14 *Law and Human Behavior* 409 (1990); and Sue et al., *supra* note 32.

44. Jeffrey Scheuer, *The Sound Bite Society: Television and the American Mind,* New York: Four Walls Eight Windows Press (1999), p. 39.

45. Austin Ranney, *Channels of Power: The Impact of Television on American Politics,* New York: Basic Books (1983), p. 73.

46. Man Sentenced to Die for Killing Two Japanese Students, *supra* note 15, at A3.

Chapter 4

1. Furman v. Georgia, 408 U.S. at 296 (1972).

2. P. Linebaugh, The Tyburn Riot Against the Surgeons, in Douglas Hay, Peter Linebaugh, J. Rule, E. Thompson, and C. Winslow (Eds.), *Albion's Fatal Tree: Crime and Society in Eighteenth-Century England* (pp. 65–117), New York: Pantheon Books (1975), p. 67.

3. N. Vidmar and P. Ellsworth, Public Opinion and the Death Penalty, 26 *Stanford Law Review* 1245, 1246 (1974). Cf., also, J. Finckenauer, Public Support for the Death Penalty: Retribution as Just Deserts or Retribution as Revenge? 5 *Justice Quarterly* 81 (1988): "Public opinion certainly seems to play a role in the setting of

criminal justice policy, including (and perhaps especially) policy regarding capital punishment." Id. at 83.

4. Philip Mackey, *Hanging in the Balance: The Anti-Capital Punishment Movement in New York State, 1776–1861,* New York: Garland (1982). Discussing the way in which the officials who presided over public executions often exercised discretion at the last minute to spare the lives of especially sympathetic persons or in cases where the death penalty seemed unwarranted, Mackey noted that: "The mood of the onlookers became a factor in determining life or death. . . . If the attendant officials at the place of execution did not look as if they were about to step forward and stop the proceedings at the last minute, the public sometimes took matters into its own hands." Id. at p. 7.

5. *Furman,* 408 U.S at 286.

6. T. Laqueur, Crowds, Carnival and the State in English Executions, 1604–1868, in A. L. Beier, David Cannadine, and James Rosenheim (Eds.), *The First Modern Society: Essays in English History in Honour of Lawrence Stone* (pp. 305–355), Cambridge: Cambridge University Press (1989), p. 355.

7. D. Hay, Property, Authority, and the Criminal Law, in Hay et al., *supra* note 2, at 17. For two general histories of the death penalty, see Stuart Banner, *The Death Penalty: An American History,* Cambridge, MA: Harvard University Press (2002); John Laurence, *A History of Capital Punishment,* New York: Citadel (1960).

8. D. Davis, The Movement to Abolish Capital Punishment in America, 1787–1861, 63 *American Historical Review* 23 (1957).

9. Id. at 46.

10. See L. Filler, Movements to Abolish the Death Penalty in the United States, 284 *Annals of the American Academy of Political and Social Science* 124 (1952).

11. R. Bye, Recent History and Present Status of Capital Punishment in the United States, 27 *Journal of the American Institute of Criminal Law and Criminology* 245 (1926).

12. L. Deets, Changes in Capital Punishment Policy Since 1939, 38 *Journal of Criminal Law, Criminology, and Police Science* 584, 594 (1948).

13. As figure 4.1 indicates, there was a 16-year hiatus between the second and third Gallup polls—1937–1953—during which time there were no reliable nation-wide estimates.

14. R. Gelles and M. Straus, Family Experience and Public Support of the Death Penalty, 45 *American Journal of Orthopsychiatry* 596, 599 (1973).

15. S. Grady, Bush's Willie Horton Legacy Lives, *San Jose Mercury News,* March 18, 1990, cols. 1–3.

16. S. Gross, Update: American Public Opinion on the Death Penalty—It's Getting Personal, 83 *Cornell Law Review* 1448, 1453 (1998).

17. A. C. Gunther, The Persuasive Press Inference, 25 *Communications Research* 486, 487 (1998).

18. In order, these headlines are from: The California Poll, April 3, 1985. J. Balzar, The Times Poll: 75% Support the Death Penalty in California, *Los Angeles Times,* Aug. 19, 1985. Gallup and Gallup, 79% of Americans Back Death Penalty, *San Francisco Chronicle,* Dec. 5, 1988, p. A-10, cols. 1–4. Death Penalty Support Hits Record High, *Raleigh (N.C.) News and Observer,* Dec. 4, 1988, p. 23A, col. 1. Support Still Strong as Execution in California Nears, Poll Shows, *Los Angeles Times,* March 15, 1990, p. A-18, cols. 2–3. Support Still Strong for Death Penalty: Poll Shows Virtually No Change Since Execution, *San Francisco Chronicle,* April 29, 1992, p. A-16,

cols. 5–6. Poll: Support Strong for Death Penalty, *San Jose Mercury News*, April 29, 1992, p. 3B, cols. 1–2. See also J. Williams, Rorty, Radicalism, Romanticism: The Politics of the Gaze, 1992 *Wisconsin Law Review* 131, n. 25 (1992): "Public opinion polls show that 70 to 80% of the American public supports the death penalty" (quoting the *Boston Globe*, July 28, 1990, p. 18), and Public Support for Death Penalty Is Highest in Gallup Annals, *Gallup Reports* (1989).

19. The Gallup polling organization had been conducting national surveys in which a death penalty question was asked since 1936. However, Gallup did not include a measure of general attitude strength ("very strongly" or "not very strongly") until 1985. That poll also included a few additional questions about reasons for respondents' death penalty support or opposition, belief in deterrence, and whether support or opposition would vary in response to information about deterrence and the alternative sentence of life without parole. See H. Zeisel and A. Gallup, Death Penalty Sentiment in the United States, 5 *Journal of Quantitative Criminology* 285 (1989).

20. Cf. P. Harris, Over-Simplification and Error in Public Opinion Surveys on Capital Punishment, 3 *Justice Quarterly* 429, 433 (1986): "Categorizing people as favoring or opposing the death penalty does not take into account the vast heterogeneity of views underlying this simple dichotomy." See also P. Ellsworth and L. Ross, Public Opinion and Capital Punishment: A Close Examination of the Views of Abolitionists and Retentionists, 29 *Crime and Delinquency* 116 (1983).

21. Some of these results are described in C. Haney, A. Hurtado, and L. Vega, "Modern" Death Qualification: New Data on Its Biasing Effects, 18 *Law and Human Behavior* 619 (1994).

22. Death penalty attitudes have been studied extensively. In fact, there may be more law and social science research conducted on the topic of capital punishment than any other, and death penalty attitudes may be the most frequently studied aspect of capital punishment. I cannot do justice to the extensive research that has been conducted on this issue and will not try. Instead, I will concentrate on my own study of death penalty attitudes and cite to other more recent or related research where appropriate. The disadvantage of this approach is that I rely heavily on a single study, done more than a decade ago, in one geographical location. The advantage is that it was an intensive study in which many different questions were asked of the same respondents, making the interrelationships between issues and variables easier to establish and explore. Among the many other important studies of death penalty attitudes, see, especially, the complex survey by Phoebe Ellsworth and Lee Ross, cited *supra* note 20, James Finckenauer's study, cited *supra* note 3. See also an early but interesting analysis of the relationship of background exposure to violence and death penalty support by Richard Gelles and Murray Straus, cited *supra* note 14. For thoughtful discussions and analyses of a number of other surveys and trends in death penalty opinion, see P. Ellsworth and S. Gross, Hardening of Attitudes: Americans' Views on the Death Penalty, 50 *Journal of Social Issues* 19 (1994); H. Erskine, The Polls: Capital Punishment, 34 *Public Opinion Quarterly* 290 (1970); Vidmar and Ellsworth, cited *supra* note 3; and the more recent review by Samuel Gross, cited *supra* note 16.

23. The survey was implemented for us by the Field Institute in December 1989. We are grateful to Amnesty International, the American Civil Liberties Unions of Northern and Southern California, Death Penalty Focus, and the Friends' Committee on Legislation for providing the funds with which to conduct this survey. To conduct

the survey, we used random digit dialing (RDD), which, as I explained in chapter 3, is a telephone survey technique in which computer-generated digits are assigned to existing telephone prefixes within the target sample area and is designed to provide a random and representative sample of respondents. Unlike the venue surveys described in the last chapter, where our target sample areas consisted of individual counties in which cases were to be tried, the target area for this statewide survey was, of course, the entire state of California.

24. For example, we explained to our respondents that capital cases typically proceed in a two-stage process and that in California a defendant is eligible to receive the death penalty only if he or she has been convicted of first-degree murder and at least one "special circumstance" has been found to be true. In addition, we explained that actual jurors would be instructed in the second stage of a capital case—the penalty trial—to be guided by the presence or absence of "aggravating" and "mitigating" circumstances in making their decision between the death penalty and life in prison without possibility of parole.

25. Items like these were first used in V. Boehm, Mr. Prejudice, Miss Sympathy, and the Authoritarian Personality: An Application of Psychological Measuring Techniques to the Problems of Jury Bias, 1968 *Wisconsin Law Review* 734 (1968), in what was termed a "Legal Attitudes Questionnaire" (LAQ). Many of the LAQ items have been modified and used by other researchers in more recent studies. We used several LAQ items as well, and substituted some others that addressed the issue of punishment more directly than previous versions of this scale.

26. For example: R. Fitzgerald and P. Ellsworth, Due Process vs. Crime Control: Death Qualification and Jury Attitudes, 8 *Law and Human Behavior* 31 (1984). See also E. Bronson, On the Conviction-Proneness and Representativeness of the Death-Qualified Jury: An Empirical Study of Colorado Veniremen, 42 *University of Colorado Law Review* 1 (1970).

27. This way of characterizing the different criminal justice perspectives held by death penalty advocates and opponents was first articulated by Fitzgerald and Ellsworth, *supra* note 26. Building on the work of Herbert Packer, they defined a "due process" perspective as one in which persons "emphasize the fallibility of the criminal process in correctly apprehending, trying, and convicting lawbreakers" (Fitzgerald and Ellsworth, at 33), while persons holding a "crime control" perspective "believe that the most important function of the criminal justice system is repressing crime" (Fitzgerald and Ellsworth, at 34). For Packer's discussion of these two perspectives, see Herbert Packer, *The Limits of the Criminal Sanction,* Stanford, CA: Stanford University Press (1968).

28. Franklin Zimring and Gordon Hawkins, *Capital Punishment and the American Agenda,* Cambridge, MA: Cambridge University Press (1986), p. 132.

29. For example, Eugene Block, *When Men Play God: The Fallacy of Capital Punishment,* San Francisco: Cragmont (1983); J. Gorecki, Capital Punishment: For or Against? 83 *Michigan Law Review* 1180, 1190 (1985); Ellsworth and Ross, *supra* note 20.

30. As table 4.2 shows, all these differences were highly significant, at the $p <$ .00001 level.

31. In each calculation, a small percentage of persons either refused to answer or said that they "did not know." Hence, the percentages do not always add to 100%.

32. These results are generally consistent with a *Los Angeles Times* poll conducted a few years before ours. It found that even persons who described themselves

as death penalty supporters in California nonetheless believed that job training, improved schools, and drug rehabilitation programs would do more than capital punishment to reduce crime. Balzar, *supra* note 18.

33. A. Doob and J. Roberts, Social Psychology, Social Attitudes and Attitudes Toward Sentencing, 16 *Canadian Journal of Behavioral Science Review* 269 (1984). See also S. Diamond, Revising Images of Public Punitiveness: Sentencing by Lay and Professional English Magistrates, 15 *Law and Social Inquiry* 191 (1990).

34. Other studies that have employed variations of these kinds of questions are Harris, *supra* note 20, who presented respondents with six aggravating but no mitigating circumstances; and J. Luginbuhl and K. Middendorf, Death Penalty Beliefs and Jurors' Responses to Aggravating and Mitigating Circumstances in Capital Trials, 12 *Law and Human Behavior* 263 (1988), who presented 325 North Carolina jurors with 9 aggravating- and 10 mitigating-type circumstances. Aggravating and mitigating circumstances are key to capital jury decision making in most states. However, as noted in chapter 1, Texas, Oregon, and Virginia use a form of what has been called "special issues" model in which several specific questions are posed to capital jurors, their answers to which determine the outcome of the penalty phase. Until the U.S. Supreme Court recently prohibited the practice, in Ring v. Arizona, 586 U.S. 584 (2002), judges and not juries were responsible for making the death penalty sentencing decision in Arizona, Colorado, and Nebraska.

35. For example, see Eddings v. Oklahoma, 455 U.S. 104 (1982). As one expert has summarized, "the overwhelming body of law permits defendants to proffer and argue virtually anything as a basis for a sentence of less than death." W. Geimer, Law and Reality in the Capital Penalty Trial, 28 *New York University Review of Law and Social Change* 273, 283 (1990–1991) (footnote omitted).

36. The figures reported in table 4.3 reflect the responses of all of the survey participants. As I discuss in the next chapter, the process of death qualification significantly changes the composition of the group of otherwise jury-eligible persons. Nonetheless, even among *only* those who were death qualified, each mitigator still was endorsed by at least 16.7% of the respondents.

37. Furman v. Georgia, 408 U.S. 238 (1972).

38. Justice Rehnquist referred only indirectly and in passing to the "popular will," from which he felt the federal judiciary was "constitutionally insulated" (*Furman*, 408 U.S. at 466) and to which the Court's connection was "remote at best" (408 U.S. at 468).

39. *Furman*, 408 U.S. at 277.

40. Id. at 299.

41. Id. at 332.

42. Ibid.

43. *Furman*, 408 U.S. at 360. Marshall underscored the connection between changing public opinion and evolving standards of decency: "The last case that implied that capital punishment was still permissible was *Trop v. Dulles*. . . . Not only was the implication purely dictum, but it was also made in the context of a flexible analysis that recognized that as public opinion changed, the validity of the penalty would have to be re-examined. *Trop v. Dulles* is nearly 15 years old now, and 15 years can change many minds about many things" [408 U.S. at 330 (citation omitted)].

44. *Furman*, 408 U.S. at 361.

45. Ibid.

46. Ibid. (emphasis added).

47. For example, see Ellsworth and Ross, *supra* note 20; Vidmar and Ellsworth, *supra* note 3; A. Sarat and N. Vidmar, Public Opinion, the Death Penalty, and the Eighth Amendment: Testing the Marshall Hypothesis, 17 *Wisconsin Law Review* 171 (1983).

48. *Furman,* 408 U.S. at 363.

49. Williams v. New York., 337 U.S. 241, 248 (1949). *Williams,* it should be noted, was an unusual case in which the U.S. Supreme Court upheld a death sentence that a trial judge imposed *over* the jury's recommendation for life. Justice Black talked about the modern philosophy of "individualizing sentences" to "fit the offender and not merely the crime." Thus, although the judge in the case purported to take into account—and use as the basis for imposing a death verdict—negative background information about the defendant that the jury did not have, the Court upheld the sentence.

50. A key figure in this movement, Andrew von Hirsch, defined "desert" as the concept that "the response to someone's behavior should depend on the good or bad qualities of that behavior." See A. von Hirsch, "Neoclassicism," Proportionality, and the Rationale for Punishment: Thoughts on the Scandinavian Debate, 29 *Crime and Delinquency* 52, 59 (1983). See also David Fogel, *"We Are the Living Proof": The Justice Model for Corrections,* Chicago: Anderson (1979); David Fogel and J. Hudson (Eds.), *Justice as Fairness: Perspectives on the Justice Model,* Chicago: Anderson (1981); and Andrew von Hirsch, *Doing Justice: The Choice of Punishment,* New York: Hill and Wang (1976).

51. *Furman,* 408 U.S. at 308.

52. Gregg v. Georgia, 428 U.S. 153, 183 (1976). Similarly, see M. Warr and M. Stafford, Public Goals of Punishment and Support for the Death Penalty, 21 *Journal of Research in Crime and Delinquency* 95 (1984): "Retribution is by far the most frequently cited justification of punishment . . . those who view retribution as the most important purpose of punishment overwhelmingly favor capital punishment" (at 104); and Harris, *supra* note 20: "[P]oll data are consistent in showing that support for the death penalty is largely a matter of emotion: revenge is a more powerful rationale than any of the utilitarian justifications" (at 453).

53. J. Fox, M. Radelet, and J. Bonsteel, Death Penalty Opinion in the Post-Furman Years, 18 *New York Review of Law and Social Change* 499, 512, n. 49 (1990–1991).

54. The question of what, exactly, is meant by retribution could itself be the subject of a complex public opinion poll. In operationalizing this concept, we relied on Justice Brennan's terse *Furman* definition: "Shortly stated, retribution in this context means that criminals are put to death because they deserve it." 408 U.S. at 304.

55. Lockett v. Ohio, 438 U.S. 586 (1978) (plurality opinion).

56. See the discussion of these issues in chapter 1

57. See, for example, K. McNally, Death Is Different: Your Approach to a Capital Case Must Be Different, *The Champion,* March 1984; J. Blum, Investigation in a Capital Case: Telling the Client's Story, *The Champion* (Aug. 1985); D. Stebbins and D. Kenney, Zen and the Art of Mitigation Presentation, or the Use of Psycho-Social Experts in the Penalty Phase of a Capital Trial, *The Champion* (Aug. 1986); D. Logan, Is It Mitigation or Aggravation? Troublesome Areas of Defense Evidence in Capital Sentencing, *Forum* (Sept.–Oct. 1989).

58. *Furman,* 408 U.S. at 345.

59. In chapter 1, I cited a number of early studies showing a lack of deterrent

effect. See chapter 1, note 30. Among others, William Bowers has provided a number of more recent, detailed analyses of this issue. For example, see W. Bowers, The Effect of Executions Is Brutalization, Not Deterrence, in K. Haas and J. Incardi (Eds.), *Challenging Capital Punishment: Legal and Social Science Approaches* (pp. 49–98), Newbury Park, CA: Sage (1988), for a comprehensive review. For a more recent review of this literature, see R. Peterson and W. Bailey, Is Capital Punishment an Effective Deterrent for Murder? An Examination of Social Science Research, in James Acker, Robert Bohm, and Charles Lanier (Eds.), *America's Experiment With Capital Punishment: Reflections on the Past, Present, and Future of the Ultimate Penal Sanction* (pp. 157–182), Durham, NC: Carolina Academic Press (1998), which concluded that "empirical evidence does not support the belief that capital punishment was an effective deterrent to murder in past years" (at 177).

60. Zimring and Hawkins, *supra* note 28, at 14.

61. For example, see J. Poulos, The *Lucas* Court and Capital Punishment: The Original Understanding of the Special Circumstances, 30 *Santa Clara Law Review* 333 (1990).

62. California Department of Justice, *Murder and the Death Penalty: A Special Report to the People* (1981), p. 8.

63. For example, see C. Haney, L. Sontag, and S. Costanzo, Guiding the Discretion to Take a Life: Capital Juries, Penalty Instructions, and the Jurisprudence of Death, 50 *Journal of Social Issues* 149 (1994); M. Sandys, The Life or Death Decisions of Capital Jurors: Preliminary Findings from Kentucky, paper presented at the annual meeting of the American Society of Criminology, San Francisco, November 22, 1991.

64. J. Culver, The States and Capital Punishment: Execution From 1977–1984, 2 *Justice Quarterly* 567, 574 (1985).

65. For example, see Comment, The Cost of Taking a Life: Dollars and Sense of the Death Penalty, 18 *University of California–Davis Law Review* 1221 (1985); J. Kaplan, The Problem of Capital Punishment, *1983 University of Illinois Law Review* 555 (1983); R. Spangenber and E. Walsh, Capital Punishment or Life Imprisonment? Some Cost Considerations, 23 *Loyola (Los Angeles) Law Review* 45 (1989); and R. Tabak, The Death of Fairness: The Arbitrary and Capricious Imposition of the Death Penalty in the 1980s, 14 *New York University Review of Law and Social Change* 797 (1986).

66. M. Dayan, R. Mahler, and M. Widenhouse, Searching for an Impartial Sentencer Through Jury Selection in Capital Trials, 23 *Loyola (L.A.) Law Review* 151, 166 (1989). See also A. Paduano and C. Stafford-Smith, Deathly Errors: Juror Misperceptions Concerning Parole in the Imposition of the Death Penalty, 18 *Columbia Human Rights Law Review* 211 (1987): "[T]he typical juror at the sentencing phase of a capital trial perceives the imposition of a sentence of 'life imprisonment' to mean there is a good chance that the capital defendant will in fact be released from prison on parole" (at 211). There was some previous research that seemed to corroborate this observation. One study found that some 70% of citizens in a national sample did not believe that defendants sentenced to life without parole would remain in prison for the rest of their lives. See Bennack, The Public, the Media, and the Judicial System: A National Survey of Citizen's Awareness, 7 *State Court Journal* 4, 10 (1983). Another survey found that the average juror in Georgia believed that a person convicted of murder and given a life sentence would be released in seven or eight years. Codner, The Only Game in Town: Crapping Out in Capital Cases Because of Juror Misconceptions About Parole, cited in Dayan et al., *supra*, at 74. More recently, the

Capital Jury Project researchers concluded more broadly: "Embedded in contemporary cultural common sense about crime and punishment is the tenet of early release which holds that state policy is too lenient and so ineffective that murderers not condemned to death will be back in society far too soon, even before they actually become eligible for parole." B. Steiner, W. Bowers, and A. Sarat, Folk Knowledge as Legal Action: Death Penalty Judgments and the Tenet of Early Release in a Culture of Mistrust and Punitiveness, 33 *Law and Society Review* 461, 496 (1999).

67. McGautha v. California, 402 U.S. 183 (1971).

68. Id. at 190, n. 4.

69. The Death Penalty Information Center reports that among the 38 states that have capital punishment, 35 of them now provide a life without parole alternative to the death penalty. Only Kansas, New Mexico, and Texas do not. See http:// www.deathpenaltyinfo.org (last visited Nov. 30, 2003).

70. The Capital Jury Project, interviewing a sample of persons who had actually served as jurors in capital cases in California, reported that an even smaller percentage—18.4% of the 152 jurors they interviewed—believed that capital defendants who got life without parole sentences actually would spend the rest of their lives in prison. See W. Bowers and B. Steiner, Death by Default: An Empirical Demonstration of False and Forced Choices in Capital Sentencing, 43 *Texas Law Review* 606, 653, n. 220 (1999).

71. Raoul Berger, *Death Penalties: The Supreme Court's Obstacle Course,* Cambridge, MA: Harvard University Press (1982), p. 58.

72. We attempted to determine whether or not there was an overall statistical relationship that would allow us to predict reversals of death penalty support when all of the variables measured by our survey were simultaneously taken into account. We used two different statistical techniques—discriminant analysis and logistic regression—to predict reversals on the basis of the respondents' answers to our other questions (including demographic variables, criminal justice attitudes, overall knowledge about the death penalty, and responses to potential aggravation and mitigation). See, e.g., William Klecka, *Discriminant Analysis,* Beverly Hills, CA: Sage (1980). We found that the two best predictors of who reversed support were the extent to which the respondent was accurately informed about capital punishment and his or her receptivity to potentially mitigating circumstances. Thus, generally accurate knowledge about capital punishment and a willingness to consider a variety of possible facts and circumstances in the mitigation of punishment seemed to render even strong death penalty supporters susceptible to change, at least when they were given an opportunity to select what they viewed as a reasonable alternative.

73. In a 1985 Gallup poll, nationwide support for the death penalty fell from 72% overall to 56% when respondents were given life without possibility of parole as an explicit alternative. Cited and discussed in Paduano and Stafford-Smith, *supra* note 66, at 223, n. 35. Zeisel and Gallup aggregated the results of 1985 and 1986 nationwide Gallup polls and showed a slightly larger drop in death penalty support (from 71% to 52%) when the life without parole option was explicitly provided. See Zeisel and Gallup, *supra* note 19, at 290.

74. See Fox et al., *supra* note 53, and reference to unpublished studies cited therein.

75. The effect of the life without parole option only (absent the restitution provision) on California respondents was measured more recently. In a December 1999 poll of just over 2,000 adults, the Public Policy Institute of California found

that 47% chose "life imprisonment with absolutely no possibility of parole" and 49% chose death. (Reported in the *Sacramento Bee*, Jan. 18, 2000.)

76. H. Bedau and M. Radelet, Miscarriages of Justice in Potentially Capital Cases, 40 *Stanford Law Review* 21 (1987); H. Bedau and M. Radelet, The Myth of Infallibility: A Reply to Markman and Cassell, 41 *Stanford Law Review* 161 (1988); Hugo Bedau, Michael Radelet, and Constance Putnam, *In Spite of Innocence: The Ordeal of 400 Americans Wrongly Convicted of Crimes Punishable by Death*, Boston: Northeastern University Press (1992).

77. For example, compare: Editorial, The Interminable-Wait Penalty, *San Jose Mercury News*, March 14, 2000, p. 6B; and R. Perez-Pena, The Death Penalty: When There's No Room for Error, *New York Times*, Feb. 13, 2000), p. 3.

78. Law professors Peter Neufeld and Barry Scheck have not only been skilled litigators but also effective public advocates on the issue. See Barry Scheck, Peter Neufeld, and Jim Dwyer, *Actual Innocence: Five Days to Execution, and Other Dispatches from the Wrongly Convicted*, New York: Doubleday (2000). In addition to the "Innocence Project" that Neufeld and Scheck direct at the Cardozo School of Law in New York, Northwestern University operates a "Center on Wrongful Convictions" that specializes in the investigation of death penalty cases in which questions have been raised about the guilt of condemned prisoners. It has been directly involved in many of the exonerations of death-sentenced prisoners in Illinois. Numerous other innocence projects have been started that are associated with law schools and legal organizations across the country. (See http://www.innocenceproject.org/about/other_projects.php for a listing.) There also have been many highly publicized news stories about wrongly convicted, death-sentenced prisoners finally being exonerated and released from prison. For example, see K. Armstrong and S. Mills, Failure of the Death Penalty in Illinois (pts. 1–5), *Chicago Tribune*, Nov. 14–18, 1999; R. Cohen, Innocents at Large, *Washington Post*, Feb. 11, 1999, p. A37. In addition, Professor James Liebman and his colleagues' national study of error rates in capital cases [*A Broken System: Error Rates in Capital Cases, 1973–1995* (2000), at http://www.law.columbia.edu/instructionalservices/liebman] was covered extensively by the press. For example, see F. Butterfield, Death Sentences Being Overturned in 2 of 3 Appeals, *New York Times*, June 12, 2000, p. A1. Documentary filmmaker Ofra Bikel has produced two PBS *Frontline* programs about exonerated prisoners and the aftermath of their wrongful incarcerations: "The Case for Innocence," which aired in 1999, and "Burden of Innocence," which was broadcast on PBS in April 2003. Playwrights Jessica Blank and Erik Jensen wrote a very successful play that was based on interviews and public records surrounding several cases in which innocent persons were sentenced to die and spent up to 22 years on death row before being released. Jessica Blank and Erik Jensen, *The Exonerated*, New York: Faber and Faber (2003).

79. The American Bar Association passed a resolution in 1997 calling for a moratorium on executions in the United States to remain in effect until the wide range of problems that the organization had identified with the administration of capital punishment was addressed. See ABA, *Report With Recommendations No. 107* (Feb., 3, 1997). A number of states, including Illinois, Maryland, and Nebraska, actually implemented such moratoria out of concerns that innocent persons might be executed in their states. For a summary of the status of these issues at the start of the 21st century, see R. Tabak, Finality Without Fairness: Why We Are Moving Towards Moratoria on Executions, and the Potential Abolition of Capital Punishment, 33 *Connecticut Law Review* 733 (2001).

80. The survey was conducted in June 2000. It used essentially the same RDD methodology as had been employed in our December 1989 statewide survey, and was done by the same California-based public opinion polling organization that we used—The Field Institute.

81. Gorecki, *supra* note 29; C. Thomas and S. Foster, A Sociological Perspective on Public Support for Capital Punishment, 45 *American Journal of Orthopsychiatry* 641 (1975), also have suggested that the public's perception of increasing crime rates will translate directly into support for punitive criminal justice sanctions, including the death penalty: "Under such circumstances, it is quite logical to suppose that the more the public comes to fear victimization, the more it will demand what it believes will be an effective deterrent" (at 645).

82. To be sure, the slight nature of the increases was in part the result of a ceiling effect—when the baseline abstract support is already near 80%, there is not much room for a factor to drive it higher.

83. See, e.g., H. O'Gorman, The Discovery of Pluralistic Ignorance: An Ironic Lesson, 22 *Journal of the History of Behavioral Sciences* 333 (1986).

Chapter 5

1. Procedures for selecting a jury—often called *voir dire* (from a French term that means "to speak truthfully")—vary widely from jurisdiction to jurisdiction in the United States. Typically, after some preliminary remarks by the judge, questions are asked of the jury panel members by the attorneys for both sides, by the judge, or by both. The answers given by prospective jurors, the "venirepersons," form the basis for challenges by either side to exclude specific persons from further participation. Through this process of elimination, a jury is selected. "Peremptory" challenges, for which attorneys need give no justification, are limited in number. "Cause" challenges are potentially unlimited in quantity but must be based on specified legal grounds, and the trial court rules on whether to grant them. For a comprehensive discussion of voir dire practices and techniques, see Beth Bonora and Elissa Krause (Eds.), *Jurywork: Systematic Techniques* (2nd ed.), New York: Clark Boardman (1983).

2. As I suggest later in this chapter, the legally preferred approach to the problem of potential publicity-created bias is to rely on jury selection to weed out the most prejudiced jurors. Yet, for psychological reasons that I discuss shortly, this technique—asking potential jurors to publicly state whether they think they are "biased" or could "set aside" whatever they may have read or heard—is not up to the task in highly publicized cases. This ineffectiveness represents a more significant problem for capital trials because they are more often plagued by significant adverse pretrial publicity.

3. Until Ring v. Arizona, 586 U.S. 584 (2002), was decided, a few states—Arizona and Colorado, for example—used judge sentencing in capital cases. *Ring* required that juries make the key factual determinations that are the basis for any death sentence. Thus, death qualification of jurors is now practiced in literally every state that has a death penalty.

4. "Reasonable likelihood that a fair trial cannot be had" is the standard endorsed by the American Bar Association. See ABA, *Standards Relating to Fair Trial and Free Press.* 8–3.3 (c) (2nd ed.) (1980). Although this standard has been adopted by most states, some jurisdictions add additional qualifying language. For example,

the New Jersey Supreme Court has articulated the standard this way: when "there is a reasonable likelihood that the trial of a capital case will be surrounded by presumptively prejudicial media publicity (as that phrase is understood in the law) the court should transfer the case to another county." State v. Harris, 156 N.J. 122, 133 (1998). However, some states have implemented an even higher prejudice threshold for changing venue. For example, Pennsylvania requires a showing of "a substantial likelihood of prejudice" and in Oklahoma persons requesting a change of venue must present "clear and convincing evidence" that a fair trial is a "virtual impossibility" in order to prevail. See Breechen v. Oklahoma, 485 U.S. 909 (1988). For two useful discussions of these issues, see: P. O'Connell, Pretrial Publicity, Change of Venue, Public Opinion Polls: A Theory of Procedural Justice, 65 *University of Detroit Law Review* 169 (1988); and M. Whellan, What's Happened to Due Process Among the States? Pretrial Publicity and Motions for Change of Venue in Criminal Proceedings, 17 *American Journal of Criminal Law* 175 (1990).

5. In some instances, a distinction is made between what is regarded as "presumed prejudice" in the publicity—publicity that is so extensive and so inflammatory that courts presume its prejudicial effect—and "actual prejudice" that is established only after questioning county residents or prospective jurors about their publicity-related bias.

6. S. Bright and P. Keenan, Judges and the Politics of Death: Deciding Between the Bill of Rights and the Next Election in Capital Cases, 75 *Boston University Law Review* 759, 766 (1995). Especially in small venues, "[t]he community demands justice and exerts tremendous pressure on the judge to keep the murder trial within its sphere of influence. . . . Since the change of venue is discretionary with the judge, is costly in terms of time and money, and is not customarily granted, most judges opt to deny the motion even though they may recognize that their decision increases the probability of conviction." C. Mullin, The Jury System in Death Penalty Cases: A Symbolic Gesture, 43 *Law and Contemporary Problems* 137, 142 (1980).

7. J. Mariniello, The Death Penalty and Pre-Trial Publicity: Are Today's Attempts at Guaranteeing a Fair Trial Adequate? 8 *Notre Dame Journal of Law, Ethics, and Public Policy* 371, 376 (1994). Similarly, psychologists Michael Nietzel and Ronald Dillehay have noted that, despite its effectiveness, "courts are reluctant to change venue because of the expense, the inconvenience, and the tradition that justice should be administered in the community where the crime occurred." Michael Nietzel and Ronald Dillehay, *Psychological Consultation in the Courtroom,* New York: Pergamon (1986), p. 68. The underutilization of change of venue as a remedy to prejudicial pretrial publicity is difficult to quantify because the pertinent data are not centralized. But there are estimates. For example, because he is one of the most experienced and respected change of venue experts in the country, Professor Edward Bronson likely succeeds more often than others in these kinds of cases. Yet he too agrees that changes of venue are difficult to achieve in capital cases. Limiting his calculations to only those extremely highly publicized capital cases in which he concluded that media-related biases could not be overcome any other way (a conclusion usually reached after not only analyzing the pretrial publicity itself but also conducting community-wide surveys that document high levels of potential prejudice), Bronson estimated that trial courts in his experience still ordered venue changes less than *half* the time (personal communication, Dec. 24, 2003). The general reactions of appellate courts to change of venue motions—admittedly, a very different issue from the way trial courts treat them—are reflected in reported caselaw. For example, see P. Guthrie,

Pretrial Publicity in Criminal Cases as Ground for Change of Venue, 33 *American Law Reports 3d* 17 (1970), who reported 21 cases where appellate judges held that a change of venue was unnecessary and only 2 in which they reached the opposite conclusion. In the 1992 supplement to Guthrie's article, there were nine pages of text reporting cases in which appellate courts denied change of venue and two pages reporting decisions in favor.

8. People v. Harris, 171 Cal. Rptr. 679 (1981).

9. R. Coronado, "Thrill Killer" Suspect Stuns Courtroom: "I Am Guilty," *Sacramento Bee*, Sept. 14, 1994, p. A1. A change-of-venue hearing had been scheduled because of the extensive case-related pretrial publicity that already had been disseminated in the community. The hearing was adjourned indefinitely following the defendant's highly publicized statement. However, when proceedings resumed several months later, notwithstanding extensive additional publicity (that included repeated mention of the defendant's in-court "confession"), and survey data that confirmed its prejudicial effect, the judge still refused to change venue.

10. Many of these issues are thoughtfully discussed in C. Studebaker and S. Penrod, Pretrial Publicity: The Media, Law, and Commonsense, 3 *Psychology, Public Policy and Law* 428 (1997).

11. N. Steblay, J. Berirevic, S. Fulero, and B. Jimenez-Lorente, The Effects of Pretrial Publicity on Juror Verdicts: A Meta-Analytic Review, 23 *Law and Human Behavior* 219, 230 (1999). See also E. Constantini and J. King, The Partial Juror: Correlates and Causes of Prejudgment, 15 *Law and Society Review* 9 (1980).

12. Courts have sometimes assumed that "factual" (as opposed to "inflammatory") publicity cannot be damaging to the fair trial rights of defendants. However, that appears not to be true. For example, see G. P. Kramer, N. L. Kerr, and J. S. Carroll, Pretrial Publicity, Judicial Remedies, and Jury Bias, 14 *Law and Human Behavior* 409 (1990); J. R. P. Ogloff and N. Vidmar, The Impact of Pretrial Publicity on Jurors. A Study to Compare the Relative Effects of Television and Print Media in a Child Sex Abuse Case, 18 *Law and Human Behavior* 507 (1994); and J. R. Wilson and B. H. Bornstein, Methodological Considerations in Pretrial Publicity Research. Is the Medium the Message? 22 *Law and Human Behavior* 585 (1998).

13. For example, see E. Constantini and J. King, *supra* note 11, J. L. Freedman and T. M. Burke, The Effect of Pretrial Publicity: The *Bernaldo* Case, 38 *Canadian Journal of Criminology* 253 (1996); G. Moran and B. L. Cutler, The Prejudicial Impact of Pretrial Publicity, 21 *Journal of Applied Social Psychology* 345 (1991); A. L. Otto, S. Penrod, and H. R. Dexter, The Biasing Effects of Pretrial Publicity on Juror Judgments, 18 *Law and Human Behavior* 453 (1994); R. J. Simon and T. Eimermann, The Jury Finds Not Guilty: Another Look at Media Influence on the Jury, 48 *Journalism Quarterly* 343 (1971); and S. Sue, R. Smith, and R. Gilbert, Biasing Effects of Pretrial Publicity on Judicial Decisions, 2 *Journal of Criminal Justice* 163 (1974).

14. Patton v. Yount, 467 U.S. 1025, 1035 (1984). For example, in one highly publicized California case, 10 of 12 jurors who were seated, and 3 of 4 alternate jurors admitted having been exposed to the case-related negative publicity. Yet the California Supreme Court minimized the extent of the potential prejudice by asserting that there was insufficient evidence that any one juror "had formed such a fixed opinion as a result of pretrial publicity that he could not make the determinations required of him with impartiality." People v. Bonin, 46 Cal. 659, 697 (1988).

15. In Mu'Min v. Virginia, 500 U.S. 415 (1991), the case of a man sentenced to death after being denied a change of venue from a community in which there had

been extensive pretrial publicity, the Supreme Court ruled that "an accused is only entitled to know whether the juror can remain impartial." Id. at 422. Yet the Court limited the opportunity to acquire the information on which that judgment intelligently might be made. The operative question that the trial judge in *Mu'Min* had posed was whether the prospective jurors could "enter the Jury box with an open mind." In essence, then, only those who were willing to admit to close-mindedness were excused for cause. Ultimately, 8 of 12 jurors were seated in the case despite having been exposed to pretrial publicity. Because none of them had indicated that they "would be biased in any way," the Supreme Court approved the refusal to change venue, the limited voir dire process, and the death sentence that ultimately resulted. See id. at 421.

16. Commonwealth v. Crews, 536 Pa. 508, 517 (1994).

17. Social psychologists have long understood that many of the persons who harbor the greatest bias and deepest prejudice believe their views to be normative or commonsensical. Others may be aware that they hold problematic counternormative views but are defensive about expressing them. Finally, there is much evidence that people are unaware of whether and how their beliefs shape and affect their judgments, decisions, and behavior. For example, see R. Nisbett and T. Wilson, Telling More Than We Can Know: Verbal Reports on Mental Process, 84 *Psychological Review* 231 (1977).

18. For a good summary of the psychological forces at work, see D. Suggs and B. Sales, Juror Self Disclosure in Voir Dire: A Social Science Analysis, 56 *Indiana Law Journal* 245 (1981).

19. C. Johnson and C. Haney, Felony Voir Dire: An Exploratory Study of Its Content and Effect, 18 *Law and Human Behavior* 487 (1994).

20. R. Seltzer, M. Venuti, and G. Lopes, Juror Honesty During the Voir Dire, 19 *Journal of Criminal Justice* 451 (1991).

21. For example, S. E. Asch, The Effects of Group Pressure Upon the Modification and Distortion of Judgments, in H. Guetzkow (Ed.), *Groups, Leadership and Men,* Pittsburgh, PA: Carnegie Press (1951).

22. One study of persons who actually had served as jurors concluded that precisely these psychological pressures—evaluation apprehension, expectancy effects—led some of them to give the answers that they thought were expected of them in voir dire, irrespective of their actual true beliefs. See L. Marshall and A. Smith, The Effects of Demand Characteristics, Evaluation Anxiety, and Expectancy on Juror Honesty During Voir Dire, 120 *Journal of Psychology* 205 (1986). For a more general discussions of evaluation apprehension, see M. Leary, B. Barnes, C. Griebel, and E. Mason, The Impact of Conjoint Threats to Social and Self-Esteem on Evaluation Apprehension, 50 *Social Psychology Quarterly* 304 (1987); A. Kazdin, Observer Effects: Reactivity of Direct Observation, 14 *New Directions for Methodology of Social and Behavioral Science,* 5 (1984); J. Cohen, Social Facilitation: Audience Versus Evaluation Apprehension Effects, 4 *Motivation and Emotion* 21 (1980); and M. Rosenberg, When Dissonance Fails: On Eliminating Evaluation Apprehension From Attitude Measurement, 1 *Journal of Personality and Social Psychology* 28 (1965).

23. On how knowledge about the beliefs of others affects our own attitudes and beliefs, see Craig Haney, *Consensus Information and Attitude Change: Modifying the Effects of Counter-Attitudinal Behavior With Information About the Behavior of Others,* doctoral dissertation, Department of Psychology, Stanford University, 1978.

24. D. Marlowe and D. Crowne, Social Desirability and Response to Perceived Situational Demands, 25 *Journal of Consulting Psychology* 109 (1968).

25. Michael Nietzel and Ronald Dillehay found that individual sequestered voir dire appeared to produced the most honest responses from prospective jurors. See M. Nietzel and R. Dillehay, The Effects of Variations in Voir Dire Procedures in Capital Murder Trials, 6 *Law and Human Behavior* 1 (1982), and M. Nietzel, R. Dillehay, and M. Himelein, Effects of Voir Dire Variations in Capital Trials: A Replication and Extension, 5 *Law and Human Behavior* 467 (1987). See also N. Vidmar and J. Melnitzer, Juror Prejudice: An Empirical Study of a Challenge for Cause, 22 *Osgoode Hall Law Journal* 487 (1984), who found that individual sequestered examination of prospective jurors was far more successful in eliciting candid information than panel questioning of the entire group. Federal judge Gregory Mize reported that he was able to elicit much more candor from prospective jurors when he interviewed them individually, in a separate room, than when he posed questions in standard, open-court, group voir dire. See G. Mize, On Better Jury Selection: Spotting Unfavorable Jurors Before They Enter the Jury Room, 36 *Court Review* 10 (1999). However, another study suggested that, in general, judges are not especially adept at eliciting candor from prospective jurors. See S. Jones, Judge- Versus Attorney-Conducted Voir Dire: An Empirical Investigation of Juror Candor, 11 *Law and Human Behavior* 131 (1987).

26. People v. Stayner, Recorder's Transcript at 3384-3385 (Santa Clara County Super. Ct., July 2, 2002) (emphasis added). Professor Bronson's discussion of the minimization issue is contained in Edward Bronson, The Effectiveness of Voir Dire in Discovering Prejudice in High Publicity Cases: An Archival Study of the Minimization Effect, unpublished manuscript, Department of Political Science, California State University, Chico (1989).

27. *People v. Stayner, supra* note 26, at 3322 (emphasis added). In the face of this kind of influence from the judge, even some prospective jurors who start off voir dire by saying that "from what I've heard—it sounds like there's no doubt that he's guilty," may end up proclaiming their open-mindedness and be retained on the jury panel. Id. at 2913.

28. G. Moran and B. Cutler, The Prejudicial Impact of Pretrial Publicity, 21 *Journal of Applied Social Psychology* 345 (1991). Ogloff and Vidmar, *supra* note 12, found essentially the same thing—that persons exposed to prejudicial material were affected by it but proclaimed their impartiality nonetheless.

29. H. Dexter, B. Cutler, and G. Moran, A Test of Voir Dire as a Remedy for the Prejudicial Effects of Pretrial Publicity, 22 *Journal of Applied Social Psychology* 819 (1992).

30. For a sampling of these studies, see N. L. Kerr, G. P. Kramer, J. S Carroll, and J. J. Alfini, On the Effectiveness of Voir Dire in Criminal Cases With Prejudicial Pretrial Publicity: An Empirical Study, 40 *American University Law Review* 665 (1991); Sue et al., *supra* note 13; S. Sue, R. Smith, and G. Pedrozza, Authoritarianism, Pretrial Publicity and Awareness of Bias in Simulated Jurors, 37 *Psychological Reports* 1299 (1975); W. Thompson, G. Fong, and D. Rosenhan, Inadmissible Evidence and Juror Verdicts, 40 *Journal of Personality and Social Psychology* 453 (1981).

31. For example, see S. Fein, A. McCloskey, and T. Tomlinson, Can the Jury Disregard That Information? The Use of Suspicion to Reduce the Prejudicial Effects of Pretrial Publicity and Inadmissible Testimony, 23 *Personality and Social Psychology Bulletin* 1215 (1997); G. Kramer, N. Kerr, and J. Carroll, Pretrial Publicity, Judicial Remedies, and Jury Bias, 14 *Law and Human Behavior* 409 (1990); and Sue et al., *supra* note 13.

32. For example: "[P]roposed remedies of brief continuance of the case, expanded voir dire, judicial instruction, trial evidence, or jury deliberation do not provide an effective balance against the weight of [pretrial publicity]." Steblay et al., *supra* note 11, at 230. Also, see Studebaker and Penrod, *supra* note 10.

33. J. Lieberman and J. Arndt, Understanding the Limits of Limiting Instructions: Social Psychological Explanations for the Failures of Instructions to Disregard Pretrial Publicity and Other Inadmissible Evidence, 6 *Psychology, Public Policy and Law* 677, (2000). See also J. L. Freedman, C. K. Martin, and V. L. Mota, Pretrial Publicity: Effects of Admonitions and Expressing Pretrial Opinions, 3 *Legal and Criminological Psychology* 255 (1998).

34. United States v. Cornell, 25 Fed. Case 650, 655 (1820).

35. Id. at 656. The same logic and presumptive style of judicial reasoning prevailed some 60 years later when the full Supreme Court first considered the propriety of death qualification and summarily approved the practice. See Logan v. United States, 144 U.S. 298 (1882).

36. Philip Mackey, *Hanging in the Balance: The Anti-Capital Punishment Movement in New York State, 1776–1861,* New York: Garland (1982), pp. 203–204.

37. Williams v. New York, 337 U.S. 241, 247 (1949).

38. Act approved July 8, 1957, ch. 1968, 1957 Cal. Stat. 3509 (codified at former Cal. Penal Code § 190.1). See Comment, The California Penalty Trial, 52 *California Law Review* 386 (1964).

39. Witherspoon v. Illinois, 391 U.S. 510 (1968).

40. Id. at 513.

41. Id. at 515.

42. Id. at 517.

43. The three studies are cited in the Court's opinion at 391 U.S. at 517, n. 10.

44. Id. at 518.

45. Id. at 520, n. 18. Despite what I have said about the Court's apparent willingness to consider social science, it would be incorrect to infer that the justices were entirely comfortable with or adept at using this kind of data. Indeed, when Justice Stewart made an explicitly empirical observation in *Witherspoon,* writing that "[c]ulled of all who harbor doubts about the wisdom of capital punishment—of all who would be reluctant to pronounce the extreme penalty—such a jury can speak only for a distinct and dwindling minority" (id. at 520), he cited writer Arthur Koestler for the proposition rather than, say, public opinion polling data.

46. Wainright v. Witt, 469 U.S. 412 (1985).

47. Scholars and researchers expressed concern over the new *Witt* standard. As Professor William Thompson noted at the time, *Witt* "expands the class of individuals who may be excluded from capital juries because of their feelings about the death penalty." W. Thompson, Death Qualification after *Wainwright v. Witt* and *Lockhart v. McCree,* 13 *Law and Human Behavior* 185, 186 (1989). By making the legal standard of exclusion less precise (from unalterable opposition to substantial impairment), and giving the trial court much latitude over the determination, *Witt* made it more difficult to subsequently contest improper death qualifying exclusions in the course of an appeal.

48. Most of the then-existing research on this topic was presented and discussed in elaborate detail in an evidentiary hearing challenging death qualification in People v. David Moore and Kenneth Moore (Alameda County Super. Ct. No. 67113) in August and September 1979. The evidentiary record in that case was incorporated

into the record of Hovey v. Superior Court (Alameda County Super. Ct. No. H–1440), argued before the California Supreme Court on May 8, 1980, and decided in a published opinion: Hovey v. Superior Court, 28 Cal. 3d 1 (1980). Essentially the same research was presented in a lengthy federal hearing that resulted in a critical decision suspending the practice of death qualification in the Eighth Circuit, Grigsby v. Mabry, 569 F. Supp. 1273 (1983), aff'd, 758 F.2d 226 (1985). Much of the research that served as the evidentiary basis for these opinions was published together in a special issue of *Law and Human Behavior*. It included legal analysis by law professor Samuel Gross, and empirical articles by social psychologists Phoebe Ellsworth, William Thompson, and others. It also contained a redacted version of the California Supreme Court's *Hovey* opinion, which was notable for its especially thoughtful discussion of the legal significance of much of this social science research. See C. Haney (Ed.), Special Issue on Death Qualification, 8 *Law and Human Behavior* 1 (1984). In this chapter, I cite to many of those studies, draw on several articles of my own that were published in this special issue, and rely on follow-up research conducted with several colleagues that was published a decade later. See also C. Haney, A. Hurtado, and L. Vega, "Modern" Death Qualification: New Data on Its Biasing Effects, 18 *Law and Human Behavior* 619 (1994).

49. Lockhart v. McCree, 476 U.S. 162 (1986).

50. Id. at p. 172. In addition to this impossible-to-meet standard, the Court analyzed the overall body of research in a manner that seemed disingenuous. Justice Rehnquist started by defining the only relevant legal issue as whether or not death-qualified juries were composed of persons who were conviction prone. This reduced the number of relevant studies from the 15 that were in the record to only the 6 that focused specifically on the issue of conviction-proneness. Rehnquist then dismissed the three studies that had been introduced in *Witherspoon* as still "too tentative and fragmentary," but for "having aged some 18 years." Id. at 171. Because two of the remaining three studies further failed to account for so-called guilt-phase nullifiers (persons whose death penalty opposition would prevent them from deciding the issue of guilt), he expressed discomfort at being asked to rest a constitutional rule on the "lone study" that remained. Id. at 172.

51. *Lockhart*, 476 U.S. at 178.

52. J. Acker, A Different Agenda: The Supreme Court, Empirical Research Evidence, and Capital Punishment Decisions, 1986–1989, 27 *Law and Society Review* 65, 76, n. 9 (1993). For one discussion of the ways in which the composition and perspective of the Court had changed between *Witherspoon* and *Lockhart*, see C. Haney and D. Logan, Broken Promise: The Supreme Court's Response to Social Science Research on Capital Punishment, 50 *Journal of Social Issues* 75 (1994).

53. National opinion polls and other surveys indicate that, although the absolute levels of death penalty opposition and the size of the difference between the groups have changed over time, the existence of the differences themselves has remained a remarkably stable social fact. For a partial summary of early data on this issue, see T. Smith, A Trend Analysis of Attitudes Toward Capital Punishment, in James David (Ed.), *Studies of Social Change Since 1948*, Chicago: National Opinion Research Center Report 127B (1976).

54. Concern for the presence of African Americans and women in jury panels in order to ensure that a cross-section of the community is represented is long-standing. See, e.g., Smith v. Texas, 311 U.S. 128 (1940) (racial groups), and Ballard v. United States, 329 U.S. 187 (1946) (women).

55. For an early analysis of this issue, see H. Alker, C. Hosticka, and M. Mitchell, Jury Selection as a Biased Social Process, 9 *Law and Society Review* 9 (1976). More recently, Hiroshi Fukurai and his colleagues have analyzed the underrepresentation of racial minorities in several books. See Hiroshi Fukurai, Edgar Bulter, and Richard Krooth, *Race and the Jury: Racial Disenfranchisement and the Search for Justice,* New York: Plenum (1993); and Hiroshi Fukurai and Richard Krooth, *Race in the Jury Box: Affirmative Action in Jury Selection,* Albany: State University of New York Press (2003). Later in this chapter I discuss the way in which the selective use of peremptory challenges further reduces the representation of African Americans on capital juries.

56. For example, several early studies showed that both blacks and women were disproportionately excluded under the *Witherspoon* standard. See E. Bronson, On the Conviction Proneness and Representativeness of the Death-Qualified Jury: An Empirical Study of Colorado Veniremen, 42 *University of Colorado Law Review* 1 (1970); and H. Zeisel, Some Data on Juror Attitudes Toward Capital Punishment, Monograph—Center for Studies in Criminal Justice, University of Chicago Law School (1968). Professor Bronson did follow-up research with separate samples of several hundred respondents each, drawn from distinct rural and urban areas of California in which he found essentially the same patterns of results. See E. Bronson, Does the Exclusion of Scrupled Jurors in Capital Cases Make the Jury More Likely to Convict? Some Evidence From California, 3 *Woodrow Wilson Journal of Law* 11 (1980). Several years later, Robert Fitzgerald and Phoebe Ellsworth published a survey of over 700 persons eligible for jury service in one California county. They found that the *Witherspoon* standard had a significant impact on the demographics of capital jury eligibility, excluding many more blacks than other racial groups (25.5% vs. 16.5%), and more women than men (21% vs. 13%). See R. Fitzgerald and P. Ellsworth, Due Process vs. Crime Control: Death Qualification and Jury Attitudes, 8 *Law and Human Behavior* 31–51 (1984).

57. See Fitzgerald and Ellsworth, *supra* note 56.

58. Duncan v. Louisiana, 391 U.S. 145, 156 (1968).

59. *Wainright v. Witt, supra* note 46.

60. Morgan v. Illinois, 504 U.S. 719 (1992).

61. The issue arose in *Hovey* itself, where the California Supreme Court ruled that comparisons of death-qualified and excludable jurors must take the automatic death penalty group into account. Two surveys done at the start of the 1980s estimated the size of this group to be approximately 1% of the population. See Field Research Corp., Fieldscope Report: Attitudes Toward the Death Penalty Among the California Adult Public (prepared for the National Council on Crime and Delinquency), San Francisco, March, 1981; and Louis Harris and Associates, Inc., Study No. 814016, 812101 (prepared for the NAACP Legal Defense and Educational Fund, Inc.), New York, Jan. 1981. Using the Field and Harris survey data, statistician Joseph Kadane estimated that "taking the automatic death penalty jurors into account will have little impact on the findings" of the earlier studies such as Fitzgerald and Ellsworth. J. Kadane, After Hovey: A Note on Taking Account of the Automatic Death Penalty Jurors, 8 *Law and Human Behavior* 115, 116 (1984).

62. As discussed in more detail in the next chapter, in actual practice, courts often frame this portion of death-qualifying voir dire in terms of "automatic" death penalty imposition, rather than using *Witt*'s "prevent or substantially impair" language. In our study, we defined our excludable category broadly, to include persons who would have been dismissed under either formulation.

63. We found that modern death qualification continued to adversely affect the demographic composition of the pool of persons eligible to sit on capital juries. The gender bias was modest: women comprised 48.4% of our overall sample but 54.7% of those excluded because of their death penalty beliefs. However, even though our overall survey sample underrepresented minorities to begin with, the impact of death qualification on race was measurable and greater than for gender: racial minorities accounted for 18.5% or our overall sample but 26.3% of the excludable group. Put somewhat differently, death qualification resulted in the loss of 27.1% of our minority respondents simply because of their death penalty beliefs.

64. For a demonstration of the relationship between juror attitudes and verdict, see V. Boehm, Mr. Prejudice, Miss Sympathy, and the Authoritarian Personality: An Application of Psychological Measuring Techniques to the Problem of Jury Bias, 1968 *Wisconsin Law Review* 734 (1968).

65. See, e.g., J. Bruner, On Perceptual Readiness, 64 *Psychological Review* 123 (1957); and H. Toch and R. Schulte, Readiness to Perceive Violence as a Result of Police Training, 52 *British Journal of Psychology* 399 (1961).

66. Social psychologist Robert Abelson suggested that the way people process information and make decisions are heavily influenced by "scripts"—preexisting frameworks about people and events in the world that become increasingly important when we are presented with ambiguous or too much information. See R. Abelson, The Psychological Status of the Script Concept, 36 *American Psychologist* 715 (1981).

67. The basic proposition that death-qualified juries might be conviction prone was first suggested by Professor Walter Oberer. See Walter Oberer, Does Disqualification of Jurors for Scruples Against Capital Punishment Constitute Denial of Fair Trial on Issue of Guilt, 39 *Texas Law Review* 545 (1961). William Thompson and Phoebe Ellsworth and their colleagues found empirical support for several of the specific psychological mechanisms at work in translating death penalty attitudes into different guilt-phase verdicts. See W. Thompson, C. Cowan, P. Ellsworth, and J. Harrington, Death Penalty Attitudes and Conviction Proneness: The Translation of Attitudes Into Verdicts, 8 *Law and Human Behavior* 95 (1984). Specifically, they found that trial testimony not only is evaluated differently by death-qualified and excludable jurors, but that "death qualified jurors perceive conflicting, ambiguous testimony in a way that follows the prosecution's version of events, perhaps because that version corresponds to a script that is readily available to them (at 111). They also found that death-qualified jurors showed a willingness "to convict on a lesser showing of guilt" than persons excluded by the death qualification process.

68. There were six studies introduced in *Lockhart* that were characterized as addressing the "conviction proneness" issue. They were: C. Cowan, W. Thompson, and P. Ellsworth, The Effects of Death Qualification on Jurors' Predisposition to Convict and on the Quality of Deliberation, 8 *Law and Human Behavior* 53 (1984); F. Goldberg, Toward Expansion of *Witherspoon*: Capital Scruples, Jury Bias, and Use of Psychological Data to Raise Presumptions in the Law, 5 *Harvard Civil Rights-Civil Liberties Law Review* 53 (1970; Louis Harris and Associates Inc., Study No. 2016 (unpublished, 1971); G. Jurow, New Data on the Effect of a "Death Qualified" Jury on the Guilt Determination Process, 84 *Harvard Law Review* 567 (1971); W. Cody Wilson, Belief in Capital Punishment and Jury Performance, unpublished manuscript, University of Texas (1964); and H. Zeisel, Some Data on Juror Attitudes Toward Capital Punishment, University of Chicago monograph (1968). In addition,

another study included in the *Lockhart* record showed that death-qualified participants were significantly more likely to vote guilty than excludables, at least in cases in which nonorganic mental disorders were used as the basis for insanity defenses. They also were less likely to believe that, in general, persons who plead insanity in court "really are" insane. See P. Ellsworth, R. Bukaty, C. Cowan, and W. Thompson, The Death-Qualified Jury and the Defense of Insanity, 8 *Law and Human Behavior* 81 (1984).

69. See Cowan et al., *supra* note 68.

70. M. Allen, E. Mabry, and D. McKelton, Impact of Juror Attitudes about the Death Penalty on Juror Evaluations of Guilt and Punishment: A Meta-Analysis, 22 *Law and Human Behavior* 715 (1998).

71. I have argued that death qualification is problematic largely because it is stuctured into the jury selection process in capital cases—that is, despite producing all of the aforementioned biasing effects, it is a legally mandated part of death penalty voir dire. In addition, however, there are ways that some of these composition-related biases can be exacerbated. Death penalty opponents who fail to meet the *Witherspoon/ Witt* standard of unequivocal opposition are prime targets for prosecutoriy peremptory challenges. This fact was documented empirically by Professor Bruce Winick who (using the *Witherspoon* standard that was applicable at the time) examined the systematic exclusion of death-scrupled veniremen by prosecutors in one Florida jurisdiction. He concluded that the tendency to use peremptory challenges on prospective jurors who expressed doubts about capital punishment or were not ardent supporters—but who were not otherwise excludable—in essence "deprives capital defendants of their due process right to an impartial jury on sentence." When considered in conjunction with the effects of the exclusions that occur under *Witherspoon,* Winick concluded that it "produces capital juries that are significantly more prone to convict than would be neutral juries, thereby depriving the capital defendant of his due process right to an impartial jury on guilt." B. Winick, Prosecutorial Peremptory Challenge Practices in Capital Cases: An Empirical Study and Constitutional Analysis, 81 *Michigan Law Review* 1, 82 (1982) (footnote omitted). Of course, Winick offered these observations before *Witt* and *Morgan* had altered the shape of the death-qualification process somewhat. It is unclear how these two later decisions affected the way that both the prosecution and defense now use their peremptories. *Morgan* gave defense attorneys an opportunity to surface strong death penalty supporters and to use peremptory challenges against those who cannot be challenged successfully for cause. However, because there are still many more death penalty supporters than opponents, it would seem that the prosecutory advantage, although attenuated, would be preserved.

This supposition seems to have been confirmed by David Baldus and his colleagues, who found that prosecutors had a significant comparative advantage over defense attorneys in using peremptory challenges to shape the composition of capital juries. Baldus et al. found that they used this advantage to eliminate larger numbers of African Americans (persons also less likely in general to support the death penalty) and that the racial composition of the jury—whether produced by the discriminatory effects of death qualification or the discriminatory use of peremptory challenges— did make a difference in death sentencing rates, especially for African American defendants. Thus, predominately black juries (with five or more black members) were significantly less likely to render death sentences than predominately white juries (with four or fewer black members). D. Baldus, G. Woodworth, D. Zuckerman,

N. Weiner, and B. Broffitt, The Use of Peremptory Challenges in Capital Murder Trials: A Legal and Empirical Analysis, 3 *University of Pennsylvania Journal of Constitutional Law* 3–170 (2001), at p. 125.

72. This commonsense relationship has been supported in a number of studies. For example, see G. Stricker and G. Jurow, The Relationship Between Attitudes Toward Capital Punishment and Assignment of the Death Penalty, 2 *Journal of Psychiatry and Law* 415 (1974).

73. J. Luginbuhl and K. Middendorf, Death Penalty Beliefs and Jurors' Responses to Aggravating and Mitigating Circumstances in Capital Trials, 12 *Law and Human Behavior* 263, 276 (1988).

74. G. Moran and J. Comfort, Neither "Tentative" nor "Fragmentary": Verdict Preference of Impaneled Felony Jurors as a Function of Attitude Toward Capital Punishment, 71 *Journal of Applied Psychology* 146 (1986).

75. Steblay et al., *supra* note 11, at 229.

76. For example, see *Ballew v. Georgia*, 435 U.S. 223 (1978). Consider, also, R. Lempert, Undiscovering "Nondiscernable" Differences: Empirical Research and the Jury-Size Cases, 73 *Michigan Law Review* 644 (1975).

Chapter 6

1. The essence of this methodological concern is captured in a classic text on research design: "Humans actively interpret the situations they enter, including experimental treatment conditions. . . ." William Shadish, Thomas Cook, and Donald Campbell, *Experimental and Quasi-Experimental Designs for Causal Inference,* Boston: Houghton Mifflin (2002), p. 77. See also Ralph Rosnow and Robert Rosenthal, *People Studying People: Artifacts and Ethics in Behavioral Research,* New York: Freeman (1997).

2. For example, see the Arizona Supreme Court opinion in State v. Melendez, 121 Ariz. 1, 599 P.2d 294 (1978), condemning the practice of conditioning jurors in voir dire.

3. For example, see F. Strier and D. Shestowsky, Profiling the Profilers: A Study of the Trial Consulting Profession, Its Impact on Trial Justice and What, if Anything, to Do About It, 1999 *Wisconsin Law Review* 441 (1999).

4. R. Beltz, Practice Pointers: Effective Use of Civil Jury Instructions, 70 *Michigan Bar Journal* 1082 (1991). Consider, also that "[j]ury selection is not the most important task during voir dire. During voir dire the attorney needs to decide which veniremen to challenge, indoctrinate the potential jurors with respect to key points of the trial story, and make a good first impression. The second and third tasks are most important." Id. at 1082. J. Call, Handling the Jury: The Psychology of Courtroom Persuasion, *Brief* (Spring 1987), pp. 48–49.

5. Berryhill v. Zant, 858 F.2d 633, 641 (11th Cir. 1988) (Clark, J., specially concurring).

6. For example, see N. Bush, The Case for Expansive Voir Dire, 2 *Law and Psychology Review* 9 (1976).

7. A. Payne and C. Cohoe, 76 *American Jury Trials* 31 (2000), at § 21.

8. This research and the discussion of underlying social psychological processes that help to explain its results first appeared in C. Haney, On the Selection of Capital

Juries: The Biasing Effects of Death Qualification, 8 *Law and Human Behavior* 121 (1984); C. Haney, Examining Death Qualification: Further Analysis of the Process Effect, 8 *Law and Human Behavior* 133 (1984).

9. Because the study was conducted before the *Witt* and *Morgan* decisions had been rendered, I relied on Witherspoon v. Illinois, 391 U.S. 510, 515 (1968), as the standard of exclusion. Thus, prospective participants who said that their opposition to the death penalty was so strong that they could not decide the issue of guilt or innocence in a fair and impartial manner were excluded from participation, as were those who said they opposition would preclude them from ever voting to impose the death penalty in any case, irrespective of the facts and circumstances.

10. A third prospective juror—who was not a confederate in the experiment— initially indicated that he was strongly opposed to the death penalty. When questioned further by both the prosecuting and defense attorney, however, he stated that there were a number of circumstances under which he could consider imposing the death penalty. Consistent with the *Witherspoon* criteria, he was retained on the jury. Although unexpected, this kind of event does occur during actual death qualification and it served to increase the representativeness of the process that was filmed.

11. It may be that, because the participants in this study were all death qualified, their crime-control perspectives rendered them more willing to relinquish the presumption of innocence and to infer guilt merely on the basis of events that occurred during death qualification. If so, the point is academic. By definition, the only persons who could survive death qualification and carry its biasing effects into the evidentiary phase of the trial are themselves death qualified.

12. Under California law, jurors are not asked to decide between the death penalty and life imprisonment until and unless the defendant has been convicted of first-degree murder *and* at least one of a list of enumerated "special circumstance" have been found to be present in the case. Prior conviction of first-degree murder is one such special circumstance.

13. For example, see W. O'Barr and J. Conley, When a Juror Watches a Lawyer, 3 *Barrister* 8 (1976). Studies also suggest that special measures need to be taken to insure that a judge's nonverbal behavior does not unduly affect jurors. See A. Halverson, A. Hart, M. Hallahan, and R. Rosenthal, Reducing the Biasing Effects of Judges' Nonverbal Behavior With Simplified Jury Instructions, 82 *Journal of Applied Psychology* 590 (1997).

14. Maryland v. Foster, Recorder's Transcript at 337 (Jan. 1982).

15. People v. Stayner, Recorder's Transcript at 3409–3410 (Santa Clara County Super. Ct., July 2, 2002). This prospective juror apparently believed that the death penalty should be imposed automatically upon a finding of guilt. She also expressed a related opinion on her questionnaire to the effect that a sentence of life imprisonment without parole would constitute "torture" for the family of the victims. Nonetheless, she was not dismissed for cause. After lengthy questioning by the judge, during which he patiently instructed her about the way the law wanted or expected jurors to function, she concluded that she could give both sides "a fair trial" on the issue of penalty.

16. People v. Scott Lee Peterson, San Mateo County Superior Court, May 6, 2004, RT 6763–4.

17. J. Carroll, The Effect of Imagining an Event on Expectations for the Event: An Interpretation in Terms of the Availability Heuristic, 14 *Journal of Experimental*

Social Psychology 88, 95 (1978). Subsequent research has confirmed Carroll's view. For example, see C. Anderson, Imagination and Expectation: The Effect of Imagining Behavioral Scripts on Personal Intentions, 45 *Journal of Personality and Social Psychology* 293 (1983); W. Gregory, R. Cialdini, and K. Carpenter, Self-Relevant Scenarios as Mediators of Likelihood Estimates and Compliance: Does Imagining Make It So? 43 *Journal of Personality and Social Psychology* 89 (1982); and L. Ross, M. Lepper, F. Strack, and J. Steinmetz, Social Explanation and Social Expectation: The Effects of Real and Hypothetical Explanation Upon Subjective Likelihood, 35 *Journal of Personality and Social Psychology* 817 (1977).

18. J. Bruner and M. Potter, Interference in Visual Recognition, 144 *Science* 424 (1964).

19. For example, see H. Shaklee and B. Fischoff, Strategies of Information Search in Causal Analysis, 10 *Memory and Cognition* 520 (1982).

20. A. Tversky and D. Kahneman, Availability: A Heuristic for Judging Frequency and Probability, 5 *Cognitive Psychology* 207 (1973).

21. For example, see S. Sherman, R. Cialdini, D. Schwartzman, and K. Reynolds, Imagining Can Heighten or Lower the Perceived Likelihood of Contracting a Disease: The Mediating Effect of Ease of Imagery, 11 *Personality and Social Psychology Bulletin* 118 (1985).

22. California v. Keenan, Criminal Case No. 100402, Recorder's Transcript at 1146–1147 (Nov. 1982).

23. People v. Bell and Martin, Criminal Case No. 122554, Recorder's Transcript at 2760 (June 1992).

24. Id. at 2760–2764.

25. Id. at 2793.

26. For example, see Joseph Wolpe and Arnold Lazarus, *Behavior Therapy Techniques,* London: Pergamon Press (1967).

27. *People v. Stayner, supra* note 15, at 2929.

28. *Maryland v. Foster, supra* note 14, at 381 (emphasis added).

29. *California v. Keenan, supra* note 21, at 926–927.

30. State v. Canipe, 240 N.C. 60, 81 S.E.2d 173, 178 (1954).

31. Id. at 177.

32. People of Ohio v. Leonard Jenkins, Case No. CR-168784, March 1982, Recorder's Transcript at 421–422.

33. It also may force prosecutors into the awkward position of arguing against death penalty imposition with prospective jurors whose support is unequivocal and appears disqualifying. Yet, in most cases, there are many fewer such persons who surface in the course of the typical death-qualifying voir dire.

34. For example: K. Lewin, Group Decision and Social Change, in E. Maccoby, T. Newcomb, and E. Hartley (Eds.), *Readings in Social Psychology* (3rd ed.) (pp. 197–211), New York: Holt, Rinehart, and Winston (1947).

35. For example, see a social psychological discussion of this phenomenon in Stuart Oskamp, *Attitudes and Opinions,* Englewood Cliffs, NJ: Prentice-Hall (1977), pp. 206–207.

36. *Jenkins, supra* note 32, at 1842 (emphasis added).

37. J. Hoffman, Where's the Buck? Juror Misperception of Sentencing Responsibility in Death Penalty Cases, 70 *Indiana Law Journal* 1137, 1156 (1995).

38. Id. at n. 38. For example, as one of capital jurors interviewed for Professor Hoffman's study put it:

Some jurors felt that we should not kill [the defendant]. This juror said she cannot give this decision for the death penalty. I then said that we were asked if we could do this at jury selection, and I asked her what she said when the judge asked you if you could come down on the death penalty. The juror told me that she told the judge during jury selection she could come down with the death penalty. I then said, "Are you feeling you cannot come down with the death penalty now even though during jury selection you said you could if the crime fits the punishment?"

This is when we had a dispute. I told these jurors, "You cannot change your mind now if the crime fits the punishment." Two jurors did this and that aggravated me, because it was as though they did not take their statements at jury selection seriously. It is a different case if the punishment does not fit the crime, then you can opt against the death penalty.

Id. at 1153. Hoffman concludes that this is one way jurors come to conclude that "the law" dictates the imposition of a death sentence.

39. Grigsby v. Mabry, 569 F. Supp. 1273, 1305 (D.C. Ark. 1983). The judge further acknowledged that he regarded the biasing effects of the death qualification process to be worse than other forms of potential juror prejudice (such as that from prejudicial pretrial publicity) because "the biasing information is transmitted to the prospective jurors inside the courtroom and is imparted, albeit unconsciously, not only by the attorneys but also by the judge." Judge Eisele suggested that these facts were so clear that "even without the strong empirical support of the Haney study, the Court could conclude on its own" that capital voir dire procedures needed to be changed. Id.

40. This bright line was reinforced the year after *Witherspoon* was decided. In Boulden v. Holman, 394 U.S. 478 (1969), the Court noted that the Alabama Supreme Court had approved the exclusion of some prospective jurors who voiced general objections to the death penalty, even though they "would hang some men." Quoted in *Boulden*, at 481. The Court rejected the practice of excluding "a person who has a 'fixed opinion against' or who does not 'believe in' capital punishment" unless the prospective juror said he or she "would automatically vote against the imposition of capital punishment no matter what the trial might reveal." Id. at 482.

41. This revised standard of exclusion was introduced in Wainright v. Witt, 469 U.S. 412 (1985).

42. Id. at 424. Indeed, the opinion went on to note that many prospective jurors "simply cannot be asked enough questions" in voir dire to definitively determine their biases because they "may not know how they will react when faced with imposing the death sentence, or may be unable to articulate, or may wish to hide their true feelings." Id. at 424–425.

43. The California Supreme Court noted that the process study had "served to alert this court to some of the pernicious consequences of our current voir dire procedures in capital cases." To better protect the fair trial rights of capital defendants, the Court ordered that: "In order to minimize the potentially prejudicial effects identified by the Haney study, this court declares, pursuant to its supervisory authority over California criminal procedure, that in future capital cases that portion of the voir dire of each prospective juror which deals with issues which involve death-

qualifying the jury should be done individually and in sequestration." Hovey v. Superior Court, 28 Cal. 3d 1, 80–81 (1980).

44. The California Legislature revised the state's Code of Civil Procedure to provide, among other things, that trial courts have discretion in the manner in which they conduct voir dire. However, the Code also directed that the voir dire of "any prospective jurors . . . shall, where practicable . . . occur in the presence of the other jurors in all criminal cases, including death penalty cases." Chapter 1, § 223. This was interpreted by the California Supreme to have "abrogated" the *Hovey* requirement to conduct death-qualifying voir dire on an individual, sequestered basis. For example, see People v. Navarette, 30 Cal. 4th 458 (2003).

45. Adams v. Texas, 448 U.S. 38, 49 (1980).

46. The comment of the federal judge in the previously cited Arkansas case describes a situation that was not uncommon until at least the mid-1980s in many jurisdictions: "Although it appears to the Court that at the time of the trials of the petitioners neither defense counsel, prosecutors nor trial judges in Arkansas were fully aware of the 'flip-side' of *Witherspoon* and consequently rarely if ever made inquiry to identify ADPs, still the law of Arkansas does, and did at the time of petitioners' trials, permit the ADP challenge despite the fact that it has been rarely used or understood." Grigsby v. Mabry, 569 F. Supp. at 1305 (footnote omitted).

47. Morgan v. Illinois, 504 U.S. 719 (1992).

48. See the discussion of this issue in chapter 5. Note that in our study we posed the life-qualifying questions as mirror opposites of the death-qualifying questions. That is, they were abstract in nature (such as, "do you favor the death penalty so much that you would always vote to impose it, in every single case, no matter what the evidence showed?"). Perhaps not surprisingly, very few people answered this question affirmatively.

49. J. Blume, S. Johnson, and B. Threlkeld, Probing "Life Qualification" Through Expanded Voir Dire, 29 *Hofstra Law Review* 1209, 1220 (2001). Another commentator has suggested the same thing: that "courts have been extraordinarily resistant to allowing the defense to challenge for cause prospective jurors whose ability to fairly consider a life sentence is substantially impaired." J. Holdridge, Selecting Capital Jurors Uncommonly Willing to Condemn a Man to Die: Lower Courts' Contradictory Readings of *Wainwright v. Witt* and *Morgan v. Illinois*, 19 *Mississippi College Law Review* 283, 290 (1999).

50. *People v. Stayner, supra* note 15, at 3150.

51. W. Bowers, M. Sandys, and B. Steiner, Foreclosed Impartiality in Captial Sentencing: Jurors' Predispositions, Guilt-Trial Experience, and Premature Decision-Making, 83 *Cornell Law Review* 1476 (1998).

52. Blume, Johnson, and Threlkeld have suggested that judges may be "quicker and more fluent in backing down" prospective jurors who identify themselves persons who would automatically impose the death penalty compared to the way they handle extreme death penalty opponents. They speculate that these tendencies may stem from the atmosphere created by death qualification itself, one that "psychologically insinuates in trial participants the assumption that death is the optimal outcome." Thus, "The mission of death qualification means that judges look at the whole process though the mental lens of this thought: 'The ability to give death is what we're looking for.' Therefore, when a juror says, 'Sure, I'd always sentence a convicted murderer to death,' the judge thinks, 'We've got just a little glitch here; we need to get rid of the 'always.' ' In contrast, when a juror says, 'Sure I'd always sentence to

life,' the judge automatically thinks, 'We've got two problems here; we would need to get rid of 'always' and get rid of 'life.' ' " Blume et al., *supra* note 49, at 1238–1239.

Courts sometimes pose life-qualifying questions in ways that encourage prospective jurors to give the desired, legally approved answer, whether or not it reflects his or her honest, candid view. For example, in one case a juror repeatedly said that he always would vote for death if he convicted a defendant in a case like the one about which he was being questioned. However, he finally relented when the judge in the case put it to him this way:

> (By the Judge) Q: . . . The question is simply this: Based upon your feelings about the death penalty, would you in that case always vote for death, or would you be willing to consider the evidence as it might bear upon life in prison without the possibility of parole, evaluate everything, and then once you reach the decision, in your conscience, give us the benefit of what you think?
> A: Yes, I would.

People v. Stayner, supra note 15, at 2329. Of course, few prospective jurors are willing to state that they would not "evaluate everything," use their "conscience" to reach a decision, and then give the court and everyone else the "benefit" of what they think, even if, virtually every time, they think death is appropriate upon a conviction for the crime of which the defendant stands accused.

53. Several different studies, including those from the Capital Jury Project (where numerous actual capital jurors were interviewed after they had served on cases in different parts of the country) have found that an average of between 14 and 30% of capital jurors—slightly fewer than 2 jurors per 12-person jury to more than 4 jurors per jury—actually were "ADPs" who would automatically vote for the death penalty upon a conviction for murder. For example, 14% of persons who actually served as capital jurors in South Carolina believed that the death penalty was the only acceptable punishment for someone convicted of murder, 30% of capital jurors in Kentucky said they would automatically vote for the death penalty in a case were the defendant was convicted of a death-eligible murder, and 70% of capital jurors surveyed in some 11 different states said that death was the only punishment they would select in sentencing a capital murderer who had been convicted of a prior murder. Blume et al., *supra* note 49, at 1220 and 1223–1224. See also R. Dillehay and M. Sandys, Life Under *Wainwright v. Witt:* Juror Dispositions and Death Qualification, 20 *Law and Human Behavior* 147, 156–164 (1996). Despite these disqualifying views, these extreme pro-death jurors managed to survive the capital jury selection process and, nonetheless, to serve as members of a capital jury. Anecdotal evidence indicates that prospective jurors who say on pre-voir-dire questionnaires that they think having someone spend the rest of their life in prison is a waste of taxpayer money, those who say that anyone who has committed a crime just like the one of which the defendant has been accused should get the death penalty if convicted, and those who say that they would not consider or give any weight to the very kind of mitigation that the defendant intends to rest his case for life on nonetheless survive the modern "life qualification" process.

And there is evidence that ADPs who would automatically reject certain kinds of mitigation that, in a given case could be the only thing on which a life sentence could turn, also survive the life qualification process. Defense attorneys sometimes term these jurors "mitigation impaired," and studies suggest that more than a few of them end up on capital juries. For example, a very high percentage of capital jurors—in some instances, as many as 90%—have reported that they would refuse to regard drug addiction as a mitigating factor. In addition, drug addiction and intoxication are equally or more likely to be regarded by capital jurors as aggravation than mitigation. See S. Garvey, Aggravation and Mitigation in Capital Cases: What Do Jurors Think? 98 *Columbia Law Review* 1538 (1998).

54. J. Cotsirilos and E. Missakian, Impact of Initial Death Qualification Questioning in Open Court, 20(3) *CACJ Forum* 30, 31 (1993).

55. S. Rozelle, The Utility of *Witt:* Understanding the Language of Death Qualification, 54 *Baylor Law Review* 677, 695 (2002).

56. The exceptions come from those very few jurisdictions that provided for judge sentencing in capital cases. The post-*Ring* status of those cases has not yet been decided by the Supreme Court.

57. A number of social scientists have underscored the importance of social attitudes in the analysis of rule-following behavior. E.g., Ellen Cohn and Susan White, *Legal Socialization: A Study of Norms and Rules,* New York: Springer-Verlag (1990); Tom Tyler, *Why People Obey the Law,* New Haven, CT: Yale University Press (1990).

58. See chapter 5's discussion of the particular characteristics associated with death-qualified juries.

Chapter 7

1. This chapter is based in part on C. Haney, Violence and the Capital Jury: Mechanisms of Moral Disengagement and the Impulse to Condemn to Death, 49 *Stanford Law Review* 1447 (1997).

2. R. Cover, Violence and the Word, 95 *Yale Law Journal* 1601, 1613 (1986).

3. See estimates contained in D. Dow, *Teague* and Death: The Impact of Current Retroactivity Doctrine on Capital Defendants, 19 *Hastings Constitutional Law Quarterly* 23 (1991); C. Smith, The Death Penalty and Juveniles, 2 *Kentucky Children's Rights Journal* 1 (Spring 1992); and V. Streib, Death Penalty for Female Offenders, 58 *Cincinnati Law Review* 845 (1990).

4. A. Bandura, Mechanisms of Moral Disengagement, in W. Reich (Ed.), *Origins of Terrorism: Psychologies, Ideologies, Theologies, States of Mind* (pp. 161–191), New York: Cambridge University Press (1989); A. Bandura, Social Cognitive Theory of Moral Thought and Action, in W. Kurtines and J. Gewirtz (Eds.), *Handbook of Moral Behavior and Development: Volume I: Theory* (pp. 45–102), Hillsdale, NJ: Erlbaum (1991). Social psychologist Herbert Kelman also understood and wrote about the way that extreme forms of state-sanctioned violence must be facilitated and maintained through a set of situational and structural conditions. These conditions and processes include what Kelman called "authorization" (the state giving its official blessing to the acts in question), "routinization" (treating otherwise extreme behaviors performed on behalf of the state as normative and routine), and "dehumanization" (depicting the targets of the state-sanctioned violence as less than human and deserving of their harsh treatment). See H. Kelman, The Social Context of Torture: Policy Process and Authority Structure, in Ronald Crelinsten and Alex Schmid (Eds.),

The Politics of Pain: Torturers and Their Masters (pp. 19–34), Boulder, CO: Westview Press (1995).

5. J. Howarth, Deciding to Kill: Revealing the Gender in the Task Handed to Capital Jurors, 1994 *Wisconsin Law Review* 1345, 1385 (1994).

6. Bandura, Mechanisms of Moral Disengagement, *supra* note 4, at 181.

7. H. Garfinkel, Conditions of Successful Degradation Ceremonies, 61 *American Journal of Sociology* 420 (1956).

8. Erving Goffman, *Asylums: Essays on the Social Situation of Mental Patients and Other Inmates*, Garden City, NY: Doubleday (1959), p. 14.

9. For example, Bandura, *supra* note 4; see also A. Bandura, B. Underwood, and M. Fromson, Disinhibition of Aggression Through Diffusion of Responsibility and Dehumanization of Victims, 9 *Journal of Research in Personality* 253 (1975); and P. Zimbardo, The Human Choice: Individuation, Reason, Order Versus Deindividuation, Impulse, and Chaos, in W. Arnold and D. Levine (Eds.), *Nebraska Symposium on Motivation* (pp. 237–309), Lincoln: University of Nebraska Press (1969).

10. T. Tyler, The Social Psychology of Authority: Why Do People Obey an Order to Harm Others? 24 *Law and Society Review* 1089, 1093 (1990).

11. For a discussion of some of the psychological changes that are necessary to prepare soldiers for warfare (which, at its core, requires individuals to somehow reverse of the internal prohibition against killing), see John Gray, *The Warriors: Reflections on Men in Battle*, New York: Harper & Row (1973), and Dave Grossman, *On Killing: The Psychological Cost of Learning to Kill in War and Society*, Boston: Little, Brown (1995). See also N. Sanford, Dehumanization and Collective Destructiveness, 1 *International Journal of Group Tension* 26 (1971); L. Stires, The Gulf "War" as a Sanctioned Massacre, 15 *Contemporary Social Psychology* 139 (1991); and O. Zur, Neither Doves nor Hawks: Marking the Territory Covered by the Field of the Psychology of Peace and War, 12 *Contemporary Social Psychology* 89 (1987).

12. R. Williams, Legitimate and Illegitimate Uses of Violence: A Review of Ideas and Evidence, in W. Gaylin, R. Macklin, and T. Powledge (Eds.), *Violence and the Politics of Research* (pp. 23–45), New York: Plenum Press (1981), p. 34. Williams's discussion of the ways in which violence is psychologically and socially transformed to become acceptable, justifiable, and "legitimate" is especially pertinent to the present analysis.

13. R. Burt, Disorder in the Court: The Death Penalty and the Constitution, 85 *Michigan Law Review* 1741, 1764 (1987).

14. Thomas Green, V*erdict According to Conscience: Perspectives on the English Criminal Trial Jury, 1200–1800*, Chicago: University of Chicago Press (1985), p. 63 (footnote omitted).

15. L. Henderson, Legality and Empathy, 85 *Michigan Law Review* 1574, 1575 (1987).

16. T. Massaro, Empathy, Legal Storytelling, and the Rule of Law: New Words, Old Wounds? 87 *Michigan Law Review* 2099, 2127 (1989).

17. Id. at 2108.

18. Gerald Lopez, *Rebellious Lawyering: One Chicano's Vision of Progressive Law Practice*, Boulder, CO: Westview Press (1992), p. 43.

19. Id. at 59.

20. Massaro, *supra* note 16, at 2116.

21. Howarth, *supra* note 5, at 1363.

22. Thus, Howarth argued further that "[t]he feminist call to revalue and rein-

corporate compassion or mercy into law implicates a core concern of penalty adjudication." Id. at 1399 (footnotes omitted). This call has not yet had much impact on mandatory death penalty sentencing procedures or standard capital trial practice.

23. L. Carter, Maintaining Systemic Integrity in Capital Cases: The Use of Court-Appointed Counsel to Present Mitigating Evidence When the Defendant Advocates Death, 55 *Tennessee Law Review* 95, 101 (1987). Handler's study of the days before bifurcated capital proceedings illustrated the tensions that surrounded the introduction of *any* humanizing background information in death penalty trials. J. Handler, Background Evidence in Murder Cases, 51 *Journal of Criminal Law, Criminology, and Police Science* 317 (1960). For example, he noted that in 19th-century California cases the courts permitted the introduction of aggravating background evidence whose "purpose . . . was to influence the jury in favor of the death penalty," but that '[w]hen it came time for the defendants to introduce background evidence in mitigation of punishment, the California courts became restrictive." Id. at 318.

24. M. Sandys, Cross-Overs—Capital Jurors Who Change Their Minds About the Punishment: A Litmus Test for Sentencing Guideline, 70 *Indiana Law Review* 1183 (1995).

25. Bandura, Mechanisms of Moral Disengagement, *supra* note 4, at 171.

26. Prosecutory closing arguments that seek to reassure jurors that the violence of the death penalty that they are being asked to impose does not compare in nature or amount to the violence that the defendant has inflicted also build effectively on this implicit psychological contrast, seeming to suggest that the point of the sentencing proceeding is to determine which side of the equation—the defendant's horrible actions or the jury's sentencing verdict—is more morally justifiable. However explicitly or implicitly the contrast is made, the logic is false—that the defendant's actions are worse, more brutal, less justified, or otherwise simply much "more wrong" than whatever the state will do to him cannot establish the moral or legal correctness of the jury's death verdict.

27. For example, see S. Bright, Death by Lottery—Procedural Bar of Constitutional Claims in Capital Cases Due to Inadequate Representation of Indigent Defendants, 92 *West Virginia Law Review* 679, 680 (1990); S. Bright, Counsel for the Poor: The Death Sentence Not for the Worst Crime but for the Worst Lawyer, 103 *Yale Law Journal* 1835 (1994); S. Bright, In Defense of Life: Enforcing the Bill of Rights on Behalf of Poor, Minority and Disadvantaged Persons Facing the Death Penalty, 57 *Missouri Law Review* 849 (1992); R. Burr, Representing the Client on Death Row: The Politics of Advocacy, 9 *University of Missouri-K.C.* 1 (1990); W. Geimer, Law and Reality in the Capital Penalty Trial, 28 *New York University Review of Law and Social Change* 273 (1990–1991); G. Goodpaster, The Trial for Life: Effective Assistance of Counsel in Death Penalty Cases, 58 *New York University Law Review* 299 (1983); and R. Tabak, The Death of Fairness: The Arbitrary and Capricious Imposition of the Death Penalty in the 1980's, 14 *New York University Review of Law and Social Change* 797 (1986).

28. C. Steiker and J. Steiker, Sober Second Thoughts: Reflections on Two Decades of Constitutional Regulation of Capital Punishment, 109 *Harvard Law Review* 355, 421 (1995) (emphasis added).

29. For example: C. Haney, Criminal Justice and the Nineteenth-Century Paradigm: The Triumph of Psychological Individualism in the "Formative Era," 6 *Law and Human Behavior* 191 (1982).

30. A cogent summary of this tendency is presented in Lee Ross and Richard Nisbett, *The Person and the Situation: Perspectives of Social Psychology,* New York: McGraw-Hill (1991), pp. 125–144. In conventional social psychological terms, the defense penalty-phase presentation must somehow correct and reverse the fundamental attribution error and educate jurors about the historical, contextual, and situational determinants of the defendant's behavior. The prosecution's approach, on the other hand, typically is to embrace and build upon this common attribution error.

31. Martha Nussbaum, *Upheavals of Thought: The Intelligence of Emotions,* Cambridge, MA: Cambridge University Press (2001), p. 447.

32. For example, for discussions of how this process operated among U.S. soldiers during the Vietnam War and after, see S. Leventman and P. Camacho, The "Gook" Syndrome: The Vietnam War as a Racial Encounter, in C. Figley and S. Leventman (Eds.), *Strangers at Home* (pp. 55–70), New York: Praeger (1980); Robert Lifton, *Home from the War,* New York: Basic Books (1973); C. Loo, Race-Related PTSD: The Asian American Vietnam Veteran, 7 *Journal of Traumatic Stress* 637 (1994); S. Shatan, Stress Disorders Among Vietnam Veterans: The Emotional Context of Combat Continues, in C. Figley (Ed.), *Stress Disorders Among Vietnam Veterans* (pp. 43–52), New York: Brunner/Mazel (1978).

33. For example: Stephen Gould, *The Mismeasure of Man,* New York: Norton (1981); Richard Lerner, *Final Solutions: Biology, Prejudice, and Genocide,* University Park: Pennsylvania State University Press (1992); and Robert Proctor, *Racial Hygiene: Medicine Under the Nazis,* Cambridge, MA: Harvard University Press (1988).

34. L. Carli and J. Leonard, The Effects of Hindsight on Victim Derogation, 8 *Journal of Social and Clinical Psychology* 331 (1989); C. Murray and G. Stahly, Some Victims Are Derogated More Than Others, 11 *Western Journal of Black Studies* 177 (1987); R. Cialdini, D. Kenrick, and J. Hoerig, Victim Derogation in the Lerner Paradigm: Just World or Just Justification? 33 *Journal of Personality and Social Psychology* 719 (1976).

35. S. Pillsbury, Emotional Justice: Moralizing the Passions of Criminal Punishment, 74 *Cornell Law Review* 655, 692 (1989).

36. M. Duncan, In Slime and Darkness: The Metaphor of Filth in Criminal Justice, 68 *Tulane Law Review* 725, 792–793 (1994).

37. Id. at 777 (footnote omitted).

38. Henderson, *supra* note 15, at 1592. Legal analysts like Joan Howarth have argued that the same process is at work at higher levels in the death sentencing hierarchy. Thus, even though the U.S. Supreme Court once recognized and protected "the obvious correlation between a decision maker's perceived connection to the defendant and the reluctance to impose death," she suggested that current death penalty trial procedures and practices serve to "increase the distance between the decision maker and the accused" so that "the Court is sending the capital defendant further and further into the distance." Howarth, *supra* note 5, at 1382.

39. California v. Brown, 479 U.S. 538, 545 (1987) (Justice O'Connor, concurring).

40. Howarth, *supra* note 5, at 1383.

41. Id.

42. For example: Jerrold Ladd, *Out of the Madness: From the Projects to a Life of Hope,* New York: Warner (1994); Nathan McCall, *Makes Me Wanna Holler: A Young Black Man in America,* New York: Random House (1994); Luis Rodriguez, *Always*

Running, La Vida Loca: Gang Days in L.A., Willimantic, CT: Curbstone (1993); Brent Staples, *Parallel Time: Growing up in Black and White*, New York: Pantheon (1994).

43. For example, see Elijah Anderson, *Streetwise: Race, Class, and Social Change in an Urban Community*, Chicago: University of Chicago Press (1990); E. Anderson, The Code of the Streets: How the Inner-City Environment Fosters a Need for Respect and a Self-Image Based on Violence, *The Atlantic Monthly* (May 1994); Daniel Coyle, *Hardball: A Season in the Projects*, New York: G. P. Putnam (1993); Alex Kotlowitz, *There Are No Children Here*, New York: Doubleday (1991).

44. For example, see N. Dubrow and J. Garbarino, Living in the War Zone: Mothers and Young Children in a Public Housing Development, 68 *Child Welfare* (1989), who concluded that children who grow up in urban housing projects are exposed to traumatic violence comparable to children living in war zones and may suffer the same kinds of psychological aftereffects and need the same kinds of treatment. See also W. Harvey, Homicide Among Black Adults: Life in the Subculture of Exasperation, in D. Hawkins (Ed.), *Homicide Among Black Americans*, Lanham, MD: University Press of America (1986), who described how numerous social pressures and a pervasive sense of hopelessness contributed to high crime rates in many inner city African American communities. Carl Nightingale, *On the Edge: A History of Poor Black Children and Their American Dreams*, New York: Basic Books (1994). For a useful summary of some of this literature and a discussion of some community-based interventions that appear to reduce the harm, see M. Greene, Chronic Exposure to Violence and Poverty: Interventions That Work for Youth, 39 *Crime and Delinquency* 106 (1993).

45. An accurate rendering of these life struggles requires an amassing of the kind of elaborate contextualizing information that, as I have suggested, the criminal law disfavors and finds so unwieldy to address. See the various articles by Lynn Henderson, *supra* note 15, Joan Howarth, *supra* note 5, and Toni Massaro, *supra* note 16. See also M. Minow and E. Spelman, In Context, 63 *Southern California Law Review* 1597 (1990). But, as I have noted, the Supreme Court recently took an important step toward requiring capital defense attorneys to do precisely these things. See Wiggins v. Smith, 539 U.S. 510 (2003).

46. Compare Massaro, *supra* note 16, who conceded that: "Although we 'know' at some level that we tend to treat people like ourselves better than those outside our spheres of familiarity, we often ignore this knowledge. If verbal reminders of this tendency are built directly into our legal discourse, they may stimulate legal decision makers to reach beyond those tendencies more consistently" (at 2123).

47. For example, see N. Finkel, K. Meister, and D. Lightfoot, The Self-Defense Defense and Community Sentiment, 15 *Law and Human Behavior* 585 (1992). In some jurisdictions, legal doctrines have been expanded to cover circumstances that were not previously recognized as "self defense"—such as when battered spouses kill their abusive mates. See, e.g., J. Greenwald, A. Tomkins, M. Kenning, and D. Zavodny, Psychological Self-Defense Jury Instructions: Influence on Verdicts for Battered Women Defendants, 8 *Behavioral Sciences and the Law* 171 (1990); and D. Follingstad, D. Polek, E. Hause, L. Deaton, L., et al., Factors Predicting Verdicts in Cases Where Battered Women Kill Their Husbands, 13 *Law and Human Behavior* 253 (1989).

48. A. Sarat, Violence, Representation and Responsibility in Capital Trials: The View From the Jury, 70 *Indiana Law Review* 1103, 1124 (1995).

49. Id. A newspaper article about a notorious criminal case with more than

the usual number of distractions underscores the degree to which graphic depictions of the violence outside the law become the emotional focal point of a murder trial:

> The antidote to the tedium [of the trial] is peppy defense attorney John-nie Cochran. While everyone else is keeping a careful eye on the TV camera mounted high on the wall above the jury, Cochran is clearly having the time of his life . . .
>
> Cochran owned the trial yesterday, turning it into his own private debating society until late afternoon. That was when (prosecutor) Clark, with no fanfare, began to put up a series of photos on the big screen behind the witness box.
>
> At one point she asked Judge Ito to cut the video, and only those in the courtroom could see the blood-drenched body of Ronald Goldman, with a detective dispassionately holding his white hiking boot up so the camera could see the sole.
>
> Suddenly, it was a murder trial again, and the jurors pulled out their notebooks and scribbled away like mad.

C. W. Nevius, Courtroom Drama Fades Into Tedium: Reality in L.A. Is Duller Than TV, *San Francisco Chronicle,* March 8, 1995, pp. A-1, A-15, cols. 2, 4.

50. T. Eisenberg and M. Wells, Deadly Confusion: Juror Instructions in Capital Cases, 79 *Cornell Law Review* 1–15 (1993).

51. For example, see J. Marquart, S. Ekland-Olson, and J. Sorenson, Gazing Into the Crystal Ball: Can Jurors Accurately Predict Dangerousness in Capital Cases? 23 *Law and Society Review* 449 (1989). See also G. Giardini and R. Farrow, The Paroling of Capital Offenders, in Thorsten Sellin (Ed.), *Capital Punishment* (pp. 169–186), New York: Harper & Row (1967), who provided an in-depth statistical analysis of the recidivism rates of capital offenders. As one commentator summarized the evidence: "Research suggests that murderers rarely kill in prison and are unlikely to engage in violence crime if they are paroled." R. Lempert, Desert and Deterrence: An Assessment of the Moral Bases of the Case for Capital Punishment, 79 *Michigan Law Review* 1177, 1189 (1981).

52. Eisenberg and Wells, *supra* note 50.

53. These data are presented and discussed at some length in J. Luginbuhl and J. Howe, Discretion in Capital Sentencing Instructions: Guided or Misguided? 70 *Indiana Law Review* 1161, 1178, tbl. 5 and 1179, tbl. 6 (1995).

54. See also C. Haney, A. Hurtado, and L. Vega, "Modern" Death Qualification: New Data on Its Biasing Effects, 18 *Law and Human Behavior* 619 (1994).

55. C. Haney, L. Sontag, and S. Costanzo, Guiding the Discretion to Take a Life: Capital Juries, Penalty Instructions, and the Jurisprudence of Death, 50 *Journal of Social Issues* 149 (1994).

56. Eisenberg and Wells, *supra* note 50, at 8.

57. See C. Haney, The Social Context of Capital Murder: Social Histories and the Logic of Mitigation, 35 *Santa Clara Law Review* 547 (1995); and C. Haney, Psychological Secrecy and the Death Penalty: Observations on the "Mere Extinguishment of Life," 16 *Studies in Law, Politics, and Society* 3 (1997).

58. For example, see C. Spatz Widom, The Cycle of Violence, 244 *Science* 160 (1989). In addition, see K. Dodge, J. Bates, and G. Petit, Mechanisms in the Cycle of Violence, 250 *Science* 1678 (1990), who also examined the impact of abuse on child development, and D. Truscott, Intergenerational Transmission of Violent Behavior

in Adolescent Males, 18 *Aggressive Behavior* 327 (1992), who reported that violent behavior in adolescence was associated with having been the victim of paternal verbal and physical aggression.

59. For example, see D. Dutton and S. Hart, Evidence for Long-Term, Specific Effects of Childhood Abuse and Neglect on Criminal Behavior in Men, 36 *International Journal of Offender Therapy and Comparative Criminology* 129 (1992), who reported that childhood "physical abuse ... increase[s] the odds [of committing] physical abuse in the family [as an adult] fivefold and the abuse of ... twofold" and that childhood "sexual abuse increases the odds of committing sexual abuse against strangers [as an adult] fivefold and within the family eightfold." See also J. McCord, The Cycle of Crime and Socialization Practices, 82 *Journal of Criminal Law and Criminology* 211 (1991), who found evidence of a generational transmission of criminality, including the role of parental criminality and parental conflict and aggression in subsequent crime among children. In addition, A. McCormack, F. Rokous, R. Hazelwood, and A. Burgess, An Exploration of Incest in the Childhood Development of Serial Rapists, 7 *Journal of Family Violence* 219 (1992), documented a high degree of childhood sexual abuse, including incest, among men who became serial rapists.

60. For example, see M. Feldman, K. Mallouh, and D. Lewis, Filicial Abuse in the Histories of 15 Condemned Murderers, 14 *Bulletin of the American Academy of Psychiatry and Law* 345 (1986); and D. Lewis, R. Lovely, C. Yeager, G. Ferguson, M. Friedman, G. Sloane, H. Friedman, and J. Pincus, Intrinsic and Environmental Characteristics of Juvenile Murderers, 27 *Journal of the American Academy of Child and Adolescent Psychiatry* 582 (1988). Other research related to these studies and those cited in the several immediately following footnotes have been more elaborately and systematically reviewed in the two articles of mine referenced *supra* note 57.

61. For example: M. Rosenberg and R. Giberson, The Child Witness of Family Violence, in Robert Ammerman and Michael Hersen (Eds.), *Case Studies in Family Violence* (pp. 231–253), New York: Plenum Press (1991).

62. V. McLoyd, The Impact of Economic Hardship on Black Families and Children: Psychological Distress, Parenting, and Socioeconomic Development, 61 *Child Development* 311, 313 (1990). McLoyd's research showed that poverty lessens the capacity for supportive parenting, renders parents more vulnerable to negative life events, and adversely affects children's socioemotional functioning. See also J. Daniel, R. Hampton, and E. Newberger, Child Abuse and Accidents in Black Families: A Controlled Comparative Study, 53 *American Journal of Orthopsychiatry* 645 (1983): "[B]lack families who abuse their children appear to suffer from poverty, social isolation, and stressful relationships with and among kin" (at 652).

63. For example, see G. Elder, T. Nguyen, and A. Caspi, Linking Family Hardship to Children's Lives, 56 *Child Development* 361 (1985), who discussed the ways in which families undergoing economic pressures are prone to unemployment and divorce which, in turn, affect the emotional, psychological, and social development of children. See also C. Kruttschnitt, J. McLeod, and M. Dornfeld, The Economic Environment of Child Abuse, 41 *Social Problems* 299 (1994).

64. For example, see McLoyd, *supra* note 62; and D. Takeuchi, D. Williams, and R. Adair, Economic Distress in the Family and Children's Emotional and Behavioral Problems, 53 *Journal of Marriage and the Family* 1031 (1991), who found that economic stress was significantly related to children's emotional and behavioral problems—specifically, to higher levels of depression, antisocial behavior, and impulsivity.

65. G. Duncan and W. Rodgers, Has Children's Poverty Become More Persistent? 56 *American Sociological Review* 538 (1991).

66. McLoyd, *supra* note 62, at 335. See also G. Duncan, J. Brooks-Gunn, and P. Klebanov, Economic Deprivation and Early Childhood Development, 65 *Child Development* 296 (1994).

67. For example, see P. Steinke, Using Situational Factors to Predict Types of Prison Violence, 17 *Journal of Offender Rehabilitation* 119 (1991).

68. For example: M. Silver and D. Geller, On the Irrelevance of Evil: The Organization and Individual Action, 34 *Journal of Social Issues* (1978).

69. Descriptions of this work can be found in S. Milgram, Some Conditions of Obedience and Disobedience to Authority, 18 *Human Relations* 57 (1965); and Stanley Milgram, *Obedience to Authority: An Experimental View,* New York: Harper & Row (1974). See also B. Eckman, Stanley Milgram's Obedience Studies, 34 *Etc.* 88 (1977).

70. S. Gilbert, Another Look at the Milgram Obedience Studies: The Role of the Gradated Series of Shocks, 7 *Personality and Social Psychology Bulletin* 690 (1981).

71. For example, see H. Tilker, Socially Responsible Behavior as a Function of Observer Responsibility and Victim Feedback, 14 *Journal of Personality and Social Psychology* 95 (1970); and Zimbardo, *supra* note 9.

72. H. Kelman, Violence Without Moral Restraint: Reflections on the Dehumanization of Victims and Victimizers, 29 *Journal of Social Issues* 25 (1973). See also Herbert Kelman and V. Lee Hamilton, *Crimes of Obedience: Toward a Social Psychology of Authority and Responsibility,* New Haven, CT: Yale University Press (1989).

73. Williams, *supra* note 12, at 34.

74. Robert Johnson, *Death Work: A Study of the Modern Execution Process,* Pacific Grove, CA: Brooks/Cole (1990).

75. R. Weisberg, Deregulating Death, 8 *Supreme Court Review* 305, 391 (1984).

76. J. Hoffman, Where's the Buck? Juror Misperception of Sentencing Responsibility in Death Penalty Cases, 70 *Indiana Law Review* 1137, 1138, n. 11 (1995).

77. See Hoffman's description of this case in his article, *supra* note 76, at 1142–1143.

78. Id. at 1146 (quoting an unidentified Indiana capital juror).

79. Id. at 1147.

80. Sarat, *supra* note 48, at 1124.

81. Payne v. Tennessee, 501 U.S. 808 (1991) authorized the use of "victim impact" testimony in capital penalty trials. The practice remains controversial, in part because most jurors already will have a deep intuitive, empathic sense of the pain of such profound loss, making additional testimony unnecessary. More important, perhaps, holding persons accountable for consequences that they did not specifically intend and could not have reasonably foreseen may be improper in proceedings where moral blameworthiness is at issue. Nonetheless, the use of victim impact testimony in capital cases is now widespread. In fact, in some jurisdictions, experts on the dying process are permitted to speculate about the nature and amount of suffering that the victim of the murder likely endured.

82. Nussbaum, *supra* note 31, at 447. See also Susan Bandes's fine analysis of this same issue: S. Bandes, Empathy, Narrative, and Victim Impact Statements, 63 *University of Chicago Law Review* 361 (1997).

83. People v. Fudge, 7 Cal. 4th 1075, 1117 (1994).

84. Id. at 1124.

85. Howarth, *supra* note 5, at 1393. For a description of *Payne*, see *supra* note 81.

86. Sarat, *supra* note 48, at 1124. Indeed, he noted further that: "To refuse to participate in the spectacle of seeing and touching those representations and instrumentalities is, in essence, to refuse to consider all the evidence and is, thus, to defy one's oath as a juror. Because the gaze cannot be legitimately averted, the juror becomes a victim of viewing" (at 1126). But it is the clear asymmetry to this victimization that serves to morally disengage them from the decision they are called upon to make and facilitates their death sentencing.

87. Haney et al., *supra* note 55, at 171.

88. Sarat, *supra* note 48, at 1133.

89. Richmond Newspapers Inc. v. Commonwealth of Virginia, 448 U.S. 555, 571 (1980) (Burger, C.J., plurality opinion).

90. J. Bessler, Televised Executions and the Constitution: Recognizing a First Amendment Right of Access to State Executions, 45 *Federal Communications Law Journal* 355, 408 (1993).

91. KQED v. Vasquez, 18 Media Law Reporter 2323 (N.D. Cal. 1991).

92. Wendy Lesser, *Pictures at an Execution: An Inquiry Into the Subject of Murder*, Cambridge, MA: Harvard University Press (1993), pp. 30–31.

93. G. Lucas, Televised Executions Bill Dies: Assembly Votes It Down for a Second Time, *San Francisco Chronicle*, Sept. 4, 1991, p. A14. See also R. Patrick, Hiding Death, 18 *New England Journal of Criminal and Civil Commitment* 117 (1992), who concluded that "hiding executions reveals a society that does not wish to confront the death it generates" (at 143).

94. T. Laqueur, Crowds, Carnival and the State in English Executions, 1604–1868, in A. Beier, D. Cannadine, and J. Rosenheim (Eds.), *The First Modern Society: Essays in English History in Honour of Lawrence Stone* (pp. 305–355), Cambridge: Cambridge University Press (1989), p. 355.

95. Bandura, Mechanisms of Moral Disengagement, *supra* note 4, at 175.

96. For example, see People v. Daniels, 802 P.2d 906, 939 (Cal.) (proper to exclude testimony about what defendant's life would be like in prison), *cert. denied*, 112 S. Ct. 145 (1991), and *People v. Fudge*, *supra* note 83.

97. In addition to the studies cited at notes 50–55, Joan Howarth reported that in one small sample of interviews "[e]very juror interviewed who voted for death incorrectly interpreted the alternative (life without the possibility of parole) as allowing for release." Howarth, *supra* note 5, at 1416.

98. Sarat, *supra* note 48, at 1133.

99. In addition to the discussion in chapter 4, see Craig Haney, Death Penalty Opinion: Myth and Misconception, 1995(1) *California Criminal Defense Practice Reporter* 1 (1995); Haney et al., *supra* note 54.

100. Sarat, *supra* note 48, at 1134.

Chapter 8

1. There were several major components to the approach that the Court approved to resolve the *Furman*-related concerns about unbridled jury discretion. One was to restrict the kinds of cases for which the death penalty was even a possibility. Thus, most states now require the prosecutor to allege in advance the special characteristics of the murder with which the defendant is charged that make it bad or

heinous enough to qualify for capital punishment. Although an analysis of the effectiveness of this reform is beyond the scope of this book, commentators have argued that the new statutes really do not significantly narrow the scope of death-eligible murders. For example, as Steven Shatz and Nina Rivkind have pointed out in their analysis of the California statute, there are some 21 categories of first-degree murder that are eligible for the death penalty, and if categories of death-eligible felony murder are included, there are an additional 12. In contrast, only 7 categories of first-degree murder are excluded. Thus, the extent of the "narrowing" brought about by a statute like this is open to question. See S. Shatz and N. Rivkind, The California Death Penalty Scheme: Requiem for *Furman?* 72 *New York University Law Review* 1283 (1997).

2. Gregg v. Georgia, 428 U.S. 153, 206–207 (1976).

3. In chapter 5, I discussed some of the studies showing that jury instructions are not very effective in addressing pretrial publicity issues. For example, see J. L. Freedman, C. K Martin and V. L. Mota, Pretrial Publicity: Effects of Admonitions and Expressing Pretrial Opinions, 3 *Legal and Criminological Psychology* 255 (1998); and J. Lieberman and J. Arndt, Understanding the Limits of Limiting Instructions: Social Psychological Explanations for the Failures of Instructions to Disregard Pretrial Publicity and Other Inadmissible Evidence, 6 *Psychology, Public Policy and Law* 677 (2000). The limitations of jury instructions in other contexts also are well documented. For example, see S. Kassin and S. Sommers, Inadmissible Evidence, Instructions to Disregard, and the Jury: Substantive Versus Procedural Considerations, 23 *Personality and Social Psychology Bulletin* 1046 (1997); J. Schmolesky, B. Cutler, and S. Penrod, Presumption Instructions and Juror Decision Making, 1 *Forensic Reports* 165 (1988); R. Wiener, K. Habert, G. Shkodriani, and C. Staebler, The Social Psychology of Jury Nullification: Predicting When Jurors Disobey the Law, 21 *Journal of Applied Social Psychology* 1389 (1991); and S. Wolf and D. Montgomery, Effects of Inadmissible Evidence and Level of Judicial Admonishment to Disregard on the Judgments of Mock Jurors, 7 *Journal of Applied Social Psychology* 205 (1977).

4. *Gregg,* 428 U.S. at 195 (opinion of Stewart, Powell, and Stevens, JJ.) (emphasis added). The leap it made in the case of the Texas statute—approved in the companion case of Jurek v. Texas, 428 U.S. 261 (1976)—that the new Texas law "clearly assures" that "the jury have before it all possible relevant information about the individual defendant whose fate it must determine" was one that the Court was forced to reconsider and retract some 13 years later. In Penry v. Lynaugh, 492 U.S. 392 (1989), the Justices decided that the absence of explicit instructions informing the jury that it could consider and give effect to certain kinds of mitigating evidence undermined its ability to provide a "reasoned moral response" in choosing between life and death. During the period in which Texas used this flawed instruction, an instruction that the *Penry* Court indirectly acknowledged did not ensure a reasoned moral response on the part of the jury, the state led the nation in the number of persons executed.

5. *Gregg,* 428 U.S. at 206.

6. McGautha v. California, 402 U.S. 183, 204 (1971).

7. Caldwell v. Mississippi, 472 U.S. 320, 333 (1985).

8. Jurors in only a few states are permitted to make sentencing decisions in noncapital cases, and even then with some limitations. The states that permit this are Arkansas, Kentucky, Missouri, Oklahoma, Texas, and Virginia. In several recent cases, the U.S. Supreme Court reversed a long-standing trend limiting jury involve-

298 Notes to Pages 166–168

ment in sentencing-related issues. In the pivotal case, Apprendi v. New Jersey, 530 U.S. 466 (2000), the Court ruled that juries must find any facts that serve as the basis for increasing the defendant's sentence above the statutory minimum, and that those facts must be proven to them beyond a reasonable doubt. Note that even after *Apprendi*, however, jurors are required to find facts that affect sentencing rather than to decide on the sentencing directly. For a useful summary of current trends and practices, see: E. Lillquist, The Puzzling Return of Jury Sentencing: Misgivings About *Apprendi*, 82 *North Carolina Law Review* 621 (2004), especially 628–652. In Ring v. Arizona, 536 U.S. 584 (2002), the Court extended the logic of *Apprendi* to the very few states where judges were responsible for death sentencing, requiring that, even in those states (Arizona, Colorado, Nebraska, and, perhaps, Florida), the existence of any aggravating factors that made a case "death eligible" would have to be found by a jury.

9. I want to be clear that I think it would be "unusual" but, depending on the factual issues decided, by no means impossible for these differences to play a significant role. Elsewhere I have written about the pitfalls of assuming a "commonsense" view of reality held by "the people," as though there were more homogeneity in the perception and experience of social reality in our society than, in fact, exists or is represented on some juries. Certain kinds of trials—largely because they involve questions of reasonableness, expectations, and likelihoods—are more likely to be influenced by differences in juror background experiences and values. See C. Haney, Commonsense Justice and Capital Punishment: Problematizing the "Will of the People," 3 *Psychology, Public Policy and Law* 303 (1997). However, these kinds of guilt phase questions are not necessarily typical in criminal trials.

10. S. Rozelle, The Utility of *Witt:* Understanding the Language of Death Qualification, 54 *Baylor Law Review* 677, 684 (2002).

11. See C. Haney and M. Lynch, Comprehending Life and Death Matters: A Preliminary Study of California's Capital Penalty Instructions, 18 *Law and Human Behavior* 411 (1994).

12. R. Weisberg, Deregulating Death, 8 *Supreme Court Review* 305, 371, n. 259 (1984).

13. A. Reifman, S. Gusick, and P. Ellsworth, Real Jurors' Understanding of the Law in Real Cases, 16 *Law and Human Behavior* 539 (1992).

14. We simplified the task that we asked our participants to perform compared to what is required of actual jurors in a real California death penalty trial. In a real case, jurors must first (1) interpret the instructional intent with respect to each factor in the template (i.e., is it supposed to be aggravation or mitigation?), then (2) determine whether or not they believe it is present in the case, (3) decide how much weight it should be given in their sentencing calculation, and finally (4) determine how it, in combination with the other factors, leads to a verdict. Our participants were asked to perform only the initial, threshold task.

15. Each participant's definitions were independently content-analyzed by two raters. Interrater reliability ranged from .83 (on whether the definition was correct or not) to .78 (on whether the definitions were "legally correct"). For each definition on which there was disagreement between raters, the definition was scored by a third rater, blind to the disagreement. In all such cases, we used the consensus score (two of three raters) in our calculation of the percentages presented.

16. For example, see W. Geimer, Law and Reality in the Capital Penalty Trial, 28 *New York University Review of Law and Social Change* 273 (1990–1991).

17. The crime focus in the way our participants understood the key sentencing terms is consistent with what Ursula Bentele and William Bowers described as the "obsessive focus on the defendant's guilt of the crime" in their analysis of a sample of interviews with actual capital jurors from a number of different states. As they put it: "The jurors do not appear to have grappled with the notion that, despite the defendant's clear guilt of an aggravated murder, they could decide that he deserved a sentence other than death. What is missing from these interviews is any real recognition of a separate choice, an independent decision about whether this defendant should suffer the ultimate penalty of death." U. Bentele and W. Bowers, How Jurors Decide on Death: Guilt Is Overwhelming; Aggravation Requires Death; and Mitigation Is No Excuse, 66 *Brooklyn Law Review* 1011, 1031 (2001). Our data suggest that, whatever else may help to account for this bias, some of it is definitional—that is, it stems from the way jurors understand (or fail to understand) the meaning of the key terms in the sentencing instruction.

18. In addition, many of the specific factors are phrased in terms of "whether or not" the factor is present (e.g., for factor "d": "*Whether or not* the offense was committed while the defendant was under the influence of extreme mental or emotional disturbance"). To avoid potential confusion about how the absence of such a factor should be interpreted (i.e., is the absence of a factor the juror decides is intended to be mitigating actually aggravation?), we rephrased these factors to focus only on their presence (e.g., "*If* the offense was committed while the defendant was under the influence of extreme mental or emotional disturbance").

19. As perhaps would be expected, our participants' ability to correctly define the terms "aggravation" and "mitigation" was related to their ability to accurately categorize the specific factors in the sentencing instruction. Thus, we gave each participant in the study an overall score for accuracy in judging the template of factors (ranging from 0 to 9, omitting factors "a" and "i" for which either response was permissible). Accuracy of overall definitions correlated significantly with accuracy of template judgments ($r = .79$, $p < .01$).

20. The two factors that may be interpreted as either aggravating or mitigating under the California instruction prompted the most equivocal responses from our participants. Thus, participants were almost evenly split on whether the circumstances of the crime were intended to be aggravating or mitigating in the instructions (56% vs. 44%). Similarly, two-thirds of the participants regarded age as mitigating and one-third as aggravating.

21. Although the motivation for this change was never officially discussed by the Commission on Judicial Instructions that made it, the intent presumably was to improve juror comprehension. The change occurred after the California Supreme Court noted that the particular definitions (which originated from *Black's Law Dictionary*) offered "a helpful framework within which the jury could consider the specific circumstances in aggravation and mitigation." People v. Dyer, 45 Cal.3d 26, 78 (1988).

22. C. Haney and M. Lynch, Clarifying Life and Death Matters: An Analysis of Instructional Comprehension and Penalty Phase Arguments, 21 *Law and Human Behavior* 575 (1997).

23. The research was published in C. Haney, L. Sontag, and S. Costanzo, Deciding to Take a Life: Capital Juries, Sentencing Instructions, and the Jurisprudence of Death, 50 *Journal of Social Issues* 149 (1994). The article included data from interviews conducted with both California and Oregon jurors. However, because the

Oregon instruction is very different from California's, and in many ways atypical of most state death penalty statutes, I discuss only the California results. Some of the results were depicted in more detail than in the published article in Dr. Sontag's dissertation on California jurors: Lorelei Sontag, Deciding Death: A Legal and Empirical Analysis of Penalty Phase Jury Instructions and Capital Decisionmaking, unpublished doctoral dissertation, University of California, Santa Cruz (1990), and in Dr. Costanzo's dissertation on Oregon jurors: Sally Costanzo, Penalty Decision-Making Under the Special Issues Framework: A Social Psychological Analysis, unpublished doctoral dissertation, University of California, Santa Cruz (1990).

24. As one juror who sat on a jury that rendered a death verdict put it: "I don't think anybody liked using those terms because when we did use them, we got confused. They were confusing and that's why we didn't elaborate on 'em, you know, we just, we probably said the same thing but in regular terms. Yeah, in our own way, not in these two words because they were just confusing and I had never really used them before in anything. So, yeah, they sit there and throw these stupid words at you and I'm like 'Well, what do they mean?' I'd get so confused 'cause they sound the same. I'm thinking 'Now which one was that again?' You know. And it totally confused me."

25. As noted at several points in previous chapters, the courts are clear on this issue—not only must a capital defendant be allowed to present whatever mitigation he or she deems relevant, but the evidence offered by the defendant at least must be *considered* by the jury as a possible reason for a sentence less than death. Thus, before reaching a sentencing verdict, the jury must take into consideration not only the crime but also "anything else" the defendant offers as the basis for a sentence less than death.

26. This juror sat on a California jury that returned a verdict of death.

27. J. Frank and B. Applegate, Assessing Juror Understanding of Capital-Sentencing Instructions, 44 *Crime and Delinquency* 412 (1997).

28. Michael Radelet, *Affidavit of Michael L. Radelet, State of Florida, County of Alachua* (1993). Professor Radelet tested the ability of 249 death-qualified University of Florida students to comprehend the Florida capital sentencing instruction. After reading a brief summary of guilt- and penalty-phase evidence from an actual case, participants heard the Florida sentencing instructions read aloud. They then were asked a series of questions designed to measure comprehension. Radelet found "widespread misunderstanding," with 50% or more of respondents answering many of the questions incorrectly, especially those that focused on the nature and role of mitigating factors that were not explicitly listed in the instruction itself—so-called nonstatutory mitigators. Radelet concluded that the effect of the instructions was to "create a very strong presumption of death."

29. In United States *ex rel.* Free v. Peters, 778 F. Supp. 431 (N.D. Ill., 1991), a federal district judge ruled that if Professor Zeisel's research was determined to be valid and unbiased, it "called into question the empirical assumptions as to juror comprehension" on which the constitutionality of the Illinois death penalty statute was predicated (at 434–435). He ordered an evidentiary hearing. The magistrate judge who conducted the hearing concluded that "there is a reasonable likelihood that a substantial number of jurors who received the [Illinois instructions] . . . believed that only the statutory mitigating factors, or factors comparable to them, could preclude the imposition of the death penalty." The district court found the 50–60% error rate by jury-eligible respondents who answered questions related to this issue

"staggering." The court concluded that, since the high error rate indicated that the majority of jurors were likely to be incorrect about this issue, deliberation would not have helped them overcome their misconceptions. See Free v. Peters, 806 F. Supp. 1098 (1992), at circa 724. Professor Zeisel's questionnaire was reprinted in the opinion, which also included a detailed discussion of many of his otherwise unpublished results. However, a three-judge panel of the Seventh Circuit reversed. Chief Judge Posner disparaged Zeisel's research, and dismissed its significance in Free v. Peters, 12 F.3d 700 (1993). The U.S. Supreme Court denied certiorari and let the Seventh Circuit's ruling stand. See Free v. Peters, 513 U.S. 967 (1994). Aspects of Professor Zeisel's research also were discussed in Gacy v. Wellborn, 994 F.2d 305 (7th Cir. 1993).

30. M. Blankenship, J. Luginbuhl, F. Cullen, and W. Redick, Jurors' Comprehension of Sentencing Instructions: A Test of the Death Penalty Process in Tennessee, 14 *Justice Quarterly* 325, 336 (1997).

31. S. Diamond and J. Levi, Improving Decisions on Death by Revising and Testing Jury Instructions, 79 *Judicature* 224 (1996).

32. R. Wiener, C. Pritchard, and M. Weston, Comprehensibility of Approved Jury Instructions in Capital Murder Cases, 80 *Journal of Applied Psychology* 455 (1995); R. Wiener, L. Hurt, S. Thoma, M. Sadler, C. Bauer, and T. Sargent, The Role of Declarative and Procedural Knowledge in Capital Murder Sentencing, 28 *Journal of Applied Social Psychology* 124 (1998).

33. Zeisel, research discussed and referred to in the opinions cited *supra* note 29; Diamond and Levi, *supra* note 31.

34. Radelet, *supra* note 28.

35. Blankenship et al., *supra* note 30.

36. T. Eisenberg and M. Wells, Deadly Confusion: Juror Instructions in Capital Cases, 79 *Cornell Law Review* 1, 12 (1993).

37. J. Luginbuhl and J. Howe, Discretion in Capital Sentencing Instructions: Guided or Misguided? 70 *Indiana Law Journal* 1161, 1167 (1995). See also J. Luginbuhl, and K. Middendorf, Death Penalty Beliefs and Jurors' Responses to Aggravating and Mitigating Circumstances in Capital Trials, 12 *Law and Human Behavior* 263 (1988).

38. Luginbuhl and Howe, *supra* note 37, at 1173.

39. The work of the Capital Jury Project appears in numerous publications. For some overviews, see W. Bowers, The Capital Jury Project: Rationale, Design, and Preview of Early Findings, 70 *Indiana Law Journal* 1043 (1995); and W. Bowers, The Capital Jury: Is It Tilted Toward Death? 79 *Judicature* 220 (1996). See also J. Luginbuhl and M. Burkhead, Sources of Bias and Arbitrariness in the Capital Trial, 50 *Journal of Social Issues* 103 (1994), who correctly observed that the specific instructional errors and the resulting general confusion that surrounds the capital decision-making process appear to have a one-sided effect, increasing the likelihood of death over life sentences.

40. Bentele and Bowers, *supra* note 17, at 1013.

41. For example, Herbert Kelman and V. Lee Hamilton, *Crimes of Obedience*, New Haven, CT: Yale University Press (1989).

42. For example, see S. Milgram, Some Conditions of Obedience and Disobedience to Authority, 18 *Human Relations* 57 (1965), and Stanley Milgram, *Obedience to Authority: An Experimental View*, New York: Harper & Row (1974). For a retrospective discussion of the meaning and significance of Milgram's research, see Tho-

mas Blass (Ed.), *Obedience to Authority: Current Perspectives on the Milgram Paradigm*, Hillsdale, NJ: Erlbaum (1999).

43. T. Tyler, The Social Psychology of Authority: Why Do People Obey an Order to Harm Others? 24 *Law and Society Review* 1089, 1093 (1990).

44. Robert Cover, *Justice Accused: Antislavery and the Judicial Process*, New Haven, CT: Yale University Press (1975), pp. 235–236.

45. Haney et al., *supra* note 23, at 166. As Robert Weisberg speculated: "In the case of the death penalty, the law has sometimes offered the sentencer the illusion of a legal rule, so that no actor at any point in the penalty procedure need feel he has chosen to kill any individual." *Supra* note 12, at 393. Empirical research cited in this chapter and the previous one appears to confirm that some capital jurors rely on this illusion to avoid the reality of the personal decision at hand.

46. Haney et al., *supra* note 23, at 167 (emphasis added).

47. Id.

48. J. Hoffman, Where's the Buck? Juror Misperception of Sentencing Responsibility in Death Penalty Cases, 70 *Indiana Law Review* 1137, 1152 (1995). Others have argued that, because of they way they are written, most penalty-phase jury instructions make it appear that the law favors death verdicts over life. For example, see W. Geimer, Law and Reality in the Capital Penalty Trial, 28 *New York University Review of Law and Social Change* 273 (1990–1991).

49. A. Bandura, Mechanisms of Moral Disengagement, in W. Reich (Ed.), *Origins of Terrorism: Psychologies, Ideologies, Theologies, States of Mind* (pp. 161–191), New York: Cambridge University Press (1989), p. 173.

50. J. Howarth, Deciding to Kill: Revealing the Gender in the Task Handed to Capital Jurors, 1994 *Wisconsin Law Review* 1345, 1410 (1994).

51. As Austin Sarat noted, jurors' widespread belief that death penalty cases are carefully and automatically appealed and reviewed can combine "to push the jurors to authorize [a death] sentence . . . even though most [are], in fact, neither deeply enthusiastic about their decision nor convinced that [the defendant] would ever be executed." A. Sarat, Violence, Representation and Responsibility in Capital Trials: The View From the Jury, 70 *Indiana Law Review* 1103, 1131 (1995).

52. Howarth, *supra* note 50, at 1411.

53. Mills v. Maryland, 486 U.S. 367 (1988).

54. Id. at 383–384. The Court ruled that ambiguity in the Maryland sentencing instruction might have confused jurors into believing that they had to *unanimously* find the *same* mitigating circumstance was present before balancing it against the aggravation.

55. Id. at 381.

56. Id. at 384.

57. Boyde v. California, 494 U.S. 370 (1990).

58. Based on nothing other than their own intuitions, the majority decided: "[W]e think there is not a reasonable likelihood that [the] jurors interpreted the trial court's instructions to prevent consideration of mitigating evidence of background and character." *Boyde*, 494 U.S. at 381. The dissent argued that this contention was "belied by both the plain meaning of the instructions and the context in which they were given." Id. at 388.

59. Buchanan v. Angelone, 528 U.S. 225 (1998). The trial judge in the case had refused the defendant's request to instruct the jury that certain evidence had been introduced to "mitigate against imposing the death penalty" and that, if the jurors

found it to be present in the case, they should consider it "in deciding whether to impose a sentence of death or life imprisonment."

60. The standard Virginia instruction told jurors only that, "if you believe from all the evidence that the death penalty is not justified, then you shall fix the punishment of the Defendant at life imprisonment." Even though the Virginia law governing the death penalty specified certain "facts in mitigation," none of those facts, or mention of the concept of "mitigation" itself, were included in the instruction the jury was given. Instead, the instruction explicitly focused the jurors on the aggravating facts that needed to be established in order to find in favor of the death penalty; it not only never mentioned mitigation but also never provided the jurors with any framework for identifying factors that would lead them to conclude that the death penalty was "not justified." See *Buchanan*, 528 U.S. at 273–274.

61. Id. at 277 (emphasis added).

62. Weeks v. Angelone, 528 U.S. 225, 236 (2000).

63. The Court cites Richardson v. Marsh, 481 U.S. 200 (1987), for this proposition. Yet *Richardson* was a case in which a trial judge instructed the jury not to use the confession of one codefendant for purposes of deciding another's guilt. Unlike *Weeks*, the issue was whether the jury had the human capacity to follow that instruction, not whether they understood it.

64. The Court cites a century-and-a-half-old contracts case, Armstrong v. Toler, 11 Wheat. 258 (1826), for this proposition. Yet *Armstrong* was a case in which the jurors had posed a confusing question to the judge that, although appearing to misunderstand it, he nonetheless answered in a legally correct manner that seemed to satisfy the jury. The *Armstrong* Court refused to reverse merely "because an answer does not go to the full extent of the question." Id. at 279. This seems fundamentally different from a case in which the jury requests guidance about a specific and central term in the instruction that the judge clearly refuses to define. This is the fact pattern in a number of capital cases and *Armstrong* does not seem to begin to address it.

65. *Weeks*, 528 U.S. at 234.

66. *Boyde*, 494 U.S. at 380.

67. Francis v. Franklin, 471 U.S. 307, 332 (1985).

68. *Free v. Peters*, 12 F.3d at 704.

69. Appellate courts continue to ignore evidence of instructional confusion simply by asserting that jurors *do* understand the key terms and that, therefore, further clarifying instructions or comments from trial judges are unnecessary. For example, according to one Indiana court, "[t]he terms 'mitigation; and 'any other circumstances appropriate for consideration' are not beyond the comprehension of the average lay juror." Wisehart v. State, 693 N.E.2d 23 (Ind. 1998). Similarly, another Indiana court held that "where terms are in general use and can be understood by a person of ordinary intelligence, they need not be defined." Roche v. State, 690 N.E.2d 1115 (Ind. 1997). A Georgia court found that "mitigation is a word "of common meaning and understanding." Smith v. State, 290 S.E.2d 43, 45 (Ga. 1982). See also Matheney v. State, 688 N.E.2d 883 (Ind. 1997), where the court concluded that the notion that "mitigating circumstances" included "virtually anything favorable to the accused" was within the common understanding of the average juror; State v. Flowers, 441 S0.2d 707, 716 (1983), where the court rejected the claim that "mitigating circumstances" is a term of art; and People v. Wader, 854 P.2d 80, 81–82 (Ca. 1993), which held that trial courts were not required to give a clarifying instruction on these terms because they were commonly understood.

70. Gacy v. Wellborn, 994 F.2d 305, 307 (7th Cir. 1993).

71. Id. at 308.

72. In People v. McLain, 249 Cal. Rptr. 630, 641 (1988), the jury sent a note to the judge asking whether there were definitions of aggravation and mitigation that were available to them. The judge replied, in writing: "Are you asking for the ordinary definition of those terms or whether there is a legal definition? If you are asking for the latter, there is no legal definition of these terms. They are to be given there [*sic*] commonly accepted and ordinary meaning." Not satisfied, and conscientiously seeking clarification of these key terms, the jury responded with another note: "Being unfamiliar with the term of mitigation we would like the dictionary meaning of both mitigation and aggravation, please." Still the trial court refused to help them. Id. at 641. The California Supreme Court, reviewing this colloquy, did not find it problematic.

73. Id. at 312.

74. People v. Malone, 47 Cal.3d 1, 55 (1988).

75. Mosk quoted *Malone* and elaborated his view in People v. Gallego, 52 Cal.3d 115, 208 (1990) (citations omitted). The California Supreme Court refused to require that trial courts "identify each factor as either 'aggravating' or 'mitigating' " in the California sentencing instruction. Indeed, "[t]o require the trial court to attach one label or the other would lead to unproductive, insoluble debates and would unduly hamper a meaningful examination of the full range of relevant consideration." People v. Cox, 53 Cal. 3d 618, 724 (1991). Moreover, the Court had asserted earlier that "the aggravating or mitigating nature of these various factors should be self-evident to any reasonable person within the context of each particular case." People v. Jackson, 28 Cal. 3d 264, 316 (1980). As I have noted, much research has shown that the meaning of these particular factors is hardly self-evident, and that many reasonable people believe their nature to be the opposite of what the instructions intend.

76. State v. Deck, 994 S.W.2d 537, 541–542 (Mo. 1999).

77. Id. at 542. Some juries that have succeeded in convincing judges that the definitions are not self-evident have been given singularly unhelpful assistance, as when one California trial court actually responded to a jury's request for clarification of the meaning of mitigation by reading a dictionary definition that included: "alleviation, abatement, or diminution of penalty or punishment imposed by law." People v. Mincey, 827 P.2d 388, 427 (1992).

78. *Deck*, 994 S.W.2d at 543. In a "postconviction" appeal (in which the standards of review are somewhat different), the Missouri Supreme Court appeared to have a change of heart. It ruled that because "defense counsel's professional incompetence" in failing to request more appropriate sentencing instructions, the jurors' confusion may have led to their discounting of the mitigation that was presented on the defendant's behalf, and reversed. The issue of whether the "correct" Missouri instruction—which also omitted any definition of the term "mitigation"—would have been comprehended and applied correctly by the jury was never reached. See Deck v. State, 68 S.W. 418 (Mo. 2002).

79. See P. Ellsworth, Are Twelve Heads Better Than One? 52 *Law and Contemporary Problems* 205 (1989).

80. Haney and Lynch, *supra* note 22, at 583–591. The confusion extended to the specific factors as well. For example, as Lynch and I noted, although the most important mitigator in the California instruction, Factor K, was identified as such in

15 of the 20 cases, defense attorneys failed to specify how or why the Factor K evidence was mitigating in nature. In fully 14 of the 20 cases, prosecutors argued in essence that there was no legitimate Factor K evidence in the case, while all of the defense attorneys in these 14 cases argued that there was. Disagreements over Factor K mitigation are particularly problematic because California trial judges often refuse to provide case-specific or "pinpoint" supplementary instructions that acknowledge the potential mitigating significance of particular kinds of Factor K evidence (like a childhood history of extreme abuse, instances of serious institutional mistreatment, or a record of excellent prison adjustment). Jurors thus must first decide what specific evidence has been offered under the rubric of Factor K and then decide whether and how much mitigating significance to attach to it (again, assuming they have managed to gain even a rudimentary understanding of how to conceptualize mitigation and the role it is supposed to play in their decision-making process).

81. For example, see S. Chaiken, The Heuristic Model of Persuasion, in M. Zanna, J. Olson, and C. Herman (Eds.), *Social Influence: The Ontario Symposium* (pp. 3–39). Hillsdale, NJ: Erlbaum (1987); R. Petty, and J. Cacioppo, The Elaboration Likelihood Model of Persuasion, in L. Berkowitz (Ed.), *Advances in Experimental Social Psychology* (Vol. 19, pp. 123–205), New York: Academic Press (1986).

82. Bandura, *supra* note 49, at 170.

83. Welsh White, *The Death Penalty in the Eighties,* Ann Arbor: University of Michigan Press (1987), p. 69.

84. Instead, they found that the bases for most of the reversals were "egregiously incompetent defense lawyers" who failed to look for or just overlooked important evidence, and police and prosecutors who suppressed evidence in order to keep it from capital jurors. They also found that appellate courts, particularly in federal habeas review, *did* reverse for "instructional error." But instructional errors, in this context, meant that trial courts had instructed improperly; rarely if ever were cases reversed because the standard sentencing instructions in use in a state were difficult or impossible for average jurors to comprehend. See James S. Liebman, Jeffrey Fagan, and Valerie West, *A Broken System: Error Rates in Capital Cases, 1973–1995,* available at http://www2.1aw.columbia.edu/ and instructionalservices/liebman/.

85. Proffitt v. Florida, 428 U.S. 242, 259 (1976).

Chapter 9

1. For example, see S. Johnson, Black Innocence and the White Jury, 83 *Michigan Law Review* 1611 (1985); S. Johnson, Comment: Unconscious Racism and the Criminal Law, 73 *Cornell Law Review* 1016 (1988); C. Lawrence, The *Id,* the Ego, and Equal Protection: Reckoning With Unconscious Racism, 39 *Stanford Law Review* 317 (1987); W. Sabol, Racially Disproportionate Prison Populations in the United States, 13 *Contemporary Crises* 405 (1989); L. Sweeney and C. Haney, The Influence of Race on Sentencing: A Meta-Analytic Review of Experimental Studies, 10 *Behavioral Science and Law* 179 (1992).

2. For example, see David Baldus, George Woodworth, and Charles Pulaski, *Equal Justice and the Death Penalty: A Legal and Empirical Analysis,* Boston: Northeastern University Press (1990); Samuel Gross and Robert Mauro, *Death and Discrimination: Racial Disparities in Capital Sentencing,* Boston: Northeastern University Press (1989); C. Haney, Let Them Eat Due Process: The Fourteenth Amendment and

Symbolic Legality, 15 *Law and Human Behavior* 183 (1991); R. Kennedy, *McCleskey v. Kemp:* Race, Capital Punishment and the Supreme Court, 101 *Harvard Law Review* 1388 (1988).

3. S. Pillsbury, Emotional Justice: Moralizing the Passions of Criminal Punishment, 74 *Cornell Law Review* 655, 707 (1989).

4. An especially insight discussion of this issue appears in A. Sarat, Speaking of Death: Narratives of Violence in Capital Trials, 27 *Law and Society Review* 19 (1993).

5. In fact, just a year after the death penalty was reinstated and the *Gregg*-approved capital sentencing reforms were implemented on an even more widespread basis, the Supreme Court offered an important clarification of the nature of the individualized justice it had in mind. In *Lockett v. Ohio,* the Court held that "the Eighth and Fourteenth Amendments require that the sentencer . . . not be precluded from considering, as a mitigating factor, any aspect of a defendant's character or record and any of the circumstances of the offense that the defendant proffers as a basis for a sentence less than death." Lockett v. Ohio, 438 U.S. 586, 604 (1977). This requirement has been reaffirmed and expanded in a series of cases. See: Eddings v. Oklahoma, 455 U.S. 104 (1982); Spaziano v. Florida, 468 U.S. 447 (1984); Penry v. Lynaugh, 492 U.S. 302 (1989); and Wiggins v. Smith, 539 U.S. 510 (2003).

6. C. Haney and M. Lynch, Clarifying Life and Death Matters: An Analysis of Instructional Comprehension and Penalty Phase Arguments, 21 *Law and Human Behavior* 575, 583–591 (1997).

7. Welsh White, *The Death Penalty in the Eighties,* Ann Arbor: University of Michigan Press (1987), pp. 53–56.

8. William Bowers, The Capital Jury Project: Rationale, Design, and Preview of Early Findings, 70 *Indiana Law Review* 1043, 1087, tbl. 2 (1995).

9. Id. at 1090, tbl. 6.

10. Id. at 1091, tbl. 7.

11. Many of these issues are discussed in more detail in C. Haney, Condemning the Other in Death Penalty Trials: Biographical Racism, Structural Mitigation, and the Empathic Divide, 53 *De Paul Law Review* 1557 (2004), on which I rely in several portions of this chapter.

12. Some of these "mechanisms of moral disengagement" were discussed at length in chapter 7.

13. For example, see C. Haney, Psychological Secrecy and the Death Penalty: Observations on "the Mere Extinguishment of Life," 16 *Studies in Law, Politics, and Society* 3 (1997).

14. Louis Masur, *Rites of Execution: Capital Punishment and the Transformation of American Culture, 1776–1865,* New York: Oxford University Press (1989), p. 6.

15. National Prisoner Statistics, *Capital Punishment 1982,* Washington, DC: U.S. Department of Justice, Bureau of Justice Statistics (1984), p. 9.

16. National Prisoner Statistics, *Capital Punishment 1995,* Washington, DC: National Criminal Justice Reference Service.

17. Amnesty International, *USA: The Death Penalty: Developments in 1987,* New York: Amnesty International (1988), p. 15.

18. Tracy Snell and Laura Maruschak, *Capital Punishment 2001,* NCJ 19020. Washington, DC: Bureau of Justice Statistics (December 2002).

19. The best archival studies reach these conclusions in varying degrees. See, e.g., Baldus et al., *supra* note 2; D. Baldus, G. Woodworth, D. Zuckerman, N. Weiner,

and B. Broffitt, Racial Discrimination and the Death Penalty in the Post *Furman* Era: An Empirical and Legal Overview, With Recent Findings From Philadelphia, 83 *Cornell Law Review* 1638 (1998); Gross and Mauro, *supra* note 2. In a congressionally mandated summary and review of some 28 studies of the topic, a Government Accounting Office report found race of victim significantly influenced death sentencing in about four out of five of the studies, and that race of defendant significantly influenced it in about half of them. See U.S. Government Accounting Office, *Death Penalty Research Indicates Pattern of Racial Discrimination* (1990).

Most recently, a nationwide study by Professors Eisenberg, Wells, and Blume found that although African American capital defendants overall were not sentenced to death in numbers disproportionate to the rates at which they were convicted of murder (a fact that this chapter attempts to put in a broader context), they *were* sentenced to die in disproportionate numbers when their victims were white. See J. Blume, T. Eisenberg, and M. Wells, Explaining Death Row's Population and Racial Composition, 1 *Journal of Empirical Legal Studies* 165 (2004). The nature and significance of cross-racial death sentencing (black defendants, white victims and jurors) is explained at least in part by the psychological dynamics discussed in the pages that follow.

20. I have discussed some of these issues more broadly in C. Haney, The Social Context of Capital Murder: Social Histories and the Logic of Mitigation, 35 *Santa Clara Law Review* 547 (1995).

21. See A. Masten and N. Garmezy, Risk, Vulnerability and Protective Factors in Developmental Psychopathology, in F. Lahey and A Kazdin (Eds.), *Advances in Clinical Child Psychology* (pp. 1–52), New York: Plenum Press (1985).

22. There is a vast literature on these issues. In this single chapter, I cannot do it justice. I have provided a partial and somewhat idiosyncratic rather than comprehensive review.

23. Carl Nightingale, *On the Edge: A History of Poor Black Children and Their American Dreams,* New York: Basic Books (1994), p. 55.

24. For example, see M. Bane and D. Ellwood, Slipping In and Out of Poverty: The Dynamics of Spells, 21 *Journal of Human Resources* 21 (1986).

25. Ethnographers have documented many of the ways in which poor children literally live different lives from children who are not poor. They have, as Annette Lareau has phrased it, "unequal childhoods." Although many of these deep consequences of these differences remain "invisible and thus unrecognized" they nonetheless have "profound implications for life experiences and life outcomes." Annette Lareau, *Unequal Childhoods: Class, Race, and Family Life,* Berkeley: University of California Press (2003), p. 257. Arguments that social class may be a more important predictor of these deep consequences than race are difficult to resolve, in part because they often overlook the way both class and race still are inextricably bound in our society.

26. For example, see J. Lempers, D. Clark-Lempers, and V. Webb, Economic Hardship, Parenting, and Distress in Adolescence, 60 *Child Development* 25 (1989). See also R. Sampson, Urban Black Violence: The Effect of Male Joblessness and Family Disruption, 93 *American Journal of Sociology* 348 (1987), who has suggested that high crime rates in urban African American communities stem from structural linkages between unemployment, economic deprivation, and family disruption.

27. C. Kruttschnitt, J. McLeod, and M. Dornfeld, The Economic Environment of Child Abuse, 41 *Social Problems* 299, 310 (1994). This fact may help to explain

the comparatively higher rates of child maltreatment reported in African American families. To the extent to which this occurs, it appears to be a product of greater levels of economic hardship faced by African American parents.

28. R. Lassiter, Child Rearing in Black Families: Child-Abusing Discipline? in R. Hampton (Ed.), *Violence in Black Families* (pp. 39–54), Lexington, MA: Lexington Books (1987), p. 39. See also J. Daniel, R. Hampton, and E. Newberger, Child Abuse and Accidents in Black Families: A Controlled Comparative Study, 53 *American Journal of Orthopsychiatry* 645 (1983); V. McLoyd, The Impact of Economic Hardship on Black Families and Children: Psychological Distress, Parenting, and Socioeconomic Development, 61 *Child Development* 311 (1990).

29. Nightingale, *supra* note 23, at 10. Many compelling urban ethnographies and other social science analyses that have been written over the last decade or so about life in inner-city minority communities. For example, see Elijah Anderson, *Streetwise: Race, Class, and Social Change in an Urban Community,* Chicago: University of Chicago Press (1990); E. Anderson, The Code of the Streets: How the Inner-City Environment Fosters a Need for Respect and a Self-Image Based on Violence, *The Atlantic Monthly* 81 (May 1994); Geoffrey Canada, *Fist Stick Knife Gun: A Personal History of Violence in America,* Boston: Beacon Press (1995); Daniel Coyle, *Hardball: A Season in the Projects,* New York: G. P. Putnam (1993); Alex Kotlowitz, *There Are No Children Here,* New York: Doubleday (1991); Darcy Frey, *The Last Shot: City Streets, Basketball Dreams,* Boston: Houghton Mifflin (1994); Jonathan Kozol, *Amazing Grace: The Lives of Children and the Conscience of a Nation,* New York: Crown (1995); Jerrold Ladd, *Out of the Madness: From the Projects to a Life of Hope,* New York: Warner (1994); Nathan McCall, *Makes Me Wanna Holler: A Young Black Man in America,* New York: Random House (1994); Luis Rodriguez, *Always Running, La Vida Loca: Gang Days in L.A.,* Williamantic, CT: Curbstone (1993); Brent Staples, *Parallel Time: Growing Up in Black and White,* New York: Pantheon (1994); and Mercer Sullivan, *"Getting Paid": Youth Crime and Work in the Inner City,* Ithaca, NY: Cornell University Press (1989).

30. C. Wright Mills, *The Sociological Imagination,* Oxford: Oxford University Press (1957), p. 161.

31. A report on foster care in California found that about two-thirds of all foster children in the state were from two minority groups—African Americans (36%) and Latino (28%). See *California Child and Family Services Review: Statewide Assessment,* Sacramento: California Department of Social Services (Aug. 2002), p. 105.

32. Dorothy Roberts, *Shattered Bonds: The Color of Child Welfare,* New York: Basic Civitas Books (2002), p. 8.

33. Id. at 9.

34. Id. at 21–23.

35. R. Skiba, Indiana Education Policy Center, *The Color of Discipline: Sources of Racial and Gender Disproportionality in School Punishment,* Policy Research Report #SRS1 (2000), pp. 13, 16. Earlier reports on the same issue found some of these same patterns of racially discriminatory treatment in public schools: in Oakland, California, at a time at which African American students comprised 28% of the students in the school system, they represented 53% of the suspensions. Commission for Positive Change in the Oakland Public Schools, *Keeping Children in Schools: Sounding the Alarm on Suspensions,* Oakland, CA: The Commission (1992), p. 1. The issue received national attention in the mid-1990s. See J. Hull, Do Teachers Punish According to Race? *Time Magazine,* April 4, 1994, pp. 30–31. Almost a decade later, the problem

had not abated. See J. Morse, Learning While Black, *Time*, May 27, 2002, pp. 50–53. See also a comprehensive statistical analysis sponsored by the *Seattle Post-Intelligencer* examining nearly 40,000 Seattle secondary school disciplinary records that found that African American students were more than twice as likely as any other group to be suspended or expelled. The statistical disparities remained even after the variables of poverty and living in a single-parent family (both of which also were associated with higher rates of school discipline) were taken into account. The differentials were particularly pronounced for vague or subjective offenses like "disobedience" and "interference with authority." R. Denn, Blacks Are Disciplined at Far Higher Rates Than Other Students, *Seattle Post-Intelligencer*, March 15, 2002.

36. Anne Ferguson, *Bad Boys: Public Schools in the Making of Black Masculinity*, Ann Arbor: University of Michigan Press (2000). See also A. Barona and Eugene Garcia (Eds.), *Children at Risk: Poverty, Minority Status, and Other Issues in Educational Equity*, Washington, DC: National Association of School Psychologists (1990); Jonathan Kozol, *Savage Inequalities: Children in America's Schools*, New York: HarperCollins (1991).

37. Ferguson, *supra* note 36, at 51. Indeed, Ferguson noted that schools are "replete with symbolical forms of violence," in part because children who are regarded by authorities as "troublemakers" are themselves "conscious of the fact that school adults have labeled them as problems, social and educational misfits" and many are also aware "that what they bring from home and neighborhood—family, structure and history, forms of verbal and nonverbal expression, neighborhood lore and experiences—has little or even deficit value." Id. at 169.

38. Id. at 89.

39. That is because, "in the daily experience of being [named as a 'troublemaker'] regulated, and surveilled, access to the full resources of the school are increasingly denied as the boys are isolated in nonacademic spaces in school or banished to lounging at home or loitering on the streets." Moreover, time spent in the school detention center "means time lost from classroom learning; suspension, at school or at home, has a direct and lasting negative effect on the continuing growth of a child" so that "human possibilities are stunted at a crucial formative period of life." Id. at 230.

40. Daniel Losen and Gary Orfield (Eds.), *Racial Inequality in Special Education*, Boston: Harvard Education Press (2002).

41. Id.

42. For example, see M. Berton and S. Stabb, Exposure to Violence and Post-Traumatic Stress Disorder in Urban Adolescents, 31 *Adolescence* 489 (1996).

43. For example, see Kimberley Leonard, Carl Pope, and William Feyerherm (Eds.), *Minorities in Juvenile Justice*, Thousand Oaks, CA: Sage (1995); Amnesty International, *Betraying the Young: Human Rights Violations Against Children in the U.S. Justice System*, AI Index: AMR 51/60/98; H. Snyder and M. Sickmund, *Juvenile Offenders and Victims: 1999 National Report*, Washington, DC: Office of Juvenile Justice and Delinquency Prevention (1999); Mike Males and Dan Macallair, *The Color of Justice: An Analysis of Juvenile Adult Court Transfers in California*, Washington, DC: Building Blocks for Youth (2000); and Eileen Poe-Yamagata and Michael Jones, *And Justice for Some*, San Francisco: National Council on Crime and Delinquency (2000).

44. These data appear in R. DeComo, *The Juveniles Taken Into Custody Research Program: Estimating the Prevalence of Juvenile Custody Rates by Race and Gender*, San Francisco: National Council on Crime and Delinquency (1993).

45. Patricia Puritz and Mary Ann Scali, *Beyond the Walls: Improving Conditions of Confinement for Youth in Custody,* Washington, DC: U.S. Department of Justice (1998), p. xi. Earlier researchers described many juvenile institutions as engendering "a constant struggle for survival" in an environment in which wards "spend much of their time either exploiting weaker youths or defending themselves against victimization." D. Davi, Chance, Change and Challenge in Juvenile Corrections, 45 *Juvenile and Family Court Journal* 47 (1982). A team of criminologists appropriately labeled the victimization of juveniles inside the very institutions where they had been sent to be helped as a "paradox." The authors described the extraordinary adaptations that were forced on young offenders trying to cope in an institutional environment that was, on the one hand, a "punishment-centered bureaucracy," and, on the other, a "terrifying . . . social world." Clemens Bartollas, Stuart Miller, and Simon Dinitz, *Juvenile Victimization: The Institutional Paradox,* New York: Halsted (1976), pp. 197, 271. The living units in the facilities they examined were "worse than the streets," places where a young inmate often was required to "feign bravery and toughness so convincingly that he is not challenged." Id. at 12. They concluded that, even in the best juvenile institutions, "very little correction, training, or adjustment occurs—or can, in fact, occur under present circumstances and social policies." Id. at 271. See also C. Bartollas, Survival Problems of Adolescent Prisoners, in R. Johnson and Hans Toch (Eds.), *The Pains of Imprisonment* (pp. 165–180), Beverly Hills, CA: Sage (1982).

46. Barry Feld, *Bad Kids: Race and the Transformation of the Juvenile Court,* New York: Oxford University Press (1999), p. 5.

47. Id. at 14.

48. For a discussion of some of the prison-related problems that ex-convicts bring with them as they reenter free society, as well as the problems they confront once they arrive, see Jeremy Travis and Michelle Waul (Eds.), *Prisoners Once Removed: The Impact of Incarceration and Reentry on Children, Families, and Communities,* Washington, DC: Urban Institute Press (2003).

49. For example, see T. Clear, D. Rose, and J. Ryder, Incarceration and the Community: The Problem of Removing and Returning Offenders, 47 *Crime and Delinquency* 335 (2001).

50. For example, see B. McCarthy and J. Hagan, Getting Into Street Crime: The Structure and Process of Criminal Embeddedness, 24 *Social Science Research* 63 (1995).

51. Bureau of Justice Statistics, *Special Report: Weapon Use and Violent Crime* (NCJ 194830) (Sept. 2003).

52. Michelle Fine and Lois Weiss, *The Unknown City: The Lives of Poor and Working-Class Young Adults,* Boston: Beacon Press (1998), p. 110 (emphasis in original). There is an extensive literature on this interrelated set of problems. For example, see W. Chambliss, Policing the Ghetto Underclass: The Politics of Law and Law Enforcement, 41 *Social Problems* 177, 183 (1994); Michael Tonry, *Malign Neglect: Race, Crime, and Punishment in America,* New York: Oxford University Press (1995).

53. D. Elliott, W. Wilson, D. Huizinga, R. Sampson, and B. Rankin, The Effects of Neighborhood Disadvantage on Adolescent Development, 33 *Journal of Research in Crime and Delinquency* 389 (1996).

54. See *supra* note 29 and the reference cited therein.

55. Nightingale, *supra* note 23, at 40.

56. For example, Sampson, *supra* note 26. See also J. Balkwell, Ethnic Inequality and the Rate of Homicide, 69 *Social Forces* 53 (1990), who reported that ethnic

inequality was a strong predictor of homicide, and J. Blau and P. Blau, The Cost of Inequality: Metropolitan Structure and Violent Crime, 47 *American Sociological Review* 114 (1982), who also found that racial and economic inequality contributed to levels of violent crime.

57. Quoted in B. Herbert, Locked Out at a Young Age, *New York Times,* Oct. 20, 2003, p. A19. See also Out-of-School and Jobless Youth Reach Crisis Levels: 87,000 Jobless Youth Walk Chicago's Streets; New Report Releases Data on State, Metro, and City Disconnected Youth, *PR Newswire,* Oct. 20, 2003.

58. J. Scott, Nearly Half of Black Men Found Jobless, *New York Times,* Feb. 28, 2004, pp. B1, B4. For the full report, see Mark Levitan, *A Crisis of Black Male Employment: Unemployment and Joblessness in New York City, 2003. Community Service Society Annual Report* (Feb. 2004).

59. W. Harvey, Homicide Among Black Adults: Life in the Subculture of Exasperation, in D. Hawkins (Ed.), *Homicide Among Black Americans* (pp. 153–171), Lanham, MD: University Press of America (1986).

60. For example, see Grace Carroll, *Environmental Stress and African Americans: The Other Side of the Moon,* Westport, CT: Praeger (1998).

61. P. Davis, Law as Microaggression, 98 *Yale Law Journal* 1559, 1565 (1989), quoting psychiatrist C. Pierce, who first coined the term. See C. Pierce, Offensive Mechanisms, in Floyd B. Barbour (Ed.), *The Black Seventies* (pp. 265–282), Boston: Porter Sargent (1970).

62. C. Nelson, Breaking the Camel's Back: A Consideration of Mitigatory Defenses and Racism-Related Mental Illness, 9 *Michigan Journal of Race and Law,* 77, 93 (2003).

63. For example, although blacks and whites use drugs at approximately the same rate, African Americans have been arrested for drug offenses at a much higher rate than whites. See A. Blumstein, Making Rationality Relevant—The American Society of Criminology 1992 Presidential Address, 31 *Criminology* 1 (1993). For a discussion of the sentencing disparities between powder and crack cocaine-related offenses, see B. Poindexter, The War on Crime Increases the Time: Sentencing Policies in the United States and South Africa, 22 *Loyola of Los Angeles Journal of International and Comparative Law Review* 375 (2000).

64. For example, see L. Cowart, Legislative Prerogative vs. Judicial Discretion: California's Three Strikes Law Takes a Hit, 47 *DePaul Law Review* 615 (1998), citing sources to the effect that "African Americans are sentenced under three strikes laws at a rate of thirteen-to-one over Caucasians" (at 652). See also Dragan Milovanovic and Katheryn Russell, *Petit Apartheid in the U.S. Criminal Justice System: The Dark Figure of Racism,* Durham, NC: Carolina Academic Press (2001).

65. A. King, The Impact of Incarceration on African American Families: Implications for Practice, 74 *Families in Society: The Journal of Contemporary Human Services* 145 (1993). Approximately one-third of all African American men between the ages of 20 and 29 are in prison, or on probation or parole. Marc Mauer and Tracy Huling, *The Sentencing Project, Young Black Americans and the Criminal Justice System: Five Years Later* (1995), p. 3. Although the rate at which white men were imprisoned in the United States rose dramatically in the 1980—growing from a rate of 528 per 100,000 in 1985 to a rate of 919 per 100,000 in 1995—it never remotely approximated the incarceration rate for African Americans. The number of African American men who were incarcerated rose from 3,544 per 100,000 in 1985 to an astonishing rate of 6,926 per 100,000 in 1995. C. Mumola and J. Beck, *Prisoners in*

1996 (Bureau of Justice Statistics Bulletin NCJ 164619), Rockville, MD: Bureau of Justice Statistics (June 1997).

66. For example, see E. Lemert, Visions of Social Control: Probation Considered, 39 *Crime and Delinquency* 447 (1993); and Jonathan Simon, *Poor Discipline: Parole and the Social Control of the Underclass, 1890–1990,* Chicago: University of Chicago Press (1993).

67. On the age-based limits to death penalty imposition, see Thompson v. Oklahoma, 487 U.S. 815 (1988), and Stanford v. Kentucky, 492 U.S. 361 (1989). On developmental disability as a bar to capital punishment, see Atkins v. Virginia, 536 U.S. 304 (2002).

68. A false dichotomy is often interposed by critics of this approach, suggesting that people either must be seen as fully autonomous agents who are not only equally responsible but completely culpable for everything they do or, otherwise, are being depicted as helpless, downtrodden victims who cannot initiate actions or make choices on their own. Of course, neither caricature is accurate. An analysis that accurately describes the way in which structural and other forces influence actions and constrain choices does not diminish the dignity of the persons to whom it is correctly applied. The social philosopher Martha Nussbaum is persuasive on this point. She writes: "[P]eople are dignified agents, but they are also, frequently, victims. Agency and victimhood are not incompatible: indeed, only the capacity for agency makes victimhood tragic." Martha Nussbaum, *Upheavals of Thought: The Intelligence of Emotions,* Cambridge, MA: Cambridge University Press (2001), p. 406. I do not understand the logic of the argument that suggests that we uphold the dignity of any group of people by holding them fully culpable and even executing them for crimes they committed in part in response to conditions created and imposed on them by others.

69. G. Goodpaster, The Trial for Life: Effective Assistance of Counsel in Death Penalty Cases, 58 *New York University Law Review* 299, 335–336 (1983) (footnotes omitted).

70. Id.

71. California v. Brown, 479 U.S. 538, 545 (1987) (concurring).

72. Id.

73. Wiggins v. Smith, 539 U.S. 510 (2003). Postconviction investigation revealed that Wiggins had a "bleak life history" that included neglect and severe forms of abuse "at the hands of his mother and while in the care of a series of foster parents" (at 516). His trial attorneys did not uncover, develop, or present any of this information at his sentencing hearing. The Court found that if the jury had been appraised of this "troubled history," which constituted "considerable mitigating evidence," there was "a reasonable probability they it would have returned a [life] sentence" (at 535–536). The *Wiggins* Court imposed a duty upon competent trial counsel to diligently seek to develop precisely this kind of information in capital cases.

74. Attribution theory was formalized in Fritz Heider, *The Psychology of Interpersonal Relations,* New York: Wiley (1958). It has been corroborated, elaborated, and extended in numerous publications since then. For thoughtful overviews, see Edward Jones, David Kanouse, Harold Kelley, Richard Nisbett, Stuart Valins, and Bernard Weiner (Eds.), *Attribution: Perceiving the Causes of Behavior,* Hillsdale, NJ: Erlbaum (1987); H. Kelley, Attribution Theory in Social Psychology, 15 *Nebraska Symposium on Motivation* 192 (1967); H. Kelley, The Processes of Causal Attribution, 28 *American Psychologist* 107 (1975); H. Kelley and J. Michela, Attribution Theory and Re-

search, 31 *Annual Review of Psychology* 457 (1980); Lee Ross and Richard Nisbett, *The Person and the Situation: Perspectives of Social Psychology*, New York: McGraw-Hill (1991).

75. There are too many studies on this topic for me to cite in a comprehensive way. One of the best syntheses of this scientific theory is Kelly Shaver, *The Attribution of Blame: Causality, Responsibility, and Blameworthiness*, New York: Springer-Verlag (1985). For a representative sample of research studies in which the theory is elaborated and extended, see N. Anderson, Psychodynamics of Everyday Life: Blaming and Avoiding Blame, in Norman Anderson (Ed.), *Contributions to Information Integration Theory* (Vol. 1, pp. 243–275), Hillsdale, NJ: Erlbaum (1990); B. Bell, Distinguishing Attributions of Causality, Moral Responsibility, and Blame: Perceivers' Evaluations of the Attributions, 17 *Social Behavior and Personality* 231 (1989); F. Cullen, G. Clark, J. Cullen, and R. Mathers, Attibution, Salience, and Attitudes Toward Criminal Sanctioning, 12 *Criminal Justice and Behavior* 305 (1985); D. Hawkins, Causal Attribution and Punishment for Crime, 2 *Deviant Behavior* 207 (1982); J. Joseph and J. Tedeschi, Perceived Responsibility and the Least of Evils Principle, 7 *Law and Human Behavior* 51 (1983); J. Sanders and L. Hamilton, Is There a "Common Law" of Responsibility? The Effect of Demographic Variables on Judgments of Wrongdoing, 11 *Law and Human Behavior* 277 (1987); A. Sinha and P. Dumar, Antecedents of Crime and Suggested Punishment, 125 *Journal of Social Psychology* 485 (1985); T. Shultz, M. Schleifer, and I. Altman, Judgments of Causation, Responsibility, and Punishment in Cases of Harm-Doing, 13 *Canadian Journal of Behavioural Science* 238 (1981); and B. Weiner, S. Graham, and C. Reyna, An Attributional Examination of Retributive Versus Utilitarian Philosophies of Punishment, 10 *Social Justice Research* 431 (1997).

76. For an excellent discussion of this and related topics, see Ross and Nisbett, *supra* note 74. For examples of fundamental attribution error in practice, see L. Hamilton, Intuitive Psychologist or Intuitive Lawyer? Alternative Models of the Attribution Process, 39 *Journal of Personality and Social Psychology* 767 (1980); E. Hansen, C. Kimble, and D. Biers, Actors and Observers: Divergent Attributions of Constrained Unfriendly Behavior, 29 *Social Behavior and Personality* 87 (2001); J. Johnson, J. Jemmott, and T. Pettigrew, Causal Attribution and Dispositional Inference: Evidence of Inconsistent Judgments, 20 *Journal of Experimental Social Psychology* 567 (1984); M. Safer, Attributing Evil to the Subject, Not the Situation, 6 *Personality and Social Psychology Bulletin* 205 (1980).

77. For example, see C. Ugwuegbu and C. Hendrick, Personal Causality and Attribution of Responsibility, 2 *Social Behavior and Personality* 76 (1974).

78. For example, see C. Banks, The Effects of Perceived Similarity Upon the Use of Reward and Punishment, 12 *Journal of Experimental Social Psychology* 131 (1976).

79. F. Banner, Rewriting History: The Use of Feminist Narratives to Deconstruct the Myth of the Capital Defendant, 26 *New York Review of Law and Social Change* 569, 579 (2000–2001).

80. Of course, these principles cannot be implemented as mere tactics or ploys. Mitigation must be rooted in the actual social history and life circumstances of the capital defendant, as reflected in and conveyed by the testimony of numerous lay and expert witnesses.

81. Nussbaum, *supra* note 68, at 409.

82. For example, see T. Pettigrew, The Ultimate Attribution Error: Extending

Allport's Cognitive Analysis of Prejudice, in Michael Hogg and Dominic Abrams (Eds.), *Intergroup Relations: Essential Readings. Key Readings in Social Psychology* (pp. 162–173), Philadelphia: Psychology Press (2001).

83. Anthony Amsterdam and Jerome Bruner, *Minding the Law,* Cambridge, MA: Harvard University Press (2000), p. 247 (emphasis in original, footnote omitted).

84. There is extensive research linking racial prejudice with death penalty support. See R. Bohm, American Death Penalty Opinion, 1936–1986: A Critical Examination of Gallup Polls, in Robert Bohm (Ed.), *The Death Penalty in America: Current Research* (pp. 113–145), Cincinnati, OH: Anderson (1991); and R. Young, Race, Conceptions of Crime and Justice, Support for the Death Penalty, 54 *Social Psychology Quarterly* 67 (1991).

85. Pillsbury, *supra* note 3, at 692. In addition to the way that death qualification is likely to increase existing differences between capital jurors and the persons they judge, research by David Baldus and his colleagues suggests that prosecutors may more successful than defense attorneys in using peremptory challenges to control the composition of the jury. Specifically, Baldus et al. concluded their study of 317 capital murder trials in Philadelphia by suggesting that the prosecutor's comparative advantage in the capital jury selection process resulted in more racial discrimination in the application of the death penalty, denied many capital defendants the right to a trial by a jury that included at least one of their peers, and resulted in a greater number of death sentences being rendered overall, and especially against Black defendants. D. Baldus, G. Woodworth, D. Zuckerman, N. Weiner, and B. Broffitt, The Use of Peremptory Challenges in Capital Murder Trials: A Legal and Empirical Analysis, 34 *University of Pennsylvania Journal of Constitutional Law* 3–170 (2001).

86. A meta-analysis is a widely used methodological and statistical technique that allows researchers to combine the results of a number of different studies to estimate overall strength of relationships and the various mediating variables that help to account for larger and smaller effects.

87. L. Sweeney and C. Haney, The Influence of Race on Sentencing: A Meta-Analytic Review of Experimental Studies, 10 *Behavioral Science and the Law* 183 (1992), p. 192.

88. This study appeared as M. Lynch and C. Haney, Discrimination and Instructional Comprehension: Guided Discretion, Racial Bias, and the Death Penalty, 24 *Law and Human Behavior* 337 (2000).

89. Davis, *supra* note 61, at 1576.

90. Indeed, David Baldus and his colleagues have conducted intensive research in at least one jurisdiction—Philadelphia—showing that the prosecutors' effective use of peremptories "enhances the probability of death for all defendants; it raises the level of racial discrimination in the application of the death penalty; and it denies defendants a trial by a jury that includes at least one of their 'peers' " See Baldus et al., *supra* note 85, p. 10.

91. Recall also that Smith, Benson, and I found that death penalty supporters were more likely to inaccurately recall closing arguments made by prosecution and defense, and were more likely to recall closing argument themes that were crime-oriented in nature. This suggests that the tendency for jury selection in death penalty cases to choose jurors on the basis of their support for capital punishment may result in juries that are especially prone to error. Death-qualified juries that favor the death

penalty appear more likely to make mistakes both in comprehending instructions *and* in accurately recalling closing argument themes.

Chapter 10

1. Stuart Banner, *The Death Penalty: An American History,* Cambridge, MA: Harvard University Press (2002), p. 39.

2. Karl Llewellyn, *The Bramblebush: On Our Law and Its Study,* Dobbs Ferry, NY: Oceana (1930), p. 144.

3. In a notable dissent published during his last year on the Court, Justice Blackmun concluded that the attempt to develop procedural and substantive rules to govern the death penalty in the United States had resulted in little more than the "appearance of fairness." He acknowledged that he felt morally and intellectually obligated to stop "tinkering with the machinery of death" and to declare instead that the nation's death penalty experiment had failed. See Callins v. Collins, 510 U.S., 1141, 1144 (1994).

4. For a discussion of some of the ways in which underfunded, undertrained, and inexperienced lawyers can make an already flawed system worse, see S. Bright, Counsel for the Poor: The Death Sentence Not for the Worst Crime but for the Worst Lawyer, 103 *Yale Law Journal* 1835–1883 (1994). The poor quality of representation at the trial level is replicated and exacerbated in many states once a defendant is sentenced to death. These post-conviction legal appeals are critically important because they are the only real opportunity to determine whether errors or mistakes or some of the kinds of problems I have discussed in the preceding chapters may have contributed the outcome in the case. Yet, as one experienced attorney described it: "Most states allow only a token fee of a few thousand dollars, or cap expenses at about the same amount, or have no standards for lawyer competence, or inflict all three plagues on the condemned. These states in fact deny any meaningful representation to men and women on death row." E. Semel, Representing Death Row Inmates at the Outskirts of the Southern Front, 26 *CACJ Forum* 37–43 (1999), at p. 40 (footnote omitted). Obviously, these problems must be solved as well if the system of death sentencing is to be made fair and just.

In addition, there have been a number of recent proposals for the reform of the system of death sentencing. Two—the American Bar Association's (ABA) guidelines for attorney performance in death penalty cases, and a report of special gubernatorial commission in Illinois—followed related recommendations for a moratorium on executions until the system could be sufficiently reformed to insure fair and reliable verdicts. The ABA established a set of guidelines governing the appointment, training, and monitoring of defense counsel in capital cases as well as a model for the proper representation of a capital client. See American Bar Association Guidelines for the Appointment and Performance of Defense Counsel in Death Penalty Cases, 31 *Hofstra Law Review* 913 (2003). Despite their reasonableness and the imprimatur of the ABA, these recommendations go far beyond what is currently required or provided in many states where death penalty statutes are in effect. The Illinois proposals for reform were even more far-reaching, including a total of some 85 recommendations that dealt not only with attorney performance but also included a number of proposals for increasing the reliability of the fact-finding in capital cases (including videotaping of interrogations, special scrutiny of eyewitness identifications and the testimony of in-custody informants, and implementing standards and providing adequate resources for forensic testing of evidence); narrowing eligibility for the death penalty (including new standards limiting the kinds of cases in which the death penalty could be sought, and statewide oversight of the decision to seek the death penalty); improving judicial performance (including giving specialized training to judges who sit in capital cases that entailed, among other things, instruction in the inherent risks and limitations of certain kinds of evidence); and broadening the nature of the mitigation that can be considered in the sentencing phase of the case (including increasing the number of specific mitigating factors the jury is instructed to consider, and permitting the defendant to address the jury in "allocution" that would occur before a sentencing verdict is rendered). See *Report of the Governor's Commission on Capital Punishment*, State of Illinois, April 15, 2002.

Largely because I have approached these issues more from a psychological than a purely legal perspective, the proposals made in this chapter are different from, but certainly not inconsistent with, these other blueprints for reform.

5. In several of the most important death penalty cases decided in the post-*Furman* era, the Court ignored or distorted social science data that addressed the way the system of death sentencing actually worked. The result was to preserve the capital punishment status quo. For example, in *Lockhart* the Court seemed to renege on its promise in *Witherspoon* [Witherspoon v. Illinois, 391 U.S. 510 (1968)] to look in a careful and balanced way at evidence on the effects of death qualification. By denying the clear implications of a series of well-designed empirical studies, the Court preserved a practice that ensured that death penalty cases would be tried before juries that were less fair than in others. [See Lockhart v. McCree, 476 U.S. 162 (1986).] In *McCleskey*, the Court turned away from the implications of a careful empirical analysis of the racial dynamics of death sentencing and retained the discriminatory status quo. [See McCleskey v. Kemp, 481 U.S. 279 (1987).] And in the *Free/Buchanan/Weeks* line of cases, the Justices have simply ignored the social science research showing that capital sentencing instructions are difficult if not impossible for many jurors to comprehend. [See Free v. Peters, 12 F.3d 700 (1993), *cert. denied* 513 U.S. 967 (1994); Buchanan v. Angelone, 528 U.S. 225 (1998); Weeks v. Angelone, 528 U.S. 225 (2000).] In each instance, the rationale for rejecting or ignoring the social science data was somewhat different, but the result was identical: Death sentencing continued on the same basis as before.

6. For example: "Much of the Court's aversion to the use of empirical data stems from the reaction to its opinion in Brown v. Board of Education. . . . [T]he Court has been exceedingly reluctant to utilize social science data ever since." M. Dorf, Foreword: The Limits of Socratic Deliberation, 112 *Harvard Law Review* 4, 55–56 (1998),

7. Gregg v. Georgia, 428 U.S. 153 (1976), at 232 (dissenting).

8. For example, in Atkins v. Virginia, 536 U.S. 304 (2002), the Court relied in part on psychological and psychiatric literature in concluding that the execution of mentally retarded persons now constituted cruel and unusual punishment. Thus, in addition to citing what the *Atkins* majority characterized as a new consensus against executing the mentally retarded, Justice Stevens cited a number of social science studies in support of the proposition that, because the mentally retarded are impaired in "the areas of reasoning, judgment, and control of their impulses" they, therefore, "do not act with the level of moral culpability" that would permit them to be sub-

jected to capital punishment. Id. at 306. More recently, in Roper v. Simmons, 125 S. Ct. 1183 (2005), a narrowly divided Court used some of the same logic about limited moral culpability that had prevailed in *Atkins* to declare that the death penalty was a disproportionate punishment for juveniles (persons under the age of 18). In categorically barring juveniles from being subjected to capital punishment, the Court cited psychological research that established their underdeveloped sense of responsibility, greater susceptibility to situational pressures, and the formative nature of their character and identity.

9. Dorf, *supra* note 6, at 56.

10. For a thoughtful discussion of this point, see Todd Gitlin, *Media Unlimited: How the Torrent of Images and Sounds Overwhelms Our Lives,* New York: Metropolitan Books (2001).

11. Indeed, CBS (the network on which *C.S.I.* is shown) banked on its continued success by introducing a third version, *C.S.I. New York,* anticipating that it would "become one of the biggest audience draws on television." CBS thus added to the original *C.S.I.,* which "remained the most watched show on television," and the second edition, *C.S.I. Miami,* which also had "improved its numbers" since going on the air with very high ratings from the start. B. Carter and S. Elliott, The Media Business: CBS Lineup to Build on Current Crop of Winners, *New York Times,* May 19, 2004, p. C7, col. 1.

12. B. Carter, Spinoff No. 2: Story Is Still King, Ka-Ching, *New York Times,* Sept. 30, 2001, § 13, p. 4, col. 1.

13. Jeffrey Scheuer, *The Sound Bite Society: Television and the American Mind.* New York: Four Walls Eight Windows Press (1999), p. 170. See also N. Postman, Critical Thinking in the Electronic Era, 65 *The National Forum* 8 (Winter 1985); and Neil Postman and Steve Powers, *How to Watch TV News.* New York: Penguin Books (1992).

14. S. Bandes, Fear Factor: The Role of Media in Covering and Shaping the Death Penalty, 1 *Ohio State Journal of Criminal Law* 585, 588 (2004).

15. L. Dorfman and V. Schiraldi, *Off Balance: Youth, Race and Crime in the News.* Washington, DC: Building Blocks for Youth (April 2001), p. 38.

16. In Apprendi v. New Jersey, 530 U.S. 466 (2000), the Court ruled that any fact that increases the penalty for a crime beyond the prescribed statutory maximum must be found by a jury beyond a reasonable doubt. Ring v. Arizona, 536 U.S. 584 (2002), extended that logic to capital penalty trials, ruling that juries, not judges, must determine whether a defendant is sentenced to life or death.

17. C. Mullin, The Jury System in Death Penalty Cases: A Symbolic Gesture, 43 *Law and Contemporary Problems* 137, 149 (1980).

18. Brecheen v. Oklahoma, 485 U.S. 909, 913 (1988), quoting *Witherspoon,* 391 U.S. at 519. Justice Marshall, in particular, complained that the Court's capital jurisprudence failed to take the special risks of prejudicial pretrial publicity in death penalty cases into account. For example, in addition to *Brecheen,* in Hale v. Oklahoma, 488 U.S. 878 (1988), he argued that a case in which six members of a capital jury admitted that they already had formed opinions concerning the case demonstrated that the extremely high threshold for changing venue imposed by the Oklahoma courts failed to protect a capital defendant's fair trial rights. In Crawford v. Georgia, 489 U.S. 1040 (1989), he argued that a death penalty defendant's rights had been violated in a trial where a majority of the jurors already knew of his past

trial and a quarter knew that he had received a prior death sentence. And in Swindler v. Lockhart, 495 U.S. 911 (1990), Marshall offered general criticism of what he thought were unduly restrictive state venue doctrines.

19. Not only would it be difficult to ensure that prospective jurors gave accurate, candid answers to questions about whether they had formed complex, subtle, and deep-seated judgments like these, but the added focus on penalty during voir dire would intensify another problematic feature of capital jury selection—the biasing effects of the death qualification process.

20. As one commentator has put it: "Because of the strong local interests involved, only a showing of actual prejudice should overcome the community's interest in a local trial and mandate a change of venue in ordinary criminal cases. In capital cases, however, the defendant's life is at stake. In such cases, in light of the severity and uniqueness of the sentence, courts should apply a more lenient standard for change of venue motions which would provide heightened protection of the capital defendant's due process rights." P. Lemanowicz, Criminal Procedure—Death Penalty Defendant Not Entitled to Change of Venue for Pretrial Publicity, 68 *Temple Law Review* 907, 907–908 (1995) (footnotes omitted).

21. S. Rozelle, The Utility of *Witt:* Understanding the Language of Death Qualification, 54 *Baylor Law Review* 677, 699 (2002). Similarly, two social science researchers have concluded: "At all stages of the trial—jury selection, determination of guilt or innocence, and the final judgment of whether the defendant lives or dies—death qualification results in bias against the capital defendant of a nature that occurs for no other criminal defendant." J. Luginbuhl and K. Middendorf, Death Penalty Beliefs and Jurors' Responses to Aggravating and Mitigating Circumstances in Capital Trials, 12 *Law and Human Behavior* 263, 279 (1988).

22. *Witherspoon v. Illinois, supra* note 5, at 529.

23. State v. Bey, 112 N.J. 123, 548 A.2d 887, 923 (1988) (Handler, dissenting, quoting *Lockhart,* 476 U.S. at 173) (emphasis in original). Similarly, Justice Durham, of the Utah Supreme Court concluded that "[i]n capital cases, the lengthiest portion of jury voir dire by far pertains to the process of death qualifying the jury, and bifurcation would permit trial courts to reserve this exhausting procedure until needed at the sentencing phase." State v. Young, 853 P.2d 327, 394 (1993) (Durham, dissenting). This reason was cited among others, by Federal District Judge Gertner when she recently ordered a bifurcated jury in a federal death penalty case. U.S. v. Green, 343 F. Supp. 2d 23 (2004).

24. Morgan v. Illinois, 504 U.S. 719 (1992).

25. J. Blume, S. Johnson, and B. Threlkeld, Probing "Life Qualification" Through Expanded Voir Dire, 29 *Hofstra Law Review* 1209, 1215 (2001).

26. At the same time, and in ways that underscore the complexity of meaningful reform in this area of the capital trial process, note that any requirement that prolongs the length of time major trial participants dwell on penalty-related issues in voir dire risks increasing the biasing effects of death qualification. These kinds of imperfect trade-offs seem to underscore the inherently flawed nature of death qualification.

27. Justice Stewart employed this approach in his plurality opinion in *Gregg,* when he characterized the capital jury as a "significant and reliable objective index of contemporary values because it is so directly involved" in death sentencing. See *Gregg v. Georgia, supra* note 7, at 181.

28. Notably, in *Atkins* and *Simmons,* the two recent cases in which the Court has significantly restricted the use of the death penalty, it has reaffirmed its ability to

bring its own "independent judgment to bear" on Eighth Amendment issues like these, rather than relying so heavily on the supposed "objective indicia" of capital jury verdicts. In fact, in *Simmons*, the Court acknowledged that an "unacceptable likelihood exists that the brutality or cold-blooded nature of any particular crime would overpower mitigating arguments based on youth as a matter of course . . . " *Roper v. Simmons*, *supra* note 8, at 1197. Although the topic is beyond the scope of this book, the Court's other index of popular support for the death penalty—the decisions of duly elected representatives in state legislatures—appears to be seriously limited as well. As one analyst has noted, politics "make the legislature a dubious barometer of public opinion regarding it acceptability." S. Krauss, Representing the Community: A Look at the Selection Process in Obscenity Cases and Capital Sentencing, 64 *Indiana Law Journal* 617, 629 (1989) (footnotes omitted). In addition, the circularity of an approach by which the Court not only defers to legislative judgments but uses them as an "objective" measure of evolving standards has been questioned by other legal commentators. As Margaret Radin put it: "Constitutional doctrine may not be formulated by the acts of those institutions which the Constitution is supposed to limit. To glean a list of permissible punishments from those enacted by legislatures . . . assumes that legislators never enact a punishment they think is, or may be, cruel or allows the legislature to define permissible punishments by its enactments. Such a view removes any role for a constitutional check." M. Radin, The Jurisprudence of Death: Evolving Standards for the Cruel and Unusual Punishments Clause, 126 *University of Pennsylvania Law Review* 989, 1036 (1978). See also S. Gillers, The Quality of Mercy: Constitutional Accuracy at the Selection Stage of Capital Sentencing, 18 *U. C. Davis Law Review* 1037 (1985).

29. W. Bowers, The Capital Jury Project: Rationale, Design, and Preview of Early Findings, 70 *Indiana Law Review* 1043, 1099, tbl. 12 (1995).

30. The Capital Jury Project did not find as large a disparity with respect to how jurors perceived the relative resources at the disposal of each side. This may be a function of the fact that the defense's disadvantage was not as obvious inside the courtroom as outside, as well as the fact that the jury could not be expected to anticipate or understand all of the things that the defense could or should or might have done if they had been given the necessary resources with which to do them.

31. For example, see C. Haney, Criminal Justice and the Nineteenth-Century Paradigm: The Triumph of Psychological Individualism in the "Formative Era," 6 *Law and Human Behavior* 191 (1982).

32. As I noted earlier, a very good summary of much of the research documenting this tendency is presented in Lee Ross and Richard Nisbett, *The Person and the Situation: Perspectives of Social Psychology*, New York: McGraw-Hill (1991), pp. 125–144.

33. L. Henderson, Legality and Empathy, 85 *Michigan Law Review* 1574, 1590 (1987).

34. S. Pillsbury, Emotional Justice: Moralizing the Passions of Criminal Punishment, 74 *Cornell Law Review* 655, 697 (1989).

35. T. Massaro, Empathy, Legal Storytelling, and the Rule of Law: New Words, Old Wounds? 87 *Michigan Law Review* 2099, 2100 (1989).

36. Pillsbury, *supra* note 34, at 669.

37. Henderson, *supra* note 33, at 1574–1575. Indeed, another legal commentator has suggested that empathy or sympathy may be less likely to occur spontaneously in a multicultural society like ours because of the "easier acceptance of one's

position as a spectator and a candid recognition of the limits of one's ability to enter into the experiences of another." Note, Sympathy as a Legal Structure, 105 *Harvard Law Review* 1961–1980, 1967 (1992). If true, this would underscore the need for more proactive legal mechanisms that encourage or better enable capital jurors to overcome their "spectator" position and better understand the formative experiences of the defendant.

38. Pillsbury, *supra* note 34.

39. Id. at 694.

40. Jeffrie Murphy and Jean Hampton, *Forgiveness and Mercy,* New York: Cambridge University Press (1988).

41. Id. at 153.

42. That is, that violent actions, like all others, need to be "understood in relation to the actions of other people, and in relation to spatial, situational, and temporal circumstances in which the actors are embedded." I. Altman, B. Brown, B. Staples, and C. Werner, A Transactional Approach to Close Relationships, in W. B. Walsh, K. Craik, and R. Price (Eds.), *Person-Environment Psychology: Models and Perspectives,* Hillsdale, NJ: Erlbaum (1992), p. 195. See also Arnold Goldstein, *The Ecology of Aggression,* New York: Plenum Press (1994).

43. People v. Lucas, 12 Cal. 4th 415, 428 (1995).

44. J. Hoffman, Where's the Buck? Juror Misperception of Sentencing Responsibility in Death Penalty Cases, 70 *Indiana Law Journal* 1137, 1157 (1995).

45. U. Bentele and W. Bowers, How Jurors Decide on Death: Guilt Is Overwhelming; Aggravation Requires Death; and Mitigation Is No Excuse, 66 *Brooklyn Law Review* 1011, 1013 (2001).

46. Richardson v. Marsh, 481 U.S. 200, 211 (1987). Unfortunately, appellate judges often adhere to this "practical accommodation" and are reluctant to grant relief on these critical instructional issues. In addition to citing the aforementioned presumption, judges often envision improbable scenarios under which the jurors "must have" derived the proper meaning from the context in which the instructions were delivered (sometimes in spite of direct expressions by the jurors that they did not). As I have noted, the Supreme Court has repeatedly ignored carefully conducted social science studies and instead relied on strained interpretations of the factual record to dismiss what appears to be reasonably clear evidence of confusion—including direct questions from juries in which they either explicitly stated that they did not understand what they were supposed to do or, indirectly, indicated the same thing.

47. Gacy v. Wellborn, 994 F.2d 305, 313 (7th Cir. 1993).

48. Weeks v. Angelone, 528 U.S. 225 (2000).

49. A. Smith and C. Haney, Get to the Point: The Use of Pinpoint Instructions to Improve Juror Instructional Comprehension in Capital Penalty Trials, unpublished manuscript, University of California, Santa Cruz (2004).

50. A. Paduano and C. Stafford-Smith, Deathly Errors: Juror Misperceptions Concerning Parole in the Imposition of the Death Penalty, 18 *Columbia Human Rights Law Review* 211 (1987). In several cases, the Supreme Court has made it clear that trial courts *must* inform jurors of the alternative sentence of life without possibility of parole when that is the mandatory alternative sentence. See Simmons v. South Carolina, 512 U.S. 154 (1994), and Shafer v. South Carolina, 532 U.S. 36 (2001). I am suggesting that, in the interest of full disclosure, capital jurors have the right to be accurately informed about all alternatives (including normative time

served for comparable crimes), even in jurisdictions where life without possibility of parole is not the only one mandated.

51. B. Steiner, W. Bowers, and A. Sarat, Folk Knowledge as Legal Action: Death Penalty Judgments and the Tenet of Early Release in a Culture of Mistrust and Punitiveness, 33 *Law and Society Review* 461 (1999).

52. J. Howarth, Deciding to Kill: Revealing the Gender in the Task Handed to Capital Jurors, 1994 *Wisconsin Law Review* 1345, 1386 (1994).

53. P. Cobb, Reviving Mercy in the Structure of Capital Punishment, 99 *Yale Law Journal* 389, 395 (1989). Cobb also observed that the "bureaucratization" of capital punishment that exempts individual decision makers from ever having to confront the personal question of extending mercy to capital defendants "affords everyone involved in capital sentencing the illusion that no one has decided that any given individual should die; in doing so, it poses the question whether we want a 'headless and soulless' institution sending people to their deaths." Id. at 404 (footnotes omitted).

54. For example, see L. Carter, Harmless Error in the Penalty Phase of a Capital Case: A Doctrine Misunderstood and Misapplied, 28 *Georgia Law Review* 125, 156 (1993). Obviously the absence of mitigating evidence presented at trial also can undermine meaningful appellate review: "Without a record containing mitigating evidence, the courts cannot conduct more than a pro forma review of the balance between aggravating and mitigating circumstances in an individual case." Id. at 127.

55. I. Fong, Ineffective Assistance of Counsel at Capital Sentencing, 39 *Stanford Law Review* 461 (1987).

56. In Lockett v. Ohio, 438 U.S. 586 (1978), the Court had ruled the states could not pass laws that explicitly excluded certain aspects of a defendant's background from being considered by the jury. In Eddings v. Oklahoma, 455 U.S. 104 (1982), the Justices said essentially the same thing. In Penry v. Lynaugh, 492 U.S. 302 (1989), the Court ruled that background evidence was "relevant." But it was not until Wiggins v. Smith, 539 U.S. 510 (2003)—decided long after the death penalty was reinstated in the United States—that the Supreme Court explicitly articulated what seemed to be implicit in these earlier cases but which was too often ignored in too many cases: the affirmative duty of defense attorneys to attempt to find and make use of mitigating social history testimony.

57. It is difficult to predict how the Court will resolve these issues. In addition to the long delay between acknowledging the importance of mitigation to the fairness of the capital sentencing process and explicitly requiring that attorneys present it, the Court's handling of this kind of issue in the preceding term raises doubts about whether the Justices understand the important difference between requiring "some" versus "adequate" amounts of mitigation. In Bell v. Cone, 535 U.S. 685 (2002), decided just a year before *Wiggins,* a Tennessee Vietnam veteran who apparently suffered from posttraumatic stress disorder and amphetamine addiction was represented by an attorney who was later shown to be mentally ill and who committed suicide as the defendant's case was being appealed. The attorney admitted that he basically had given up once his client was convicted in the guilt phase (expressing the belief that a death-qualified jury was "fixed" and was "going to find a death penalty" in any case in which it convicted), also said that he did not believe in humanizing his client, had no idea why capital trials were bifurcated into guilt and penalty trials (he replied, "God only knows" when asked this question in postconviction proceedings), conceded that he did not understand "the separate nature" of

the penalty trial, did no penalty-phase mitigation investigation and, as a result, did not develop any separate penalty-phase testimony or present any mitigation witnesses at the penalty trial. Only Justice Stevens was troubled enough by this performance to find that it fell below the constitutionally required minimum.

58. For a broad discussion of some of the ways that racial diversity can be ensured on juries generally, see Hiroshi Fukurai and Richard Krooth, *Race in the Jury Box: Affirmative Action in Jury Selection,* Albany: State University of New York Press (2003). See also P. Butler, Affirmative Action and the Criminal Law, 68 *Colorado Law Review* 841 (1998).

59. For a discussion of the nature of and need for a Racial Justice Act, see D. Edwards and J. Conyers, The Racial Justice Act—a Simple Matter of Justice, 20 *University of Dayton Law Review* 699 (1995); and E. Chemerinsky, Eliminating Discrimination in Administering the Death Penalty: The Need for the Racial Justice Act, 35 *Santa Clara Law Review* 519 (1995).

60. C. Haney, The Social Context of Capital Murder: Social Histories and the Logic of Mitigation, 35 *Santa Clara Law Review* 547, 561 (1995).

61. Tuilaepa v. California, 512 U.S. 967, 995 (1994).

Concluding Thoughts

1. John Locke, *Two Treatises of Government* (P. Laslett, Ed., 2nd ed.), Cambridge: Cambridge University Press (1963), p. 286.

2. In fact, in part as a result, a panel of distinguished experts in Illinois has called for a "sweeping overhaul" of their state's system of death sentencing and imposed a moratorium on executions until it has been reformed. J. Wilgoren, Illinois Panel: Death Sentence Needs Overhaul, *New York Times*, April 15, 2001, pp. A1, A19. Some 85 separate reforms were recommended that the authors of the report deemed "indispensable" to "better ensure a fair, just and accurate death penalty scheme." Illinois had been operating under a gubernatorially imposed moratorium on executions after some 13 persons had been exonerated from the state's death row in a single decade. There is no reason to believe that the widespread unreliability that plagued the system of death sentencing in Illinois was entirely unique to that state.

3. The Supreme Court has articulated and, at least in the abstract, continued to affirm this view. For example: "The 'unique' nature of modern capital sentencing proceedings . . . derives from the fundamental principle that death is 'different' and that heightened reliability is required at all stages of the capital trial." Schiro v. Farley, 510 U.S. 222, 237 (1994) (citations omitted). Or: "In capital proceedings generally, this Court has demanded that factfinding procedures aspire to a heightened standard of reliability. . . . This especial concern is a natural consequence of the knowledge that execution is the most irremediable and unfathomable of penalties; that death is different . . ." Ake v. Oklahoma, 470 U.S. 58, 87 (1985) (Chief Justice Burger, concurring in judgment).

4. Indeed, for many critics of capital punishment, one of the most troubling features of the modern death penalty is that—because the protection of society can be accomplished so effectively in other ways—killing even the worst criminal has become gratuitous.

Index

conducted in open court, 117, 127, 137

sequestered, 133, 136–137

Wainright v. Witt, 104, 122, 133, 136, 137

Weeks v. Angelone, 236

Weisberg, Robert, 155, 167

Weiss, Lois, 198

Wells, Martin, 178

West, Valerie, 188

White, Welsh, 191

Wiener, Richard, 177–178, 185

Witherspoon v. Illinois, 103–104, 108–110, 115, 122, 132, 223

Witherspoon/Witt standard, 108, 112, 122

Woodson v. North Carolina, 211

World War I, 69

World War II, 69

wrongful convictions, 87–88, 91, 109

innocent people freed, 4, 42, 47, 73, 98

Young, Robert, 38

Zeisel, Hans, 177–178

Zimring, Franklin, 74, 82